ALSO BY HOWARD M. SACHAR

The Course of Modern Jewish History

Aliyah: The Peoples of Israel

From the Ends of the Earth: The Peoples of Israel

The Emergence of the Middle East

Europe Leaves the Middle East

The Man on the Camel

Egypt and Israel

Diaspora

A History of Israel from the Aftermath of the Yom Kippur War

A History of the Jews in America

Farewell España: The World of the Sephardim Remembered

A History of Israel: From the Rise of Zionism to Our Time

The Rise of Israel: A Documentary History (edited, 39 volumes)

ISRAEL AND EUROPE

An Appraisal in History

ISRAEL AND EUROPE

AN APPRAISAL IN HISTORY

HOWARD M. SACHAR

 ALFRED A. KNOPF   NEW YORK   1999

THIS IS A BORZOI BOOK
PUBLISHED BY ALFRED A. KNOPF, INC.

Copyright © 1998 by Howard M. Sachar
All rights reserved under International and Pan-American
Copyright Conventions. Published in the United States by
Alfred A. Knopf, Inc., New York, and simultaneously in
Canada by Random House of Canada Limited, Toronto.
Distributed by Random House, Inc., New York.

www.randomhouse.com

Library of Congress Cataloging-in-Publication Data
Sachar, Howard Morley.
Israel and Europe: an appraisal in history / Howard M.
Sachar.—1st ed.
p.   cm.
Includes bibliographical references and index.
ISBN 0-679-45434-9 (alk. paper).
1. Israel—Foreign relations.   I. Title.
DS119.6.S33   1999
327.5694—dc21   98-15453   CIP

Manufactured in the United States of America
First Edition

For Raphael and Ori

CONTENTS

IV   A MARRIAGE OF WESTERN CONVENIENCE

V   ALTERNATING PERSPECTIVES ACROSS THE RHINE

VI   A TRAUMA OF DIPLOMATIC RECONCILIATION

VII   A WIDENED SOVIET WINDOW ON
THE MEDITERRANEAN

VIII   1967: A TRANSPOSITION OF WESTERN
ALLIANCES

ACKNOWLEDGMENTS

Israel is the product of Europe more than of any other civilization. Zionism from its inception was the Jews' ideological response specifically to European romantic nationalism, their political response to European antisemitism. Since 1948, moreover, in Israel's nostalgia for the amplitude of European culture and in Europe's afflicted conscience for the Holocaust, in each side's political and economic vulnerability to Middle Eastern conflict, in the sensitivity of each to the other's perceived moral and diplomatic gravamen, Israel and Europe have found themselves linked in an often abrasive configuration of mutual dependence. The connection may be worth further scrutiny. To that end, this brief overview is offered as a supplement to the many valuable published accounts of Israel's relationship with the Arab world, the United States, and individual European nations.

The following persons have generously shared their insights with me: Dr. Yonah Alexander, director, Terrorism Studies Program, George Washington University; Mr. Shimshon Arad, former Israeli ambassador to the Netherlands; Mr. Yehuda Avnair, former Israeli ambassador to Great Britain; Dr. Yoel Barani, former director, Vatican Department, Israeli foreign ministry; Mr. Yechezkel Barnea, former Israeli "diplomatic representative" to Greece; Mr. Chanan Bar-On, vice-president for international operations, Weizmann Institute of Science; Mr. Michael Bavli, former deputy director general, Israeli foreign ministry; Mr. Asher Ben-Natan, former Israeli ambassador to the Federal Republic of Germany, to France; Dr. Chanan Chefer, professor of comparative literature, Tel Aviv University; Mr. Michael Elizur, former Israeli ambassador to Australia, to Austria; former deputy director general, Israeli foreign ministry; Mr. Moshe Erel,

adviser on Vatican affairs, Israeli foreign ministry; Dr. David
Ettinger, director, Interlibrary Research Service, Gelman Library,
George Washington University; Mr. Emanuele Ferrugia, director,
economic office, Italian embassy in Israel; Mr. Moshe Gilboa, former
Israeli ambassador to Greece; Mr. Friedrich Grommes, minister for
public affairs, German embassy in Israel; Ms. Eva Gruber, former
Israeli agriculture ministry representative to the European Commu-
nity; Mr. Yosef Gubrin, former Israeli ambassador to Austria; Mr.
Moshe Hadas, former Israeli ambassador to Belgium; Ms. Rachel
Hirschler, office of commercial affairs, Israeli Embassy in the United
States; Dr. Emmet Kennedy, professor of history, George Washing-
ton University; Dr. Ruth Lapidot, professor of law, and director,
Helmut Kohl Institute, the Hebrew University; Mr. Wavel Megar,
director, commercial office, British embassy in Israel; Mr. Yochanan
Meroz, former Israeli minister plenipotentiary to France; former
ambassador to the Federal Republic of Germany; Mr. Sergio
Minerbi, former Israeli observer to the European Economic Com-
munity; former ambassador to Belgium, to Italy; Mr. Binyamin
Navon, former Israeli ambassador to the Federal Republic of Ger-
many; director, Daimler-Benz Investment Office in Israel; Mr.
Yitzchak Oren, director, office of congressional affairs, Israeli
Embassy in the United States; Mr. Michael Peled, former director,
office of German affairs, Israeli foreign ministry; Dr. Vladimir
Petrov, professor emeritus of political science, George Washington
University; Brigadier General Yigal Pressler, adviser on terrorism,
Israeli prime minister's office; Mr. Gideon Rafael, former director
general, Israeli foreign ministry; former ambassador to the United
Nations, to Great Britain; Mr. Meir Rosenne, former Israeli ambas-
sador to France, to the United States; Mr. Bradford Rothschild, former director of communications, Israeli Mission to the United
Nations; Mr. Moshe Sasson, former Israeli ambassador to Italy; Mr.
Nadav Tamir, office of political affairs, Israeli embassy in the United
States; Ms. Brita Waggoner, director, commercial office, German
embassy in Israel; Mr. Aharon Yaar, minister-counselor, Israeli
embassy in the United States; Mr. Ehud Ya'ari, Middle East correspondent, Israel Television Services; Dr. Moshe Yegar, former Israeli
ambassador to Romania, to Sweden, to Czechoslovakia; Dr. Moshe
Zimmermann, professor of contemporary history; director, Center
for European Studies, the Hebrew University.

I am grateful as well to the following individuals for their participation in a symposium on German-Israeli relations, cosponsored in

April 1996 by George Washington University and the Friedrich Ebert and Friedrich Nauman Stiftungen. Their contributions added significantly to this volume:

Dr. Dieter Dettke, director, North American Office, Friedrich Ebert Stiftung; Dr. Lily Gardner Feldman, scholar-in-residence, Center for German and European Studies, Georgetown University; Mr. Ari Rath, former editor, *Jerusalem Post*; Mr. Bernd Scheitterlein, director, Washington Office, Friedrich Naumann Stiftung; Mr. Klaus Schütz, former German ambassador to Israel; former director general, Deutsche Welle; Mr. Werner Sonne, deputy bureau chief, ARD German Television, Washington, D.C.; Dr. Angela Stent, associate professor of government, Georgetown University; Dr. Hans Stercken, former chairman, foreign affairs committee, Bundestag; former European desk officer, German Government Press Office; Dr. Hans-Georg Wieck, former German ambassador to the Soviet Union, to NATO; former president of the Bundesnachtrichtendienst.

Ms. Aryeh Somer of George Washington University conscientiously helped arrange delivery of bibliographical material from libraries in the United States and abroad. Mr. Michael Weeks, also of George Washington University, offered invaluable help in the printing and dispatch of successive draft chapters. Mr. Eri Steimatzky of Tel Aviv generously provided me with books often still unavailable in the United States. My wife, Eliana, has proofread my manuscript with her customary diligence and devotion. Other "collaborators" in this endeavor, as in so many others over the years, have been Ms. Jane Garrett and Mr. Melvin Rosenthal, my editors and cherished friends at Alfred A. Knopf, Inc.

ISRAEL AND EUROPE

An Appraisal in History

I AN INDETERMINATE FAREWELL

THE PANGS OF WITHDRAWAL

On February 14, 1947, Foreign Secretary Ernest Bevin informed the House of Commons that he was referring the fate of Britain's embroiled Palestine mandate to the United Nations. The decision to abandon imperial rule in a tiny Middle Eastern country was influenced not alone by the Labor government's failure to reconcile Jewish and Arab claims in the Holy Land. Some two years after the war, Britain was teetering on the edge of bankruptcy. The economic and human costs of maintaining overseas political administrations and military garrisons had become insupportable. Indeed, scarcely a week after Bevin's Palestine announcement, Prime Minister Clement Attlee declared that his government also intended to terminate its rule in India and its military and financial commitments to Greece and Turkey. As the smallest component in this once historic sphere of British influence, Palestine too now apparently was expendable.

The Zionists had contributed mightily to its expendability. Desperate to rescue their surviving kinsmen from postwar Europe's archipelago of displaced persons camps, to pry open the doors of their National Home, Jewish guerrilla organizations were intensifying their attacks on British personnel and installations in Palestine, and Jewish refugee vessels were challenging the Royal Navy's extensive blockade of Palestine's coast. The message to the British taxpayer was a harsh one, and it registered. By the late winter of 1947, the United Kingdom had stationed no fewer than eighty thousand troops in Palestine, had dispatched still additional naval craft to the eastern Mediterranean. At a time of grim austerity in the home islands, the burden of maintaining order in the Holy Land no longer was worth the effort. Others would have to cope with Palestine. So it was, during the spring and summer of 1947, that a United Nations Special Com-

mittee on Palestine studied the competing demands of Jews and
Arabs, and on August 31 produced a majority report that recommended partitioning the little country into separate Jewish and Arab
states, with the Jerusalem area to be placed under United Nations
administration.

On September 26, as the UN General Assembly debated this
recommendation, and as the Jews frantically mobilized support for
partition and the Arabs issued dire imprecations against it, Britain's
colonial undersecretary, Arthur Creech-Jones, announced that
British forces in any case would be unavailable to enforce a settlement
that was "unacceptable either to Arabs or Jews." Plainly it was Arab
friendship, and the safety of British bases and British oil supplies in
the Arab world, that dared not be forfeited. Six days earlier, in a memorandum to his staff, Foreign Secretary Bevin had denounced partition as "manifestly unfair to the Arabs," and likely to inflame the
entire Moslem world. A British deal struck with the Zionists, he
warned, "would be poor compensation for the loss of Arab goodwill."

On November 29, 1947, the UN General Assembly approved partition, to take effect on May 15 of the following year. Immediately,
then, the British declared that they would terminate their mandate in
Palestine not later than August 1 (actually two and a half months
beyond the United Nations deadline), and would assume no responsibility for implementing the General Assembly resolution. It was
at this point, too, that London's conception of "even-handedness"
became rather clearer. On December 1, 1947, David Ben-Gurion,
chairman of the Jewish Agency Executive—the Zionist quasi-government in Palestine—paid a call on High Commissioner Sir Alan Cunningham at British government headquarters in Jerusalem. To cope
with the responsibilities of impending Jewish statehood, Ben-Gurion
explained, he needed copies of land records and information on supplies of food and fuel in the country. Would the high commissioner
provide these? Cunningham would not. Neither would he cooperate
with the United Nations commission that had been appointed to
monitor Palestine's transition from mandate to partition. When the
six commissioners turned up in January 1948, Cunningham allotted
them an unventilated Jerusalem basement, where they were gradually
reduced to foraging for food and drink, and blocked from accom-
plishing anything.

The mandatory government's obduracy reflected not only concern
for Arab friendship. Human frustration and bitterness were also a factor. Beyond the scores of its personnel killed and wounded in Palestine at the hands of Zionist terrorists, Britain had been shamed before

the world by the tatterdemalion flotilla of Jewish refugee vessels, and exposed to the endless diplomatic harassment of U.S. President Harry Truman. An insight into Ernest Bevin's rage was provided by Richard Crossman, a Labor MP who met with the foreign secretary in August 1947, and then was obliged to sit through an anti-Jewish tirade. The Jews had successfully organized a worldwide conspiracy against Britain and against him personally, Bevin complained; the whole Jewish "pressure" was a gigantic "racket" operated from the United States; the Germans might have learned their worst atrocities from the Jews. Exposed to this outburst, Crossman concluded sadly that Bevin had become insane on the Palestine issue.

The foreign secretary and his colleagues in fact were preoccupied not only with Arab goodwill in the Middle East but specifically with the need to preserve a residual British influence in Palestine, or at least in the eastern sector controlled by the Hashemite Arab Legion (pp. 6, 10). It was with this leverage in mind that Whitehall—the Foreign Office—froze the currency deposits belonging to the Jewish Agency and to private Jewish firms, banks, and other institutions that had maintained accounts in London. The measure threatened to bankrupt the embryonic Jewish state at the outset. Thus, as the mandatory administration gradually relinquished its grip on the Holy Land, and ceased to operate Palestine's railroads and postal services, it denied the Jews a concomitant opportunity to take over these facilities. At the very time Britain continued to sell weapons to Iraq and Transjordan, moreover, it barred the Jews from organizing an official militia or from gaining access to crucial defense installations. In his war memoirs, Iraq's General Taha Hashimi acknowledged receiving detailed advance notice of Britain's timetable for evacuating its police fortresses in Safed, Nebi Yusha, and Samakh. All these stockades were immediately occupied by Arab irregulars. Similarly, by Hashimi's account, the British deputy police commander in Jerusalem provided an advance schedule of military evacuation from several Jewish neighborhoods north of the city, with the same consequences of Arab occupation.

Yet there is little evidence that Bevin, for all his grievances against the Zionists and his concern for Arab goodwill, actively favored strangulation of the incipient Jewish state. His purpose, rather, was to limit its expansion (p. 20). Moreover, some of the worst of British derelictions often reflected plain and simple confusion over final authority. No clear line of policy existed between High Commissioner Cunningham and General Sir Gordon Macmillan, the military commander in Palestine. If there were two compelling objectives of British policy during the mandate's last months, one was to carry out a swift, efficient evacuation, and the other was to assure that King Abdullah of Transjordan, a dependable British client, would preempt the allocated Arab state in Palestine for his own Hashemite kingdom.

A PATRONIZATION OF SURROGATES

Britain's underlying political strategy for the Holy Land became somewhat clearer as the end of its tenure approached in the spring of 1948. By then a loose British understanding had been reached with King Abdullah that a full-scale Hashemite war with the Jews not only could prolong disruption in the Middle East but could possibly threaten Abdullah's hegemony even in his own realm. As early as February 7, 1948, therefore, when Transjordanian Prime Minister Tewfiq Abu'l-Huda met with Ernest Bevin in London, he assured the foreign secretary that Hashemite forces would operate exclusively within the Arab-designated sector of Palestine. "It seems the thing to do," replied Bevin approvingly. "By all means, do not go and invade the areas allocated to the Jews." "We could not do so even if we wanted to," agreed Abu'l-Huda. Thus, as the British mandate ended on May 14, and the armies of five Arab nations attacked the newly proclaimed State of Israel, one of those armies limited its operations essentially to eastern Palestine. This was Abdullah's tightly disciplined Arab Legion, commanded by British officers. It was in the eastern sector, directly abutting the Hashemite Kingdom's western—Jordan River—frontier, that the Legion within less than two weeks achieved its objective of investing some three-quarters of the Holy Land's Arab-inhabited areas, including the Old City of Jerusalem and its small Jewish quarter.

Afterward, however, Britain's Foreign Office confronted an unanticipated danger. By late May 1948 the Jews had weathered the initial Arab onslaught. Consolidating their armed forces, integrating new recruits and weapons, they were threatening to launch a counteroffensive of their own against Hashemite-occupied eastern Palestine and Egyptian-occupied southern Palestine. Until then, ironically, Britain's ambassador to the United Nations, Sir Alexander Cadogan, had blocked all efforts in the Security Council to achieve a four-week truce in the Holy Land, and he did not relent until May 29, when the Hashemites had conquered the lion's share of the territory allocated to the Arabs. Once the truce finally came into effect, moreover, on June 11, Britain decided also to exploit one of its key features. The UN General Assembly had appointed Count Folke Bernadotte, a respected Swedish diplomat, to "mediate" an end to the Arab-Israeli conflict. With their extensive governing experience in the Holy Land, the British plainly anticipated guiding the mediator's diplomacy in the "proper" direction.

Thus, in his diary, Bernadotte recalled that the first "outsider" to call on him when he arrived in Paris on June 15, en route to Palestine, was Ashley Clarke, Britain's chargé d'affaires in France. Discreetly, Clarke intimated to Bernadotte the lines of mediation that would enjoy British support. These included a revision of the partition formula, with the southern part of the Negev Desert (which the United Nations had allocated to the Jews) to go to Abdullah of Transjordan, while the Jews would receive as compensation western Galilee (an area the United Nations had allocated to the Arabs but which the Jews already had overrun). Finally, Jerusalem, originally designated for United Nations administration, should be given over to Abdullah in its totality, including the Jewish New City, whose inhabitants would enjoy autonomy.

Evidently Bernadotte was impressed by this scenario. In his own version, which he presented to the Security Council on June 27, he followed Britain's proposals with only minor alterations. Entirely gratified, Ernest Bevin then informed the House of Commons that "the recommendations of Count Bernadotte have the whole-hearted and unqualified support of the Government." Bevin's enthusiasm was understandable. The formula would have provided Britain with surrogate bases in the Negev Desert and Jerusalem mountains. Hector McNeil, minister of state in the Foreign Office, then met privately in New York with Aubrey (later Abba) Eban, Israel's "observer" at the United Nations, to seek Zionist support for the Bernadotte proposal.

McNeil got nowhere. Unwilling to abandon their claim to the Negev Desert, or the reality of their military control of Jerusalem's New City, the Israelis vehemently rejected the Bernadotte plan. So did the Syrians and Egyptians, who were not interested in legitimizing Abdullah's rule over eastern Palestine. Chagrined at this rebuff, the Foreign Office then feverishly set to work drafting a new scenario for Bernadotte. Completed in late July 1948, the revised draft was intended to be more palatable at least to the Israelis and the Hashemites, if not to the rest of the Arab world. It envisaged an exchange of territories, in which the Israelis still would be allowed to keep the Galilee, but in return would relinquish the southern Negev, a sector they had been awarded under the original partition resolution but had yet to conquer. Finally, Jerusalem this time would be placed under an international trusteeship (as envisaged in the original partition plan). For the British the new arrangement had the transparent advantage of preserving a land route from their Egyptian emplacements to their bases in Hashemite Transjordan.

The United States State Department too initially regarded alteration of the partition plan as useful for Western strategic interests. Thus, in early September 1948, a State Department official, Robert McClintock, joined with John Troutbeck of Britain's Foreign Office in an effort to sell the plan to Bernadotte. After some hesitation, the UN mediator agreed. But when he submitted the new formula to the Arabs and Israelis, he evoked as hostile a response from King Abdullah as from Prime Minister Ben-Gurion. Neither leader was interested in renouncing his nation's respective share of Jerusalem. The Israelis assuredly were not prepared to forfeit their part of the Negev. Indeed, Bernadotte soon paid dearly for his naiveté in functioning as a British surrogate. On September 17, driving through a heavily scarred battle area in Israeli-occupied Jerusalem, he was shot dead by Jewish terrorists.

The fortunes of war, meanwhile, had long since shifted in Israel's favor. The initial four-week truce, beginning on June 11, 1948, had allowed both Jews and Arabs to replenish their forces. The Jews did a better job of it. On July 8, as the truce expired, and as the Egyptians sought to renew their offensive in the Negev, the Israelis needed only ten days to repel the enemy assault, to stabilize the southern front, then to launch a pulverizing campaign of their own that drove the last remaining Iraqi and Syrian units out of north-central Israel. By the time a second United Nations cease-fire took effect, on July 18, Israel's military position had become impregnable. Only the Egyptians remained precariously ensconced in the Negev's northwestern quadrant. "This is a complete disaster," lamented Hector McNeil.

For Britain, worse was to come. The Israelis were keenly aware that even a minimal Egyptian foothold in the Negev Desert would preserve Britain's opportunity for surrogate bases on Israeli territory. On October 14, 1948, therefore, they launched a major offensive against the Egyptian expeditionary force. Within a week they captured Faluja, a village controlling the highway net to the Mediterranean coast. They followed this conquest by overrunning Huleiqat, a stockade anchoring the Egyptian line in the northwestern desert, and finally seized the neighboring little Arab caravansary of Beersheba, "capital" of the Negev. Thirty-five thousand Egyptian troops now faced the possibility of entrapment.

Witnessing this debacle, Sir Alexander Cadogan, Britain's ambassador in the UN Security Council, pressed urgently for sanctions against the "Zionist aggressors." Somewhat bemused by Cadogan's reincarnation as an apostle of peace, the other delegates allowed three days to go by before simply demanding a third cease-fire, on October 22. David Ben-Gurion acquiesced. Yet the Israeli prime minister's compliance was entirely tactical. Convinced that a final, triphammer campaign would evict the Egyptian enemy from Israeli soil altogether and decisively confirm the Jewish state's sovereign viability, he and his generals needed time to regroup and reprovision. To that end, during the months of November and December 1948, replenishing their supplies of manpower and weapons, the Israelis prepared for a climactic offensive. They launched it on December 22, and within two days overran al-Auja, the last Egyptian staging base on the Negev-Sinai border. On December 28 an Israeli armored column actually crossed the Egyptian frontier and began rolling into the Sinai Peninsula. The Egyptian people were appalled by this unimaginable turn of events. Indeed, by December riots were erupting in the streets of Cairo and Alexandria, and Egyptian Prime Minister Mahmud Fahmi al-Nuqrashi was assassinated by members of the Ikhwan, the Moslem Brotherhood.

Help came to the Egyptians from another quarter. Under the terms of the 1936 Anglo-Egyptian Treaty, Britain was obliged to assist Egypt against any attack by an outside party. On December 29, 1948, as the UN Security Council ordered still another Arab-Israeli cease-fire, Foreign Secretary Bevin was prepared to exploit the treaty to validate Britain's presence in Egypt. In fact, the Egyptians in recent years had been seeking to abrogate the treaty, for it prolonged Britain's control of the Suez Canal; but now, in their desperation, they were prepared to accept British military help on their behalf. In turn, Bevin's warning to the Israelis was terse and specific: Unless they obeyed the latest Security Council resolution, Britain would "fulfill its treaty obligations" to Egypt. For Ben-Gurion the ultimatum was a chilling one. He dared not risk a frontal collision with a Great Power, still less with a state whose residual claims on Palestine were barely disguised. Accordingly, on January 2, 1949, he ordered his troops to withdraw from the Sinai. At the same time, however, faced with an urgent appeal from his military commanders, Ben-Gurion authorized a last-minute assault on the heights above the border town of Rafa. Control of this ridge would have sealed the Egyptian army's final escape route from the Negev.

For several weeks, as it happened, RAF Spitfires had accompanied Egyptian air patrols over the Egyptian-Israeli frontier. On January 7, 1949, Israeli planes shot down five of these British fighters. London waited no longer. Declaring that Israel had made "unprovoked aggressions" against Egyptian territory, it put a squadron of naval destroyers in the eastern Mediterranean on "highest alert," then rushed two British army battalions from East Africa to the Suez Canal Zone, and advised British citizens in Israel to leave the country forthwith. In truth, the Foreign Office was interested in considerably more than Israeli withdrawal from Sinai. It preferred that the Israelis should also be obliged to relinquish the largest part of the Negev.

It was specifically this wider objective that Ernest Bevin now pressed on Washington, emphasizing the strategic advantages for the West if the British maintained de facto control of a desert land bridge from Egypt to Transjordan. But the foreign secretary was also pressing his luck. Britain's effort to muscle its way back into the Palestine equation did not resonate well among the American people, who by then had developed much sympathy for the Jews and admiration for their reborn state. Harry Truman's patience with the British similarly was exhausted. On January 10, 1949, the president summoned Britain's Ambassador Sir Oliver Franks to the White House. "I don't like what you people are doing," Truman coldly informed Franks. "Your planes have no business over the battle area in Palestine." It was a view fully shared by France, the Netherlands, and Norway, whose governments also expressed grave reservations. At this point Bevin finally stepped back from the brink. He ordered British forces to stay clear of the Israelis in the Negev.

If the foreign secretary was deterred from a military confrontation with Israel, it was due not least to growing criticism of his policy within Britain itself. No denunciation of his Middle East brinksmanship was more unsparing than Winston Churchill's. As leader of the Conservative opposition, Churchill for weeks had been taking the Attlee government to task for rejecting Israel's legitimacy as a sovereign nation. "[The Jews] have established a government which functions effectively," the old statesman declaimed before the House of Commons in December 1948. "They have a victorious army at their disposal and they have the support both of Soviet Russia and the United States. . . . [T]he government of Israel . . . cannot be ignored and treated as if it did not exist." The criticism gained in urgency after the Anglo-Israeli air battle of January 7, 1949.

Two weeks later, in a stormy parliamentary session, Ernest Bevin lashed back at his critics, protesting the "unfair political pressures" directed at government policy on Palestine. He and his colleagues at least had been responsive to Arab feelings about "a new and alien State to be carved out of Arab land by a foreign force," insisted Bevin,

"against the wishes and over the protests of the native population."
That "foreign force" had driven half a million Arab refugees from
their land and conquered large areas of terrain. It was the United
States that had exploited the Palestine issue, complained Bevin, and
exclusively for domestic political purposes. But Churchill would not
allow Bevin refuge in self-pity:

> Whether the Right Hon. Gentleman likes it or not [Churchill
> replied] . . . the coming into being of a Jewish State . . . is an
> event in world history to be viewed in the perspective, not of a
> generation or a century, but in the perspective of a thousand,
> two thousand, or even three thousand years. . . . [N]ow that it
> has come into being, it is England that refuses to recognize it,
> and, by our actions, we find ourselves regarded as its most bitter
> enemies.

Indeed, for months after May 15, 1948, Cadogan at the United
Nations refused even to allude to Israel by name, resorting instead to
such circumlocutions as "the Jewish authorities in Palestine." This
was the protective reaction of a "cuttlefish," sneered Churchill,
"beclouding friend and foe alike in an opaque, inky liquid."

By mid-January 1949 Conservative criticism was striking home.
Although the Attlee government survived a parliamentary vote of
confidence on Palestine, one hundred fifty Labor delegates joined the
opposition or abstained. Since the previous May, and for half a year
even after termination of the Palestine mandate, Britain had continued to detain Jewish male refugees whom earlier it had intercepted at
sea en route to Palestine and interned in Cyprus. Only now, on January 18, 1949, did a chastened Bevin authorize their release. Eleven
days afterward, the Labor cabinet announced *de facto* recognition of
Israel. Yet, as late as March 24, Britain's Ambassador Cadogan
abstained when the UN Security Council voted to admit Israel to the
United Nations, and more than another year would pass before
Whitehall, in April 1950, upgraded its recognition from *de facto* to *de
jure*.

A GRUDGING RECONCILIATION

Neither Britain nor Israel would find it an easy matter to overcome
the resentments engendered by this prolonged confrontation.
Throughout 1949 the Foreign Office dealt with Israel's first diplomatic representative, Mordechai Eliash, with caution and reserve.
The Israelis responded in kind. When Sir Alexander Knox Helm

arrived in Tel Aviv as Britain's first chargé d'affaires (and later minister), he and his staff initially were treated with suspicion and more than occasional rudeness. Yet substantive dialogue with the British could not long be postponed. Hundreds of thousands of refugees were streaming into a near-bankrupt little republic. They had to be fed and housed. The Ben-Gurion government regarded it as critical to win release of the Jewish Agency's—now Israel's—frozen sterling balances in England. In May 1949, therefore, David Horowitz, director general of Israel's ministry of finance, departed for London to seek access to these funds.

Horowitz did not anticipate an easy mission. The acrimony of recent years was certain to have left a bitter residue in the home island. But upon arriving in England, the Israeli emissary was pleasantly surprised to be granted a cordial private meeting with Sir Wilfred Eddy, a senior Treasury official. "You shot your way out to freedom," Eddy genially reassured Horowitz, "and now we can become friends." Yet he warned that difficulties remained, for Britain's own economic circumstances were grave. Hoping to ease the way, Eddy then arranged a meeting for Horowitz with Henry Wilson-Smith, the Treasury's permanent undersecretary. But Wilson-Smith, far from offering help, declared his intention to use the impounded sterling balance as payment of a counterclaim for Israel's "sequestration" of British government property in Palestine. The gap between the two sides was too wide to be bridged in these initial discussions.

In late June 1949 negotiations were resumed in Israel. Britain's Minister Helm led his country's delegation, while Horowitz was flanked by Minister of Finance Eliezer Kaplan and Foreign Minister Moshe Sharett. The Israelis by then had decided to use Wilson-Smith's argument to make their own case. It was Britain, they contended, that had turned over several of its key military installations to the Arabs in the last months of the mandate. In capturing these "Arab" facilities, at heavy cost of life, Israel had merely conquered property that Britain had given the Arabs in the first place, and thus Britain was not justified in "reselling" it to Israel. But Helm and his colleagues remained unmoved. Israel had assumed the role of successor government in Palestine, they insisted, and thus had inherited all outstanding obligations. The Anglo-Israeli discussions soon reached an impasse.

In the early autumn of 1949, Horowitz decided to return to England, to negotiate directly with Sir Stafford Cripps, Chancellor of the Exchequer. In fact the two men had met briefly on Horowitz's earlier trip, and had related well to each other. "From the moment I met him," Horowitz wrote later, "I sensed his sincere desire to make amends for Britain's hostile dealings with us." Doubtless much of that goodwill reflected Cripps's ideological sympathy for the plight of a fellow Socialist government. "Give us a little time," the chancellor suggested to Horowitz. "We're facing another election in two weeks. Afterward, many things may be possible." And once Labor was reelected with a triumphant majority, Cripps personally formulated a deal with the Israelis. Horowitz recalled:

> [T]he agreement with Britain in its finalized form went far beyond all our expectations. It transferred, finally and legally, to the State of Israel the vast British properties in Palestine, in return for a token payment and a negligible proportion of the original demands—a sum that was to be paid in installments over a period of fifteen years, with interest of only one percent a year.

Yet it was not ideological fraternalism that ameliorated still another lingering Israeli economic crisis. In 1950 the nation's fuel supply was all but exhausted. During the Palestine War, Iraq had severed the oil pipeline from Mosul to the refineries of Haifa. Israel thereafter would be obliged to purchase its crude oil from the United States and Latin America before processing it in Haifa. And it was specifically over those refineries that a new difficulty arose. Their owner, the Anglo-Iranian Petroleum Company, was unwilling to activate them; and without access to these giant cracking vats, Israel would be obliged to import refined oil at prohibitive cost. Thus, in June 1950, David Horowitz once again departed for London, to intercede with Anglo-Iranian's board of directors. This time he met a stone wall. Any move to activate the refineries, the directors argued, would outrage the Arab world and thus jeopardize Anglo-Iranian's other vast installations in the Middle East.

The Englishmen were not dissembling. On learning of Horowitz's mission, Prime Minister Nuri es-Saïd of Iraq, one of Britain's most valued allies in the Arab world, flew immediately to London. Indeed, Nuri rushed straight from Gatwick Airport to Ernest Bevin's hospital room, where the foreign minister was recovering from surgery. Activation of the Haifa refineries, Nuri warned, would torpedo a wide-ranging Anglo-Iraqi financial agreement even then under negotiation between the two governments. Taken aback (and doubtless physically vulnerable), Bevin promised to veto any agreement with Israel. But Horowitz in turn resorted to a counterstrategy, one that made no further appeal to compassion. Horowitz knew that the British govern-

ment's voting shares in Anglo-Iranian were under the legal control of
the Treasury—in effect, of Sir Stafford Cripps. Through a mutual
friend, Horowitz then sent word to the chancellor that Israel could
not allow the refineries to remain idle. Even nationalization was a
possibility, he intimated. The hint was palpable. Should Israel take
that draconian step, other Middle Eastern governments might discern a useful precedent for Anglo-Iranian's installations in their own
territories. After two days of suspense, Horowitz received word from
Cripps that the Haifa refineries would be reopened within three
months. They were.

Beyond currency deposits and oil installations, could the physical
protection of the British Commonwealth also be retrieved? Israel
found itself not only economically beleaguered but militarily isolated.
The issue became relevant in the late autumn and early winter of
1950–51. By then two years had passed since the Rhodes Armistice
Agreements of January–April 1949 (pp. 18–19), officially ending the
Palestine War, and not a single one of Israel's Arab neighbors had
moved decisively toward the anticipated second step of formal peace.
Overwhelmed by the economic burdens of its early statehood, the
Jewish nation would have been hard pressed to face yet another full-
scale enemy invasion. It needed allies. In Prime Minister Ben-
Gurion's calculations, too, his country had something to offer. The
Korean War was raging, and the threat of Communist aggression in
Europe, perhaps in the Mediterranean, was by no means remote.
Would not a democratic nation like Israel, toughened in the battle for
military survival, possess alliance value?

In fact, Ben-Gurion's quest for a strategic partnership was paralleled in London. By 1950 Britain's senior military staff was carefully
appraising Israel's logistical value. The Jewish state, after all, was the
inheritor of Britain's former roads, bridges, and ports in the Holy
Land. In the event of a future Soviet threat to the Middle East, those
facilities could well prove indispensable for Britain's strategic purposes, as they had during World War II. Should an effort not be made
to determine whether, and under what conditions, the Israelis would
make them available? But when the general staff submitted its proposal to the Attlee cabinet, the reaction at first was unenthusiastic.
Too much bad blood had flowed between the two countries to permit
even the narrowest degree of functional cooperation. This also
appeared to be the Israeli view. Indeed, in September 1950, Alexander
Helm, Britain's emissary in Tel Aviv, had cautiously raised the issue of
bases with General Yigael Yadin, Israel's chief of staff. The response
was not encouraging—although Yadin had assured Helm that, in the

event of war, Israel of course would be on the side of the West, and then (but only then) would offer its cooperation.

Nevertheless, the British general staff continued to importune the government, seeking authorization to explore the possibility at least of transit rights through Israel in times of "military emergency." By December 1950, as it happened, the chances of reaching an agreement appeared somewhat brighter. Teddy Kollek, minister of information at the Israeli embassy in Washington, had acknowledged to the State Department that Israel's policy of "nonidentification" in the Cold War had been a failure (pp. 61–3), and that Israel was willing now to place its army at the disposal of the West. In return for military aid, Kollek intimated, Israel would even allow the United States use of its military facilities. But State Department officials reacted to Kollek's proposal with caution, even bemusement, and suggested instead that Britain, with its wide network of Middle Eastern connections and commitments, might prove to be a more logical partner for Israel. Kollek hesitated, citing "psychological barriers" in dealing with the British. Nevertheless, when an account of this meeting reached London early in 1951, the foreign ministry discerned a window of opportunity. Negotiations with Egypt were going badly on a renewal of British treaty rights at Suez (p. 22). Discussions with the Israelis accordingly might prove useful in exploring an alternative relationship.

In London, on January 14, 1951, Sir William Strang, permanent undersecretary for foreign affairs, sounded out Israel's Minister Eliahu Elath on the chances of establishing bases in Israel, particularly in the Gaza area, as well as a strategic corridor for British troops through the Negev to Hashemite Jordan. Intrigued by the possibility of a major strategic alliance, Elath soon afterward flew to Israel on leave and communicated the proposal to Ben-Gurion directly. But the prime minister regarded the suggestion as nothing less than an "insult." While acknowledging that a tripartite arrangement with the United States and Britain was conceivable, he rejected the very notion of a bilateral relationship exclusively with Britain, a country that had "inflicted only harm on Israel." Indeed, the presence of British bases on Israeli soil would curtail the government's freedom "to deal with" the Arabs, Ben-Gurion insisted, should they infringe the armistice agreements. Elath was sobered. Returning to London, the ambassador somewhat embarrassedly informed Strang that the issue of bases was "premature."

Even then, however, the British Foreign Office and the general staff were allowed to search out areas of cooperation. The following month, General Sir Brian Robertson, commander of British armed forces in the Middle East, arrived in Israel on a secret exploratory visit. Robertson's instructions were firm. He was to deal cautiously with the Israelis, to elicit their views on a possible tactical military accommodation, but to withhold any specific proposals lest the Israelis demand too high a price. Robertson met with Ben-Gurion on February 19, 1951, and outlined his government's views on Middle Eastern security. It was in this geographic region, Robertson explained, where Britain still possessed extensive land, naval, and air facilities, that the West was in its strongest position to blunt any possible Soviet military initiatives. Ben-Gurion then interjected: "What are your plans in the event of an actual war with the Soviet Union?" Robertson's answer was equally forthright. If Russia were to thrust southward toward Iraq, he explained, "[w]e shall advance northward from our bases in Egypt by way of Israel, Jordan, and Iraq." The response offended the prime minister. "Do you think we're a British colony?" he protested. "Before deciding to turn us into a 'transit route' for your armies, you must come to an agreement with us." Robertson immediately apologized, explaining that he had been speaking only in theoretical terms.

Yet Ben-Gurion now had his opening. Did not Britain also wish Israel to play an active role in the Western war effort as a full partner? he asked. If that was the case, Israel then had its own price for cooperation. This was Western help in developing its military industries and transportation network. Once constructed, those facilities surely would be useful to the West in the event of war. Would Great Britain not regard its help to Israel as an expression of enlightened self-interest? General Robertson's reaction was amiably noncommittal. The extent of Britain's support would depend on the extent of Israel's cooperation, he replied vaguely. The two men plainly were engaged in a game of cat-and-mouse, each feeling out the other.

It was in his second meeting with Robertson, two days later, that the prime minister caught his visitor off guard. He proposed now that Britain deal with Israel as if the Jewish state were a member of the British Commonwealth. "We could establish an interrelationship like the one you have with New Zealand," he suggested. It was a breathtaking concept. In effect, Ben-Gurion was seeking a privileged position for Israel in the Middle East. If his nation really was of such critical strategic importance to Britain, the prime minister wanted material proof, a commitment to mutual defense evidently as far-reaching as the guarantees Britain was offering its Commonwealth allies. Taken aback by the sheer magnitude of the proposal, Robertson played for time. He was only a soldier, he explained. Political matters should be left to his government.

Upon his return to England, the general transmitted an account of his conversation to Herbert Morrison, who lately had replaced the ailing Bevin as foreign secretary. Morrison and his Whitehall colleagues did not react well to Ben-Gurion's offer. A special status for Israel would have doomed Britain's already fragile position in the Arab world. Nevertheless, in April 1951, under pressure from the general staff, which dearly coveted Israel's communications network, the foreign secretary responded circumspectly to Ben-Gurion:

> We believe that it is possible to establish a relationship between our two peoples which . . . shall constitute a bond between us and which shall be capable of progressive development. In our view, this must be a gradual process and one which comes about naturally as a result of continual contact with exchanges of views and individual acts of cooperation in the military field.

Ben-Gurion did not reply. Regarding the letter as deliberately evasive, he concluded that "Morrison is a fox, and should not be trusted."

In October 1951, however, the Conservatives won Britain's general election, and Winston Churchill was returned to power. Accordingly, that same month, Ben-Gurion at last felt emboldened to reply—to Anthony Eden, Morrison's successor as foreign secretary. "We are willing to do our share," he wrote, "in safeguarding the interests of our two countries . . . in the Middle East. . . . To enable us to play our role effectively, it will be necessary to strengthen our industrial [and infrastructure] potential . . . to improve the training and equipment of our armed forces . . . and to provide stocks of food and fuel." Ben-Gurion then proposed direct discussions on concrete plans. This time he made no further mention of a special relationship with the British Commonwealth.

A week later Eden, a veteran Arabist and godfather of the Arab League, kept his brief reply diplomatically cryptic: "His Majesty's Government agree to your suggestion that direct conversations on specific matters should now be initiated . . . [and] accordingly suggest that a small British mission should visit Israel for the purpose of exploratory discussions of the type mentioned in your message." The British delegation of five officers, none more exalted than a brigadier, duly arrived in late October, and Israel's chief of staff, General Mordechai Makleff, was charged with conducting talks on "nuts and bolts." But the series of meetings was conducted in an atmosphere of elliptic generalities. When they ended, after four days, their single conclusion was to hold further meetings in England. In fact, none ever took place, in England or Israel, and gradually the matter dropped off Ben-Gurion's agenda. Neither, in future years, would it be revived in London. For Anthony Eden and the professionals at Whitehall, the notion of a formal military partnership with the Jewish state had always been the remotest of possibilities. By January 1954, engaged at last in revived and productive discussions with Egypt on Britain's residual access to the Suez Canal Zone, Eden concluded that his government should now abandon any further notion of basing its military policy in the Middle East "either wholly or mainly on cooperation with Israel."

THE HASHEMITE FACTOR

Rather, from the very onset of the Palestine crisis in 1947–48, the Foreign Office nurtured a more fundamental understanding with its most reliable Arab protégé, King Abdullah of Transjordan. If partition of the Holy Land was unavoidable, Bevin and the Hashemites agreed, its terrain should be divided exclusively between Transjordan and the emergent Jewish state (p. 6). It was on the basis of this tacit Anglo-Hashemite accord that Britain anticipated maintaining a foothold at least in eastern—Hashemite—Palestine, and thus a residual staging area in the Holy Land for its Middle Eastern lifeline. The Jews accepted this scenario. Indeed, on the very eve of the Palestine War, private conversations between King Abdullah and Mrs. Golda Myerson (later Meir), a senior official of the Jewish Agency, confirmed their expectations of a mutual territorial accommodation. Although it was not possible to avoid a fierce series of battles for Jerusalem, by late summer of 1948 a de facto segmentation of the city into Jewish- and Hashemite-controlled zones essentially terminated the war between Israel and Transjordan. For his part Abdullah was not dissatisfied. With the approval of Bevin in London, and the even more vigorous support of Sir Alec Kirkbride, Britain's "resident" in Amman, the king had extended his realm across the River Jordan and fended off last-minute Egyptian efforts to establish a rival puppet regime for Arab Palestine. Ruling over his enlarged kingdom, Abdullah was prepared to negotiate the final details of a settlement with the Israelis.

Officially those negotiations were conducted in the late winter and early spring of 1949 on the island of Rhodes, under United Nations auspices. There a tandem series of Arab-Israeli discussions produced armistices between the Jewish state and Egypt and Transjordan, and set the precedent for agreements concluded slightly later with Lebanon and Syria along their respective frontiers (Iraq alone refused to negotiate an armistice with Israel). But in the case of the Hashemites, the decisive bargaining occurred well beyond Rhodes. In February 1949, even as discussions continued on that island, Abdullah invited an Israeli delegation to meet with him secretly at his winter palace in Shune, near the Dead Sea. It was consequently at Shune, in this and in other intermittent Israeli visits over the next weeks, that the final territorial issues between the two countries were resolved. Most of the adjustments were comparatively minor. Indeed, the single most important provision was to freeze the status quo for Jerusalem. The New City would remain in Jewish possession, the Old City in Arab—Hashemite—possession.

While no British representatives sat in on these clandestine negotiations, their progress was carefully monitored by Sir Alec Kirkbride. It was at his encouragement that Abdullah's ministers explored with the Israelis longer-range strategic accommodations between the two countries, with a view to a formal peace treaty. Significantly, Ernest Bevin was prepared by then to revise his earlier suspicion of the Jewish state as a threat to Britain's Middle East interests. As the foreign secretary envisaged it, a permanent Israeli-Transjordanian understanding might even assure stability for the little Hashemite client state. "The Israelis are now ready to look to us for practical advice," Bevin informed a conference of Britain's Middle East ambassadors in July 1949, and thus an Israel-Hashemite territorial settlement could be regarded as a settlement between two potential allies of the West. It was not an easy or an entirely accurate sell to these veteran Arabophiles, but the foreign secretary held firm.

With Bevin's encouragement, then, Abdullah initiated still another round of direct contacts with the Israelis, in October 1949. The king's hope, and Britain's, was to negotiate additional advantages for his realm. Abdullah sought access to the Mediterranean through the Negev, the return of Arab neighborhoods in Jerusalem's New (essentially Jewish) City, and a free port in Haifa. In return he offered Israel access to its lost potash works on the north shore of the Dead Sea, and a free port on the Hashemite side of the Gulf of Aqaba. In principle Ben-Gurion was interested. After six weeks of additional Israeli-Hashemite talks, the Israeli prime minister agreed to offer Transjordan a demilitarized, northern Negev easement to Haifa. A more difficult issue was extension of the 1946 Anglo-Hashemite military treaty to the Transjordanian-annexed West Bank of Palestine. Ben-Gurion initially opposed this provision, fearing an intimidating network of British army bases hard by Israel's fragile new borders.

Yet, facing a new United Nations demand to internationalize Jerusalem (p. 200), a development inimical to both Israel and Transjordan, the two sides decided to intensify their negotiations at Shune, and to evince greater flexibility. This time Kirkbride participated actively in the discussions. The Israelis dropped their objection to territorial extension of the Anglo-Transjordanian Treaty. The Hashemites for their part abandoned their demand for minor boundary adjustments in Jerusalem's New City, and consented to augmented Israeli access to the Hebrew University and Hadassah Hospital buildings on Mount Scopus in East Jerusalem, facilities Israel had lost in the recent war. In March 1950, finally, Israel and Transjordan agreed to initial a peace agreement.

Yet the moment news of the accord leaked to the Arab world, a storm broke over Abdullah's head. He faced a crisis within his own cabinet. The West Bank refugee population seethed. Syria threatened to close its frontier with the Hashemite Kingdom. Egypt and Saudi Arabia proposed to expel Transjordan from the Arab League. Thereupon, given pause by the vehemence of his neighbors' reaction, Abdullah decided to hold the treaty in limbo, at least until excitement died down in the Arab world. The British, too, were sobered. They had pinned their hopes on an enlarged "Hashemite Kingdom of Jordan" (as Abdullah had renamed his realm in late April 1950), a nation to be locked in a stable peace with its vibrant new Jewish neighbor. But with a formal Israeli-Hashemite treaty threatening to disrupt Abdullah's enlarged realm, the British now cast about for another formula. By early May 1950, after two months of discussions with Washington and Paris, they produced their own, alternative solution for Arab-Israeli stability. This was the Tripartite Declaration, issued jointly by Britain, the United States, and France. Under its terms the three governments committed themselves to preserve a balance of power between Israel and the Arab states by monitoring and rationing the sale of weaponry to them, and, if necessary, by intervening militarily to forestall aggression between them.

Interpreted by outside observers as a guarantee principally of Israel's security, the declaration in fact reflected Britain's commitment to the security of its Hashemite client—both against Israel and against other Arab nations. It was significant, after all, that Britain (and the other signatories) issued their announcement only five days after Abdullah formally proclaimed his nation's reconstitution as the enlarged Hashemite Kingdom of Jordan. In effect Abdullah's neighbors now were put on notice: Any retaliatory violence against the Hashemite realm would trigger not only implementation of the 1946

Anglo-Transjordanian Treaty but possibly even intervention by the French and Americans. If the Israelis henceforth drew any reassurance of stability with Jordan, it was less from the declaration itself than from the manifest goodwill of the Hashemite king. It was Abdullah they trusted, assuredly not the British. He, not they, was their best guarantee against instability along Israel's precarious eastern border with the Hashemite kingdom. The guarantee would prove a fragile one. Only a year and a quarter later, on July 30, 1951, as Abdullah was descending the steps of the al-Aqsa Mosque in the Arab sector of Jerusalem, a Palestinian gunman in the pay of Egypt shot the little monarch dead.

THE EGYPTIAN FACTOR

For Israel, during the months following the Palestine War of 1948–49, the auguries for peace with its neighbor to the south appeared almost as hopeful as those with the Hashemites. In January 1949 the Egyptians were the first of Israel's Arab enemies to begin armistice negotiations in Rhodes. Within a few days the acting United Nations mediator, Ralph Bunche, who had succeeded the murdered Bernadotte, cajoled the Arab delegations into face-to-face conversations with the Israelis. Among those delegations it was the Egyptians who evinced both pragmatism and a certain cautious flexibility. Thus, as a first step, they agreed that the armistice agreement should be drawn essentially along the existing military lines. The Negev would remain within Israel, except for the narrow Gaza coastal strip occupied by Egyptian troops. Each side assumed that the armistice rapidly would be supplanted by a permanent treaty of peace.

By the summer of 1949, however, once the shock of defeat began to ebb, and as intermittent peace talks in Lausanne, Switzerland, under a "Palestine Conciliation Commission," failed to make progress, several of the Arab governments reappraised their ability to strangle the upstart Jewish state—if not in direct battlefield conflict, then by economic quarantine. To that end, it was the Cairo government that resorted to a particularly effective weapon. This was closure of the Suez Canal and, later, the Gulf of Aqaba to Israel-bound shipping. Over the years it was an embargo that would become increasingly painful to the Jewish state (p. 82). Beyond its economic costs, the blockade signified foreclosure of a once promising opportunity for peace with the largest and most powerful of Israel's Arab neighbors.

Meanwhile, Britain's own quest for a strategic accommodation with Egypt would prove of comparable diplomatic frustration. By

1952, over 100 million tons of shipping passed through the Suez Canal annually, and of this tonnage, 35 million was British. Through Suez, British troopships foreshortened by half the Cape route to Malaya, Hong Kong, and Korea. If the Egyptians, in violation of international treaty obligations, closed this waterway to Israeli shipping, might they not also discriminate against British shipping in the future? Moreover, the Canal Zone was of even greater value to the British as a military base than as a shortcut for maritime passage. With its thirty-eight army camps and ten airfields in use during World War II, this huge reticulation, extending two-thirds the length of the waterway, supported forty-one British divisions and Commonwealth units and air forces totaling sixty-five squadrons. In the event of future conflict with the Communist empire, the Suez complex offered unmatched capabilities both for defensive and offensive operations. Within the 2,500-mile range of Suez-based RAF bombers lay the entirety of industrial and oil installations in the southern Soviet Union. None other of Britain's Middle Eastern emplacements possessed comparable military advantage.

And, by the same token, it was this vast British extraterritorial presence that the Egyptian people regarded as a galling affront to their national sovereignty. Seven decades of British occupation were enough, they insisted. In fact London was not insensitive to their cri de coeur; it was prepared to respond in a forthcoming manner. But even if the elaborate Suez defense complex were to be abandoned, a treaty arrangement was required to guarantee British troops renewed access in the event of a future military threat to the Commonwealth. A residual peacetime force of British technicians would also have to stay on to maintain (and guard) the Suez facilities. It was specifically on these issues that Anglo-Egyptian negotiations remained deadlocked through the late 1940s and early 1950s.

No nation followed the trajectory of these discussions with more acute presentiments than did Israel. In 1952 a military cabal had overthrown the Farouk monarchy and taken power in Cairo. Its leader, and later the nation's president, Colonel Gamal Abd al-Nasser, had required less than a year to project himself as a champion of Arab unity throughout the Middle East. It soon became plain that there would be little room for accommodating Israel's security needs in Nasser's pan-Arabist vision. Accordingly, if the British military presence were removed from Suez, Egypt under Nasser would gain possession of a cornucopia of military installations, further tilting the military balance against Israel. Access to Britain's abandoned RAF bases would shorten by one hundred miles Egypt's bombing route to

Israel, and thus provide Egyptian aircraft with an additional fifteen minutes' flight time over Israeli targets.

In fact Israel's worst fears were to be realized. On July 27, 1954, following years of intermittent and acrimonious negotiations, Egyptian and British diplomats at long last initialed a "Heads of Agreement"—a short, ten-paragraph treaty outline that represented a near-total victory for Egypt. By its provisions Britain would withdraw from Suez altogether, preserving the option of return only in the event of a "direct attack" (not a mere "threat of attack") on Egypt itself, and, at that, an attack by a non–Middle Eastern nation—thereby foreclosing the Arab-Israel conflict as a pretext for a renewed British presence. Egypt's only concessions were to allow Britain two years to wind up its affairs at Suez and complete its evacuation, and to permit a small group of British civilian personnel to remain for maintenance purposes. The bulk of the Suez installations would devolve into Egypt's hands.

The moment news of the Heads of Agreement was announced, a burning issue for the Israelis was the compensation their own nation would receive. Would the British be prepared to recompense Israel for the additional danger they were imposing on a tiny and still fragile nation? Would they consent to store their heavier weaponry and engineering equipment on Israeli territory? At a minimum, as a feature of the impending treaty, would they require the Egyptians first to open Suez to oil tankers bound for Israel? But when Israel's Ambassador Eliahu Elath raised these questions at Whitehall, he evoked only polite smiles.

Colonel Binyamin Gibli, chief of Israel's military intelligence branch, could have anticipated Britain's nonresponsiveness. Well before completion of the Heads of Agreement, Gibli was convinced that the time for diplomatic fantasizing had run out. More urgent measures were needed. There was a chance, he felt, that the "Suez Rebels," a small group of Conservative hard-liners in the House of Commons, would seize upon any evidence of Egyptian bad faith to deter or at least delay a British evacuation from the Canal Zone. In Gibli's view, Israel should find a way to provide that "evidence," even if it had to be manufactured. Israel's defense minister, Pinchas Lavon, may not have been fully apprised of Gibli's intended conspiracy. Prime Minister Moshe Sharett assuredly was not. But the intelligence director was determined to move ahead, if necessary on his own.

The groundwork for the Israeli plot in fact had been laid three years earlier, in 1951, when the nation's military intelligence branch recruited a dozen young Egyptian Jews who had been engaged in secret emigration activities, and trained them in the manufacture of rudimentary explosive devices. In June 1954, as Anglo-Egyptian negotiations gained momentum, Colonel Gibli dispatched an agent to Cairo to contact and "activate" the little Jewish underground group. On July 2, at the agent's instructions, the conspirators set about placing their incendiary devices at carefully selected public buildings in Cairo and Alexandria, in post offices, public checkrooms, movie theaters, and United States Information Centers and consulates. Several of the "bombs" exploded. Damage was slight, and there were no injuries. It was Gibli's hope that the sabotage would be attributed to Egyptian extremists.

One of the Jewish spies was caught in the act, however. Arrested, he was tortured into revealing the identities of his companions. These too were arrested and forced to confess. To the accompaniment of a farrago of sensationalist Egyptian press accounts of a Zionist spy plot, the prisoners were scheduled for trial before a military court on December 11, 1954. Ten days before the proceedings, one of the defendants committed suicide in his cell. By the time trial ended, in late January 1955, two others had been sentenced to death, and all but two of the remaining eleven received sentences varying from seven years to life.

Meanwhile, within days of their arrest, Israel's Prime Minister Sharett issued an indignant denial of an Israeli spy plot against Egypt, and called upon Western governments to intercede with Cairo. Most of these governments responded. For them the accusation of "Jewish treason" evoked only ugly reminders of the recent Nazi era. The British Foreign Office in any case was uninterested in seeing the Jewish prisoners hanged, lest the Israelis be provoked into retaliatory military action against Egypt—a warning that was discreetly transmitted to Cairo by Lord Stansgate, a retired diplomat with close ties to Nasser. But the Egyptian government disregarded the appeals and warnings. On January 31, 1955, two of the condemned prisoners were hanged in the courtyard of Cairo's military prison. In Israel a day of public mourning was declared. With hardly an exception, the Western nations expressed their revulsion and outrage.

Only in later years did the authentic circumstances of the spy plot begin to emerge, first in Israel and then, belatedly, in Western intelligence circles. Yet even without awareness that the conspiracy was no mere fabrication of the Nasser government but rather an Israeli intrigue, Britain's Suez Rebels in 1954 almost certainly would have failed to block an Anglo-Egyptian deal on Suez. During the summer and autumn months of 1954, the period when Britain's press condemned the arrest and trial of the Egyptian Jews as mere crude propaganda, no second thoughts were raised on Britain's departure from Suez. The Heads of Agreement document was routinely initialed on October 19, 1954, and ratified by Parliament on December 6. In their last-ditch effort to block the treaty, the Suez Rebels did not so much as allude to the spy trial. With the passage of time, to be sure, the British would have ample cause to regard Gamal Abd al-Nasser as a loose cannon in the Middle East; but Israel's misguided and inept excursion into sub rosa intrigue would play no role in determining London's Middle Eastern policy.

Meanwhile, with the exchange of Anglo-Egyptian ratifications on December 6, 1954, the first stage of Britain's evacuation began. Each ensuing month between 3,000 and 4,000 troops, together with huge quantities of equipment, were loaded onto transports and freighters. By June 13, 1956, when the last British officer stepped from the Alexandria wharf onto a troopship bound for Cyprus, the United Kingdom had left behind supplies valued at eighty million pounds sterling. These included, beyond an embarras de richesses of military camps, airfields, and training installations, some 50,000 tons of ammunition, 2,000 vehicles, and sufficient personal equipment to outfit 50,000 troops. As its final legacy to Nasser, Britain also left behind an open arena for potential military action eastward—across the Sinai Peninsula.

Well before then, in any case, neither Israel nor even Egypt was the principal focus of British strategic concerns in the Middle East. Rather, the Foreign Office was shifting its attention from Suez toward Iraq, Turkey, Iran, even Pakistan. As the repository or transit route of Britain's largest complex of oil fields, refineries, and pipelines, it was specifically these "northern tier" countries that appeared the likeliest targets for Soviet penetration. Indeed, on their own, in February 1955, Turkey and Iraq entered into a mutual defense agreement. Months later, prodded by London and Washington, Iran and Pakistan joined this so-called "Baghdad Pact." When Britain soon afterward added its own substantial weight to the agreement, and the United States joined the pact's military committee, it became evident that Anglo-American funds, weaponry, and strategic guidance eventually would be made available to a new and more powerful configuration of Middle Eastern states. It was not a development to be regarded congenially by Egypt's President Nasser. Only the year before, he had won Britain's commitment to end its imperial presence in Egypt. Were the British now returning to their former Middle Eastern preeminence through a back door? In his outraged response to the Baghdad Pact, the Egyptian president soon would have recourse to an alternative Great Power sponsor (pp. 75–6).

For Israel, meanwhile, the shift in the region's military balance evoked even graver concern. Liquidation of Britain's "buffer" presence at Suez was ominous enough. But if Iraq were to be allowed widened access to British and American military resources, of what use to Israel was the pious Tripartite Declaration of 1950? Would the Western Powers be prepared to offer Israel an equivalent membership in the Baghdad Pact? In fact, the opposite was the case. From 1954 on, London had structured its Middle East strategy on a classified blueprint formulated by Sir Evelyn Shuckburgh, a senior Foreign Office official. Known as the Alpha Plan, the scenario anticipated that, for the sake of peace in the region, Israel sooner or later would have to make significant territorial concessions. In Washington, Secretary of State John Foster Dulles concurred in this assumption. It appeared to be the only way of placating Nasser, who had demanded the southern sector of the Negev Desert as a basis for negotiating even the most grudging, functional accommodation with the Jewish state.

If the Alpha Plan at first remained secret, the Israelis were not slow in grasping London's chill reserve on their security needs. After an unproductive meeting with Foreign Secretary Selwyn Lloyd in July 1954, Shimon Peres, director general of Israel's ministry of defense, noted in his diary: "Overall, I have the impression that the English still have not recognized the State of Israel." Peres was at least partly right. Well into the mid-1950s, Britain's Conservative government was unprepared to recognize the permanence of Israel's frontiers. At a Guildhall banquet on November 9, 1955, Anthony Eden, now prime minister, obliquely acknowledged the Alpha Plan when he broached the possibility of attenuating the Negev in favor of Egypt. Upon learning of the speech, Israel's Prime Minister Sharett all but abandoned hope that Britain might serve as an honest broker in the Middle East. Ben-Gurion, on leave at his desert retreat in Sde Boker, remained more implacable yet in his distrust of the British.

A CONTEMPLATED SECOND RESCUE

Even as Whitehall pinned its faith on a chain of Middle Eastern clients, its attention was drawn increasingly to Jordan, the weakest link in that chain. From the early 1950s the Hashemite desert kingdom was drawn into an escalating series of brutal confrontations with Israel. The crisis between the two countries was less one of national rivalry than of mutual human vulnerability. The Israeli-Jordanian borders, sculpted by the Palestine War and the Rhodes Armistice, had been regarded as subject to later negotiated adjustments. Yet the assassination of King Abdullah doomed any likelihood of further discussions or compromises. The frontiers accordingly remained frozen, and reflected no concession to civilian needs. They cut Arab villagers off from their fields and wells, from their homes and chattels, and often separated members of extended Arab families.

Soon Arabs marooned on the Hashemite side of the line began crossing a boundary that to them was indeterminate, to rejoin their kinsmen in Israel, to reclaim their possessions, occasionally to harvest their abandoned crops, or to steal from Israeli farms. At first the Mixed Israel-Jordan Armistice Commission, established as a feature of the Rhodes Agreement, managed to resolve issues of crop and chattel pilferage. By the early 1950s, however, the theft or vandalism of Israeli farm property became virtually uncontrollable, and the Israeli response became increasingly forceful—even brutal. Soon Israeli border police began shooting infiltrators almost as a matter of routine. In 1952 alone 394 Arabs were killed and 227 wounded. The Arabs in turn compounded theft and arson with armed attacks, and by 1953 hardly a week passed without the slaying or wounding of Israeli civilians by infiltrators crossing over from Hashemite territory. The Israelis' response was to force King Hussein, grandson of the murdered Abdullah, to accept full responsibility for the mayhem. They retaliated in organized military raids of increasing severity.

The mutual violence reached a crescendo of sorts in 1953. In October, Arab marauders from Jordan threw a grenade into an Israeli home, killing a mother and two children. This time the Israeli cabinet decided to strike back decisively at a cluster of known Palestinian infiltration bases. One of the most notorious of these was the village of Qibya, just within the Hashemite border. The Israeli army launched a pulverizing assault on the community. Yet, owing to faulty intelligence, the attack extended beyond the targeted guerrilla base, and forty-two innocent Arab civilians were killed, fifteen wounded. The Mixed Armistice Commission sternly condemned Israel's action, as did the UN Security Council. Acknowledging the tragedy, the Israeli government sought to make financial amends to the bereaved families. Nevertheless, it could not allow its Arab enemies to assume that a revived Jewish state was incapable of protecting its citizens. The retaliations continued, with mounting ferocity, into 1954, 1955, and beyond.

At the same time, it was Israel's devastating Qibya attack that intensified Britain's solicitude for its Hashemite client. Serving as foreign secretary in 1953, Anthony Eden favored invoking the Anglo-Transjordanian Treaty's military provisions in Hussein's behalf. But Prime Minister Churchill, a veteran pro-Zionist, hesitated to authorize more than a gesture. This took the form of an additional British armored infantry squadron dispatched to Jordan. The warning was taken seriously by Moshe Sharett, who had replaced Ben-Gurion as prime minister in December 1953; yet Sharett failed to dissuade Chief of Staff Moshe Dayan from continuing to launch periodic ripostes. "The centre of infection in the region is Israel," insisted Sir John Nicholls, Britain's ambassador to the Jewish state, in his dispatch to Whitehall of September 14, 1954. ". . . [I]t is not reasonable to expect that a nation made up of individuals so psychologically unstable should be capable of a mature foreign policy." Nicholls added that Britain should not "depend on the Jews coolly reckoning the odds of British intervention against them." They might well risk war with Jordan.

The ambassador's views were shared at the Foreign Office. By late 1954 Britain's Middle East preoccupations were shifting to the threat of Nasser's escalating countercampaign against the Baghdad Pact. Inasmuch as Jordan, too, was regarded as a logical component in the emergent Middle East Treaty Organization, London set about sweetening its inducement to the Hashemite government. In December 1955, Field Marshal Sir Gerald Templer, Britain's military chief of staff, visited Amman and offered increased funds and equipment for Jordan's Arab Legion and air force. Templer added, meaningfully, that membership in the Baghdad Pact would fortify Hashemite defenses not only against the Soviet threat or against Nasserist intimidation, but equally against Israeli "aggression." Hussein and his military leadership were receptive to the proposal.

Not so the festering Palestinian refugee population on Jordan's West Bank. In December 1955, when it appeared that Hussein was prepared to accept Templer's offer, the Palestinian members of the Jordanian cabinet resigned en bloc. Inspired by Egyptian propaganda, they proclaimed that "the salvation of Palestine is more important than imperialist alliances." The mass resignation in turn became the signal for a series of tumultuous pro-Nasserist riots among the Palestinians, both in Amman and in the swollen West Bank refugee camps. Continuing into early 1956, the violence aborted Jordan's membership in the Baghdad Pact, and even intimidated Hussein into dismissing Brigadier John Baghot Glubb, the Arab Legion's British commander. Britain's worst-case Middle East scenario had come to pass. By falling into Nasser's orbit, the Hashemite government evidently was abdicating its initiative in foreign and military policy to the Egyptian dictator.

It was in January 1956, therefore, that Nasser, orchestrating an augmented Palestinian guerrilla campaign of his own against the Jewish state (p. 73), enjoyed the leeway to begin shifting the launching base for these operations from Gaza to the long and porous Hashemite border with Israel. Predictably, the Israelis gave better than they took, striking back across the frontier in military operations of increasing depth and scope. By then Anthony Eden had succeeded Churchill as Britain's prime minister. His foreign secretary, Selwyn Lloyd, as well as the latter's deputy, Anthony Nutting, and the Foreign Office's permanent undersecretary, Sir Ivone Kirkpatrick, shared Whitehall's traditional pro-Arab orientation. All were convinced that Jordan—even under Nasserist influence—remained central to Britain's interests in the Middle East. All then worked closely with the defense ministry in devising a possible course of British action in the event that full-scale warfare should break out between Israel and the Hashemite Kingdom.

Their efforts were rewarded on January 26, 1956, when Eden gave his qualified approval to a new military blueprint. Titled "Operation Cordage," the formula envisaged "neutralization" of the Israeli air force, a naval blockade of the Israeli coast, and the "punishment" of Israeli ground forces. The "punishment" would be undertaken by two bomber squadrons and five fighter/ground-attack squadrons based on Cyprus. Even under this scheme, it was anticipated that Israel might inflict serious damage on the Arab Legion and possibly overrun parts of the Hashemite West Bank. Nevertheless, six months of ensuing naval blockade were regarded as sufficient to induce the Israelis to "withdraw and sue for peace."

By June 1956 the Israeli-Hashemite border was flickering in almost daily violence. By then, too, the British had dispatched an additional armored infantry company to Jordan, together with an RAF fighter squadron from their neighboring Habbaniyah air base in Iraq. These units would now be available to supplement the British forces in Cyprus that similarly had been alerted for possible operations against Israel under Operation Cordage. Yet it was no longer certain that even these reinforcements would suffice. In September 1955 heavy clashes between Israeli and Jordanian army units reduced King Hussein to near-panic. Swallowing his pride, the young monarch then ignored the strictures of the Nasserites in his cabinet and turned unreservedly to his British patron. In the event of full-scale warfare, he asked, would London honor the 1946 Anglo-Transjordanian

Treaty? The response, on October 1, was affirmative. Yet it was also conditional. The British by then were preparing simultaneous military operations against Egypt, whose government lately had nationalized the Suez Canal Company (pp. 86–7). They would be in a better position to meet their responsibilities to Hussein if an Iraqi infantry brigade could also be stationed in Jordan. Would King Hussein agree to this proposal? He would. So would Iraq's Prime Minister Nuri es-Saïd.

Not so Israel's Ben-Gurion, who had returned as his country's prime minister in November 1955. In his chronic suspicion of Whitehall, Ben-Gurion regarded Iraqi troops on Hashemite territory as still another British plot to attenuate Israel's eastern border. He decided then to send Britain and its Arab allies an emphatic message. On October 10, 1956, the Israeli army launched a heavy-artillery bombardment along a twelve-mile stretch of the Jordanian frontier. The following night an Israeli infantry force of near-brigade strength crossed into the West Bank to assault the Jordanian police fortress of Qalqilya, which it had targeted earlier as a center of guerrilla concentration. Although the fortress eventually was destroyed, the battle lasted well into the next afternoon, and both Israelis and Jordanians suffered extensive casualties. It was the single heaviest battle between the two countries since the 1948–49 Palestine War.

Four days later, on October 14, the counsellor of Britain's embassy in Tel Aviv, Peter A. G. Westlake, informed Golda Meir, Israel's foreign minister, that his government "stood ready" to honor its treaty obligations to Jordan, and was "inviting" Iraqi troop units to protect key Jordanian "security installations." Mrs. Meir did not flinch. Any Iraqi move into Jordan, she replied, would adversely affect the military balance of power against Israel, and her government accordingly would "reserve its freedom of action." By then, on the weekend of October 13–14, Air Marshal Sir William Dickson, RAF commander for the Middle East, had placed half his aerial strength on a six-hour alert. His staff was intensively completing the details of a major series of strikes against Israel. At the same time General Sir Charles Keightley, commander in chief of "Operation Musketeer," the impending Anglo-French assault against Egypt (pp. 87, 95), was reviewing the possibility of an amphibious operation against Israel's southern port of Eilat. "With forces now available," he reported to London, "[we] are in a strong position to overcome any Israeli resistance in a few days." Yet, for insurance, Keightley recommended shifting a wing of Venom fighters from British air bases in Germany to Cyprus, and assigning Canberra bombers already deployed in Malta "for offensive action against Israel as well as Egypt."

In fact, Dickson's and Keightley's preparations had become obsolete. Late on the evening of October 14, 1956, Anthony Eden issued orders canceling the planned transfer of Iraqi units to Jordan. The military scenario against Israel was similarly dropped. Almost at the last moment, the prime minister had decided where his priorities lay. Discerning in Gamal Abd al-Nasser the preeminent regional threat to Britain's Commonwealth lifeline, and to Middle Eastern stability altogether, Eden was prepared at last to reappraise his government's approach to the little Zionist republic. For him and for other veterans of Whitehall's Arabophile fraternity of Middle East specialists, the process of reevaluation had taken not less than eight years. But now, finally, with a much graver, Egyptian danger looming on the Mediterranean horizon, no further provocations of the Israelis were to be risked, no further scenarios devised of returning to Palestine through a Hashemite back door. However belated, Britain's farewell to the Holy Land by then had become irreversible.

A DIALOGUE
        OF EMBITTERED
        MEMORY

At war's end Germany was a wasteland, its cities shattered hulks, its population reduced to foragers of bread and shelter. Not the least of the nation's ordeal was uncertainty of its political and economic future. Under agreements reached at the Teheran and Yalta conferences of 1943 and 1945, the conquered land would be divided into zones of Allied occupation, with each of the occupying powers to impose its own economic reparations on the Germans. The agreements did not survive the Cold War. The Soviets were uninterested in calculating a final bill. In their own eastern zone, they simply began carrying off to the USSR vast quantities of German industrial equipment. The Western Allies in their zones soon abandoned the notion of reparations altogether in favor of economic and political reconstruction. The latent power of German industry was becoming indispensable to the economic revival of Europe as a whole, even as the developing East-West schism was transforming the German people into a potential ally of the free world.

Thus, in 1947 the West Germans were included in the ambit of Marshall Plan generosity. Soon afterward the British, the Americans, and later the French restructured their zones of occupation into a single, integrated "trizonia," with its own uniform currency, the revalued deutschmark. In 1949 the Allies negotiated the establishment of a West German successor state, the Federal Republic of Germany, with its capital in Bonn. Henceforth, under the leadership of Chancellor Konrad Adenauer, the new *Bundesrepublik* embarked on a trajectory of economic revival, even of prosperity, unprecedented in German history since the days of the Wilhelmine Empire. By the time Marshall Plan aid was phased out, in 1952, the number of German unemployed had dropped to less than one million, industrial plant destroyed in the war had been entirely replaced by modern equipment, and the

Bundesrepublik was emerging as the economic locomotive of Western Europe altogether.

In these same years the contrast between West Germany's circumstances and those of Israel could not have been more vivid. Exhausted by war and overwhelmed by a tidal wave of destitute refugees, the little Jewish republic in 1949 was facing insolvency. Although emergency loans were secured from Denmark, Belgium, Sweden, and the United States, these infusions brought only temporary relief. By 1951 Israel's imports were exceeding its exports by five times, and the lack of raw materials and electric power created prolonged factory work stoppages. With the Israeli pound collapsing, even veteran citizens had become dependent on food parcels sent by relatives overseas. This was the crisis that impelled the Israeli government to look to Germany for help.

It was the unlikeliest of alternatives. The very name "Germany" was a stench and abomination for the Israeli people. The country's chief rabbinate seriously debated imposing a ban of excommunication on Jews who chose to return from Israel to their former homes in Germany. For years after 1948, Israeli passports were stamped: "Not valid for Germany." In a Knesset foreign-policy session of September 1950, Prime Minister Ben-Gurion deplored the Bundesrepublik's recent application for observer status in the United Nations. "The government of Israel cannot imagine," he declared, "that the gates of the cultured and peace-loving world will be opened to the German people, not only because their hands are still smeared with blood, but also because their plunder is still under their cloak."

Ben-Gurion's public rhetoric belied his private diplomacy, however. By 1950 the prime minister sensed that it was no longer possible to ignore the potential of German economic help. He was aware, too, that a substantial infrastructure of legal research had been accumulated on German accountability. As early as 1941, Nahum Goldmann, then executive vice-president of the World Jewish Congress, first mooted the notion of postwar German compensation to the Jews. Subsequently a British-based committee, the Council for the Protection of the Rights and Interests of German Jews, led by Dr. Siegfried Moses, explored in some depth the concept of German redress, and by war's end had outlined its basic components. These included restitution of Jewish property and indemnification of Jews, or heirs of Jews, for possessions that no longer could be restored, and compensation to the Jewish people as a whole for the Nazi trauma, with payment to take the form of "reparations" to the Jewish National Home in Palestine as the legal sanctuary of the Jewish people. In September

1945 it was essentially this formula that was adopted by the Jewish Agency, Palestine Jewry's quasi-government, and presented to the four Allied Powers as the first postwar Jewish claim against Germany. The Allied representatives filed the document without action or comment.

Until 1949, in any case, there existed no central German government to meet a collective impost. The three Western Powers had initiated their own separate directives for restitution or indemnification in each of their respective zones. In the American zone, Jewish property confiscated by the Nazis was to be sold and its proceeds used to rehabilitate Jewish claimants. Britain and France later approved similar laws for their own occupation areas. Yet the regulations soon proved hopelessly inadequate. They applied only to former German Jews or their heirs, and in practice required individual Jews to file claims. Even after establishment of the Bundesrepublik in 1949, each claim had to be approved by one or another of West Germany's separate *Länder* (states). The bureaucratic ordeal was endless. By 1953 barely eleven thousand applications had been filed, and a niggardly eighty-three million dollars paid out. As for collective German reparations to the Jewish National Home—and later Israel—the Allies regarded the notion as too exotic for serious consideration.

Well before 1953, however, Nahum Goldmann of the World Jewish Congress and other Jewish spokesmen had succeeded in making their case with a number of sympathetic interlocutors in the Bundesrepublik itself. The latter included Kurt Schumacher, leader of the opposition Social Democratic party, and Dr. Herbert Blankenhorn, director of the Chancellor's Office and Konrad Adenauer's closest political adviser. Goldmann and his colleagues sensed the vulnerability of the German political leadership and their need for international goodwill. In November 1949, only two months after his election as the Bundesrepublik's first chancellor, Adenauer assured the editor of the *Allgemeine Wochenzeitung der Juden in Deutschland*, a German-Jewish weekly, that "[t]he German people are resolved to make good the wrong done to the Jews in the name of a criminal regime. . . . This reparation we regard as our duty." Initially, to be sure, the chancellor's notion of "reparation" was decidedly, even grotesquely, limited. It was to offer expropriated German Jews a lump sum of DM10 million (approximately $2.5 million). The World Jewish Congress, which estimated the value of plundered Jewish property at $6 billion, disdained to acknowledge the offer.

By autumn of 1950, nevertheless, the Israelis in their economic desperation were putting their own imprint on the claim for German funds. This was to resuscitate and amplify the notion of reparations specifically to the Jewish state. The formula's most vigorous advocate was David Horowitz, director general of his country's finance ministry. In meetings with Prime Minister Ben-Gurion, Horowitz made a powerful case for en bloc reparations as the centerpiece of Israel's demands on Germany. Indemnification of individual Jews was vital, he agreed, but only reparations to Israel would make the difference between economic survival or collapse, and possible mass hunger. Ben-Gurion concurred. So did his coalition cabinet, in January 1951.

By then the Israeli government was able to base its case on a formula lately refined by Professor Leo Kohn of the Hebrew University, political adviser to the foreign ministry. Its central premise was that Israel had been "afflicted" by Germany. Since 1948 the Jewish state had been deluged with five hundred thousand impoverished refugees, most of them direct or indirect victims of the Nazi Holocaust. The cost of feeding and housing these newcomers, of providing for their medical, educational, and social services, was estimated conservatively at $3,000 each. Of the $1.5 billion total, therefore, two-thirds should appropriately be borne by the West German Bundesrepublik, one-third by the East German Deutsche Demokratische Republik. It was this formula, in the spring of 1951, that the Israeli government prepared to submit to the governments of West and East Germany, and to the Allied Occupation Powers. Time was of the essence. Beyond Israel's own parlous economic situation, West Germany's political circumstances were subject to imminent change. Konrad Adenauer was known to be negotiating for a revision of the Allied Occupation Statute. Should the Bundesrepublik achieve an even wider degree of political independence, its need for Jewish and liberal goodwill in the West might be reduced.

Contacts with Bonn intensified. With Herbert Blankenhorn serving as Adenauer's principal intermediary, David Horowitz secured an interview with Adenauer himself in April 1951. The meeting took place at the Hotel Crillon in Paris, where the chancellor was on an official visit, and it was secret. Israeli public opinion would have bridled at contacts with German officials, within or beyond German territory (Horowitz and Maurice Fischer, Israel's ambassador to France, actually entered the Hotel Crillon through a rear entrance). Adenauer then began the discussion by asserting his willingness to do all in his power to atone for the Nazi crimes. Horowitz in turn presented the formal draft of Israel's case.

The draft was composed of two parts. The first claimed indemnification for individuals spoliated by the Germans. The second, lengthier portion dealt with the reparations claim for $1.5 billion. Horowitz paraphrased both documents in his own language, his voice thick with emotion. "The Government of Israel cannot reconcile itself to the enjoyment by Germany of the fruits of its rapine and murder," he declaimed, "while the victims of an unholy regime are denied all comfort and redress." With statesmanlike dignity, the chancellor then assured Horowitz that "[w]e would like somehow to make amends for the great wrong that has been done." Horowitz asked: Would the chancellor commit himself to a solemn, public declaration before the world? Adenauer agreed in principle. Both sides then concluded the discussion with expressions of goodwill, and with the understanding that their interview would remain secret.

Meanwhile, three weeks before the Adenauer-Horowitz meeting, the government of Israel dispatched notes to the four Allied Powers, formally setting out its two claims. By then the United States, Britain, and France were evaluating Adenauer's request to move the Bundesrepublik closer to full independence. It was thus Ben-Gurion's contention that Germany could not be permitted to achieve that sovereignty until the issue of reparations was addressed. If the Allies agreed, were they prepared to act as go-betweens in negotiating the details of German payment? The Allies were not (the East German government did not so much as respond). For one thing, there was no precedent in international law for "reparations" to a state that had not come into existence until after the war. More fundamentally, it troubled Western diplomats that the Bundesrepublik should be hobbled with a vast new financial obligation to Israel at a time when a vibrant, unencumbered German economy was needed to augment Western defenses against the mounting Soviet threat.

Still an additional factor weighed in Allied considerations. A conference in London even then was negotiating the scope of Germany's prewar debts to non-German creditors worldwide. The most commonly cited figure was $20 billion. Unless that Nazi-era obligation were paid off, the Bundesrepublik would never be regarded as creditworthy. Could Bonn sustain a triple obligation now, one to its creditors, another to its joint defense commitment in Europe, and yet a third to Israel? Allied statesmen were uneasy. They would not discourage the Bundesrepublik from meeting its Jewish responsibilities, but their governments could not function as lawyers for the Jews, and assuredly not for Israel, with its own abrasive territorial and military policies. The rejection accordingly was conveyed to Jerusalem in July 1951. The Allied governments could not officially require Bonn to pay reparations to Israel, it stated; it would be more appropriate for

Israeli and other Jewish representatives to negotiate directly with the Bundesrepublik.

TO NEGOTIATE FOR "BLOOD MONEY"?

With no alternative to direct, official negotiations with the Germans, Ben-Gurion recognized that legal authority to cross that fathomless psychological barrier now would have to be sought from the Knesset. If the prospect was daunting, it was not unanticipated. Indeed, to help resolve it, the prime minister had authorized David Horowitz's earlier meeting with Adenauer. In turn, much would depend on the chancellor's willingness to ease Ben-Gurion's task in advance by making public his private—Hotel Crillon—commitment to Horowitz.

Adenauer's motives at best were an amalgam. A Rhinelander, brother of the Catholic bishop of Cologne, the chancellor took his religious obligations seriously. After 1933, driven by the Nazis from his office as mayor of Cologne, Adenauer for long stretches of privation was sustained by dollar remittances from two Jewish friends, Daniel Heinemann and Otto Kraus, who had reestablished themselves in the United States. These private obligations doubtless weighed heavily on the chancellor's conscience. Nevertheless, as the postwar Bundesrepublik's first political leader, Adenauer could not be indifferent to pragmatic as well as personal and moralistic considerations. In his dealings with the Allied Powers, his priority objective was to negotiate a relaxation of the Occupation Statute, and thereby to revive his nation's political freedom of action. In that effort, Western trust and goodwill were indispensable.

Thus, in 1949, Adenauer guided the Bundesrepublik to membership in the Organization for European Cooperation; in 1951, to the Council of Europe and to the incipient European Coal and Steel and European Defense Communities. It was in return for this commitment to *Erfüllungspolitik*—acceptance of international obligations—that the chancellor anticipated a widening latitude of functional West German independence. Even as late as 1951, however, quasi-sovereignty was dependent on German participation in the EDC, the (West) European Defense Community, a membership that itself was hostage to lingering French suspicions of treaty partnership with a revived and remilitarized Germany. For France, as for other Western nations, additional evidence was needed of the Bundesrepublik's reincarnation as a thoroughly penitent and democratized nation.

Here it was that Adenauer still remained vulnerable. His program of denazification had never been altogether consistent. In the early years of his chancellorship, one of his most trusted collaborators, Hans Glöbke, was an ex-Nazi. Two of his ministers, Theodor Oberländer and Hans-Christoph Seebohm, were ardent right-wing nationalists. Fully 80 percent of the judges in the Bundesrepublik's early years had served under the Nazis, and the sentences they handed out to Nazis convicted of capital crimes tended to be less than punitive. Altogether, for political reasons, Adenauer did not seem to be in a hurry to provoke a wrenching confrontation with Germany's recent past. In the immediate postwar, his own Christian Democratic Union, the nation's largest party, had little to say about the need for *Wiedergutmachung*—making amends—to the Jews.

Adenauer himself meanwhile would not venture a public utterance on the Jewish question until his 1949 interview with the *Allgemeine Wochenzeitung*. His purpose at best was ambivalent. To his cabinet, in the aftermath of the interview, the chancellor then acknowledged that "[o]ne should not underestimate the power of the Jews, particularly in America." And as the issue of German acceptance into the complex of Western economic and defense structures gained momentum, Adenauer paid greater heed to Blankenhorn and other political advisers who had developed a close dialogue with Nahum Goldmann and with Noah Barou, a vice president of the World Jewish Congress. It was they who finally persuaded the chancellor to make a decisive personal commitment to the Israeli emissaries, David Horowitz and Maurice Fischer, in the Hotel Crillon meeting of April 1951.

Lacking official Allied sponsorship, the Israeli government on its own then promptly established a special "reparations" department within its foreign ministry. Directed by Felix Shinnar, a German-born lawyer, it was this bureau that embarked upon the formulation of a detailed prospectus of financial claims against Germany. At the same time, Nahum Goldmann set about organizing a confederation of American and European Jewish communal agencies, the "Conference on Jewish Material Claims against Germany," that would function as a central "address" for negotiating Diaspora Jewry's schedule of demands. Those latter claims would encompass both restitution and indemnification to individual Jewish survivors or their heirs, and—where there were neither survivors nor heirs—"global" indemnification to the Jewish people at large for destroyed or confiscated property. As the issue of formal discussions with Germany drew closer, meanwhile, the Israelis too continued to use Goldmann as their principal liaison with Bonn.

Lithuanian-born and educated in Germany, Goldmann was a man of rare linguistic and diplomatic virtuosity. His skill in organizing the

Claims Conference testified to the fact, as did his tact and eloquence in dealing with Blankenhorn and other German representatives. It was he as well as David Horowitz who secured the Germans' understanding that only the chancellor's public, formal commitment to reparations would enable Ben-Gurion to seek Knesset authorization to negotiate. In July 1951, Adenauer reaffirmed that original Hotel Crillon promise. Over the next weeks, then, drafts of the chancellor's impending statement went back and forth between Bonn, New York, and Jerusalem, until all parties approved its final text. Finally, on September 27, 1951, Adenauer delivered his address before the Bundestag.

The speech began cautiously, stressing the need to educate all Germans in the spirit of religious tolerance, and warning that antisemitic activity of any kind would be severely punished. Only at the end of the address did the chancellor turn to issues of recompense. Inasmuch as Nazi crimes, he declared, "if not committed by all Germans, had been committed in the name of all Germans," his government was "ready, jointly with the representatives of Jewry and the State of Israel, which has received so many homeless Jewish refugees, to bring about a solution of the problem of material restitution." Adenauer qualified his pledge by noting that the amount of compensation had to be weighed against the nation's capacity to provide for its own war victims and the influx of refugees from East Germany. Nevertheless, the declaration represented the first official allusion to German moral responsibility and willingness to make financial amends. It was followed then with supportive endorsements by representatives of the Social Democratic and Free Democratic parties. Afterward, the Bundestag members rose to their feet for a moment of silence in memory of Hitler's victims.

Adenauer had mentioned no hard figures. The Israelis accordingly required a more tangible German commitment even before negotiations could begin. This time it was Goldmann who served as intermediary. His meeting with the chancellor took place on December 6, 1951, when Adenauer was on an official visit to London. The private conference, at Claridge's Hotel, proved decisive. Assessing once more the magnitude of Jewish losses, Goldmann emphasized that *Wiedergutmachung* could not be regarded as a political issue but as one of essential morality. The sum of $1 billion for Israel was the minimum amount acceptable as a basis even for discussions, he insisted, with an additional $500 million to be sought for the Claims Conference. If the figure were to be subjected to routine financial haggling, negotiations should not so much as begin. The chancellor heard Goldmann out, then responded with quiet passion: "Dr. Goldmann, . . . my desire for restitution is sincere. I regard it as a great moral problem and a debt of honor for the new Germany. . . . I am prepared to approve the undertaking you request on my own responsibility. If you will give me the draft of such a letter after our talk, I will sign it in the course of the day." Goldmann in fact had already prepared the draft of a letter. He left it with Blankenhorn, who had participated in the meeting, and that same afternoon the written commitment to a negotiating figure of $1 billion was back in his hands, signed by the chancellor.

With the issue of direct German-Israeli negotiations now joined, Ben-Gurion in Jerusalem waited no longer to prepare his case for the Knesset. Henceforth, it required all the prime minister's skill to win approval even from his own Mapai party, on December 30, 1951, and afterward from the minority members of his government coalition. On January 7, 1952, at last, he brought the issue before the Knesset. Asking permission to negotiate with Germany, the prime minister reminded the legislators that, if his request were not granted, Israel would forfeit more than a billion dollars' worth of heirless Jewish property. "Let not the murderers of our people also be their heirs!" he cried. But the opposition parties in turn now gave full vent to their hostility. The leftist Achdut HaAvodah and fellow-traveling Mapam factions denounced Adenauer's government as a neo-Nazi lackey of the United States State Department, and thus as a threat to peace.

The right-wing Cherut party, led by the militant territorialist Menachem Begin, went rather further. For Begin, the very notion even of speaking directly to Germans, let alone asking them for a "handout," signified "the ultimate abomination." On that same January 7, the Cherut chairman addressed a crowd of fifteen thousand in Jerusalem's Zion Square. "Today I give the order [to march]—Yes!" he shouted. "This will be a war of life or death." Lines of demonstrators began converging on the Knesset, forcing their way through police cordons, torching automobiles, hurling rocks and brickbats at the Knesset building, threatening to batter their way into the Knesset chamber. Troops had to be called in to drive back the mob. The crisis by then had escalated into the gravest political threat ever confronted by Israel's fragile young democracy.

Would it lead to civil war? Begin raised this possibility when he warned his fellow Knesset members: "There are things in life that are worse than death. This is one of them. For this we will give our lives. We will leave our families. We will say good-bye to our children, but there will be no negotiations with Germany." Ominously, Begin then warned that he and his supporters could not promise to respect the personal safety of any Knesset member who voted to negotiate with Germany. The threat of physical intimidation was explicit. Ben-Gurion faced it head-on in a broadcast to the nation the following morning: "Yesterday," he declared, "the hand of evil was raised against . . . democracy in Israel. . . . I want to reassure the nation [that] all necessary measures have been taken to safeguard democratic institutions, and law and order." The prime minister's calm resolve had its effect. On January 9 the Knesset gave him a solid vote of approval to enter negotiations with Bonn. Begin promptly wilted and called off further demonstrations.

IN FRONTAL DIALOGUE

During the same months of their preliminary discussions with the Bundesrepublik, the Israeli government and the Claims Conference simultaneously reached agreement between themselves on the two categories of demands they would negotiate directly with the Germans. The first, for $1.5 billion, anticipated a global indemnification to the Jewish people at large. The largest proportion of this claim, $1 billion, should be paid as "reparations" to a state, Israel, that was bearing the heaviest burden of refugee absorption. The smaller proportion of the initial claim, $500 million, should be paid to the Claims Conference as indemnification to Jewish welfare organizations that were bearing the burden of reviving Jewish life outside Israel. The second claim category encompassed restitution or (more commonly) indemnification to individual Jewish survivors or heirs of survivors for property and other personal losses suffered at German hands. No sum could yet be projected for this category. The machinery for its calculation would have to be negotiated in the forthcoming conference.

A "neutral" venue meanwhile was approved for the conference. This was Wassenaar, in the Netherlands. A suburb of The Hague, Wassenaar would allow convenient access to the German and Israeli embassies in the Dutch capital. Its former ducal castle, the Oudkasteel, now a hotel, lent itself to modern security arrangements. Here three parties gathered on March 21, 1952. The Israeli delegation comprised Felix Shinnar, director of the foreign ministry's reparations department, and Giora Josephthal, also German-born, treasurer of the Jewish Agency. The Claims Conference was represented by Moses Leavitt and Alex Easterman, executives of the American Jewish Joint Distribution Committee. The German delegation was com-

posed of Professor Franz Böhm, dean of Johann Wolfgang Goethe
University in Frankfurt, and Dr. Otto Küster, director of the Restitutions Department for the *Land* of Baden-Württemburg. Both were
men of unblemished anti-Nazi reputations. Böhm had been a concentration camp prisoner. As a youth, Küster had been a classmate and
friend of Shinnar's in Stuttgart. Talks between the delegations nevertheless began in a chilly atmosphere, without handshakes. English
was the language of negotiation.

The Israelis opened the proceedings by restating the historical
basis for Israeli and Jewish claims, then presenting the bottom line of
their demands: $1 billion in reparations to Israel (60 percent in cur-
rency, 40 percent in commodities), to be paid out over six years; with
another $500 million to be disbursed to the Claims Conference.
Responding, the Germans then dropped a bombshell. In principle,
they explained, their government had accepted the obligation of
financial reparations, but the actual sums and terms of payment would
depend on another set of negotiations taking place simultaneously in
London. This was the Allied German Debt Conference.

In London, the twenty-three assembled Allied delegations were
determined that the Bundesrepublik should not be permitted to
achieve full sovereignty before meeting its prewar financial obligations to their respective governments. These debts now were assessed
at 13.5 billion deutschmarks. The figure was disputed by Hermann
Abs, president of West Germany's Central Bank and leader of his
country's delegation to London. The Bundesrepublik could not
assume a financial burden of more than DM7.3 billion, he argued.
Indeed, Abs had pleaded with Adenauer for postponement of any
commitments to Israel and the Jews until the debt issue was resolved.
The chancellor, in turn, although refusing to delay the Wassenaar
Conference, agreed to impose no restrictions on his delegations'
negotiating positions—either in London or in Wassenaar. Rather, the
two conferences were to be used as bargaining tools, each against the
other.

At Wassenaar now, Josephthal, Shinnar, and the Claims Conference delegates were appalled. For them the notion of "linkage"
between the London negotiations and their own was unthinkable.
This had not been the understanding, they protested, under which
they had consented to direct discussions with the Bundesrepublik.
Their sense of outrage was duly conveyed to Bonn. At Adenauer's
request, then, Abs and Finance Minister Fritz Schäffer arrived in
Wassenaar to seek a "compromise" formula. Well apprised of Israel's
financial desperation, the Germans offered the Jewish state and the

Claims Conference a total of DM3 billion—$713 million—less than half the amount Israel and the conference had accepted as a basis for negotiations. Two more weeks of tense discussions brought no progress. On April 9 the conference recessed. It was also on April 9 that forty thousand demonstrators gathered in Tel Aviv to roar their opposition to any further contacts with the Germans. The city's mayor announced his readiness to go on a hunger strike. Press criticism of the "new" Germany was withering. Ben-Gurion's early hopes for a forthright German commitment to *Wiedergutmachung* apparently were shattered.

At this point, intercession came from an unlikely source. John McCloy, the United States high commissioner in Bonn, conferred urgently with Blankenhorn and Walter Hallstein, Adenauer's closest advisers. At a time when German membership in the European Defense Community was under Allied evaluation, McCloy noted, was not the issue of Germany's image crucial? The implicit threat of American displeasure registered. Adenauer personally cabled Nahum Goldmann an invitation to confer with him. The secret meeting took place on April 20, this time at the chancellor's private residence in Rhondorf. The discussion was businesslike but cordial. Adenauer promised Goldmann to formulate a proposal acceptable enough to restart the Wassenaar talks. Goldmann declared his gratification. Two more weeks passed. The new offer did not materialize. Israel was teetering on the brink of insolvency. Yet even then its government would not budge from its original negotiating figure.

Fortunately for the Israelis, Adenauer was beginning to respond more decisively to a widened confluence of pressures. These arose in the Bundesrepublik itself. Between 1945 and 1951 an eerie silence on the Jews had reigned in Germany. By the summer of 1951, however, as the Jewish claims issue evoked reminders of the Holocaust's ongoing impact upon Israel's struggle for economic survival, a responsive chord suddenly welled up in German liberal circles. It was then that Erich Lüth, director of the Hamburg State Press Office, published an article in the *Neue Zeitung* entitled: "We Beg Israel for Peace." The appeal called for meaningful recompense to the Jewish state as a precondition for Germany's acceptance into the community of civilized nations. Lüth's cri de coeur was echoed almost immediately by another Hamburg journalist, Rudolf Küstermeier, whose entreaty was published in *Die Welt*. Both articles evoked an avalanche of letters, newspaper columns, and editorial expressions of support. In the ensuing months a series of lectures, rallies, meetings, and church prayer sessions were organized throughout Germany in passionate endorsement of the Peace with Israel movement. By no coincidence, the upswell reached its apogee during the spring 1952 interruption in the Wassenaar Conference.

A second reservoir of pro-Israel sentiment was the oldest of Germany's political parties, the Social Democrats. German socialism's historic repudiation of political antisemitism, and the grim ordeal of its leadership during the Hitler era, were testimony enough that the Social Democrats had paid their dues in the struggle for German democracy. And now, in the postwar period, the party chairman, Dr. Kurt Schumacher, who had lost an arm and a leg in a Nazi concentration camp, emerged as the most forthright champion of pro-Israel support on the political scene. By 1952 it was Schumacher's Social Democratic opposition bloc in the Bundestag that became a particularly vocal critic of the government's evident ambivalence on Germany's "moral obligation" to Israel. Possibly shamed by this initiative, the Bundestag's Foreign Affairs Committee—with its Christian Democratic majority—gathered in emergency session in May 1952 to resolve unanimously that the "moral" claims of Israel and the Jews deserved priority over the "sordid commercial claims" under discussion at the London Debt Conference. Virtually all the Bundesrepublik's leading newspapers supported this resolution.

For Adenauer, however, the most sobering development of all was a revolt within Germany's own Wassenaar delegation. In late May, as a statement of "moral conscience," Küster and Böhm tendered their resignations to the chancellor. Adenauer was shaken. Summoning the two men to his office, he prevailed on them to change their minds. The Bundesrepublik would find a way to honor its obligations, he promised. This time he kept his word. Meeting afterward with Abs and Schäffer, Adenauer insisted upon a more forthcoming compromise proposal to Israel. In fact the compromise was Böhm's. It was to offer the Israelis DM3 billion, with an additional DM445 million to be made available to the Claims Conference. Adenauer decided too that there would be no further linkage between reparations and the London Debt Conference. If necessary, Bonn would meet its outstanding commercial obligations by raising a new loan. To allay his financiers' concerns, the chancellor agreed simply that the bulk of the payments to Israel would be made in locally produced commodities, not in currency, and would be spaced out over twelve years, rather than the six requested by the Israelis.

It was this formula that subsequently was transmitted to Shinnar and Goldmann. Both men favored accepting it as a basis for resuming the Wassenaar negotiations. Although Ben-Gurion and his advisers required two additional weeks of detailed calculations to evaluate the new proposal, the nation's economic circumstances simply were too critical to allow for rejection. On June 9, 1952, the prime minister approved a resumption of discussions with the Bundesrepublik. Adenauer was gratified. The following evening, June 10, he attended a scheduled banquet with the assembled prime ministers of West Germany's Länder. As the dinner concluded, Adenauer ceremonially informed his guests that a basic understanding on financial compensation had been reached with Israel and the representatives of world Jewry. "I regard this agreement," he proclaimed, "as an event no less vital for our future than the restoration of German sovereignty." Thereupon the ministers rose to their feet in sustained applause.

A TREATY SIGNING IN LUXEMBOURG

The Wassenaar negotiations resumed on June 28, 1952, and continued until August 22. With the principal sum essentially in place, discussions focused now on terms and methods of delivery. Both sides refined and rerefined draft after draft. Finally, on September 3, the Adenauer cabinet approved the text initialed by both sets of negotiators. The Israeli cabinet's approval was forthcoming on September 5. Two weeks earlier, at the chancellor's vacation residence on the Bürgenstock, Goldmann and Adenauer had worked out the signing scenario personally. The venue would be Luxembourg, and the target date was September 10, when Adenauer would be en route to Paris to sign another historic treaty, this one bringing the Bundesrepublik into the European Coal and Steel Community.

And so it happened. At Luxembourg, Foreign Minister Sharett represented Israel. Goldmann was present to sign for the Claims Conference. Before the hundreds of journalists who witnessed the ceremony in the Luxembourg City Hall, Adenauer praised the Jewish delegations' "moral courage and good faith." Sharett in turn gallantly acknowledged that the chancellor and his representatives, "by fulfilling their obligations to Israel and the Jewish people, had demonstrated their readiness to right a historic wrong." These statements won editorial endorsement from every major West German newspaper. All discerned historic significance in the fact that the Bundesrepublik's first international treaty had been signed with representatives of world Jewry and Israel, an event that signified nothing less than a turning point in Germany's return to the community of free nations. In Israel, however, public and private reaction was entirely subdued, even cynical. Characteristic was an editorial in

Ma'ariv, then the nation's largest daily: "They tore the gold teeth from our sisters' mouths and they return it now, not in gold but in something which is equal to gold. They do not let us buy freely but force us to take it in the form of goods produced by their bloodstained hands."

The treaty consisted of four related but separate protocols. The first was the reparations accord between Israel and the Bundesrepublik. Under its terms, Bonn would pay Israel DM3 billion (by then, $720 million), principally in goods and services. The second and third protocols, between the Bundesrepublik and the Claims Conference, committed Bonn to enact legislation for the indemnification of surviving Holocaust victims or their heirs, and to pay an additional DM450 million (approximately $110 million) for the work of Jewish relief and welfare organizations in countries outside Israel. To avoid spending its hard currency, however, Bonn was allowed to provide the equivalent of this amount in the form of goods and services to Israel; Israel in turn would reimburse the Claims Conference in cash. The fourth protocol, a minor one, related to the land, buildings, and chattels of Palestine's German Templar community, which had been sequestered by the British mandatory government in 1941. Israel later had taken over this property. Now it was obliged to refund its value—$54 million—to Bonn.

Manifestly, the key provision in this nexus of protocols was Bonn's reparations obligation to Israel. Adenauer had signed the Luxembourg Treaty at a time when more than a third of the Bundesrepublik's citizens still lived in substandard housing, and one-fifth of its population consisted of refugees from East Germany. Under Allied military occupation, the nation's political future remained enveloped in uncertainty. Little wonder that the Bundestag, charged with ratification of international treaties, would spend fully six months in often stormy committee debate on the likely economic and diplomatic consequences of the new financial commitment. The issue no longer was one of moral obligation but of economic scope. The impact of a DM3.4 billion payment would ramify even through the Bundesrepublik's foreign policy. Reference was made to Germany's historically friendly ties with the Moslem world, extending back to Kaiser Wilhelm II's diplomatic and military alliance with the Ottoman Empire. Indeed, protests already were mounting from the Arab League that reparations to Israel constituted a breach of German neutrality on the Middle East conflict, and thus would threaten German-Arab relations.

Although Adenauer himself refused to be dissuaded by these cautionary notes, German industrial circles were unprepared to disregard Arab threats of an economic boycott. Their anxieties in turn registered on the nation's conservative middle classes, and on the politicians who represented them. The latter included the Free Democratic, German, and Center parties, and even important elements within the Christian Social Union, the Bavarian wing of Adenauer's own Christian Democratic Union. In September 1952 the CSU chairman, Franz-Josef Strauss, authored a joint letter with the heads of the other parties, entreating Adenauer to reconsider the magnitude of the reparations commitment to Israel.

As if to validate their concern, the Saudi government in October 1952 peremptorily canceled its substantial order with Siemens for telecommunications equipment. Almost simultaneously, the Syrian government threatened to terminate negotiations with three German companies for enlargement of port facilities in Latakia and Tarsus. That same month the Saudi and Lebanese governments went further yet, intimating a possible recall of their ambassadors from Bonn. Adenauer was not insensitive to these warnings. Thus, while holding firm on the reparations agreement, he signaled his willingness to assist the Arab nations in their own economic development programs. In February 1953 his minister of economics, Ludwig Erhard, dispatched a mission to Cairo, offering Egypt credits of some DM300 million. Comparable offers of economic help were transmitted to Saudia Arabia and Syria. Yet the Arab governments remained uncongenial. They wanted nothing less than cancellation of the Treaty of Luxembourg.

By late winter of 1953, Adenauer sensed that the treaty issue had to be resolved without additional delay. The intensifying political backlash threatened not only ratification but the international goodwill for Germany that had been achieved at Luxembourg. On March 4, 1953, therefore, the chancellor personally submitted the treaty to the Bundestag for its first reading. Once again invoking the nation's moral obligation, he reminded the legislators that "[t]he name of our fatherland must regain the esteem appropriate to the historic accomplishments of the German people in cultural and economic matters." To defuse criticism both from German business circles and from the Arab world, the chancellor in his Bundestag address then emphasized that payments to Israel would be made not in currency but in goods locally produced and purchased with local deutschmarks. Munitions and weaponry of any kind would be excluded from the shipments. Finally, in a meaningful barb at Communist charges of West German "neo-Nazism," Adenauer added: "[L]ately, race hatred and race persecution have been exploited as political weapons within the sphere of the Communist regime." The chancellor was alluding to the recent trial of Rudolf Slansky in Prague, with its transparent exploitation of local Czech antisemitism (pp. 64–5). He concluded by expressing the hope that "acceptance of [the Treaty of Luxembourg] . . . will take effect as a German contribution toward strengthening the spirit of human religious tolerance in the world."

The auguries for ratification appeared at least even. Indeed, the treaty passed its initial Bundestag reading within hours of Adenauer's address, and a second reading was scheduled for March 18. Yet the government's four-year term of office was due to expire only a week afterward, on March 24, 1953. Under the nation's *Grundgesetz*, its constitution, any pending legislation still uncompleted had to be renewed ab initio on the agenda of a successor government. Months could pass before the Treaty of Luxembourg achieved ratification—if a new Bundestag were inclined to ratify it at all.

Thereupon Nahum Goldmann resorted to another gamble in personal diplomacy. On March 5 he made a long-distance telephone call from New York to Erich Ollenhauer, chairman of the Social Democratic party (the former chairman, Kurt Schumacher, had recently died). In a lengthy conversation, Goldmann appealed to the Social Democrats to forgo the usual practice of committee scrutiny, and to support the treaty as it stood. Ollenhauer was receptive. He asked only for several hours to discuss the proposal with his colleagues. Later that same afternoon the chairman was able to telephone Goldmann with an affirmative reply. Indeed, Ollenhauer did better than that. At his request the Social Democrats then maneuvered the Christian Democrats and other parties of the government coalition to match their own initiative. The treaty accordingly passed its second and third readings in a single day, March 18, and by a final, overwhelming 239 votes in favor, 35 against, with 86 abstentions. And once the Bundestag ratified the document, the upper chamber, the Bundesrat, followed pro forma, two days later. President Theodor Heuss signed the treaty that same March 20, 1953.

Under Israeli law there was no requirement for Knesset ratification. On March 19 Prime Minister Ben-Gurion submitted the treaty to the Knesset Foreign Affairs and Defense Committee, where it passed by a vote of 7 to 5, with one abstention. The votes precisely reflected the political configuration of the original January 1952 Knesset vote. For Ben-Gurion, however, it was a bittersweet moment. Much as he appreciated the vital importance of reparations for Israel's economy, he viewed the Treaty of Luxembourg more as a historic moral vindication than as a legal guarantee of the Bundesrepublik's future compliance. Its significance lay in the ability of a sovereign Jewish state to bring mighty Germany to a public gesture of guilt and contrition. "This is a great day," the prime minister observed privately of the Bundestag's vote on March 18, "but the Germans will never pay."

REPARATIONS AND RESTITUTION

If Ben-Gurion equated Bonn's credibility on reparations with that of Weimar in the 1920s, he was wrong. Under Adenauer's stern tutelage, the Germans were destined to fulfill the terms of their agreement punctually and conscientiously. Once a special committee of Israel's ministry of finance—"the Horowitz Committee"—approved a list of purchases, the schedule was sent on for implementation to a German-Israeli Mixed Commission. It was this group of economists, representing each nation's central bank and a spectrum of relevant ministries, that bore responsibility for determining annual delivery schedules. From the outset, the Germans surprised the Israelis with their goodwill and flexibility. By then, the Bundesrepublik had undertaken other, heavier debt obligations, specifically a DM13.5 billion accounting recently negotiated at the London conference. Yet it was understood that Israel was "special," that payments to the Jewish state took priority over all other financial commitments. The German members of the Mixed Commission gave substance to this understanding. Under the treaty, the Bundesrepublik was authorized to stretch out its delivery installments over fourteen years. Yet, at Israel's request, the commission agreed to foreshorten the schedule to twelve years, and then help Israel meet the interest charges for this concession with a Bundesbank loan.

Once approved, commodity orders were dispatched to Israel's Special Purchasing Mission in Germany, which opened its office in Cologne in May 1953. The mission's director, Felix Shinnar, was almost ideally equipped to launch the new undertaking. He had participated with David Horowitz in the 1949–50 London visitations to unlock Israel's sterling balance, then to reopen the Haifa oil refineries (pp. 12–14). In 1951 it was Shinnar who organized Delek, a public energy company, to conserve his nation's meager foreign currency reserves through centralized oil purchases and allocation. And with his recent Wassenaar experience in negotiating with German officials, Shinnar was prepared to deal no less pragmatically with German businessmen in the Bundesrepublik itself. As projects approved by the Mixed Commission reached his desk, Shinnar and his staff set about inviting and evaluating bids from a wide variety of German contractors.

Moreover, the Israeli Mission in Cologne soon transcended its official function as a mere purchasing agency, and took on a quasi-diplomatic status. Bonn cooperated. It exempted the Mission's senior officials from the jurisdiction of German courts and taxes. At public events Shinnar was tendered the deference normally extended to an ambassador. His deputy functioned in effect as consul general, selectively issuing Israeli visas for German visitors to Israel, interpreting Israeli political and cultural developments to German press and academic circles, and transmitting to Israel information on German political and economic activities. Nevertheless, during the Mission's twelve-year existence, its principal efforts were to orchestrate the dispatch of not less than 1,440,000 tons of German goods to a beleaguered and impoverished homeland.

Ironically, these shipments achieved a bonus for the Bundesrepublik itself. Israel's thousands of reparations contracts often were decisive in reviving idle or underused sectors of the West German economy, particularly in the telecommunications and maritime industries. Long after reparations installments ended, in 1966, Israeli companies would remain dependent on their German contractors for spare parts and upgraded equipment. For Israel, of course, these deliveries proved an even more indispensable economic lifeline. While purchases were approved for some two thousand private Israeli enterprises—dairies, flour mills, sugar refineries (the owners paying Israeli currency into a government savings fund)—the principal industrial shipments were of capital goods intended to develop the Jewish republic's fragile economic infrastructure. These included rolling stock and support equipment for the national railroad system; pumps and pipe-manufacturing machinery for irrigation and oil; telecommunications equipment; electric power stations; the entirety of the machinery required to develop the Timna copper mines, the Koor iron foundry, the Lachish regional development complex, the ports of Haifa and Ashdod; fifty ocean freighters with a combined tonnage of 450,000—in effect, the totality of Israel's new merchant marine. By the time reparations ended, in 1967, Israel's industrial output had increased by 250 percent, capital stock in industry by 300 percent, the number of employed individuals by 83 percent. It was progress achieved at a time when mass immigration had to be absorbed and a war—in 1956—had to be fought. Growth of this magnitude was due first and foremost to the infusion of German reparations.

Still another transfusion flowed into Israel's survival. This was the payment of German indemnifications to surviving victims of the Nazi regime who currently lived in the Jewish state. Under the Treaty of Luxembourg, Bonn had agreed to enact laws providing both for restitution of property and for personal indemnification. In meeting these obligations the Bundesrepublik subsequently produced two legislative landmarks. The first and most important was the Federal Indemnification Law (BEG), passed in 1953. The second was the Federal Restitution Law (BRUEG), passed in 1957. The latter authorized the restitution of property, or its monetary equivalent, to individuals who had been pillaged by the Nazi regime.

The former, BEG, was considerably more extensive in scope. Under its provisions victims of the Nazis, or victims' dependents, would be indemnified from a central fund for loss of life or health; for loss of business or professional careers; for deprivation of liberty, for interruption of vocational training, and for loss of pension and insurance rights. The payments varied for each category, but none was less than fair, even generous. Unlike the provisions of BRUEG, moreover, which authorized confiscated-property compensation exclusively to former citizens of Germany, the beneficiaries of BEG included all victims of Nazism who had been "stateless persons" as of January 1, 1947, that is, those European Jews who later, as displaced refugees, poured into Israel. The indemnification was administered equitably, indeed, was repeatedly amended in ensuing years, making adjustments for inflation, and each time adding new categories of beneficiaries—among them Jews who were belatedly released from Communist-bloc nations after 1953, and then, later, after 1989 (pp. 332–3).

Beyond its reparations obligations to Israel, therefore, Bonn had assumed a prodigious financial obligation under the BEG and BRUEG commitments. By 1973, twenty years after ratification of the decisive BEG legislation, some 4,277,000 claims had been submitted and 95 percent had been processed. By then, too, fully 278,000 annuities to Nazi victims were in force, requiring monthly payments totaling DM11,680,000. Not less than 75 percent of the payments went to Jews residing outside Germany; and, of these, 40 percent lived in Israel. Twenty-five years later yet, by 1998, the totality of German expenditures for reparations, indemnifications, and restitutions exceeded DM100 billion, and the single largest beneficiary of these distributions was the nation of Israel. Altogether, the infusion of *Wiedergutmachung* payments had saved the little country during its most precarious early years of economic vulnerability.

During the Sinai War of 1956 (pp. 96–8), anticipating United Nations sanctions against Israel, the Eisenhower administration in Washington queried Bonn on a possible suspension of reparations payments to Israel. Adenauer instantly shot the proposal down. His government would recognize no punitive measures, he responded icily. The Treaty of Luxembourg was to be regarded as a moral obligation of the German people, a commitment that transcended all issues of conventional statecraft. The chancellor's obdurateness impressed even Menachem Begin and other Israeli right-wingers. They were prepared afterward to mute their reservations about the Bundesrepublik. Indeed, more than any other factor, it was Bonn's forthright implementation of *Wiedergutmachung* that laid the psychological basis for other political and economic German-Israeli accommodations in the decades ahead. For Israel, well into the 1950s, the Bundesrepublik assuredly would not be confused with a paradigm of moral transfiguration. Yet neither by then could it be regarded any longer as the incarnation of irremediable evil. However tentative, the line of communication between Germans and Israelis henceforth would remain open.

III AN ATTENUATED
         SLAVIC HONEYMOON

AN UNANTICIPATED ADVOCACY

In their quest for statehood the Jews entertained fewer expectations of help from the Soviet Union than from any other European power, not excluding Great Britain. Before the war Zionism was as illegal a movement among Soviet Jewry as political nationalism among others of the USSR's heterogeneity of races and peoples. The Kremlin's tactics changed only during the Nazi invasion. To cultivate Western Jewish sympathies, Ivan Maisky, vice commissar for foreign affairs, served as liaison with the Zionist movement in England. Visiting Palestine in October 1943, Maisky conferred with David Ben-Gurion and other leaders of the Jewish Agency Executive. In February 1945 the Soviet representative at a London trade union conference supported a resolution that "the Jewish people must be enabled to continue the rebuilding of Palestine as their national home."

But these and other expedient pro-Zionist gestures ceased as abruptly at war's end as did other genuflections to Jewish goodwill. Evaluating the political ferment in the Middle East, the Soviets reconfirmed socialism's historic antipathy to Zionism. The aim of Zionism in any case was not Jewish statehood, they insisted, but perpetuation of the British mandatory regime in Palestine. Accordingly, well through 1946 and into 1947, the Kremlin opposed any notion of partitioning the Holy Land into separate, independent Jewish and Arab states. Even Palestine Jewry's local Communist chairman, Meir Vilner, took up the antipartitionist refrain. The one acceptable formula for Jews and Arabs alike, Vilner explained to a British journalist in May 1947, was "immediate recognition of [undivided] Palestine as an independent binational state and . . . withdrawal of the British army from the country." Vilner's final clause was the key. The party's, the Kremlin's, overriding objective was termination of Britain's presence in Palestine.

Yet it was also in 1947 that puzzling new discrepancies appeared in Moscow's position on the Arab-Jewish conflict. In February of that year, as Britain announced its decision to refer the Palestine question to the United Nations, the Soviets unexpectedly muted their anti-Zionism and adopted an uncharacteristic stance of noncommitment. In the emerging Cold War, Moscow's policy planners now began reappraising their Middle Eastern strategy altogether. It appeared that Britain's support of reactionary plutocracies in Iran and Iraq rendered these states newly vulnerable to Soviet penetration. For that matter, the entirety of Britain's puppet Arab League federation now seemed fair game, and all the more at a time when the Attlee government was evaluating the possibility of withdrawing costly garrisons along the nation's traditional Commonwealth lifeline.

To accelerate Whitehall's reassessment, the Soviets in the early postwar period organized and fostered subversive elements throughout the entirety of the Middle East. These included Kurdish guerrillas in Iraq, a dissident junta in Iran's northern provinces, a leftist insurgency in Greece. Support of the Jews in Palestine would mesh with the Kremlin's larger strategic opposition to British colonialism. Locked in struggle with Britain's Palestine administration, the Jews appeared less likely than the region's subservient Arab governments to accept continuation of the British presence. The Soviets entertained few expectations of a Marxist Jewish regime in Palestine, to be sure. It was assumed nevertheless that Palestine's dedicated and articulate enclave of Jewish leftists would at least establish a substantial Soviet bridgehead in the region. Doubtless such hard-core apparatchiks as Meir Vilner could not by themselves secure that enclave. Yet the fellow-traveling (although ardently Zionist) partisans of the Mapam faction, small in numbers but vibrant in decibel power, maintained their own extensive contacts with Communist-bloc officials abroad. In their missionary zeal, they impressed these diplomats as a potentially significant "anti-imperialist" force in Palestine. They were worth cultivating.

Even as late as February 1947, however, no observer could have predicted that Soviet Ambassador Andrei Gromyko, then leader of his country's United Nations delegation in New York, would have spoken out in direct support of the Zionist cause. But on March 14, addressing the UN Security Council, Gromyko launched into an extended disquisition on the Palestine issue. Only in mid-speech did he observe that, if a federative arrangement should prove "unfeasible," his government then would favor partition. The speech left the Zionists jubilant, the Arabs in consternation. On October 16, 1947, moreover, Gromyko unequivocally endorsed the majority recommendation of UNSCOP, the United Nations Special Committee on Palestine, and then cast his vote for the UN General Assembly's partition resolution of November 29. That same day, the Soviet press office in New York vigorously defended Gromyko's vote, even denouncing its Arab critics as "reactionaries . . . tools of the imperialists."

For their part, the British and Americans grasped Moscow's purpose unerringly. It was to support the Zionist cause in hope of gaining entry into the Middle East, either by participating in a United Nations "peacekeeping force" or by exploiting the chaos that partition would foster. In some degree it was this concern over ulterior Soviet intentions that impelled Washington in March 1948 to back away from partition and favor a "temporary" United Nations trusteeship for the Holy Land. The move infuriated Gromyko, provoking him to accuse the "Anglo-American Bloc" of plotting to prolong British rule in Palestine. At this juncture, Aubrey Eban, pleading the Zionist case at the United Nations, found himself "conferring conspiratorially" with Soviet representatives almost every night on a strategy for blocking the trusteeship proposal.

The proposal in any case was moot. The British mandate ended on May 14, and Israel was born. Yet, once more it was the Soviets who trumped Washington's immediate *de facto* recognition of the Jewish state by extending *de jure* recognition two days later. Afterward it was the Soviets, not the Americans, who denounced the Arab invasion of Israel with particular vehemence. "In their ill-judged support of aggression against Israel," editorialized *Pravda* on May 25, the "Arab masses [are] unwittingly fighting to preserve the hydra of British imperialism." On June 4 Gromyko repeated the acccusation in the UN Security Council: "We can only wonder at the course taken by Arab states that have not even achieved their own full liberation from foreign influence, and some of which have not even real national independence."

FROM ADVOCACY TO WEAPONRY

The Soviets moved swiftly to translate their patronage of the Zionist cause from diplomatic to military support. Palestine Jewry's defense force was ill-equipped for large-scale warfare. Its ordnance consisted essentially of purloined or salvaged British army stocks, and light weapons manufactured locally and secretly. Thus, well in advance of statehood, Ben-Gurion dispatched a network of agents to seek out matériel in the world's arms markets. The most rewarding of those sources turned out to be Czechoslovakia. Early in 1947, Ehud Avriel, the Jewish Agency's principal liaison official in Europe, learned that Czech weaponry might be available to the Jews, provided the transactions were secret and payments were made in dollars. Within days, Avriel prepared his shopping list, then dispatched it to Prague. It was personally approved by Czechoslovakia's foreign minister, Jan Masaryk. Upon receiving their cash payment, Czech officials then signed bills of sale made out to the "Government of Ethiopia." The initial purchase, in January 1948, included 10,000 rifles, 4,500 heavy machine guns, and 3 million rounds of ammunition. Originally manufactured by the Skoda works for the Wehrmacht, the equipment was now redundant, as Czechoslovakia's armed forces switched to Soviet armament. The Czechs even surprised Avriel by offering to sell a number of Skoda-manufactured Messerschmitt-109 fighter planes. Ideology played no role in these initial transactions. They were exclusively commercial.

It was the Stalinist takeover of the Prague government in February 1948 that transformed a financial relationship into one of ideological and strategic policy. Soon the range of Czechoslovak arms sales to the Zionists widened dramatically. Nor were there to be additional fake invoices to "the Government of Ethiopia." General Bedrich Reicen, Czechoslovakia's deputy minister of defense, himself a Jew, now threw the entire weight of his military establishment behind the Jewish supply effort, providing much larger quantities of Czech equipment, from artillery pieces to fighter planes. By the time of Israel's birth, the only limitation on Czech supplies was the Jewish state's ability to arrange for their transport. At first the method of delivery was by Danube River shipment from Bratislava to the Yugoslav port of Sibenik. The Yugoslavs were entirely cooperative. During World War II, Ehud Avriel had established close relations with Tito's partisans, and these now were renewed. An old friend, Alexander Rankovic, was Yugoslav minister of the interior, and personally ensured swift passage for the Zionist munitions. Once at Sibenik, the equipment was transferred to Zionist vessels.

Several weeks before May 15, however, as British withdrawal and full-scale Arab invasion became imminent in Palestine, the Jews were obliged to shift their efforts to air delivery. To meet that need, Bedrich Reicen granted the Zionists access to a Czech military air strip at Zatek. The Jewish Agency in turn chartered several Czech DC-3 civilian transports, and Jewish and Czech personnel cooperated in loading them with munitions. The initial flight departed

Zatek on March 31, 1948, carrying some two thousand rifles and machine guns, with accompanying ammunition. Refueling at a Yugoslav air force base in Montenegro, the plane reached a secret Zionist airstrip in Palestine the next morning. Its cargo proved indispensable to the Jews in the battle for the Tel Aviv–Jerusalem highway. In ensuing weeks even heavier equipment was airlifted from the Zatek base.

Meanwhile, as the first ten Messerschmitt fighters became available for departure to Palestine—and, later, a number of surplus Mosquitoes and Spitfires—the Czech air force agreed to provide specialized instruction for the Jewish air crews and for several dozen foreign mercenaries. Their efforts to ferry planes across the width of the Mediterranean were complicated by limited fuel capacity. Headwinds forced down several of the fighters in Greece, where they were interned. Eventually, however, with supplementary fuel tanks, most of the planes reached Israel. By late summer of 1948, when the supply effort gradually was phased out, Czechoslovakia had supplied Israel with 84 fighter planes, 22 tanks, 16 artillery pieces, 60,000 light arms, and tens of millions of rounds of ammunition.

Additionally, in September 1948, the Prague government authorized formation of a "Czech Brigade," a unit of volunteers trained to fight under Israeli command. The notion was the brain wave of Shmuel Mikunis, secretary-general of Israel's tiny Communist party. Arriving in Czechoslovakia in late 1947, and operating without authorization from Ben-Gurion or Ehud Avriel, Mikunis toured the Communist bloc in an effort to mobilize Jewish youth for military service in Palestine. Meeting with Czech Communist leaders, he invoked the precedent of the International Brigade that had fought in the Spanish Civil War. Although intrigued, the Czechs suggested that Mikunis first refer his proposal to the Kremlin. Eventually, in June 1948, after preliminary negotiations with Soviet officials in Prague, Mikunis telephoned Moscow, and spoke to Gyorgy Malenkov, a senior Communist official (and future prime minister). Soviet approval was forthcoming within hours. In mid-September, the Czech government also concurred. The Prague government's ulterior motive may have been less ideological, or even diplomatic, than functional. The permanent departure of a large number of Jews would have facilitated the reclamation of their jobs and housing for "integral" Czechs.

The Czech-Jewish brigade was organized by a non-Jewish officer, Major Antonin Sochor, who in fact was a Red Army major general and World War II hero. Within weeks Sochor had recruited a thousand Jews and some non-Jews, most of these also Red Army veterans.

Assigned to Czech camps that Bedrich Reicen had placed at Sochor's disposal, the recruits were given additional training by Israeli liaison officers. From the outset, however, the venture suffered from confusion of purpose. Reicen and his associates had anticipated keeping the brigade intact in Israel. Its commanding officer would be Sochor himself—whose principal loyalty, of course, was to Communist Czechoslovakia. Ben-Gurion would not hear of it. Eventually the Czech government backed down. The Czech volunteers would be dispersed throughout the Israeli army.

In November 1948, a modest force of six hundred volunteers departed on specially chartered vessels. By February 1949, when the last of the trainees arrived, the Palestine war had all but ended. Although Sochor and some two hundred of his men saw limited action in a few skirmishes, their role was essentially superfluous. The Czech Jews remained on, to settle in Israel. Sochor himself returned to Prague following the Rhodes Armistice Agreements, and in 1950 was killed in a mysterious automobile accident. Perhaps by no coincidence, it was the identical fate decreed by Stalin in the 1930s for numerous Soviet veterans of the Spanish Civil War. They had been "infected" by Western idealism.

Even as the Czechoslovak brigade project was running its course, other, parallel ventures were under exploration. Mordechai Oren, a member of Israel's far-left Mapam party, and Nahum Shadmi, a senior Haganah training officer based in Paris, traveled through Eastern Europe, seeking to recruit young Jews for military service in Israel. Their effort was less than successful. Local Communist officials generally were suspicious, and the few hundred Hungarian and Romanian Jewish volunteers received only hurried and superficial military training. Those who reached Israel in the spring of 1948 were unfamiliar even with the use of rifles. Hurled posthaste into the battle for the Jerusalem highway at Latrun, they suffered heavy casualties.

AN INFUSION OF HUMAN "MATERIAL"

But if military recruitment essentially failed, the wider upsurge of Jewish civilian immigration from Eastern Europe more than fulfilled Israel's state-building purpose. Thus, of Czechoslovakia's 51,000 surviving Jews in the early postwar period, 35,000 departed for the displaced persons camps of Allied-occupied Germany, and eventually continued on to Israel. President Edvard Benes and his government provided the Jewish Agency with office space in Prague to coordinate this emigration, even made railroad and bus facilities available to the

Jews. In any case, the largest numbers of émigrés in transit through Czechoslovakia were not of local origin. Some 220,000 arrived from Poland. A tiny fraction of that nation's once vast Jewish population of 3.2 million, virtually all now were fleeing a resurgence of Poland's malevolent folk antisemitism. Although in 1948–49 the Warsaw government systematically closed all Zionist institutions, including the Jewish Agency emigration office, it permitted a final contingent of 67,000 refugees to depart before sealing the gates. By then the bulk of the Polish-Jewish exodus was resettled in Israel.

Their numbers were augmented by streams of immigrants from other East European nations. In Bulgaria, approximately 44,000 Jews remained alive at the end of the war. Destitute, heirs to a long Zionist tradition, they required no further incentive to leave for the ancestral homeland. In 1947, moreover, the Sofia government dutifully adapted to Soviet Middle Eastern strategy by allowing some 7,000 younger Jews to depart for Palestine as "fighters against British imperialism." A year later the Jewish Agency negotiated an even wider-ranging deal with the Bulgarian Communist regime. All Jews who chose to leave for Israel would be allowed to do so, provided they renounced their homes and chattels. Most did. By 1950, fewer than 5,000 Jews remained, essentially older people. In Yugoslavia, some 18,000 of the nation's prewar Jewish population of 55,000 had escaped the Holocaust. During these same postwar years, approximately two-thirds of the survivors chose to depart for refugee camps in the West, and from there to Palestine. The Tito government made no attempt to stop them.

The 210,000 Jews who remained alive in Hungary at war's end comprised less than a third of that country's once substantial Jewry. In earlier years Zionism had failed to become a dynamic movement among this highly acculturated population. Even after 1945, Jewish emigration to Palestine remained proportionately smaller from Hungary than from Poland or Romania. Age was a factor. The survival rate of middle-aged Jews was rather larger here than elsewhere in Europe, and these older people were less inclined to face the hardships of refugee camps or Israeli relocation centers. Until May 1949, when Jewish emigration was choked off altogether, not more than 70,000 Hungarian Jews departed for the American zone of Germany—and Israel. Virtually all were younger men and women. But if they were a minority even of Hungary's postwar remnant, they also represented indispensable human "material" for the Jewish state.

An even farther-ranging boon for Israel was to be found in Romania, a nation that before the war had encompassed nearly 800,000

Jews, Europe's second-largest Jewish population outside the USSR. The Holocaust wreaked its fury here, too, of course, but Romania's 360,000 surviving Jews represented a still formidable critical mass. They had been an intensely Zionist community even before the war. After 1945 their impulse for departure to Palestine was overwhelming. The Bucharest government placed few obstacles in their way. Indeed, it saw only advantage in reducing its historically suspect and now impoverished Jewish minority. In the first two postwar years, tens of thousands of these people were quietly allowed to leave. Afterward, however, Jewish emigration did not always flow smoothly. In 1948, following the Soviet break with Yugoslavia's Marshal Tito (pp. 63–4), Zionism came under renewed suspicion as a "deviationist" movement, and in June of that year, the Communist regime attached Zionist funds and training farms.

Yet Jewish emigration even then was not foreclosed. Foreign Minister Ana Pauker, herself a Jew, negotiated an arrangement with Israel's ambassador, Reuven Rubin, for the departure of 4,000 Jews monthly. The decision was not uninfluenced by a handsome Jewish Agency subvention to the Bucharest government in dollar currency. Possibly a certain lingering *Judenschmerz* also influenced Pauker's decision. This hard-edged Communist had been a Hebrew teacher in her youth. Her father and brother lived in Israel. The foreign minister's authorization in any case was coldly selective. It applied mainly to ruined businessmen and to other economically "redundant" Jews. There were not a few of these. Between the end of the war and December 1951, fully 115,000 Romanian Jews emigrated to Israel, an exodus second only to the Polish outpouring. Altogether, by then, the Soviet bloc, if not the Soviet Union itself, supplied the largest component of Israel's postwar European population.

AN ENVELOPING CHILL FROM THE EAST

Israel's diplomatic relations with the Soviet Union meanwhile unfolded equably. In August 1948 a Soviet legation set up shop in Tel Aviv, and its senior staffers were ceremonially received by Prime Minister Ben-Gurion and Foreign Minister Sharett (both in full formal dress, complete with top hats and striped trousers). Grateful for Soviet help, the Israeli government extended itself in gestures of reciprocal friendship. One of these related to Russian Orthodox Church grounds and buildings in Jerusalem. After the Bolshevik Revolution, a schism had developed between Soviet claimants to this property and claimants representing the exiled "White" ecclesiastical headquarters in New York. The dispute had not been resolved during the twenty-five years of British rule in Palestine. Upon achieving independence, Israel resolved it forthwith. It recognized "Red" authority over the properties. As another gesture of goodwill, the government extended legal recognition to the Communist party, reversing the ban that had been imposed by the British administration.

Moscow in fact was disappointed at the party's feeble showing in the first Knesset election of January 1949. The Communists won a mere 4 of 120 seats. Yet distinctly more encouraging was Mapam's success in capturing 19 Knesset seats, thereby ranking this far-leftist faction as second only to Ben-Gurion's moderate Socialist Mapai party. The Soviets also drew reassurance from Israel's evident non-alignment in the Cold War. On numerous occasions Ben-Gurion affirmed his government's commitment to a policy of "friendship with all," of "nonidentification" with either power bloc. Aware of the vulnerability of Jews living behind the Iron Curtain, the prime minister emphasized repeatedly that "as long as there are millions of our people on both sides, we must guard our independence of action."

Within his nation's political arena, however, Ben-Gurion would not indefinitely tolerate the far left's threats to public order or security. Despite their small numbers, and the focus of their efforts principally upon Israel's Arab population, the Communists also proved ruthless in exploiting the pressures of mass Jewish immigration, organizing the newcomers in clamorous demonstrations for housing and employment. In October 1949 Israel's Communist newspaper, *Kol HaAm*, described the cabinet as "traitors to their country and enemies of the workers," and Ben-Gurion himself as "an American agent." The provocation was too much for the prime minister. He instituted a criminal-libel suit against the Communists, even attempted to suppress *Kol HaAm* until the Israeli supreme court quashed the effort as an infringement of free speech. In turn the Soviet press denounced the prime minister for an act of "Israeli McCarthyism." Ben-Gurion remained implacable. On the basis of internal security reports (pp. 67–8), he ordered several members of the Communist party arrested for illegal possession of military documents. And the Soviet press in turn riposted with even harsher accusations of "racial and discriminatory policies" toward Arabs and working people, and "imperialist penetration in the Middle East."

The incremental shift in Moscow's approach to Israel was no mere reflexive endorsement of its Communist protégés. During the early postindependence years, Ben-Gurion's efforts, and those of Foreign Minister Sharett, to steer a discreet course between the camps of East and West became increasingly difficult. In May 1950, the United States, Britain, and France issued their Tripartite Declaration, ostensibly "guaranteeing" the Arab-Israel territorial status quo. For the Israeli government the moment was an awkward one. Acceptance of the "guarantee" (which in fact was directed more toward Hashemite Jordan than Israel) would place the Jewish state exclusively under Western protection. Ben-Gurion accordingly informed the Knesset that he regarded the Western declaration as "unilateral" and "not binding on Israel." Yet, at the same time, he welcomed the pronouncement "to the extent that it was designed to increase security and peace." The Soviets were unimpressed by the prime minister's circumlocution. Their press denounced the Western commitment as "a new aggressive act directed against the Soviet Union . . . dictated . . . by the military interests of American imperialism."

The crisis in Israeli diplomacy intensified the following month. On June 25, 1950, the Korean War broke out, and Israel found itself caught up in Soviet-American rivalries as never before. The government's approach initially was to support the attempt of "nonaligned" nations to end the war through negotiation. Within the United Nations, Israel's Ambassador Abba Eban sought out opportunities to play a mediative role. But the neutralist effort soon came under heavy American pressure. Washington demanded that Israel "stand up and be counted," that its United Nations delegation vote unequivocally to condemn North Korean aggression.

Within the Jewish state, policy-makers sensed that they had reached a diplomatic fault line. Like the Communists, the Mapam faction interpreted the Korean conflict as a revolt of oppressed citizens against a corrupt and reactionary South Korean regime. Even nonleftists were given pause. Israel owed the Soviet bloc so much, they noted. Why should it be more pro-Western than Egypt, which similarly remained uncommitted? But, in the end, the cabinet felt obliged to remember which side of the Atlantic Israel's bread was buttered on. The decision was couched in moralistic language: The independence of small nations had to be respected. On July 4, 1950, after a sharp debate, the Knesset majority gave its support to the UN Security Council vote of condemnation. Soon afterward the government dispatched a medical team to South Korea as a gesture of solidarity.

Moscow's response was predictable, if still unofficial. The Soviet *New Times* attacked Israel in an article entitled: "A Toady of American Imperialism." Other press criticism was equally harsh. In turn Ben-Gurion and Sharett scrambled to reassure the Soviets of their unwavering friendship. They organized ceremonial receptions to commemorate the Soviet role in defeating Nazi Germany; dispatched congratulatory messages to Stalin on the anniversary of the Bolshevik Revolution and on the Soviet dictator's own birthday; affirmed and reaffirmed Israel's commitment to East-West détente. By 1951, however, the tightrope effort became too difficult for a vulnerable little nation. In that year London and Washington were exploring ways of extending NATO into a Middle East alliance system, with Iraq and possibly several other Arab states to be invited as future members. Alerted to this development, Ben-Gurion in turn felt obliged to raise the possibility of his own government's participation. In February of that year, he held his conversation with General Sir Brian Robertson (pp. 16–17).

News of the prime minister's conversation leaked. Reaction was not long in coming. Within Israel itself, Mapam began organizing protest demonstrations. In the Soviet Union, *Pravda* and the *New Times* furiously denounced the specter of an "Anglo-American-Turkish-Israeli Axis" in the Middle East. By then, ironically, the Western Powers themselves discerned little advantage in Israeli participation. Even as the anticipated Middle East alliance went through various drafts in 1951, Israel gradually was excluded from consultation. When Sharett repeatedly queried Washington on his nation's standing in the emergent Baghdad Pact, he was politely fended off. By the autumn of 1951 Israel's diplomatic position thus had been undermined among both sets of Great Powers. Dunned by the Knesset's Mapam faction, Sharett continued to insist that "Israel has never agreed, and will not agree, to support any aggressive plans aimed against the Soviet Union." Yet, to Moscow the protestations rang hollow. Israel, it appeared, had irretrievably abandoned its status of nonalignment in the Cold War.

AN EXECRATION OF "TRAITORS"

In these same early years of Israel's precarious neutralism, between 1948 and 1951, the postwar emigration of East European Jews slowly dried up. In one Soviet-bloc nation after another, Zionist activities were snuffed out and Jewish communal institutions were closed or taken over by Communist apparatchiks. More ominously yet, the Communist satellite governments launched an "anti-Zionist" offensive that exploited many of the classic wellsprings of nativist antisemitism. The new campaign by no coincidence followed hard upon Stalin's break with Yugoslavia's Marshal Tito, in February 1948. The threat of "Titoism" within the Communist empire henceforth became

Stalin's nightmare. Identifying that danger with the earlier bête noire of "Trotskyism," the Soviet dictator would stamp out all other potentially deviationist movements behind the Iron Curtain. Zionism was regarded as one of these, and the Jews altogether as a potential fifth column. Which others of Eastern Europe's minority peoples, after all, possessed the largest numbers of their kinsmen among the Western "imperialist" nations? In Hungary, as in Bulgaria (and later in Romania), the Jewish exodus was brought to a peremptory halt. In 1949 Hungarian Foreign Minister Laszlo Rajk, a Jew, was put on trial for "Zionist-bourgeois" plotting, and later executed. In Bulgaria that same year, another Jew, Deputy Prime Minister Traicho Kostov, was imprisoned on the identical charge. In Bucharest, three years later, Ana Pauker was removed from office and scores of Zionist leaders were sentenced to long prison terms.

It was in Czechoslovakia, however, that the residual tradition of democratic—non-Stalinist—socialism was longest-lived, and in which the Moscow-inspired campaign against putative deviationism was shifted most flagrantly from "Titoism" to "Zionism." In the autumn of 1951 Prague announced the arrest of fourteen leading officials of the party and government. Imprisoned and intermittently tortured for nearly a year, the defendants eventually were placed on trial in November 1952. They included Rudolf Slansky, secretary-general of the Czech Communist party, and thirteen other senior party and government figures. All but three were Jews. After the name of each Jewish defendant, the indictment added the words "of Jewish origin." Their alleged crime, "Zionist conspiracy," was depicted as a widely based plot, led by prominent Jews in the United States and Israel, to undermine the Socialist order. The American Jewish Joint Distribution Committee was identified as the conduit of this Zionist penetration, its techniques purportedly ranging from espionage and sabotage to black-market operations and smuggling. Once on the stand, the prisoners vied with one another in confessing their alleged crimes, and the trial proceedings were widely published and broadcast.

Among those testifying were two Israeli defendants, former Czech citizens. They were the Mapam activists Mordechai Oren and Shimon Orenstein. Both men, on their own, were engaged in the Jewish emigration effort at the time of their arrest in late 1951. They too now were intimidated into confessing their participation in the "Zionist plot." In November 1952, the court handed down sentences of death by hanging for Slansky and ten other defendants, with three receiving life terms. The executions were carried out the next month. From the outset of the trial, moreover, Jews in every echelon of public life were expelled from their positions in government, party, and industry. Numbers of Jewish communal leaders were jailed on charges of "economic crimes."

In Israel, reaction to these developments was one of shock and outrage. Although Meir Vilner and his Communist faction dutifully endorsed Prague's charges against "the Slansky gang of spies and traitors," the leadership of Mapam was entirely discountenanced. There appeared no way any longer to reconcile Zionism and pro-Sovietism, or to explain the arrest of their own party emissaries, Oren and Orenstein, in Czechoslovakia. The result was a gradual erosion of Mapam strength in Israel, and a near-total loss of sympathy for the Communist party among the nation's Jewish population. The Israeli government response was one of unequivocal condemnation. Addressing the Knesset in November 1952, Sharett scornfully observed that

> only those to whom espionage and sabotage come naturally as a matter of daily practice can invent such stories of sinister plotting about the government of Israel. . . . The liberation of Czechoslovakia from Hitler's storm troopers stands desecrated before the whole world by this attempt to revive Hitler's vile spirit within her borders.

Recriminations between Israel and the Eastern bloc were followed soon by more tangible diplomatic consequences. In December 1952, the Czech government declared Arie Kubovy, Israel's minister in Prague, persona non grata, accusing him of "espionage contacts" with the late Slansky and other convicted Jewish Communists. Inasmuch as Kubovy doubled as Israel's minister to Warsaw, the Polish government echoed Prague's accusations and similarly demanded his recall. In February 1953, Budapest expelled Israel's cultural attaché, Yosef Walter, also on charges of espionage.

Ultimately, the campaign against Zionism and Jews as agents of Western imperialism achieved its direst virulence in the Soviet Union itself. Directed by Stalin's deputy Andrei Zhdanov, until his death late in 1948, the offensive initially was waged against Jewish institutions, and specifically against the Jewish Anti-Fascist Committee. Twenty-five former members of this ad hoc former wartime group were arrested, imprisoned for four years, and eventually put on trial in 1952. They were charged with plotting, in collaboration with Washington, to "amputate" the Crimea and transform it into a "Zionist bourgeois state"—and thereby into a base for American imperialism. The defendants were found guilty, and in August of that year twenty-four of them were executed. The one woman in the group was sentenced to life imprisonment. Arrested, too, were hundreds of prominent Jewish intellectuals, almost all of whom later would die in prison. Thousands of other Jews were dismissed from leading positions in party, state, and professional life.

Moscow's anti-Zionist terror reached its climax in January 1953, shortly after the Slansky trial in Czechoslovakia, when *Pravda* announced the arrest of a dozen "physician-saboteurs," most of them with Jewish names. In recent years, it was alleged, the physicians had poisoned to death a number of eminent Soviet officials. As in the case of the Jewish Anti-Fascist Committee, these "monsters in human form" were identified as hirelings of "the international Jewish bourgeois organization" the American Joint Distribution Committee, which had been appointed by Washington to "destroy the leading cadres of the Soviet Union." In fact, many of the named Soviet victims had been "murdered" years before, among them Andrei Zhdanov himself in 1948, but the world evidently had to wait until 1953 for the "true facts" of their deaths to emerge.

As the imprisoned physicians awaited their trial, public accusations against other Jewish doctors circulated throughout the Soviet Union, and many hundreds of these men and women were dismissed from their hospital positions. Stalin's campaign to arouse "revolutionary vigilance" against the "Zionist nests" assuredly reflected his fear of Titoist deviationism. Yet this was not the danger he publicly proclaimed: That honor was reserved instead for the "imperialist West." And from 1950 on, it was Israel and international Zionism that were irretrievably linked with that putative menace.

On February 9, 1953, a small explosive device went off in the garden of the Soviet legation in Ramat Gan, Israel, slightly injuring the wife of the Soviet minister and two local employees. The Israeli government was horrified. In the Knesset the next day, a shaken Ben-Gurion furiously denounced the outrage, then read out the message he had dispatched to Moscow: "This act of criminal folly stands condemned in the eyes of all decent citizens," he asserted, "who will recognize that it is directed not merely against a formal diplomatic mission but at the heart of the State itself. Every effort will be made to find [and prosecute] the perpetrators of this foul deed." The perpetrators in fact were not found, then or later. Very possibly the Soviets had staged the bomb incident themselves. Meanwhile, on February 12, only three days after the episode, Moscow exploited the crisis, depicting Ben-Gurion's expressions of regret as camouflage for his government's ultimate implication in the deed, then announcing that it was closing the Soviet legation in Israel, and requiring Israel similarly to close its legation in the Soviet Union.

THE SECRET GAME

Fortunately for Israel, and even more for the Jews of Eastern Europe, Joseph Stalin died a month later, in March 1953. The imprisoned Soviet Jewish doctors were soon released, and gradually the antisemitic terror campaign abated throughout the Communist empire. In July, the Soviet and Israeli legations reopened. During the ensuing year and a half, Soviet-Israeli diplomatic relations continued functionally. Indeed, in June 1954, both governments raised their legations to embassy status. Moscow's revived forbearance plainly evinced no sudden upsurge of benevolence for Israel or the Jews. Rather, in the aftermath of Stalin's death, the Kremlin leadership became increasingly embroiled in an internal political power struggle. In need of a breathing space, they were prepared to exercise restraint in negotiating an end to the Korean and Vietnamese wars, even in countenancing a reconciliation with Tito in Yugoslavia. Israel shared in this moratorium of Cold War abrasiveness.

Yet the restored normalcy of Soviet-Israeli diplomatic contacts belied a clandestine underground intelligence struggle. As early as 1948, the KGB wiretapped Israel's legation in Moscow; while in Israel the Soviets vastly enlarged their undercover penetration efforts. It was a subversive campaign that actually had been directed toward Palestine Jewry as early as the 1920s and 1930s. Suspended during the war, the clandestine operation was resumed in 1945. Indeed, it was facilitated by the massive postwar emigration to Palestine of East European displaced persons. In November 1947, a special KGB unit directed by Colonel Aleksandr Korotokov began recruiting and training likely "anti-Fascist" elements among these embarking refugees. Korotokov's deputy, Lieutenant Colonel Vladimir Vertiporokh, later became the first KGB *rezident* in Israel. Functioning as an "attaché" in the Soviet legation, Vertiporokh continued to recruit agents and to seek out new information on Israeli military and foreign policy developments. By the mid-1960s most of the sixty Soviet embassy staffers were actively engaged in this intelligence campaign. Their efforts were supplemented by intelligence personnel in the Czech, Romanian, Polish, and Bulgarian legations, and also by their own network of Israeli contacts.

Early on, Israel's *Shin Bet*—internal security service—had placed most of these people under continual surveillance. Isser Harel, the service's director, well understood that Communist subterfuge was far more sophisticated than the Arab variety. He also grasped the historic depth of pro-Soviet loyalty among Israel's Communist and Mapam factions. In their ideological vulnerability, these far-leftists had to be watched as carefully as the East European diplomatic personnel. One of them, in fact, Aharon Cohen, was a senior Mapam political theorist. In April 1958 Shin Bet operatives spotted Cohen in clandestine meetings with Vladimir Sokolov, the Soviet "press attaché," and a known intelligence agent. Ongoing vigilance revealed Cohen in further secret discussions with other Soviet intelligence figures. Harel suspected him of sharing with these agents his party's access to national security information. At Ben-Gurion's orders, however, no arrests were made. Cohen was a rather unworldly scholar, and almost certainly not animated by disloyalty to the state. At that time, too, Mapam belonged to the government coalition, and the prime minister was uninterested in a political crisis. But after monitoring three additional years of Cohen's clandestine meetings, the Shin Bet and the police finally were allowed to seize their quarry. In July 1961 Cohen was tried *in camera*, convicted, and sentenced to five years' imprisonment.

By then Israel's population had become well apprised of Communist subversion. One particularly shocking case involved a long-term KGB "mole." This was Ze'ev Avni, a senior staff member of Israel's embassy in Belgrade. Born Wolf Goldstein in Switzerland, Avni was the son of Socialist idealists who had briefly sheltered Lenin during World War I. In 1948 he settled in Israel, and immediately joined the young state's foreign service. Multilingual, a trained economist, Avni was a logical choice as Israel's first commercial attaché to the Benelux countries. Soon his manifold talents attracted the attention of the *Mossad*, Israel's "CIA," its foreign-intelligence-gathering arm (p. 121). Recruited, Avni thereafter used his diplomatic cover to serve as a "mailbox" between the Mossad and its European agents. And, simultaneously, Avni transmitted the names of those agents to his Soviet contacts. Four years passed before the man's double role came under suspicion, and eventually was confirmed. Lured back to Israel, Avni was tried *in camera* and given a fifteen-year prison sentence. Still another entrapped Israeli spy was Yitzchak Zilberman, a Bessarabian engineer and 1949 immigrant. Employed in the metals division of Koor, a major Israeli industrial conglomerate, Zilberman was privy to numerous classified military projects. He transmitted the information to his Soviet contacts. In 1959, finally, the Shin Bet discovered Zilberman's activities. He too was swiftly tried, convicted, and sentenced to nine years' imprisonment.

In no instance was Soviet espionage undertaken in Israel primarily for financial reward. The inducement was hard-core ideological commitment to the Soviet cause. Nor was that loyalty confined to East European Jewry. As early as the 1930s, as fugitives from Central Europe migrated to Palestine, the Communist recruitment effort gained momentum among them as well. Thus it was that the most notorious Soviet spy in Israel's history emerged from the German-speaking "fifth wave" of immigrants. He was Israel Beer. Arriving in Palestine in 1938, this articulate young Viennese Jew brought with him unique military credentials. By his own account, he had graduated from the Austrian military academy and had earned a doctorate at the University of Vienna; fought as an officer in the 1934 Schutzbund (Social Democratic) armed revolt against Austria's Dollfuss government; in 1937 served as a lieutenant colonel in the Loyalists' International Brigade during the Spanish Civil War. It was a dazzling background, impressive enough to win Beer immediate officer status in the Haganah, the Palestine Jewish underground defense force.

Afterward Beer progressed rapidly through Haganah ranks, becoming one of only six Israeli colonels at the time of the 1948 War of Independence. Soon he was promoted to assistant chief of planning and military operations at Israel's general staff headquarters. In 1949, once the war ended, Beer left the army to become military correspondent for the Labor newspaper *Davar.* Again the man's powerful gift for exposition made its mark. By the mid-1950s, he had become professor of military history at Tel Aviv University and a trusted military adviser to Ben-Gurion himself. Indeed, Beer convinced the prime minister that the Soviets would move vigorously to protect their expanding interests in the Middle East. It was an argument that weighed heavily in Ben-Gurion's later decision to heed Soviet threats and abandon the Sinai, in the aftermath of the 1956 war (p. 102).

Beer's impact upon his listeners and readers was extraordinary, and soon extended well beyond Israel. By the latter 1950s, he was a frequent lecturer in West Germany before academic societies and military circles. In 1958, as he addressed the annual meeting of the German Association for Military Science, Defense Minister Franz-Josef Strauss was in the audience, and was impressed. Through Strauss, in turn, Beer came to know numerous senior officers of the Bundeswehr. They reacted gratefully to this visiting Israeli's support for a vigorous policy of German military preparedness. By 1959, however, Beer's numerous visits to Germany had caught the attention of Isser Harel, now chief of Israel's joint security services. Harel was particularly concerned that Beer lately had made several excursions into East Berlin. From there, it was learned, he had been flown to Warsaw to meet with Poland's defense minister, Ignacz Kummer, ostensibly a former comrade in the International Brigade.

It was discovered, too, that Beer simultaneously had become an intimate of General Reinhard Gehlen, chief of the Bundesrepublik's intelligence service. Indeed, almost from the moment Beer met Gehlen, in May 1960, the two agreed to work together, to exchange intelligence data. "We began to take a more professional interest in the Israelis," acknowledged Gehlen some years later. "We gave them expert advice on the development of their small but powerful secret service . . . because we recognized that Israel was as much an outpost of the free world as West Berlin." For Beer, the relationship with Gehlen opened access to privileged NATO military information, data he could well have been taking with him on his periodic trips to Eastern Europe. The possibility did not escape Isser Harel.

In 1960, urgently concerned that Beer might be serving as a conduit of Israeli—and Western—secrets to the Soviet bloc, Harel put him under twenty-four-hour surveillance. Soon the intelligence director's worst suspicions were confirmed. In Tel Aviv, on March 30, 1961, Beer was caught and arrested in the act of passing a briefcase to Vladimir Sokolov, Russia's ubiquitous "press attaché." The briefcase was found to contain photographed extracts from Ben-Gurion's private diary, including references to several key Mossad personnel. Although Harel's men allowed Sokolov to make a hurried departure to the USSR, they now set about grilling Beer intensively. They also belatedly investigated his earlier background in Europe. The ensuing revelations proved a shock. Almost all of Beer's European bona fides now were discovered to be fraudulent: his University of Vienna "doctorate," his purported officer's ranking in the 1934 Schutzbund, in the International Brigade, even his participation in the Spanish Civil War. Rather, he had belonged to a Communist cell in Vienna, and between 1936 and 1938 had attended the Soviet intelligence school in Moscow. Indeed, it appeared that Israel Beer was not even Israel Beer. There was evidence that the actual Israel Beer may have been a poor Jewish student in Austria who mysteriously disappeared just at the time the man bearing his name departed for Palestine. Thereafter the Soviets waited nearly two decades before putting their mole into action.

In March 1962, Beer was tried *in camera* and given a ten-year sentence. He died in prison four years later, still maintaining his innocence, still protesting that all his activities had been carried out to "protect" Israel. The "protection" had done the nation grievous harm. Many of Israel's most valuable Mossad agents had to be withdrawn from Central Europe. Vital Western military information had been turned over to the Soviets, including details of NATO bases in Turkey constructed by Israeli contractors. Not least of all, Ben-Gurion had been sold on Beer's assessment of Moscow's 1956 threat to drive Israel from the Sinai, a threat that belatedly proved a massive bluff.

Yet the Soviet-Israeli game of cloak-and-dagger was by no means a one-way operation. Israel had an agenda of its own to fulfill behind the Iron Curtain. It was to maintain a viable connection with the Jewish hinterland within the Soviet empire, and specifically within the USSR itself. The Nazi invasion had cruelly depleted that hinterland. As late as 1958 an official Soviet census recorded the Jewish population within the pre-1939 Soviet frontiers as 1,760,000. The figure signified a reduction by fully one-third of prewar Soviet Jewry— although Jewish survivors in annexed eastern Poland, in Moldova (formerly Bessarabia), and in the three Baltic republics, who had fled eastward during the war, raised the figure to 2,268,000.

And after 1945, it was this cruelly ravaged minority that was subjected to the Stalinist campaign of cultural strangulation and political oppression. The psychic trauma inflicted by the anti-Jewish onslaught was difficult to gauge. The Jews had never been a monolithic entity. Until 1941 many had been village dwellers who had preserved their Jewish culture intact, particularly in the Baltic republics, in eastern Poland, and in far-off Soviet Asia. Others were marginal Jews, citizens of the "heartland" Soviet republics—Ukraine, Belarus, Russia itself—who functioned between the Jewish and Gentile spheres. By the eve of the war, hundreds of thousands were well along the road to assimilation. Yet even among these, a residual Jewish identity conceivably endured. If so, they might yet be envisaged as a future source of Israeli immigration.

For David Ben-Gurion, there never had been a question of writing off Soviet Jewry as "lost" to Israel. From the moment diplomatic relations were consummated with Moscow, in September 1948, the prime minister was intent on organizing a network of contacts between the USSR's widely dispersed Jewish population and the new Jewish state. At the direction of Ben-Gurion's security adviser, Shaul Avigur, the task of forging the linkage was assigned initially to Nechemia Levanon. Estonian-born, a Russian-speaker and a kibbutz member, Levanon in earlier years had served as a highly successful Zionist youth emissary in England. In January 1953, still in his thirties, he was dispatched to Moscow ostensibly to serve as agricultural attaché at the Israeli Embassy, but in practical fact to operate as "liaison" to Soviet Jewry.

In July 1953, following the brief interregnum of severed diplomatic relations, Levanon returned to Moscow, and under his official embassy title was permitted routinely to tour outlying Soviet agricultural areas. It was during these visits that he managed to revive a number of Jewish contacts from his youth, and to arrange for the discreet circulation of Russian-language publications that had been prepared in Israel. The KGB knew what these diplomatic personnel were up to, but rarely intervened. The Israelis did not appear to be interested in secret intelligence. So long as Levanon and his staff restricted themselves to the distribution of Jewish and Zionist information, Moscow chose not to create a pretext for Israel to block the reciprocal free movement of Soviet personnel in the Jewish state. As late as the 1950s, few Middle East specialists in the Soviet government—or Kremlinologists in the Israeli government—could have anticipated that these early, comparatively innocuous excursions by a handful of second-level embassy staffers were shaping the future destiny of Israel. In fact, they were laying the groundwork for a migratory explosion that four decades later would revolutionize the demography, the very character, of the little Jewish republic.

A SOVIET INCURSION INTO THE MIDDLE EAST

In March 1954 Colonel Gamal Abd al-Nasser outmaneuvered his rivals within Egypt's revolutionary military junta to assume his nation's prime-ministry, and soon afterward its presidency. His principal objectives thenceforth, aside from keeping himself in office, were to liquidate the British occupation in Egypt and to continue his predecessors' struggle against internal poverty and social stagnation. Nasser fulfilled his initial objective in July 1954, winning Britain's agreement to evacuate the Suez Canal Zone. Yet he was less successful in achieving his economic and social goals, for Egypt's internal problems gradually revealed themselves to be all but insoluble. By the summer and autumn of 1954, therefore, Nasser began shifting the emphasis away from the domestic agenda to offer his people the diversion of a militant new program of pan-Arabism. It was Egypt's destiny, the president announced in a series of public addresses, to foster the struggle against imperialism everywhere in the Middle East as leader of a federation of Arab nations.

Yet the new policy orientation was threatened that same year, 1954, when Iraq entered the Baghdad Pact. In Nasser's eyes the Western Powers, which only recently had begun a selective evacuation of the Middle East, appeared to be returning through a Pakistani-Iranian-Turkish—and now Iraqi—back door. Worse yet, Nasser's cherished role as leader of the Arab world was now being threatened by Iraq's Prime Minister Nuri es-Saïd, a British ally. The young president accordingly set about meeting the new challenge with imagination and ruthlessness. All the resources of Egyptian bribery, diplomacy, and Nasser's considerable personal charisma were thrown into the campaign to rally Arab nationalism against the Baghdad Pact.

It was to assure credibility in that offensive, moreover, that Nasser was obliged increasingly to adopt an unanticipated role, this one as champion of Arab revanchism against Israel. Thus, from late 1954 on, his military commanders in the Egyptian-occupied Gaza Strip directed a widening series of Palestinian guerrilla incursions into Israeli territory, inflicting a heavy toll of Israeli civilian lives. Retaliating with characteristic vigor, the Israeli army in turn launched its own counterattacks across the Gaza border, striking directly at Egyptian military installations. The violence reached a climax of sorts in February 1955, when Palestinian bands from Gaza penetrated deep into central Israel, killing a dozen civilians, among them a group of village schoolchildren studying in their classroom. Immediately Ben-Gurion authorized a reprisal of brigade strength against Egyptian army headquarters in Gaza. Launched on February 28, the attack killed thirty-eight Egyptian troops and wounded twenty-four.

Shocked and humiliated by the Gaza debacle, Nasser henceforth shifted the full weight of his military preparations toward the Zionist enemy. "February 28, 1955, was the turning point," he argued later. ". . . We at once started to examine the significance of peace and the balance of power in the area." Until early 1955 there had been a certain functional military equilibrium between Egypt and Israel. The United States, Britain, and France had ensured this balance, monitoring and restricting the sale of weapons within the framework of their May 1950 Tripartite Declaration. If Israel's air and army equipment remained numerically inferior to Egypt's, the Jewish state nevertheless maintained its narrow operative edge through superior training and esprit de corps. But it was a functional parity that now would be altered profoundly, as Nasser made the decision to turn to Moscow.

It will be recalled that tensions between Israel and the Soviet Union had eased following the death of Stalin in March 1953. By summer, mutual diplomatic relations were restored, and the Soviets maintained a cautious even-handedness on Arab-Israeli issues. That restraint would undergo change in February 1954. It was then, dealing with a Syrian-Israeli border dispute on irrigation rights, that the UN Security Council formulated a compromise proposal. By its terms, Israel might resume its irrigation activities under the selective approval of the UN Truce Supervision commander on the spot. But when the resolution was submitted to a formal vote, the Soviet delegate, Andrei Vishinsky, vetoed it. Indeed, from then on, the Soviets vetoed every Security Council resolution in behalf of Israel's complaints, supported every Arab-inspired resolution, large or small, against Israel. Plainly the tentative Soviet-Israeli reconciliation now was all but moribund.

It had been torpedoed by the Cold War. Soviet distrust of the Jewish state reflected a succession of developments: the atrophy of Israel's far-leftist parties; Israel's painful decision to condemn North Korean aggression; its growing financial dependence on West Germany and the United States; its tentative outreach campaign to East European Jewry. Beyond all else, however, the shift in Moscow's support from Israel to the Arab nations evinced distrust of the emergent Baghdad Pact. In the Soviet "dialectic," it appeared inconceivable that Israel, already linked by a nexus of ties to the West, should not also be lured under the protective umbrella of this multilateral treaty. In the summer of 1955, Israel's Ambassador Abba Eban was in San Francisco to participate in a tenth-anniversary celebration of the founding of the United Nations. Soviet Foreign Minister Vyacheslav Molotov had arrived for the occasion, and invited Eban to lunch. During their lengthy conversation Molotov spoke bluntly. "His information was that the United States was going to get Israel to sign a defense treaty," Eban recalled. "This would be a tragic development; the central aim of Soviet policy was to avoid being encircled by American and other imperialist bases. The Soviet Union had helped Israel come into existence in the hope that it would never lend itself as a base for the hostile actions of one power against the other."

Eban listened to Molotov's admonition with incredulity. His own government feared the Baghdad Pact no less than the Soviets did. Under the treaty's provisions, after all, the West was arming Iraq and perhaps, later, other Arab states that chose to join. In cosmeticizing the exclusion of Israel from this pact, American Secretary of State John Foster Dulles earlier had explained to Eban that, by involving

Arab states in a "northern-tier" defense against Soviet expansion, together with such non-Arab states as Iran and Turkey, the United States would be substituting communism for Zionism as the major foe of the Arabs, and thereby would divert Arab preoccupation from the Israel issue. "It was hard to listen to such talk," recalled Eban, "without a violation of courtesy." And now here was Molotov sharing a fantasy of his own, of Britain and the United States wooing Israel as an ally.

Fantasy or not, the Russians since the early postwar period had lived with the fear of a Western-controlled military alliance "in proximity" to their southern frontiers. As they saw it, the impending northern-tier alliance would have to be outflanked, at every juncture and at any cost. By February 1955, as it happened, Nikita Khrushchev had emerged as his country's Communist party chairman (and later prime minister). Unlike Stalin, Khrushchev had never subscribed to a simplistic two-camp view of the world. Rather, in the new chairman's perspective, there existed three principal blocs: the Socialist bloc, the capitalist-imperialist bloc, and the Third World. It was the Third World that now should be cultivated and, with Soviet economic and military help, eventually weaned away from the imperialist West. Here the Arab Middle East, with its own recent experience of imperialist subjugation, appeared a logical target. Although several Arab nations were ruled by fundamentalist clans that remained endemically suspicious of godless Russia, it was not a profile that characterized them all. Since 1954 it assuredly had not characterized Nasser's Egypt.

For Nasser, by 1955, the search for a patron was dramatically accelerated by the Israeli raid on Gaza. In April of that year, the Egyptian president traveled to Bandung, Indonesia, to attend a conference of "nonaligned" nations. There he sought Chinese Prime Minister Chou En-lai's intercession in acquiring weaponry from the Soviet Union. Several weeks later, Chou sent word to Nasser that Khrushchev was prepared to help. As in their earlier support of Israel, the Soviets preferred to arrange their help through Czechoslovakia. Thus, in August, discussions were transferred to Prague, and by September were consummated in an agreement. It was a shocker. As Western intelligence agencies evaluated the deal's key features, the Soviets and Czechs would provide Egypt with 170 medium tanks, 60 heavy tanks, 200 armored personnel carriers, 300 antitank guns, 140 light and heavy howitzers, 60 field artillery pieces, 134 light and heavy antiaircraft guns, 4 radar installations, 2 destroyers, 4 minesweepers, 12 torpedo boats, and 6 submarines. More intimidating yet was the equipment Moscow and Prague would supply Egypt's air force. It would include 100 MiG-15 fighters, 48 Ilyushin-28 bombers, and 20 Ilyushin-14 transport planes.

Together with vast quantities of support vehicles, small arms, ammunition, and spare parts, the total value of this Soviet-bloc equipment was calculated at $200 million. In February 1956 the infusion would be augmented by a squadron of even more advanced MiG-17 fighters, worth another $160 million. No money would actually change hands, however. Egypt would cover the purchase through barter, by providing virtually unlimited shipments of cotton and rice to the Soviet bloc, to be delivered in installments over twelve years. In return Egypt gained access to a cornucopia of military hardware far surpassing the experience of any Arab nation.

The Israelis were stunned. Before then the quantity of weapons in the hands of their Arab enemies had not exceeded a 3-to-1 ratio. Now the ratio would soar to 9 to 1. The imbalance was qualitative as well as quantitative. By General Moshe Dayan's calculations, the MiG-17 fighters and Ilyushin-28 bombers were "two stages ahead" of Israel's obsolescent force of 50 British Meteors and French Ouragans, while the Soviet T-41 and Stalin-III tanks were "infinitely better" than Israel's aged Shermans. Once again the Jewish republic was confronted with a threat to its survival, and this time from a source that had not earlier evoked Israel's principal concern. Until 1955, after all, Britain had functioned as the Arabs' perennial benefactor. It was the British, and the Americans, who had begun to arm Iraq under the Baghdad Pact.

By contrast, the Communist bloc had godfathered Israel's birth and supported the Jewish state in its initial battle for independence. If the East European governments by the mid-1950s had withdrawn their diplomatic patronage, they had chosen nevertheless to direct their animus first and foremost against their own Jewish citizens. But now, it appeared, the Soviet leadership had entered into a new appraisal of their Middle East strategy. At the very moment that they mitigated their own domestic terror campaign against East European Jewry, Khrushchev and his colleagues had decided to equip the largest and most powerful of the Arab "confrontation states" for a definitive military onslaught against Israeli Jewry. The worst of Ben-Gurion's nightmares evidently was approaching realization. Bereft of allies in the East or West, his country now found itself entrapped between the competing juggernauts of the Cold War.

IV

A MARRIAGE OF WESTERN CONVENIENCE

THE FOUNDATIONS OF SENTIMENT

French bitterness in the early postwar period was directed not alone at the recent Nazi enemy but in some degree even at Great Britain. Between 1943 and 1946 London had given diplomatic support to the Arab nationalist movements that had undermined France's ruling presence in Syria and Lebanon. Foreign Secretary Bevin's Palestine policy exacerbated this French resentment. With General Bernard Montgomery's army in occupation of France's Mediterranean ports, British intelligence agents operated freely, even arrogantly, to impede the clandestine Jewish refugee traffic flowing through the Riviera.

Compassion, and displaced guilt for France's wartime treatment of the Jews, may also have played a role in Paris's approach to the refugee issue. Wherever possible, French officials allowed the Jewish Agency to operate without interference on their territory, to provide shelter and care for Jewish displaced persons, to purchase, repair, and equip the vessels that would carry the survivors to Palestine. The disjointed nature of postwar French governance offered leeway for this pragmatic Franco-Jewish collaboration. Entire ministries operated virtually as autonomous fiefdoms. Thus, the prefect of Bouches-du-Rhône, the police commissariat of the Midi, and port officials along the Côte d'Azur allowed refugees to pass through without hindrance. In the summer of 1947, French public opinion and official policy converged as the refugee vessel *Exodus*, intercepted by British destroyers en route to Palestine, was escorted back to Marseilles. When Bevin threatened to transship its 4,500 passengers back farther yet, to the displaced persons camps in Germany, Prime Minister Paul Ramadier immediately offered them asylum on French soil.

Government policy toward an independent Jewish state was more ambivalent. France's tradition of cultural homogeneity did not accommodate easily to the concept of the Jews as a national entity. Nor were the foreign ministry's professional diplomats interested in antagonizing the Moslem populations of France's North African empire, or in undermining a wide network of French Catholic institutions in the Levant. When the United Nations debate on Palestine reached its climax, therefore, in November 1947, France's attitude toward partition remained uncertain. But here too anti-British resentments played their role, as did compassion. So did a transatlantic telephone call from Chaim Weizmann, the Zionist elder statesman then in New York, to Léon Blum, French socialism's elder statesman. Blum's influence still mattered, even within Prime Minister Robert Schuman's non-Socialist government. Only two hours before the final General Assembly vote on November 29, the French UN delegate received instructions to support partition.

Yet there was no equivocation whatever on the issue of arms sales to the Jews. Only weeks after the partition vote, French surplus weaponry was made available to the Haganah's purchasing agents. Soon the arms traffic picked up momentum under the benign approval of Minister of the Interior Jules Moch. At the key dispatch site in Ajaccio, Corsica, Moch's personal staff dispensed with bureaucratic formalities. No questions were asked as Zionist transport planes loaded up with French equipment. Nor were supplies withheld even from elements beyond control of the emergent Israeli government. One of these elements was Etzel, the paramilitary arm of Menachem Begin's right-wing Revisionist movement. Foreign Minister Georges Bidault personally authorized the sale to this group of 5 tanks, 150 antitank guns, 300 machine guns, 5,000 rifles, and millions of rounds of ammunition. In June 1948 the equipment was loaded onto an Etzel LST vessel, the *Altalena*, at Port-de-Bouc. It was accompanied by human "cargo," some nine hundred young North African and French Jewish volunteers. In this instance the supply effort was at least partially aborted. The *Altalena*'s subsequent arrival in Israel provoked a bitter jurisdictional clash with regular Israeli army units. Although a majority of the volunteers survived, nearly all the weaponry was lost. In later years, France would replace this equipment—and more.

THE QUEST FOR ARMS

The war of independence left the Jewish state with a skeletal air force, a potpourri of Messerschmitts, Spitfires, and a few converted American civilian transports. Through persistence and hard bargaining,

Israel's defense ministry was able to purchase thirty additional obsolescent Spitfires and Mosquitoes from the Italian air force, and some fifty surplus Mustangs and Harvard trainers from the United States. But under the constraints of the 1950 Tripartite Declaration, Britain and the United States monitored and carefully limited sales of modern jet aircraft. France was obliged to share in this supervisory task.

As early as 1953, however, Shimon Peres, the youthful director general of Israel's defense ministry, had come to envision France as a likely future source of military equipment. France had not been invited to join the emergent Baghdad Pact, he noted, for its ongoing involvement in Indo-China's colonial wars evidently had made it an unacceptable partner. Conceivably, then, the nation's resentment might leave it susceptible to a "private" deal with Israel. Peres knew that France's North African responsibilities, even its commitment to protect Lebanon's Christian minorities, had not precluded its earlier weapons sales to Israel. Although much of Israel's military training was based on its pre-independence experience in the British armed forces, the potential availability of French equipment was worth a reorientation effort. Prime Minister Ben-Gurion agreed. He gave Peres free rein to explore the arms market in France.

By 1953, moreover, Peres and the chief of his arms-purchasing mission in Paris, Colonel Yosef Nachmias, had grasped the opportunity for discreet transactions within the concentric circles of France's governmental bureaucracies and armed services. Amid the confusion of postwar decentralization, it was the technocrats and professional officers who often determined the fate of overseas military contracts. Many of these functionaries tended also to view civilian politicians as the root cause of France's humiliating withdrawal from Syria and Lebanon, and of its equally painful exclusion from the Baghdad Pact negotiations. Typical of the hard-liners was Abel Thomas, director general of the ministry of the interior, and later of the ministry of defense. Thomas and his personal staffs in both ministries were anti-British and anti-Arab. By contrast, they had nothing but admiration for the Israeli army, which had defeated both the British and the Arabs. Indeed, Thomas was convinced that Israel's victory in its 1948–49 war of independence had delayed nationalist Moslem uprisings in French North Africa by at least ten years.

Cultivated by Peres and Nachmias, Thomas put the Israelis in touch with procurement officers in the ministry of defense, and with key executives of France's major armament firms. These latter, in turn, were particularly eager to promote overseas sales at a time when the United States and Britain still enjoyed a virtual monopoly of weapons contracts for the North Atlantic Treaty Organization. Substantial orders of French equipment for Israel might even help jump-start and rationalize the nation's military production. Thus, by 1953, France's defense ministry was effectively bypassing the foreign ministry in approving Israel's initial purchase orders. Contracts were signed for light tanks, artillery pieces, and twenty-five Ouragan jet fighters. The Ouragans in fact represented Israel's first major government-to-government acquisition since its war of independence.

Within the ensuing year and a half, relations between the two nations warmed even further. As Shimon Peres had anticipated, the development came in tandem with France's humiliating exclusion from the impending Baghdad Pact. Moreover, in November 1954, at the very moment when Paris was negotiating the independence of its former protectorates Tunisia and Morocco, a nationalist revolt erupted in Algeria, a region historically defined as an extension of metropolitan France itself. The role of Egypt's President Nasser in support of this uprising soon became evident. Algerian rebel headquarters actually were established in the Egyptian capital. Radio Cairo transmitted Algerian nationalist broadcasts. From 1954 onward, as Britain's evacuation from Suez gained momentum, the Egyptian government began dispatching weaponry to the Algerian insurrectionists.

By then, a congruence of French and Israeli interests had developed. Its principal objective was to block Gamal Abd al-Nasser's campaign to advance Egyptian imperialistic designs under the banner of pan-Arabism. Even traditionalists in the French foreign ministry now muted their earlier reservations on Israel's armaments requests, while the army opened its war college to Israeli officers. At the suggestion of Pierre Gilbert, France's recently appointed ambassador to Israel, Shimon Peres moved even more vigorously to cultivate his relationships with French defense ministry officials. Thus, when the Radical Socialist (and Jew) Pierre Mendès-France assumed the premiership early in 1954, Peres sensed that the moment was opportune to reach an understanding at the highest government level. His instincts were right. Agreement was quickly reached for the two nations' military intelligence branches to share information on Egypt. The weapons provided to Israel similarly were upgraded, and included important quantities of new tanks and artillery.

In January 1955 Mendès-France was replaced as premier by another Radical Socialist, Foreign Minister Edgar Faure. Receiving Israel's Ambassador Ya'akov Tsur in May of that year, Faure reminded his visitor that he, Faure, was descended from an old Protestant family, and had been raised on the folklore of Huguenot persecution. He would not allow a little people like Israel to be placed at unreasonable risk. "Tell Sharett and Ben-Gurion that I shall always do my best to help you. You may count on me." It was significant that Faure retained key figures from his predecessor's government. One of these, General Pierre Koenig, the defense minister, required no directives from the premier. A renowned war hero, Koenig had led Free French troops in the North African campaign against Rommel, and under his command a unit of Palestinian Jews had fought with memorable gallantry at the Battle of Bir Hachim. To Peres now, Koenig gave assurance of his willingness to develop a closer relationship with Israel. More than wartime nostalgia animated the general's friendship, of course. "For us," he acknowledged later, "it was clear . . . that we had to do everything possible to weaken Egyptian military power."

Koenig and his close associate, Minister of Aviation Diomède Catroux, encouraged discussions between Peres, Colonel Nachmias, and the French aviation industry. The Israelis were keenly interested in a new fighter, the Mystère IV. Under manufacture by the Dassault Aviation Company, it was a plane they regarded as superior to anything yet available to the Egyptian air force. Would they be allowed to order it? In principle, the Faure government was willing to authorize a limited sale to Israel of twelve Mystères, with the promise of an additional twelve later. But even for this token number, complications soon developed. Foreign Minister Antoine Pinay, although personally sympathetic to Israel, feared difficulties with France's NATO partners. The Mystère IV was assigned to NATO use, and development of the plane had largely been underwritten by NATO's most important member, the United States. Speaking for the Eisenhower administration, Secretary of State John Foster Dulles had warned of the dangers of a new Middle Eastern arms race. He preferred that the limitations of the 1950 Tripartite Declaration remain in force.

Washington based its opposition to the Mystère transaction on the need for a "military balance." Yet by September 1955 the massive Soviet-Egyptian arms deal had taken place. Israel's most powerful enemy now was acquiring sophisticated weaponry, including modern jet fighters and bombers. Indeed, twelve or even twenty-four Mystères would hardly restore the "military balance"; Israel required dozens to mount a credible deterrent. In October 1955, therefore, Moshe Sharett—then serving as prime minister—risked his diplomatic bona fides by arriving uninvited in Geneva, where a Four-Power conference was taking place on Vietnam. At the Palais des Nations, Sharett buttonholed Secretary of State Dulles and Britain's Foreign Secretary Harold Macmillan, to seek their understanding of

Israel's military procurement needs. Neither man was forthcoming. Unknown to Sharett, Dulles's and Macmillan's staffs recently had drawn up a confidential statement of joint policy. "We must avoid being pushed by the Russians into a position of opposition to Arab interests . . . ," it declared. "It must be our purpose not to allow a substantial increase in the striking power of Israel's armed forces."

BEN-GURION SEEKS A FRIEND

Six months earlier, in February 1955, following a two-year absence, David Ben-Gurion had returned from his desert retreat to assume the portfolio of defense minister. The "old man" by then no longer was prepared to tolerate acts of Egyptian belligerence, whether the mounting cycle of Egyptian-directed guerrilla raids, the closure of Suez to Israel-bound shipping, or, most recently, the ominous blockade of Israel-bound vessels through the Gulf of Aqaba. It was this latter development that was particularly galling to Ben-Gurion. Since 1953, the Egyptian coast guard unit at Ras Nasrani, at the southern tip of the Sinai Peninsula, had closed off Israeli maritime passage through the Strait of Tiran, and in September 1955, began turning back the vessels of other nations bound for Israel's Negev port of Eilat.

In November 1955, his patience exhausted, Ben-Gurion—who that month also had resumed the office of prime minister—raised the issue of a preemptive campaign against the Egyptians. Moshe Sharett, who remained as foreign minister, and a majority of his cabinet colleagues, rejected the proposal. Israel could not yet risk international condemnation as an "aggressor," they argued. It was not a danger that impressed Ben-Gurion or Chief of Staff Moshe Dayan. As they saw it, the infusion of Soviet weaponry into Egypt was drastically shifting the Middle Eastern balance of power. Sooner rather than later, they warned, Israel would have to strike.

It was to anticipate that inevitable confrontation that Shimon Peres intensified his search for modern weapons. The quest did not go unrequited. By autumn of 1955, the French defense ministry had become even more warmly cooperative, providing Israel with significant new quantities of guns, tanks, and ammunition. Yet Prime Minister Faure's promise of twenty-four Mystères continued to remain ensnarled in bureaucratic and diplomatic uncertainty. Indeed, the Faure government itself fell on November 28, and elections took place in January 1956. In February a new coalition cabinet was assembled under the premiership of Guy Mollet. Although Mollet himself was a veteran Socialist, his government presented an initial uncertainty to the Israelis. One of the premier's first appointments was Robert Lacoste as minister-resident of Algeria. Lacoste was known to favor an accommodation with Algeria's Moslem population. Mollet's choice as foreign minister, Christian Pineau, reportedly was intent on achieving improved relations with the Arab world at large.

Israel's Ambassador Tsur was not discountenanced. Pineau, he knew, had been active in the wartime resistance, and had spent eighteen months as a prisoner in Buchenwald. His empathy for the Jews could never be doubted. Neither could the friendship of another key Mollet appointment. This was Maurice Bourgès-Maunoury, who became minister of defense. Earlier, as interior minister under Mendès-France and Faure, Bourgès-Maunoury had interceded ardently with government colleagues in Israel's behalf. His deputy, Abel Thomas, had been the single most important link between Israel's military liaison office and the French armaments industry; and Thomas now accompanied Bourgès-Maunoury to the defense ministry, serving again as chef de bureau. Soon, then, Tsur's hopes for the new government were vindicated. In March 1956 President Eisenhower and Britain's Prime Minister Eden met in Washington to develop a strategy for achieving a wider Arab acceptance of the emergent Baghdad Pact. For Eden a key inducement in this endeavor, one he had floated earlier in his 1955 Guildhall speech (p. 26), was a renegotiation of Israel's frontiers. The French had not been invited to the conference, but their views on the Middle Eastern territorial issue were solicited. Where would they stand?

By chance the proposal was relayed to Paris at the very moment that Israeli intelligence was supplying France with credible new evidence of Nasser's accelerated arms shipments to the Algerian rebels. Foreign Minister Pineau's response to Washington accordingly was instantaneous, and its indignation undisguised. France would approve no Middle Eastern security arrangements negotiated at Israel's expense, it declared; Middle Eastern stability required assurance of a balance of power between Israelis and Arabs. In Jerusalem, news of the French stance was received with a rush of gratitude. It was enhanced when Abel Thomas informed Israel's military attaché, Colonel Nishri, that the earlier, promised delivery of twelve Mystères now would be fulfilled. It was. On April 11, 1956, piloted by Israeli crews, the jets departed their French military base. Awaiting them at a Negev airfield were France's Ambassador Gilbert, together with Israel's senior military and defense officials, and Ben-Gurion himself. In his excitement, the prime minister insisted on drinking tea with the young pilots.

The Mystères arrived at a moment when the Mollet government had resolved its final, lingering equivocation on France's relationship with Israel. The next day, April 12, Peres met with Abel Thomas in Paris to state his nation's military intentions straightforwardly: "War [with the Arabs] is inevitable during the forthcoming six months," he explained. ". . . Briefly, we have decided not to run the mortal risk of a defensive war. . . . We are practically resigned to launching a preventive offensive." That same day Ambassador Tsur confirmed Peres's sense of urgency by delivering a personal message to Mollet from Ben-Gurion. Stressing the threat that Nasser's vast rearmaments program represented to Israel's very existence, the prime minister sought a major commitment from France: "At this dangerous time," he wrote, "the small and young Republic of Israel appeals to the older and great French Republic with the certainty of mutual understanding." These appeals evoked resonance at all levels of the French government, even at the foreign ministry, where Christian Pineau now fully endorsed a pragmatic alliance with Israel. The doors of French military warehouses from then on would be opened wide to the Jewish state.

Ironically, it was Moshe Sharett who entertained reservations about the developing alliance. In earlier months the foreign minister had opposed Moshe Dayan's harsh retaliatory forays against guerrilla bases in Egypt, Jordan, and Syria. And now, in the spring of 1956, he feared that a preemptive military offensive in the Sinai would result in Israel's diplomatic isolation. The notion of acting in concert with Western, colonialist powers was especially repugnant to the foreign minister; such an alliance would gratuitously antagonize Israel's potential friends in Africa and Asia. During increasingly tense discussions, Ben-Gurion failed to dissipate Sharett's misgivings. With much sadness, therefore, the prime minister on June 18 replaced his old friend with Mrs. Golda Meir, Israel's former minister of labor, who entirely shared Ben-Gurion's willingness to meet force with force.

Three days later, on June 21, 1956, a military transport plane lifted off from an Israeli air force base in the northern Negev. Its passengers included Chief of Staff Dayan and General Yehoshafat Harkabi, director of Israel's military intelligence. The following afternoon, in a Paris suburb, the group conferred secretly with General Pierre Boursicot, Harkabi's counterpart as director of French military intelligence, and with General Maurice Challe, France's deputy chief of staff. By the time discussions ended, a day and a half later, agreement had been reached on the farthest-reaching arms transaction in Israel's history. France would provide Israel with an additional seventy-two

Mystères. In ensuing months the planes would be flown over in three flights of twenty-four each. Additionally, three French LST vessels would land on Israel's shores, again in three cycles, bringing 160 tanks of various sizes, 118 heavy artillery pieces, and vast quantities of ammunition and spare parts.

The unprecedented supply operation would require detailed cooperation between French and Israeli defense personnel at all levels. Dubbed "Operation Jonah" by the Israelis and "Operation Fog" by the French, the deliveries later would be described jokingly by Prime Minister Mollet as the secret "French invasion" of Israel. Yet Ben-Gurion and his closest associates welcomed the "invasion" in a mood not of bemusement but of euphoria. On July 24, 1956, in the dead of night, as the initial French LST unloaded its cargo of thirty tanks and sixty tons of munitions on a beach south of Haifa, the prime minister and Shimon Peres were there to greet it. Tight press censorship was in effect, and the troops who shared in the unloading were sworn to secrecy. Even so, Ben-Gurion could not resist bringing a trusted friend to witness and commemorate the delivery. It was a renowned poet, Natan Alterman.

The prime minister had a purpose in mind. The Israeli people were tense with apprehension as the Egyptians absorbed their wealth of Soviet and Czech weaponry. On June 19, in a public speech, Nasser had exhorted his armed forces: "We must be strong in order to regain the rights of the Palestinians by force." Marshal Abd al-Hakim Amer, the Egyptian army commander, had informed his troops on July 5: "The hour is approaching when [we] . . . will stand in the front ranks of the battle against imperialism and its Zionist ally." In these summer months Israeli citizens were taxing themselves to the limit in an effort to strengthen the nation's defenses. Israeli women were contributing their family jewelry to a special army fund. Civilian volunteers were digging antitank ditches along Israel's southern frontier.

But now at last Israel had secured a powerful ally. On July 4 Foreign Minister Pineau informed Ambassador Tsur that all former limitations on weapons delivery to Israel were canceled, regardless of American or British policy. France would reserve its liberty of action in supplying its "true friends." Indeed, the French people by then shared that commitment. In their hatred of Nasser and resentment of Washington's "even-handed" Middle Eastern policy, newspaper editorials and public figures alike increasingly lauded "brave little Israel." Amid this effusion of French goodwill, Ben-Gurion now felt it important for Israel's citizenry to be allowed at least an oblique intimation that they were no longer alone. And thus, in mid-October, the poet Natan Alterman's veiled allusion to a new hope was read out in the Knesset and printed in *Divrei HaKnesset,* the official transcript:

> *Perhaps this is a night of dreams, but wide awake, and*
> *What it saw was the melting away of the terror gap*
> *Between ourselves and the forces of destruction. Iron comes*
> *On steadily and the bowels of the earth tremble.*

FROM FRIENDSHIP TO ALLIANCE

Months earlier, on February 28, 1956, British Foreign Secretary Selwyn Lloyd arrived in Cairo, still hoping to dissuade Nasser from his campaign of subversion against the Baghdad Pact. Lloyd was rebuffed. On March 14, French Foreign Minister Pineau also visited Cairo in a bid to forestall Egyptian support of the Algerian rebellion. This effort foundered as well. By summer the West's exasperation with Nasser's obstructionism, his progressively intimate relationship with the Soviet bloc, boiled over at last. On July 19 Washington and London formally retracted earlier offers to help underwrite the Egyptian president's favored domestic project, construction of a high dam at Aswan, on the Nile River.

But Nasser had cards of his own up his sleeve. The previous month, the last contingents of British troops had evacuated Egypt (pp. 23, 25). On July 25, therefore, the Egyptian president dropped a bombshell. Inviting the Americans to "go choke on your fury," he announced his intention to nationalize the Suez Canal Company, and to apply its future revenues to construction of the Aswan Dam. That night delirium reigned throughout Egypt. In his own country Nasser was hailed as a national hero; in the Arab world at large, as the hero of anticolonialism. London and Paris were stunned. The British government owned the largest block of stock in the Suez Canal Company, and private French investors owned much of the rest. Nearly a quarter of British imports passed through the canal. These were now at risk. At stake, too, was Britain's prestige in the Middle East altogether. Prime Minister Eden needed little reminder of the fruits of appeasement. Neither did Guy Mollet, whose anti-Munich reflex was as strong as Eden's, and who characterized Nasser as the "Hitler of the Nile."

Frantic to avoid hostilities, and a possibly irretrievable alienation from the West of the Afro-Asian bloc, Secretary of State Dulles promptly rushed off to London to organize a conference of maritime nations. But in ensuing weeks Nasser rejected all compromise formulas. Accordingly, on August 5, a joint team of British and French staff officers established a combined headquarters in Cyprus and set to work preparing a strategy for invading Egypt and seizing control of the Suez Canal. The impending operation, dubbed "Musketeer," envisaged a combined naval armada of 130 British and French warships and hundreds of landing craft. Air units would comprise three British bombing squadrons and four French fighter squadrons. The actual invasion force would encompass some fifty thousand British and thirty thousand French troops. The invasion scenario anticipated a heavy air bombardment, to be followed by the descent of several thousand paratroops for initial landings. The bulk of the expeditionary force would reach Egypt afterward by sea, establish a beachhead on the Egyptian coast, then drive ahead toward Alexandria and Cairo.

It was not simply Operation Musketeer's engorged dimensions (which prefigured those of Operation Desert Storm decades later) that forced the Allies to postpone their offensive. Washington's horrified opposition also played a role. At President Eisenhower's insistence, the Allies were obliged to give Secretary of State Dulles time to explore nonmilitary alternatives. Nevertheless, weeks of additional negotiation proved fruitless. By late September 1956, Eden and Mollet concluded that all peaceful recourse was exhausted. D-day was set initially for October 8. Yet the hiatus at least had given the Allies time to rethink their invasion strategy, and eventually to abandon their plan for driving on Alexandria and Cairo. Instead, the objective would be shifted exclusively to the Suez Canal area. Greater reliance, too, would be placed on air bombardment before the paratroop and amphibious landings. It was this alteration, in turn, that now provided the opening for collaboration with Israel.

The possibility of Israeli involvement had been raised as early as July 27, 1956, only two days after Nasser announced nationalization of the canal. Shimon Peres was then in France on yet another arms-purchasing mission. That day Bourgès-Maunoury invited Peres to his office. Straight out, the defense minister asked: How much time would the Israeli army require to fight its way across the Sinai toward the Suez Canal? Although surprised, Peres needed only a few moments to react. The accepted estimate in Israel was approximately a week, he answered. Bourgès-Maunoury then asked if Israel intended to strike along its southern border, and if so, where? Peres replied only that "our Suez is Eilat. We would never agree to it being closed off." Thereupon Bourgès-Maunoury put the most crucial question: Would the Israeli government "in principle" be willing to share in an Anglo-French military operation against Egypt? "In principle," Peres thought that it would.

Upon returning to Jerusalem, Peres apprised Ben-Gurion and Dayan of the fascinating overture. Neither man, however, showed enthusiasm for an offensive directed toward Suez. Their single objective was liberation of the Gulf of Aqaba and the Strait of Tiran. Indeed, to that limited end, Dayan and his staff had been at work for months, developing plans for an initial straight-line offensive into the Sinai, then shifting southward to invest the peninsula's eastern sector, and ultimately Sharm es-Sheikh on the Tiran coast. The canal was irrelevant to their plans.

By September, nevertheless, as the British and French redirected their own strategy to a more limited move against Suez, the queries from Paris became more insistent. In turn Ben-Gurion cautiously authorized Peres to explore in greater detail the notion of collaboration. Yet the prime minister and Dayan emphasized that Israel would insist on fulfilling its priority objective, the capture of Sharm es-Sheikh. On that understanding Peres flew back to Paris on September 18, meeting again with Bourgès-Maunoury. The French defense minister was not fazed by Israel's conditions. France wished to launch a war against Egypt "before the winter, before the resignation of the present Cabinet," he explained. Moreover, riots in Poland lately had drawn the Kremlin's attention away from the Middle East toward Eastern Europe, and America's attention was largely focused on its presidential elections. Would Ben-Gurion be interested in sharing in an early offensive? That same day, on telephoning Jerusalem, Peres was able to give a qualified yes.

Arrangements were made for more extensive discussions in Paris. This time Peres would be joined by Golda Meir, Moshe Dayan, and Moshe Carmel—the latter a trusted confidant of the prime minister. Before the group's departure, however, on September 27, Ben-Gurion outlined his own conditions. These were daunting. Israel would not initiate action against Egypt on its own. It would not participate in a joint venture unless Britain agreed to refrain from intervening at the side of Jordan or Iraq, in the event Israel were obliged to take defensive action along its eastern, Hashemite border. Washington would have to be given prior notice of the impending action against Egypt. And, finally, Israel required assurance that it would exercise ultimate control of the shoreline along the Strait of Tiran. With this understanding, Peres, Dayan, Carmel, and Mrs. Meir departed for Paris on a converted French bomber that Bourgès-Maunoury had placed at their disposal.

In the French capital the next day, September 28, meeting at the private apartment of Colonel Louis Mangin, the Israelis entered into discussions with Bourgès-Maunoury, Pineau, and other senior civilian and military officials. Tentative and explorative, the talks were based on the likelihood that Britain, continually dithering over the terms of an offensive, might actually pull out in the end. Would Israel then join France in moving against Egypt on their own? The Israelis' response was affirmative, on condition that Britain did not support Jordanian and Iraqi provocations along Israel's eastern frontier. Pineau in turn was confident that he could win London's understanding on this point. The Israelis asked him then: Would the United States make difficulties? The French foreign minister thought not, but still preferred to avoid alerting Washington in advance.

For the Israelis, another key issue was the quantity of additional equipment France was prepared to supply, and the aerial protection it would offer Israel's cities. Here Peres submitted an enlarged shopping list that included hundreds of additional tanks, half-tracks, front-wheel-drive transports, and vastly augmented quantities of ammunition and fuel. Bourgès-Maunoury agreed on the spot. French aerial protection also would be provided. On October 1, as the Israelis departed for home, they were accompanied by General Maurice Challe, the French deputy chief of staff, and a staff of aides from all branches of the French armed services. The latter would examine Israel's military circumstances and organize a French liaison structure in Israel.

It will be recalled that Ben-Gurion's commitment to the emerging alliance was paralleled by acute disquiet at Britain's threatening response to Israel's counterattacks across the Hashemite border (pp. 27, 28). The tension reached its climax on October 10, when Israel responded to a series of Jordan-based guerrilla assaults with a heavy counterattack of its own against the Hashemite police fortress at Qalqilya. Both sides took heavy losses, and it was then that London made plans to dispatch units of the Iraqi army into Jordan. An adverse Israeli response, warned the British, would invoke the 1936 Anglo-Transjordanian Treaty. Indeed, under the guidelines of "Operation Cordage," RAF units in Cyprus were alerted for possible bombing raids on Israeli military bases (pp. 29–30). It was only at the last moment, on October 12, that an urgent phone call from Prime Minister Mollet in Paris apprised Eden of the ongoing Franco-Israeli negotiations, and of Israel's possible role in an Allied offensive against Egypt. Thereupon Eden notified Whitehall that he wanted Anglo-Israeli tensions eased. When Foreign Undersecretary Anthony Nutting telephoned Eden to press the case for moving Iraqi troops into Jordan, the prime minister shouted: "I will not allow you to plunge this country into war merely to satisfy the anti-Jewish spleen of you people in the Foreign Office!"

On October 14 General Challe arrived from Paris to confer with Eden at the prime-ministerial retreat at Chequers. The French deputy chief of staff presented a straightforward proposal: The Israelis should be encouraged to attack Egypt; Britain and France should then order the Israelis and Egyptians to draw their forces back from the canal. To ensure compliance the Allies soon afterward would dispatch a "police force to separate the combatants" and occupy the complete length of the canal. The scheme's novelty impressed Eden. So did the need for secrecy. The prime minister shared the proposal at first with only a single confidant at the foreign ministry, Sir Ivone Kirkpatrick, his Middle East adviser, who liked it. In Paris an equivalent secrecy was maintained. All planning centered on Bourgès-Maunoury, Abel Thomas, General Challe, and Colonel Mangin. Except for Pineau himself, even the foreign ministry was kept out of the loop.

The Israelis, too, were out of the loop. They were aware of course that their envisaged offensive toward Sharm es-Sheikh would serve French purposes at Suez. But General Challe, studying the little nation's military capabilities during his early October visit, concluded that Dayan's army was sufficiently tough and well led to confront the Egyptians for a short while as far west as the canal. Ironically, the notion of a thrust westward also formed part of Dayan's strategy. The Israeli commander anticipated dropping one or two paratroop platoons deep in the Sinai for the limited purpose of harassing Egyptian supply lines and sowing confusion. Yet the scheme was marginal to his larger strategy of driving south toward Sharm es-Sheikh. By contrast, Challe envisaged an Israeli drive toward Suez as the pretext for Allied intervention. An ultimatum would be given to both the Egyptians and the Israelis to "withdraw" from the vicinity of the canal. Israel would accept; Egypt manifestly would not, and the Allies thereupon could launch their offensive against Egypt. It was this strategy that Challe later brought back to Bourgès-Maunoury and Mollet— and then on October 14 to Eden at Chequers.

Two days later, Colonel Nishri, Israel's military attaché, was summoned to Bourgès-Maunoury's office and given the essential outlines of the French scenario, and the likelihood of British cooperation. Ben-Gurion was informed at once. The prime minister reacted angrily. The notion of serving as agent provocateur for the Allies was altogether distasteful to him. Worse yet, it depended upon British cooperation. And the prospect of Britain, whose government only days before had threatened to come to Jordan's aid against Israel, now suddenly agreeing to bomb Egypt's Suez bases, struck the prime minister as an entirely unacceptable risk. Informed then of Ben-Gurion's reaction, Mollet urgently appealed to Eden to accommodate his strategy more closely to France's earlier understanding of a full alliance with Israel. On the same night of October 16, Eden and Foreign Minister Selwyn Lloyd flew to Paris and conferred with Mollet and Pineau.

It was in Paris, at last, that Eden agreed to the essence of the new formula, and agreed also to transmit a personal message of reassurance to Ben-Gurion in Israel. Issued by the prime minister in London, the message was a cautious two-paragraph document. "In the event of any threat of hostilities in the neighbourhood of the Canal," it acknowledged, "the French and British Governments would call the belligerents to halt and to withdraw from the immediate vicinity of the Canal." If one or both refused, Allied forces would intervene to "ensure the free passage of the Canal." Eden then obliquely confirmed that, should Egyptian-Israeli hostilities break out, Britain would not come to the assistance of Egypt. Yet the assurance was coupled with a veiled warning that "[d]ifferent considerations would of course apply [to] Jordan, with whom [the British] have, in addition to their obligation under the Tripartite Declaration, a firm treaty."

Eden's commitment struck Ben-Gurion as anemic, and its reminder of Britain's obligations to Jordan did nothing to dissipate the Israeli prime minister's suspicions. Ben-Gurion could not know it, of course, but Eden was using the possibility of an Israeli attack on Jordan mainly for internal political reasons, to justify "collusion" with the Israelis and French. Indeed, he tipped his hand at an inner cabinet meeting of October 18. There were signs, he noted, that the Israelis "might be preparing to make some military move . . . against Jordan." This would put Britain on the spot. If then the Israelis were going to attack someone, "far better if they attacked Egypt."

Ben-Gurion meanwhile continued to distrust Eden. His experience of British Middle Eastern policy altogether continued to rankle. On October 16 Dayan noted in his diary: "[Ben-Gurion] is . . . suspicious of Britain. He feels that Britain may wish to demonstrate her friendship for the Arabs by employing her forces against us in going to the help of Jordan." And Peres observed in his own diary entry of the same day: "Another problem . . . [is] the deep distrust which Ben-Gurion harbor[s] towards the British Government—and to Eden in particular." It required all of Mollet's diplomacy to dissuade the Israeli leader from breaking off negotiations, and at least to explore the possibilities for joint action. Conferring with their prime minister on October 17, Peres and Dayan added their own appeals to Mollet's. The opportunity for alliance with major Western powers should not be lightly forfeited, they argued. Thereupon Ben-Gurion decided that a personal meeting with the Allied leadership was critical. To Mollet he sent word of his desire to fly to Paris for the purpose of discussing fundamental alterations in the Allied scheme. The French premier's formal invitation arrived within hours.

THE TREATY OF SÈVRES

On October 21 Ben-Gurion, Peres, Dayan, and an entourage of civilian and military officials flew off secretly to Paris, accompanied by General Challe and Colonel Mangin. Landing at the French air force base of Villacoublay, the Israelis were sped off immediately to a secluded villa placed at their disposal in the Paris suburb of Sèvres. The next day, following a sumptuous luncheon in their honor, the Israelis were joined by Mollet, Pineau, and Bourgès-Maunoury. Ben-Gurion was invited to begin the discussions. After a brief tour d'horizon of the Middle East, the prime minister turned to the issue at hand.

The notion of Israeli military action simply as a pretext for Anglo-French intervention was unacceptable, Ben-Gurion emphasized, particularly since Britain was unwilling to recognize Israel as a full ally. Notwithstanding all the military protection France was prepared to offer, he had just learned from Colonel Nishri that Britain and France were suggesting a seventy-two-hour gap between Israel's attack and the Allied bombardment of Egyptian airfields. The interval was too long; it would expose Israeli troops to Egyptian air attack. The prime minister also feared the danger of Soviet "volunteers" pouring in. Neither did he look forward to a possible denunciation by Eisenhower. Repeatedly he adverted to a pet project: The operation should be launched at a later date, once American support was assured, and only after Britain had been persuaded to accept the Israeli plan for wresting open the Strait of Tiran.

Pineau then interjected the observation that, if Eden's help was to be forthcoming, it had to be now, and under the British prime minister's own terms. To reject the current plan meant scrapping the entire project for good. Bourgès-Maunoury then sweetened the offer, suggesting that the time gap before Allied bombardment could be reduced. France would use its veto on Israel's behalf in the UN Security Council. It was also Bourgès-Maunoury's view that the Soviets were likely to be absorbed by their own problems of national restiveness in Poland and Hungary, even as the United States would be preoccupied with its impending presidential election. France, too, could wait no longer, he warned. "The beginning of November is the last possible date."

Here it was that Moshe Dayan came up with his own "private" proposal. It was based on his initial strategy for a Sinai offensive. Israel would launch a deep foray into Egyptian territory; yet the operation would be limited rather than a full-scale offensive. That way, if the British changed their minds at the last moment about attacking Suez, Israel could retreat, describing its action as simply an extensive reprisal raid. The proposal in fact was intended more to allay Ben-Gurion's fears than to reconcile the French. It succeeded. The prime minister softened, although still insisting on "full partnership" with Britain and France. Mollet and the others were sympathetic. They promised the Israelis that the issue would be reviewed with "a senior British representative," who was due to arrive that very afternoon.

In fact, the visitor turned out to be Selwyn Lloyd, the British foreign secretary. Upon reaching Sèvres, Lloyd first closeted himself in another room with Pineau and Bourgès-Maunoury to be apprised of the Israeli position. The scheme displeased him. He had expected the Israelis to launch a "real act of war," one that would justify an Allied ultimatum and intervention, and at least spare Britain the obloquy of the Afro-Asian world, and possibly of its own Commonwealth. Moreover, the notion of accepting the Israelis as "full partners," rather than merely as provocateurs, was unacceptable.

For that matter, upon entering the salon, Lloyd barely concealed his distaste at meeting with the Israelis altogether. His manner was chill and patronizing. Mordechai Bar-On, secretary to the Israeli delegation, recalled that Lloyd gave the impression of "having a dirty smell under his nose." And Ben-Gurion, for his part, did not bother to disguise his own suspicions. In terse staccato sentences, the prime minister emphasized that Israel would not be seen as an aggressor against the canal or be served an ultimatum. Nor, upon entrance into the Sinai, would Israel accept a delay of longer than twelve hours until the onset of the Allied bombing runs against Egyptian airfields. Lloyd demurred, pointing out that Britain then would be condemned as an aggressor throughout the Arab world.

As the Frenchmen's faces fell, Dayan suddenly filled an awkward vacuum. On the back of a cigarette box he sketched out his plan for a "deep-penetration raid," but this time extending its range to the

Mitla Pass, only forty miles from the canal—and some twenty miles farther than his original scheme. In return for this concession, the Allies would refrain from branding Israel an aggressor, and issue an "appeal" rather than an "ultimatum" for Israeli withdrawal. The Allies also should agree to shorten the time period before their bombing attack on Egyptian bases, refrain from objecting as Israeli troops drove through the southern Sinai toward Sharm es-Sheikh, and from assisting Jordan or Iraq if either nation attacked Israel. Talks continued for another two hours. By late afternoon, a tentative consensus had emerged. Lloyd then departed for London to confer with Eden.

Meanwhile, pursuing their own—far less contentious—discussions, the Israelis and the French reached an understanding that same evening. Before Dayan launched his invasion of the Sinai, France would station two of its own air squadrons at Israeli bases to protect Israel's cities. It would send additional pilots to man those Israeli Mystères whose crews had not completed their training, and deploy three French naval vessels along Israel's coastline. Ben-Gurion reacted affirmatively to the proposal. The next day, October 23, Pineau flew to England, and the following morning, at Chequers, he pressed the full scenario on Eden and Selwyn Lloyd. For Eden, the priority was to achieve Nasser's downfall, and the Franco-Israeli formula appeared likely to achieve that objective. On the spot, then, and over Lloyd's lingering reservations, he accepted all of Israel's demands, and also agreed to a reduction of the bombing time gap to thirty-six hours. Thereupon Pineau returned to Paris. Accompanying him were Patrick Dean, Whitehall's Middle East intelligence director, and Dean's assistant, Daniel Logan. The three groups resumed discussions in the midafternoon of October 24, and swiftly refined the last details. Ben-Gurion insisted on formalizing the tripartite understanding in writing. The request was approved, and the protocol was duly typed up in six brief paragraphs and signed by Dean, Pineau, and Ben-Gurion. The Israeli prime minister felt strongly the need for a contractual, "nonaggressor" equivalence for his country with Britain and France. In the "Sèvres Treaty" he achieved it, and similarly distanced his government from Allied war aims at the Suez Canal.

Just before midnight of October 24, Ben-Gurion and the Israeli entourage boarded their awaiting aircraft at Villacomblay, and departed for home. En route the prime minister wrote in his diary: "If, on arriving home, we find the ratification of the British government, we will face great days in our history. But I am highly doubtful whether London's approval will be forthcoming." Ben-Gurion was aware that an agreement signed by second-ranking Whitehall officials could yet be disavowed by Eden. At any moment a clash between Israeli and Hashemite forces could torpedo all the negotiations of the last two and a half days. By then, however, he was underestimating Eden. Through Britain's ambassador in Tel Aviv, John Nicholls (who remained uninformed of the Sèvres agreement), the British prime minister sent a veiled message: "Eden is aware that Ben-Gurion suspects the English and does not believe that Eden is convinced of the need to eliminate Nasser. Eden therefore wants to reassure Ben-Gurion emphatically and most personally that there are no grounds for his suspicions."

The French meanwhile were fulfilling their part of the Sèvres commitment, in both letter and spirit. Two squadrons of Mystères and F-84 interceptors were flown to Israel, with maintenance crews arriving on transport planes. These squadrons were divided between an air base in northern Israel and Lod International Airport, where their tricolor markings were replaced by Israeli Stars of David. Command structures were established to integrate French and Israeli air force units. Three French destroyers also now took up their positions along Israel's coast. Together with personnel that had arrived in earlier weeks, France's air, military, and naval contingents in Israel reached three thousand men by the last week of October. To the mystification of the public, Israel State Radio began now to devote much of its broadcast time to French melodies. Barely forty-eight hours before the scheduled Israeli offensive, two hundred indispensable front-wheel drive trucks arrived by freighter.

From the moment Dayan returned from Sèvres, meanwhile, Israel began calling up its military reserves. To disguise the operation, its military intelligence branch leaked "disinformation" of an impending move of Iraqi forces into Jordan. Duly reported to Washington, this evoked Eisenhower's urgent, last-minute appeal to Ben-Gurion for restraint. Even Britain's military high command had not yet been alerted to the impending offensive against Egypt. Only on October 26 was British invasion headquarters in Cyprus informed that "Operation Cordage," the blueprint for RAF attacks on Israel, was to be scrapped in favor of "Operation Musketeer." It was then, too, that General Keightley, the Allied commander, learned of the impending Israeli connection (stunned, Keightley muttered disbelievingly to his adjutant: "They're bringing in the hook-nosed boys"). Neither was the intelligence shared with the Foreign Office or with Britain's diplomats abroad. In Israel, Britain's Ambassador Nicholls met with Foreign Minister Golda Meir on the morning of October 29, still requesting assurance that the Israeli army was not preparing to attack Jordan.

A WAR OF MILITARY COLLUSION

At 3:30 p.m. on October 29 a squadron of Israeli transport planes crossed the Negev-Sinai frontier. Upon reaching an identification point six miles from the Mitla Pass, the paratroop battalion jumped. By 7:30 that evening it had reached its assigned position along this key east–west axis through the Sinai. There the paratroopers dug in. Meanwhile the larger body of the paratroop brigade moved by land into the Sinai, with the aim of linking up with the units at Mitla. It was reprovisioned en route by supplies parachuted from French transport planes. As the offensive unfolded, the Israeli government was obliged to lift its veil of secrecy. Early on October 30, Ben-Gurion approved the deceptive announcement that "Israeli defense forces entered and engaged [guerrilla] units in Ras Nakhl . . . and seized positions west of the Nakhl crossroads in the vicinity of the Suez Canal. This action follows the Egyptian assaults . . . designed to cause destruction and the denial of peaceful life to Israeli citizens." Just enough had been revealed to enable Paris and London now to carry out their part of the joint operation.

Immediately following the Israeli announcement, Mollet and Pineau flew to London, and on the afternoon of October 30, the latter and Sir Ivone Kirkpatrick at the Foreign Office handed notes to the Israeli and Egyptian ambassadors "requesting" that their forces "withdraw," respectively, to points ten miles east and west of the canal. The Allied governments demanded an answer to their "request" within twelve hours. "If at the expiration of that time one or both Governments have not undertaken to comply with the above requirements, [British] and French forces will intervene in whatever strength may be necessary to secure compliance." The warning plainly was a fake in its alleged purpose of separating the combatants, for the Allies were ordering the victim (Egypt) to withdraw to the west bank of the canal, and allowing the invader (Israel) to advance to a distance ten miles east of the canal. Thus, at midnight on October 30, in compliance with the Sèvres scenario, Golda Meir transmitted Israel's reply. Accepting the Anglo-French "request," the foreign minister added: "In giving this undertaking, it is assumed . . . that a positive response will [be] forthcoming also from the Egyptian side." The assumption could not have been serious. As anticipated, Nasser rejected the Allied demand.

Fortunately for the Israelis, throughout October 30, Egyptian air action was minimal. Ineffective training was one factor. In dogfights

over the battle zone, no Israeli fighters were downed. French interceptors also were on the alert—and often airborne—although none of
their planes was engaged in combat. For the time being, the bulk of
Israel's air force was able to concentrate on ground support, strafing
Egyptian armor moving from the west. Nevertheless, during the
night of the 30th and morning of the 31st, the Israeli command
tensely awaited the promised Anglo-French air bombardment of
Egyptian fields. More than thirty-six hours had passed since Israel
had launched its offensive. At British headquarters in Cyprus, the
decision had been reached to postpone air operations from the morning until the evening of the 31st, when Egyptian antiaircraft fire
would be less effective. Ben-Gurion's direst fears seemed now to be
realized. Indeed, Israel's advance units at Mitla already were suffering
heavy casualties from entrenched Egyptian infantry. On the morning
of the 31st, Ben-Gurion used his "red telephone" personally to call
Abel Thomas, Israel's most reliable interlocutor in Paris, to express
his concern. At Thomas's request, Pineau then telephoned Eden,
who promptly communicated with General Keightley in Cyprus to
demand action.

Finally, at 7:00 p.m. on the 31st, the Allies launched their bombardment of Egypt's principal air bases. Late as it was, the air attack
was effective. Ultimately two hundred British and French fighter-
bombers, operating from aircraft carriers and from bases in Cyprus
and Malta, swept back and forth over the delta and canal fields,
destroying a major portion of the Egyptian air force on the ground.
Egypt's capacity for air activity against Israeli troops in the Sinai, let
alone against Israeli cities, was eliminated. On the night of October
31, Nasser ordered a general withdrawal from Sinai, concentrating
his defenses against the impending Allied invasion. For Israel, the
switch in Egyptian strategy now opened the opportunity to fulfill
Dayan's maximum plan of operations.

Pounding ahead swiftly, Israel's armored columns invested Egypt's
key bases in the central Sinai and the Gaza Strip. By November 2 the
Sinai was an open door for the Israeli army. Driving westward along
the coastal road toward Suez, Dayan's troops reaped a windfall of
some 385 Egyptian military vehicles still in running order, including
40 tanks. Yet even the Sinai breakthrough was essentially a sideshow.
Ben-Gurion's and Dayan's ultimate objective lay deep at the south-
eastern tip of the peninsula. For Israel's Ninth Brigade of farmer-
reservists, the challenge was less to overcome isolated Egyptian
resistance than to traverse a nightmare of lunar topography. But after
three days of steady march, the Ninth Brigade reached its objective.

At 9:30 p.m. on November 4, the Egyptian garrison in Sharm es-Sheikh surrendered. The Sinai war was over. At a cost of 180 men killed and 4 captured, Israel in a hundred-hour campaign had occupied the entirety of the Sinai Peninsula and the Gaza Strip, shattered three Egyptian divisions, and captured 7,000 tons of ammunition, half a million gallons of fuel, 200 artillery pieces, 1,300 vehicles, and a naval frigate trapped off the coast of Haifa by the French destroyer *Kersaint*, then rocketed into surrender by Israeli planes.

A WAR OF BRITISH EQUIVOCATION

Whatever the Israelis' thrilled relief at the eradication of the Egyptian threat, the response elsewhere was markedly different. Even Britain, Israel's putative ally, was characteristically ambivalent in justifying the one-sided ultimatum to Egypt and Israel. On October 30, Whitehall distributed a statement to the various Arab governments. It observed that "[t]he Israeli attack on Egypt seems undoubtedly to be an act of aggression," but insisted that "Egypt has called this on herself . . . [by blockading Israel's maritime freedom of passage] and . . . threatening to encompass the destruction of Israel." Conversely, in a note to Eisenhower that same day, Eden acknowledged that Israel had a case for acting in self-defense, but added: "Nevertheless, we would not wish to support or even condone the action of Israel." And in the House of Commons the prime minister adopted a conventionally pro-Arab stance, emphasizing his government's intention of standing by Jordan, and Israel's pledge not to attack Hashemite territory.

The convoluted rationale did not satisfy the rest of the world. In New York, the UN Security Council met in emergency session on October 31 to condemn Israel's move into Sinai and to demand an immediate withdrawal of Israeli forces. For the first time in the history of the world body, Britain and France both cast negative votes—in effect, vetoes. In a transatlantic phone conversation with Eisenhower, Eden sought to fend off the president's censure by repeating his labored justification, of the need to block equivalent Egyptian and Israeli threats to the canal. The following day, November 1, when the General Assembly was summoned to circumvent the Allied vetoes in the Security Council, Britain's representative, Sir Pearson Dixon, once again insisted that "by our swift intervention, the Israeli advance has already been halted and this threat to the Canal has been averted." Secretary of State Dulles was not impressed. He asked for a resolution condemning Britain, France, and Israel alike, and demanding immediate Israeli withdrawal and the cessation of Allied bombardment. The resolution was carried the next day by 64 votes to 5, with only Australia and New Zealand joining Britain, France, and Israel in opposing it.

The situation was acutely uncomfortable for the British and French. By November 3 Dayan's army had virtually cleared Sinai. But Operation Musketeer—the occupation of the Suez Canal Zone—was still hanging fire, with the vast Allied armada still five hundred miles off Egypt and airborne troops waiting in Cyprus. In the United Nations frantic efforts were afoot to devise a solution before the British and French landed their amphibious forces. The next day, the Canadian delegate, Lester Pearson, came up with a formula that won overwhelming General Assembly approval. It was to create a UN Emergency Force that would anticipate Britain and France in "separating the combatants" along the canal and elsewhere in Sinai. In effect the Allies were ensnared by their own declared rationale for Operation Musketeer. What need was there now for an invasion?

On the eve of the General Assembly vote, Pineau flew to London to urge that Allied paratroops be dispatched to the canal without further delay. He suggested that Israel could provide flank support during the three-day interval until the amphibious force reached Egypt. Indeed, he had broached the idea to Dayan the day before. With Ben-Gurion's approval, the Israeli commander agreed to seize al-Qantara on the east bank of the canal, in order to protect the sector designated for the French paratroop landing. It was London now that rejected the proposal, and with scarcely less than horror. Allied-Israeli collusion should not be even further exposed.

But on the night of November 3, with his nation's strategic objectives all but fulfilled, Israel's Ambassador Abba Eban informed the UN General Assembly that his government was accepting the cease-fire, provided a similar response were forthcoming from Egypt. In fact, Egypt had accepted the Assembly's resolution the previous day. More even than the arrival of the UN Emergency Force, Eban's statement foreclosed the rationale for Allied landings. Pineau accordingly dispatched an urgent appeal to Jerusalem for a retraction. It angered Ben-Gurion profoundly. The Allies had enjoyed six days, he noted, from October 29 to November 4, to exploit Israel's invasion, but throughout those six days the British had plodded on in meticulous preparations for Operation Musketeer. Once again Eden was expecting Israel to pull his chestnuts out of the fire.

Yet, whatever his exasperation, the prime minister saw no alternative to compliance. At his instructions, Eban on November 4 "clarified" his government's earlier acceptance by interposing several conditions: assurance that Egypt no longer regarded itself as in a state of war with Israel, was prepared to embark upon peace negotiations, would terminate the economic boycott and maritime blockade against Israel, and would put an end to guerrilla attacks against Israel from the Gaza Strip. Nasser of course gave the qualifications short shrift—and the pretext for Allied landings consequently remained intact.

The French understood Israel's predicament. To resolve it, Foreign Minister Pineau telephoned Prime Minister Eden on the afternoon of November 4, again pleading for an immediate paratroop landing along the canal. Yet, even at the last moment, seeking to defuse world obloquy, Eden came up with still another backhanded swipe at the Israelis. At his insistence, the French concurred in a joint declaration. Its key provision stated: "The two governments continue to believe that it is necessary [to interpose Allied forces] . . . *to secure the speedy withdrawal of Israeli forces* [italics added], to take the necessary measures to remove obstructions to traffic through the Suez Canal, and to promote a settlement of the problems in the area."

When the text of this declaration reached Jerusalem, Ben-Gurion reacted explosively. What kind of gratitude was this, he asked, after Israel had agreed to retract its acceptance of a cease-fire? In an urgent cable to Paris the Israeli prime minister protested bitterly that France's identification with the declaration "will be an act of unfriendliness against us if [the Allied entry into Suez is based upon] . . . protection from Israel. . . . We urge [the French government] in all friendship not to do this thing." Ben-Gurion's appeal reached its mark. Considerably embarrassed, Mollet then clarified the declaration, alluding to the need to ensure Israeli withdrawal specifically from the Suez Canal Zone, rather than from the entirety of the Sinai Peninsula.

At last, on the morning of November 5, a wave of Allied paratroops dropped outside Port Saïd, and a second wave descended in the afternoon. Throughout the night the first ships of the Allied flotilla arrived off Port Saïd, and at dawn on November 6 they began their shelling of Egyptian emplacements. The town surrendered in the early afternoon. Immediately afterward an armored column pushed on toward Suez City. British patrols were only twenty-five miles short of this southern exit of the canal when, at 6:00 p.m., London announced that it was accepting the United Nations demand for a cease-fire. It developed that the accumulation of pressures, domestic and international, by then had shaken Eden's commitment to Operation Musketeer. One of these catalysts was the upswell of outrage from Britain's Labor opposition and from a substantial Conservative minority. It was matched by a wave of execration from the Afro-Asian members of the British Commonwealth.

Yet it was not domestic or Commonwealth condemnation alone that cracked Eden's resolve. On November 6, Washington informed the prime minister that Britain's impending $1 billion loan from the International Monetary Fund was contingent on a cease-fire. A sick man by then, Eden became completely unnerved. He telephoned Mollet. "I am cornered," he protested. "I can't hang on. I'm being deserted by everybody. . . . I can't even rely on unanimity among the Conservatives. . . . The Commonwealth threatens to break up. . . . Eisenhower phoned me. I can't go it alone without the United States. . . . No, it is not possible." Mollet pleaded for only a little more time for his own forces to complete the seizure of the canal. But French operations were too intimately combined under British leadership at every level. Frustrated and bitter, Mollet in the end was obliged to act jointly with the British. Operation Musketeer would end at midnight, November 6—and within the month, Eden would resign as prime minister in favor of Harold Macmillan.

In reaching their decision, the British and French took note also of a warning from Moscow. At first, Soviet press and radio condemnation was muted. On October 31 the USSR called only for United Nations action to restrain the Israelis and Western Allies. The Russians plainly had their hands full then with an anti-Communist uprising in Hungary. But on November 4, Soviet tanks launched a final, brutal suppression of the rebels in Budapest. With world outrage all but unanimous, the Kremlin accordingly seized upon the Sinai-Suez crisis as a useful propaganda diversion. On November 5 Prime Minister Nikolai Bulganin dispatched messages to the governments of France, Britain, and Israel. His notes to the two Western governments asked, rhetorically: "In what situation would Britain [or France] find [themselves] if [they] were attacked by stronger states, possessing all types of modern destructive weapons? And such countries could . . . [send] naval or air forces to the shore of Britain [and France] and use other means—for instance, rocket weapons." In fact, the Soviets in 1956 possessed only one model of long-distance rocket in large quantity, a rather primitive German V-2 type capable of delivering an eight-hundred-pound warhead to a maximum range of 450 miles. Harold Macmillan later confirmed that the British leadership never took Bulganin's threats "too seriously."

Instead it was Bulganin's warning to Ben-Gurion that appeared particularly ominous. In his message of November 5 the Soviet prime minister accused Israel's government of

> playing with the fate of the whole world, with the fate of its own people. It is sowing hatred of the State of Israel among the peoples of the East. Its actions are putting a question mark on the very existence of Israel as a State. . . . We suggest that the Government of Israel should weigh its actions as long as there is still time.

Although Ben-Gurion reacted to the threat calmly, he was aware that Soviet weaponry was pouring into Syria, and that rumors abounded of Soviet "volunteers" mobilized for service in the Middle East. In his diary the Israeli prime minister wrote: "From Rome, Paris, and Washington there [are] . . . reports on a stream of Soviet planes and 'volunteers' to Syria, or a promise to bomb Israel—airfields, cities, and so on. . . . The Soviet tanks' rampage in Hungary testifies to what these Communist Nazis are capable of doing." It was not unlikely, too, that Ben-Gurion recalled the warnings of Israel Beer, the Soviet "mole" in Israel: that Moscow would not passively accept the humiliation of its Egyptian protégé. Thereupon, Ben-Gurion dispatched Shimon Peres and Golda Meir to Paris to seek Mollet's evaluation. The French premier similarly advised his visitors "not [to] belittle Bulganin's warning." In fact Ben-Gurion neither belittled the warning nor flinched before it. His reply to Bulganin was courteous but firm. Israeli forces were not going to withdraw from Sinai, he insisted, unless and until Nasser ended his campaign against Israel's fundamental security.

The Israeli prime minister did not know it, but on November 5 Bulganin had also dispatched a letter to Eisenhower, proposing that the United States and the Soviet Union act together militarily to halt the fighting in Egypt. Rejecting the suggestion, Eisenhower instead promptly dispatched U-2 surveillance aircraft to overfly Syria and Israel. At the same time he informed Eden and Mollet that, if Soviet forces were found to be intervening in the Middle East, "we would be justified in taking military action." The president's warning actually was intended as an oblique reminder to the Allied leaders of the potential global consequences of their armed intervention in Egypt. Ultimately it was the confluence of these dangers—military, diplomatic, economic—that registered on Eden (and in lesser degree on Mollet), and impelled them to abort their painstakingly contrived Operation Musketeer.

A WAR OF DIPLOMATIC ISOLATION

Ben-Gurion would prove far less timorous than the Western leaders. He had accomplished his long-held strategic objective. The blockade of the Strait of Tiran was broken. So was the back of the Egyptian army in Sinai. The Gaza Strip no longer would be a launching ground for guerrillas; on November 4 the General Assembly had approved dispatch of a UN Emergency Force—UNEF—to serve as a buffer between Egypt and its enemies, the Western Allies and Israel alike. But on November 8 Britain suddenly chose to back away even further from its tactical alliance. Selwyn Lloyd urged Israel to evacuate the Sinai in return for certain "assurances." These included a peace treaty with Egypt, defensible frontiers guaranteed by the Allies, and free Israeli passage through the Suez Canal and the Gulf of Aqaba. By his request the foreign secretary hoped to salvage the already shaken partnership of the Baghdad Pact, and Britain's precarious access to Arab oil. He received no answer from Jerusalem. If Ben-Gurion earlier had entertained few illusions about the British, by now he evinced nothing but contempt for their premature decision to accept a cease-fire. Indeed, after November 8 the prime minister simply ignored London in weighing Israel's options. The following month, in an interview with Richard Crossman, a visiting British MP and veteran friend of Israel, Ben-Gurion recalled that several years earlier he had offered to bring Israel into the British Commonwealth (p. 16). "Well," he added drily, "that offer is withdrawn."

Among the Great Powers, France remained Israel's single dependable ally. Both publicly and privately, Mollet, Pineau, and their colleagues were unshakable in their loyalty. They provided diplomatic support for Israel's security demands in the United Nations, and military cover in the Sinai itself to give Israel's army time to carry off its treasure trove of captured weaponry. Thus, during November and early December, Israeli troops enjoyed a certain leeway in negotiating their slow, incremental withdrawal. Throughout these weeks, the main United Nations efforts in any case focused on replacement of Allied troops along the canal with UNEF contingents. But on December 22 the last French and British soldiers finally departed Port Saïd. With the Suez phase of the episode over, Israel alone now confronted the heaviest weight of international pressure.

During the ensuing four months, the Jewish state waged a stubborn diplomatic campaign to avoid unconditional withdrawal to the 1949 Rhodes Armistice lines. In that struggle their principal ad-

versaries were the Soviet and Afro-Asian blocs. Together with UN
Secretary General Dag Hammarskjöld, these delegations pressed
unremittingly for total Israeli evacuation from the Sinai and Gaza.
Although the Western governments were by no means oblivious to
the provocations Israel had endured in recent years, their private
sympathies were vitiated by "objective" factors. Their economies
were critically dependent on the passage of oil through Suez. At the
beginning of the Allied landings, Nasser had scuttled vessels
anchored in the canal, and refused to allow clearing operations in
the blocked waterway until the Israelis departed. Under the circumstances the European delegations then felt obliged to support the
series of UN General Assembly resolutions for prompt and unconditional Israeli evacuation. Washington fully endorsed these demands.
By then, the Eisenhower administration scarcely disguised its threat
to impose economic sanctions on Israel.

On January 15, 1957, Ben-Gurion finally announced his government's decision to evacuate the entirety of the Sinai within the month.
Yet he exempted from this commitment the Sharm es-Sheikh emplacement, guarding the Strait of Tiran, and the Gaza Strip, directly abutting integral Israel. For security reasons these areas should never be
returned to direct Egyptian rule. In the United States, as it happened,
Ben-Gurion's anxiety had registered on congressional leaders of both
political parties. In turn, they made known their own reservations to
the White House. In seeking a compromise formula with the Israelis,
Secretary of State Dulles then raised with Ambassador Eban the
notion of permanent UNEF contingents at Gaza and Sharm es-
Sheikh. The scheme's basic outlines in fact had been devised in Paris.
The French had monitored Israel's situation with intense solicitude.
In late January 1957 Foreign Minister Pineau warned UN Secretary
General Hammarskjöld that "France would not recognize any Gen-
eral Assembly resolution imposing sanctions on Israel. . . . The
French Government is determined to provide Israel with all the help
needed to meet her just demands."

Ironically, the obstacle to a final understanding was the secretary
general himself, who opposed the notion of a UN administration at
Gaza or Sharm es-Sheikh. As Hammarskjöld saw it, the United
Nations was exclusively a peacekeeper rather than a sovereign government. "Not a single spark of political imagination illuminated the
arid wastes of his legalism," Eban wrote later. On February 18, 1957,
however, Dulles and Eisenhower met with Mollet and Pineau, who
had flown to Washington to deal firsthand with the Americans on the
Middle East crisis. It was then that the French statesmen offered a

fascinating proposal. As Pineau later outlined it to Eban, representatives of the United States, France, Britain, and other maritime nations would declare in the UN General Assembly that every nation had the right to freedom of navigation in the Gulf of Eilat and the Strait of Tiran, and consequently that they recognized Israel's right to safeguard its own vessels against any aggression. The declaration, issued by the maritime nations independently, would not require approval by a two-thirds UN General Assembly majority—and thus could not be thwarted by the Afro-Asian and Communist blocs.

As for the Gaza Strip, it was France's view that no issue of United Nations "governance" would arise—as Hammarsjköld had contended—if UNEF troops simply occupied this vital border region on an "interim basis" to safeguard refugees and to provide effective civilian administration. To avoid any formal derogation of Egyptian rights, it would be understood that the presence of UNEF troops in Gaza, an enclave already overflowing with refugees, would preclude the simultaneous reoccupation of this region by the Egyptian army. Further to spare Egyptian amour-propre, the scenario would be attributed to a "neutral" author, Lester Pearson, Canada's delegate to the United Nations. In Pineau's understanding, the formula, through this veil of subterfuges, would be acceptable to the Egyptian government.

It was. Egyptian Foreign Minister Mahmoud Fawzi had instantly discerned in the proposal a face-saving alternative for his country. It would not be formulated by written agreement. Rather, the arrangement should simply be allowed to develop pragmatically. Sharm es-Sheikh too now could be added to the plan, for the solution there, as in Gaza, avoided any public derogation of Egyptian authority. "If they [the Israelis] would keep their mouths shut," Mahmoud Fawzi suggested to Hammarsjköld, "we would keep our eyes shut." Eban reacted well to the scheme, as Dulles had. Upon his recommendation, the Israeli government similarly accepted the plan. Within the next few days it became clear that there existed a General Assembly consensus, rather than a formal "resolution," for sending UNEF contingents into Gaza and Sharm es-Sheikh. Eban observed later that it would have been difficult to "overstate the still under-appreciated role" played by the French in resolving the impasse.

Nevertheless, the Israelis remained concerned that the UNEF at some future time might be precipitously withdrawn, and that Israeli shipping might again be obstructed. They sought Hammarsjköld's commitment that any future proposal to evacuate the UNEF must first be submitted to the General Assembly. The secretary-general confirmed the understanding on February 26, 1957, in a memorandum, and Dulles endorsed it in writing. Three days later, appearing before the UN General Assembly on March 1, Foreign Minister Golda Meir reiterated these conditions in her announcement of Israeli withdrawal from Gaza and Sharm es-Sheikh. Following Mrs. Meir to the rostrum, United States Ambassador Henry Cabot Lodge endorsed her statement on the Gulf of Tiran and free navigation. Alluding to Gaza, however, Lodge deviated significantly from the Pineau-Dulles-Eban understanding. He made specific reference to the 1949 armistice agreement, which gave Egypt jurisdiction in Gaza, and thereby underscored Egypt's legal position in the area. Furious, Mrs. Meir and Eban immediately and vehemently protested this interpretation.

Once again it was France that came to Israel's rescue. Pineau demanded a written "correction" from Dulles. He got better than that. It was a letter from Eisenhower himself to Ben-Gurion, endorsing the "assumptions" under which Israeli forces were being withdrawn, "assumptions" that were endorsed by fifteen maritime members of the UN General Assembly. At the same time Pineau telexed a personal letter to Ben-Gurion. If Israel again were forced to defend itself against Egyptian aggression, the foreign minister emphasized, "France . . . will not only refuse to associate itself with any sanctions, but will continue to aid Israel in seeking a just solution to the problem." The Israeli government accepted these assurances, and on March 4 began evacuating its troops from Gaza and Sharm es-Sheikh, to be replaced immediately by six UNEF battalions.

Only two days later, local Palestinians in the Gaza Strip issued strident calls for the return of an Egyptian administration. Agreeing to meet these "demands," Nasser promptly dispatched a civil governor to the Gaza Strip with an appropriate staff. Although no troops accompanied them, the development astounded and outraged the Israelis. Ben-Gurion and his cabinet then rushed into urgent session to debate a possible resumption of military action. And once more the French stood by their side. On March 8, Defense Minister Bourgès-Maunoury informed the United States that France was making preparations to supply air cover in the event the Israelis resorted to armed force.

But in London Selwyn Lloyd, who had remained on as foreign secretary after Eden's resignation, took precisely the opposite position. The notion of military action was "absolute nonsense," he insisted. At this point, even Christian Pineau began to have second thoughts, and joined with Dulles in urging the Israelis not to overreact. What did it matter if an Egyptian governor had returned in Gaza, asked the French foreign minister, so long as UNEF troops provided a safeguard against future guerrilla incursions? Grudgingly, then, Ben-Gurion and his cabinet agreed not to press the issue.

After Israel's long diplomatic isolation, after the condemnation it had suffered for its collusion with Britain and France, had the Sinai Campaign in the end been worthwhile for the Jewish state? Nasser, after all, had emerged from his battlefield disaster with his prestige reasonably intact. He had camouflaged the brutal shellacking his army had suffered at Israel's hands under the palpable evidence of Anglo-French bombardment. The Sinai Campaign also reconfirmed Ben-Gurion's mordant evaluation of his putative British ally. Meeting with Eisenhower and Dulles in Bermuda on March 20, 1957, less than two weeks after Israel's withdrawal from Gaza and Sharm es-Sheikh, Prime Minister Harold Macmillan and Foreign Secretary Lloyd reviewed the Middle Eastern situation. Once again Lloyd adverted to a favorite British theme: Israel's current frontiers, he emphasized, could not be "justified" and "would have to be adjusted." Nevertheless the French connection at least held firm, and even began to take on the characteristics of an ongoing alliance. In May 1957 a French naval squadron took up positions along the Strait of Tiran to guarantee the safety of Israeli shipping there, while smaller French naval units hovered around the Red Sea approaches to the Suez Canal to ensure passage through the waterway of non-Israeli vessels bearing cargo for Israel.

Meanwhile, guerrilla infiltration from Gaza ended. Israelis in their nation's outlying border settlements now could work and sleep in peace for the first time in nearly a decade. The Gulf of Aqaba was open, and Israel's freedom of passage there would remain unchallenged until May 1967. Those ten and a half years were sufficient to consolidate the Jewish state's trade and diplomatic relationships with the Orient and Africa, where (notwithstanding Moshe Sharett's earlier reservations) Israel's image was enhanced and its reputation admired. The time frame was sufficient, too, to inaugurate a series of pipelines that transformed the Zionist republic into a major oil entrepôt between Iran and Europe, and to launch it on a period of impressive economic growth. Altogether, from November 1957 on, and not least as a consequence of its tactical alliance with a stalwart European patron, Israel achieved its "takeoff" and established itself as a sovereign entity to be treated with circumspection and respect in the councils of nations.

V

ALTERNATING PERSPECTIVES ACROSS THE RHINE

As the dust of the Sinai-Suez conflict settled, each of its participants began to appraise the episode's likely future consequences. For Britain, the aborted invasion doomed more than Anthony Eden's political career. A historic sphere of imperial influence in the Middle East plainly was drawing to a close. Indeed, only two years later, in July 1958, Iraq's traditionally pro-British government was overthrown by partisans of Gamal Abd al-Nasser. The Iraqis' ensuing defection from the Middle East Treaty Organization scuttled the Baghdad Pact altogether. It was in 1958, too, that Prime Minister Harold Macmillan accepted the recommendation of a Whitehall task force to focus Britain's "Arab" diplomacy less on the eastern Mediterranean than on the oil-rich Persian Gulf. With this shift in emphasis, leeway opened for a more relaxed approach to Israel, a nation that had proved its staying power against the common Egyptian enemy.

Relations between the two governments never again would revert to the suspicions that had flared up as a consequence of Israeli-Jordanian border violence. In the next decade Britain's exports to Israel would reach twice the volume of its shipments to the entirety of the Arab world. The Foreign Office dropped its traditional ban on Israeli military purchases. British munitions manufacturers were free to sell Israel their latest-model tanks and other ordnance. In 1964, when Harold Wilson formed Britain's first Labor government in thirteen years, he invited Israel's Prime Minister Levi Eshkol for an official visit. Upon arrival, Eshkol was tendered a warm public and fraternally Socialist reception.

Franco-Israeli cordiality ran even deeper in the late 1950s and early 1960s. In Israel, during the euphoric aftermath of the Suez-Sinai alliance, French bookstores, films, and cultural events were widely attended. In 1957 the nation's first French-language daily, *L'Information,* made its appearance. With the substantial immigration of francophone Jews from North Africa and Romania during the early 1960s, French even briefly superseded English as the second language of choice in numerous Israeli high schools. More fundamentally, the Israeli government was prepared now to accept a certain diplomatic guidance from Paris. Thus Prime Minister Ben-Gurion, and later his successor, Levi Eshkol, became uncharacteristically reticent on issues of European colonialism where French policy in Algeria was concerned; and in the United Nations, Israel's delegates kept silent in all discussions relating to the Algerian nationalist insurrection. For some years, at Paris's request, Israel sought (with only intermittent success) to exercise an unwonted restraint toward periodic Syrian incursions along the northern, Syrian-Israeli demilitarized zone. If possible, nothing should be done to prejudice France's efforts to reestablish its influence in the Levant.

In France, too, after 1956, admiration for "brave little Israel" remained the defining mood in both private and government circles. The Alliance France-Israël included among its members some of the nation's most respected cultural, military, and political figures. Its president was the renowned war hero General Pierre Koenig. The press gave extensive coverage to Israeli affairs. Under instruction from Paris, France's residents-general in North Africa actively cooperated with the Jewish Agency in the emigration of tens of thousands of Maghreb Jews to Israel. The French government joined with the Rothschild consortium to invest $24 million in Israel's first oil pipeline, extending from Eilat to the Mediterranean port of Ashdod. In personally authorizing the venture, Prime Minister Guy Mollet emphasized that he regarded Israel as the West's principal buffer against Soviet expansion in the Middle East (a meaningful swipe at the Baghdad Pact, and its Anglo-American sponsors).

It was to fortify that strategic alliance, moreover, that Paris encouraged collaboration between French and Israeli armed forces and intelligence services. From 1957 on, a joint French-Israeli planning committee met regularly to explore ways of protecting both nations' interests in the Mediterranean and Red seas. In 1958 France and Israel conducted joint naval exercises in the Mediterranean. Perhaps of greatest importance, Paris allowed Israel carte blanche in its purchases of French weaponry, and specifically of military aircraft, including the updated Mirage III-C and the Vautour light bomber, both regarded as superior to the equipment Moscow was providing its Arab clients.

Beyond the strategic alliance, the weapons relationship manifestly served France's commercial interests. By 1963 Israeli military purchases accounted for some 13 percent of the country's export orders, thus allowing French manufacturers to exploit economies of scale in developing their weaponry. Ultimately contracts with Israel reduced the assembly-line price of French military aircraft by one-third. The relationship also served the research needs of both nations. In 1959, Israel was allowed to invest in Marcel Dassault's Sud-Aviation Company, and thereby to collaborate in projects of special value to Israeli defense needs. The development of the French Matra air-to-air missile was essentially a joint French-Israeli venture. So, in 1961, was the production of Israel's two-stage, solid-fuel "meteorological" rocket, the Shavit II, developed for Israel by Sud-Aviation, and given its first test launching in the French Sahara.

And so was the most highly classified of all Israel's military-research projects. From the beginning of statehood, Ben-Gurion had been convinced that the nation required a nuclear power source to meet its energy needs. By 1952, moreover, he was persuaded that a nuclear reactor might also serve as a military deterrent. In that year he established Israel's Atomic Energy Commission, and placed it—significantly—under the chairmanship of Shimon Peres, director general of the defense ministry. The commission's first appointed director was Dr. David Ernst Bergmann, a German-born chemist and former research director of the Weizmann Institute of Science. A man of broad scholarly and administrative talents, Bergmann over the years had developed excellent connections with French nuclear scientists, not a few of whom also were Jews. In 1954, one of these, Bertrand Goldschmidt, together with the chairman of the French Atomic Energy Commission, Frédéric Joliot-Curie (a non-Jew), persuaded the Mendès-France government to explore means of helping Israel develop its own enriched uranium plant.

Three years later, in complete secrecy, the government of Prime Minister Bourgès-Maunoury signed an agreement with Israel for cooperation in nuclear research. France would help Israel construct a 24-megawatt reactor near the isolated northern Negev town of Dimona. Israel in turn would share its research data with France. Thus, from late 1957 on, several hundred French engineers and technicians traveled to Israel on long-term contracts. Their assignment was to construct and put into operation the Jewish state's first nuclear reactor—whose purpose was distinctly not limited to research. Bourgès-Maunoury's commitment was unprecedented, for it was undertaken three years before France detonated its own atomic bomb, and it was made not to a NATO ally but to a tiny nation with which France had no official alliance of any kind.

DE GAULLE AND REASSESSMENT

In May 1958, in its effort to bring an end to four years of debilitating struggle with Moslem insurrectionists in Algeria, the French government suddenly confronted an unanticipated new danger. This was the imminent likelihood of an army coup in behalf of Algeria's ruling European minority. Confused and alarmed, French political leaders turned reluctantly to a historic icon, Charles de Gaulle, as the single figure capable of defusing the threat of civil war. On June 1, the National Assembly voted the charismatic general into office as prime minister with interim full ruling powers. In the ensuing six months, de Gaulle succeeded in consolidating his executive authority and in winning a mandate as president of a new, Fifth Republic.

Only then did de Gaulle reveal his intention of achieving a political settlement in Algeria, one that would accommodate the basic aspirations of the Moslem population. The task required still another four years of painstaking negotiations, interspersed by yet another abortive army mutiny and a sequence of assassination attempts inspired by Algeria's European settlers against the president himself. By April 1962, however, the feat of diplomatic surgery was completed. Algeria became independent, and soon its European population would repatriate itself en masse to metropolitan France. In effect, de Gaulle had cauterized the infection that had poisoned France's relations with Algeria's Moslems—and with the largest part of the Arab world.

No people followed these developments with more acute attention and concern than did the Israelis. De Gaulle, they knew, was no stranger to Middle Eastern realities. He had been in Palestine in 1941 when Free French army units joined Britain's in liberating Syria and Lebanon from Vichy rule, and he had received both moral and military support from the Jewish Agency. In 1947, as the fate of Palestine was debated in the United Nations, de Gaulle privately acknowledged to Maurice Fischer, the Jewish Agency representative in Paris, that partition "appeared reasonable." In April 1955, when Ambassador Ya'akov Tsur visited him at his family estate in Colombey-les-Deux-Églises, de Gaulle expressed admiration for Israel's growth and progress. "Your presence in the Middle East is a reality," he proclaimed, "and . . . the Great Powers [must be convinced] that it is indispensable to assure the existence of Israel in the region." The general similarly approved the 1956 French-Israeli military collaboration against Nasser. In February 1957, interviewed by Menachem Begin at his Paris office, the general strongly recommended that Israeli troops continue their occupation of the Gaza Strip. Thus far there appeared to be no divergence between de Gaulle's Middle Eastern views and those of the Mollet government. Neither did a political shift become evident after de Gaulle assumed power in 1958. In an interview soon afterward with the American journalist Cyrus Sulzberger, the new president vented his spleen at the Americans and British for their recent troop landings in Lebanon and Jordan. Without so much as consulting France, de Gaulle complained, the "Anglo-Saxons" had engaged in a feckless attempt to salvage the Baghdad Pact. The Israelis could only have taken heart from de Gaulle's attitude.

On the other hand, it did not escape them that commercial relations between the two countries remained ominously thin. In October 1959, under Arab pressure, the Renault Company canceled a contract for the assembly of its Dauphine automobile in Haifa. Renault was a nationalized firm, and the cancellation plainly had been decided on the governmental level. Air France, another nationalized company, also prepared to capitulate to the Arab boycott by ending its flights to Israel. Only Ben-Gurion's personal appeal to de Gaulle reversed that decision. By the late 1950s Paris evidently had decided that hard economics would determine its trade relationship with the Jewish state. Long-term credits no longer were extended for Israeli purchases of French equipment, even military equipment.

Nevertheless, it was specifically France's export of weapons to Israel that continued without interruption. Shimon Peres's cultivation of French armament manufacturers had ensured a formidable industrial lobby in favor of the Israeli connection. France's defense establishment was equally supportive, and within the key Conseil Supérieur de Défense (comprising both foreign and defense ministry officials), de Gaulle invariably cast the deciding vote with the defense group. Israeli pilots and other officers continued to share in specialized French military training programs. Israeli aeronautical engineers were seconded to French aircraft plants. None of France's policymakers needed reminders that Israel's military prowess "advertised" the superiority of French equipment in the world arms market. Thus, as late as 1964, de Gaulle personally approved a major new Israeli order of fifty Mirage Vs. Representing the apotheosis of French military aircraft design, this new fighter in Israeli hands might prove its superiority to the American Phantom for possible NATO acquisition.

Nevertheless, as the Israeli government anxiously monitored its relationship with France, it noted several troubling changes within the Gaullist administration. Upon coming to power in 1958, the general had moved decisively to curb the rebellious Algérie-Française elements that had brought France to the verge of civil war. Henceforth, under the Fifth Republic, military and foreign affairs would fall strictly within the president's domain, and de Gaulle would exercise that authority with no further tolerance for private bureaucratic fiefdoms. The political consequences of this alteration would bar special pleaders for Israel from interference with the orderly, centralized direction of foreign and defense policies. When Jacques Soustelle, one of the most militant of the Algérie-Française right-wingers, approached de Gaulle late in 1958 to propose a formal Franco-Israeli alliance, the president's response was cool. "Matters are fine as they are," he replied. "There is no need for an official text." Conceivably de Gaulle was expressing the view of his foreign minister, Maurice Couve de Murville. An austere professional diplomat, a former ambassador to Egypt, Couve de Murville strongly favored a restoration of France's ties with the Arab world. To that end he worked assiduously with the president to achieve an orderly French withdrawal from Algeria. By 1962, when the process finally was completed, France at long last was in a position to seek a rapprochement with the Arab Middle East.

But, in truth, even before the Algerian issue was resolved, Couve de Murville was moving discreetly to uncouple France from its intimate embrace of "gallant little Israel." Upon assuming his portfolio at the foreign ministry, one of his first acts was to replace the ardently pro-Zionist Pierre Gilbert as ambassador to Israel. In March 1959, Couve de Murville appointed a special body of foreign ministry experts, the "Jeanneney Commission," to reevaluate France's Middle East policy. The commission's report four months later recommended that diplomatic efforts in the region be focused more intensively upon Lebanon, Syria, Jordan, and Iran. Whereupon, acting on the report, the government soon began extending wider economic credits to these nations. Within a half decade, some 21,000 French teachers and 6,000 French engineers and technicians were at work in the Moslem world (most, to be sure, in North Africa), while only thirty-three French teachers, and no technicians at all, remained in Israel. From 1959 on, de Gaulle rejected any further suggestions of developing a joint Red Sea strategy with Israel. In the UN General Assembly, France's delegate refused to support a 1961 African initiative calling for direct negotiations between Arabs and Israelis.

Witnessing the subtle shift in French policy, Israel's Prime Minister Ben-Gurion sought out ways of developing a personal relationship with the French president. Finally, in June 1960, de Gaulle somewhat reluctantly consented to a meeting, although on condition that Ben-Gurion's visit to France be regarded as strictly private, and limited to twenty-four hours. No Israeli flag flew over Ben-Gurion's hotel in Paris. The lunch at the Élysée Palace was brief and perfunctory. Yet, in a long, private conversation afterward, Ben-Gurion and de Gaulle related well to each other. The Israeli prime minister outlined the danger of renewed Arab military action against Israel, and emphasized his country's ongoing need for France's "superb" military equipment. He asked then if Israel might proceed with negotiations to purchase the new Mirage V fighter. In response, de Gaulle turned to Pierre Messmer, the minister of defense: "Messmer, see to it," he declared magisterially.

But only two months later, Couve de Murville shocked Israel's Ambassador Walter Eytan by declaring that France no longer would provide uranium for Israel's nuclear reactor. The foreign minister also requested that the Dimona facility be placed under international supervision. The bolt did not come entirely out of the blue. By then American U-2 surveillance planes and additional CIA investigation had confirmed the existence of the nuclear project, and Washington was pressing France and Israel to open the reactor to international controls. De Gaulle himself would have preferred that the cooperative enterprise be discontinued altogether. In his *Memoirs* he wrote that he had opposed construction "of an installation . . . from which, one bright day, atomic bombs could emerge." For Israel now, the president's evident intention to reduce France's involvement in the Dimona project demanded an urgent response. Thus, visiting Couve de Murville several weeks later, Shimon Peres came up with a warning of his own. The original bilateral agreement beween the two governments, he noted, had committed both to absolute secrecy on its plutonium-producing feature. If France now persisted in unilaterally abrogating the contract, Israel, at risk, might not be able "to preserve its commitment to secrecy." The threat of a move likely to provoke Arab retaliation against France was all but explicit, and it registered. For the time being, Couve de Murville allowed uranium deliveries to continue.

In March 1961 the Israelis thought they discerned an opportunity to remind Paris of their nation's reciprocal usefulness to France. It was a period when the Organisation de l'Armée Secrète, a cabal of embittered irredentists, was engaged in efforts to assassinate de Gaulle for his "betrayal" of the Algérie-Française cause. That month an Israeli visitor with right-wing contacts in France was alerted to yet a new plot against the president's life. If it succeeded, the conspirators intimated, they would be in a position to offer Israel "dramatic" help against its Arab enemies. Horrified, the Israeli immediately contacted Walter Eytan, his country's ambassador in Paris. The ambassador in turn alerted Jerusalem. Ben-Gurion's reaction was reflexive: de Gaulle should be warned forthwith. Eytan then conveyed his information to Colonel Alain de Boissieu, de Gaulle's son-in-law and director of the president's security office. The conspirators soon afterward were arrested.

Whatever de Gaulle's gratitude, it was in some measure neutralized by persistent rumors of other, less benign Israeli activities. The following month, in a last-ditch effort to abort the impending French withdrawal, a group of senior French generals in Algeria mutinied against Gaullist authority. The uprising was quashed within a week. Then, soon afterward, press reports circulated of an alleged Israeli involvement in the uprising. Although the reports were still inconclusive, agents of Menachem Begin's right-wing Cherut party were known to maintain close ties with Jacques Soustelle, still a leading Algérie-Française activist. Incensed by the rumors, de Gaulle promptly ordered his ministers and military commanders to sever their ties with the Alliance France-Israël.

At this point, determined to salvage the relationship with the French president, Ben-Gurion intervened personally again. In June 1961 he paid a second visit to Paris. Remarkably, his meeting with de Gaulle this time proved even more cordial than the year before. The president assured his guest that France would make available to Israel "the finest planes we possess," then ended the luncheon with a formal toast to Israel, "our friend and ally." A few months later, conferring with Foreign Minister Couve de Murville and Defense Minister Messmer, Shimon Peres won assurances that French participation in the Dimona nuclear project would continue. Three years after that, in the summer of 1964, de Gaulle tendered a warm reception to Prime Minister Levi Eshkol, Ben-Gurion's successor. As in the 1961 luncheon for Ben-Gurion, the president offered a toast "to Israel, our friend and ally," then fortified his earlier commitment on the Mirage V fighters with a pledge to sell Israel a squadron of Super-Frélon helicopters.

It would be the French president's last public gesture of friendship to the Jewish state. On October 29, 1965, Mehdi Ben Barqa, a Moroccan political revolutionary whom King Hassan II earlier had exiled to France, was abducted from his Paris apartment and presumably murdered (his body was never found). A formal inquiry and trial in France suggested that the crime had been instigated by General Muhammad Oufqir, the Moroccan minister of the interior, and that a number of rogue French police and intelligence officials had been involved. And so, too, apparently, had the Israeli Mossad, whose agents may actually have perpetrated the kidnapping as a favor to both their Moroccan and their French political contacts. Outraged at this violation of national sovereignty, the Gaullist government issued an international warrant for General Oufqir's arrest, and in January 1966 severed diplomatic relations with Morocco. At the same time, following a thorough survey of military-intelligence relations between France and Israel, de Gaulle ordered a reduction of these contacts to a minimum.

Meanwhile, France also was moving vigorously to repair its ties with the Arab world. Diplomatic relations with Arab capitals, severed following the 1956 Suez episode, were gradually being restored: with Syria, Jordan, and Saudi Arabia in 1962; with Iraq in 1963; and finally with Egypt itself in 1965. Mutual visits of French and Arab ministers became more frequent. Would de Gaulle accept the 1963 evaluation of his Middle East adviser, Jean Chauvelle, that French-Israeli relations "do not in any way serve the credit of France in the Arab world"? Not officially. As late as July 1965 Alain Peyrefitte, France's minister of information, could assure a contingent of visiting Israeli journalists that "the good relations that we are developing with both [the Arabs and Israel] will permit the maintenance of peace in the Middle East." In March 1966, queried on the upsurge of French arms sales to Egypt and Syria, Defense Minister Messmer insisted that "the increase of our influence [among all parties] in the Middle East augments the chances for peace."

Yet, in practical fact, the Franco-Israeli relationship of the mid-1960s had devolved into its original, essentially mercantile configuration of the early and mid-1950s, with French manufacturers reaping handsome profits from their sale of military and nuclear hardware to Israel. The 1956–57 honeymoon was over. Moshe Dayan acknowledged the fact with characteristic bluntness in a press interview of 1965: "Israel's position today . . . is determined by various international organizations, such as [NATO] and the Common Market, and not by the Suez-Sinai alliance, which now is seen as no more than a passing episode."

BONN RENEWS A FINANCIAL TRANSFUSION

During the same decade, from the mid-1950s to the mid-1960s, it was the Bundesrepublik that continued to ease the heaviest of Israel's economic burdens. Together with its indemnity payments to victims of Nazi persecution living in the Jewish state, Bonn's reparation installments to Israel continued year in and year out, on or ahead of schedule. By the late 1950s criticism of German "blood money" had all but disappeared from the Israeli political arena and the public media. Nor was the indispensable role of the annual transfers the only factor softening distrust of the Germans. During the Sinai-Suez crisis, Bonn sharply rebuffed Washington's appeal to suspend these payments. Morality aside, explained Foreign Minister Fritz Schäffer, the Bundesrepublik did not belong to the United Nations and consequently was under no obligation to help enact its punitive resolutions. Adenauer went rather further. Invoking the unique legal and moral obligations of the Luxembourg Treaty (p. 52), he reminded the Bundestag that "Israel's armed intervention against Egypt was a natural reaction to a real danger." The chancellor's stance was heartily supported by every West German political party. In Israel editorial reaction to this display of German commitment was one of gratification.

With the Sinai Campaign representing yet another litmus test of Bonn's evident sincerity of purpose, it became somewhat easier for Israel to offer hospitality to a growing stream of German public figures. These included Bundestag members, trade union leaders, academicians, mayors, and delegations from the Länder parliaments. In May 1960 the Bundesrepublik's first president, the now retired Theodor Heuss, arrived in Israel to deliver a lecture at the Hebrew University. Two years later Eugen Gerstenmaier, president of the Bundestag, also delivered a guest lecture at the university. Both men were received with rare grace and honor; Gerstenmaier was a house guest of Ben-Gurion's. As recently as 1954, two years before the Sinai-Suez War, Franz Böhm, who played the leading role in the Wassenaar negotiations, had been obliged to arrive incognito for his secret tour through the country. But in 1963, on the tenth anniversary of the Treaty of Luxembourg, Böhm returned for a public reception in which great tribute was paid him.

Ben-Gurion, who lost no opportunity to proclaim that "the Germany of today is not the Germany of Adolf Hitler," had never been indiscriminate in dispensing compliments. As pragmatic in his diplomacy as Adenauer, the prime minister remained acutely sensitive to the importance of German economic help. By 1958, too, it was becoming apparent that reparations alone would not cover the bill for the substantial merchant fleet Israel had ordered from West German shipyards. None of these vessels was expendable. After its Sinai victory Israel required millions of tons of shipping to exploit its new opportunities of maritime passage through the Strait of Tiran. Industrial development of the Negev now also became crucial, once the Sinai War opened the desert's southern, Eilat outlet. Late in 1958, to be sure, Finance Minister Eshkol managed to secure a DM1.5 billion ($450 million) loan from Germany's Deutsche Bank. It would be repaid in the final two installments of Bonn's reparations schedule. But with only seven and a half years left on that schedule, a longer-term arrangement plainly had to be negotiated with the Bundesrepublik.

As Ben-Gurion saw it, only a face-to-face meeting with Adenauer himself could establish the appropriate *Stimmung* for negotiations. And, for his part, the German chancellor was receptive. His nation's painfully restored reputation as a liberal democracy lately had come under renewed scrutiny. In the spring of 1959 a series of swastika daubings had appeared on a Cologne synagogue and on Jewish graves in several German cemeteries. The episodes were extensively reported in the United States, and Adenauer feared that his official visit to Washington, scheduled for March 1960, might be compromised by a revival of Germany's racist image. Accordingly, a formula was devised for Ben-Gurion and Adenauer to meet during that same March on "neutral" American territory. Brandeis University would invite the prime minister to receive an honorary doctorate. Afterward Ben-Gurion would travel to New York, where he would confer with Adenauer at the latter's suite in the Waldorf-Astoria Hotel.

In fact, a general understanding already had been reached between Finance Minister Eshkol and Hermann Abs, chairman of Germany's Bank for Reconstruction. The Israelis would seek a long-term, low-interest loan of $250 million, and the Germans in principle would regard such a loan as feasible. Only hours before the March 14 meeting, however, Ben-Gurion's advisers had prevailed on him to double his request, to ask for $500 million, at least as a negotiating figure. Thus, on meeting at the Waldorf-Astoria, and after a cordial exchange of amenities, the prime minister explained to Adenauer that the Negev Desert, if properly developed, would serve as the key to Israel's most important potential markets in Africa and Asia. Without that development, he added meaningfully, Israel would be hard-pressed to make up the sheer economic loss the Holocaust had inflicted on its potential manpower resources. Would not the German people derive great "moral" satisfaction in providing Israel with the resources for this crucial undertaking? Ben-Gurion then capped his exposition with the request for the $500 million loan, to be repaid over a ten-to-twenty-year period.

Adenauer's response was an immediate "We will help you." There would be no haggling. The chancellor gave his commitment for the entire amount, on the spot, with only the details remaining to be negotiated. The two statesmen then engaged in a brief tour d'horizon of the world scene. An hour and a half later, on taking his leave of Adenauer, Ben-Gurion once again repeated to the crowd of newsmen waiting in the hotel corridor that "the Germany of today is not the Germany of yesterday." Widely publicized, the prime minister's encomium could not have come at a more opportune moment for Adenauer. To his aides the chancellor acknowledged of Ben-Gurion: "A great man. We had a most rewarding talk." In a later message to the Israeli prime minister, Adenauer repeated his assurance that "I will do my best to obtain German financial assistance for Israeli development projects." In his own reply of August 5, Ben-Gurion reiterated his wish "to establish pioneering enterprises here in Israel which—when German young people see or hear about them—will give them moral satisfaction by showing that Adenauer did as much as could be done to atone for the sins of Hitlerite Germany."

In ensuing discussions, carried out in Brussels between Levi Eshkol and the Bundesrepublik's minister of economics, Ludwig Erhard, the terms of the financial package were carefully explored and refined. Under West Germany's constitution, a loan in the magnitude of $500 million would require Bundestag approval. But therein lay a complication. The ensuing parliamentary debate would immediately alert the Arab governments. Both sides then agreed that the commitment would have to remain secret and informal, in the nature of a "gentleman's agreement." Yet, an additional twenty-one months of complex discussions were needed before the terms of the "gentleman's agreement" were completed. Beginning in January 1966, when the last of the reparations would expire, payment of the $500 million package would take the form of annual installments at low interest rates, each payment not to exceed $37,500,000, the maximum allowed within the chancellor's executive discretion. The funds would be earmarked for specific projects to be proposed year by year, and would be evaluated by Bonn on an ad hoc basis. Israel in turn agreed to make every effort to ensure that the envisaged goods and services would be supplied by German firms. Finally, Israel would be vouchsafed a twenty-five-year period of repayment, and that to begin only after an initial seven-year moratorium.

The arrangement worked well. With few exceptions Bonn accepted Israel's suggested projects. These dealt principally with construction of urban centers in the Negev, including the port of Eilat. The agreement also confirmed Ben-Gurion's deeply held conviction that Germany, even more than France, remained Israel's likeliest European source of economic development.

EICHMANN FORCES A REAPPRAISAL

The prime minister's letter to Adenauer of August 5, 1960, outlining his loan proposal, contained a significant prefatory comment: "I do not know whether the German youth of today are aware of what was done by Nazi Germany, but I have not the slightest doubt that some day [they] will know the terrible truth, and every young German will feel sorrow and shame." Ben-Gurion by then was keenly aware of the information likeliest to mobilize that "sorrow and shame." Three months earlier, on May 23, he had revealed it before the Knesset:

> I have to inform the Knesset that a short while ago the Israeli Security Services captured one of the greatest Nazi war criminals, Adolf Eichmann, who together with the Nazi leaders was responsible for . . . the destruction of six million European Jews. Eichmann is already in detention in Israel and will soon be put on trial here under the Nazi and Nazi Collaborators Punishment Law, 1950.

After the postwar Nuremberg trials and sentences, only a few of the most notorious mass murderers remained unaccounted for. One of these was the Austrian-born Adolf Eichmann, the SS officer who had directed the Jewish section of Nazi Germany's Reich Main Security Office, and in that capacity had presided over a major phase of the "Final Solution." Hiding on a remote German farm during the next four years, Eichmann had secured the help of ODESSA, the Organisation der SS ehemaligen Angehörigen—Association of Former SS Members—which smuggled him out of Austria to Italy, and eventually from Italy to Argentina in July 1950. Bearing the name "Ricardo Klement," he secured modest employment in Buenos Aires. Two years later Eichmann felt secure enough to send for his family. The children, who had been small when their father left them in 1945 and who had been informed that he was dead, were told that he was "Uncle Ricardo." Subsequently Eichmann "married" their mother, and she became "Mrs. Klement."

In ensuing years, working in a Buenos Aires branch factory of

Daimler-Benz, Eichmann became increasingly confident that the search for him was over. He was not entirely wrong. The official pursuit was indeed ended once the West began courting the Bundesrepublik. Even for Israel the quest no longer was a priority during the Jewish state's early years of military and economic struggle. In the late 1950s, however, the Mossad—Israel's overseas intelligence branch— resumed its search for ex-Nazis. For Isser Harel, who had moved from the Shin Bet to become director of the Mossad, information on Eichmann's whereabouts had always remained a matter of urgency. And at last, in 1960, Harel was alerted to an Austrian newspaper obituary announcing the death of Eichmann's father on February 5 of that year. One of the signatories was "Vera Eichmann, née Liebl." The announcement proved that her reported "second marriage" in Argentina was a fake. She still called herself Eichmann.

Soon afterward, in Germany, Dr. Fritz Bauer, attorney general of Hesse, himself a Jew, was informed by his own sources that Eichmann actually was living in Buenos Aires under the name of Ricardo Klement. Bauer transmitted the report to Isser Harel. Within the week Harel dispatched one of the Mossad's ablest investigative teams to Argentina. It swiftly located the Klement family house and managed also to snap a long-range telephoto of Klement himself. It was sent back to Israel and compared with an old wartime photograph of Eichmann. Experts tentatively reconciled the pictures. In early March 1960, four additional Mossad agents arrived in Buenos Aires. They maintained a close watch on Klement, and after several weeks their vigil was rewarded. Klement returned home with a bouquet of flowers. It was a day of no meaning if he were the second husband of his wife. But the day commemorated the original anniversary, March 21, 1935, of the Eichmanns' marriage in Austria.

At Ben-Gurion's orders, and under the personal direction of Isser Harel, who now flew to Buenos Aires, plans were laid to kidnap Eichmann—it was surely he—and bring him to Israel. The Argentine government was unlikely to be interested in arresting and prosecuting the man; it had taken no action against other former Nazis on its territory. Instead, at Harel's request, an El Al airliner was chartered for a flight to Buenos Aires in mid-May, ostensibly to bring Abba Eban on a goodwill visit. During the unsuspecting Eban's stay, the plane would be available for an unscheduled return trip to Israel. Thus, in the late afternoon of May 11, the Israelis waited near their quarry's bus stop. As he disembarked at his customary time, they seized him and hustled him into an automobile, then carried him away to a "safe house." Under questioning, Eichmann confessed his identity. Fearful of being liquidated on the spot, he also signed a previously prepared declaration of "consent" to proceed to Israel for trial. On the evening of May 14, the Israelis drugged him, drove him to the airport, and stretcher-carried him onto the awaiting El Al plane as an "ill traveler." The plane departed immediately for Israel. At Lod Airport, Eichmann was disembarked at a far corner of the runway and sped off to prison. On May 23, Ben-Gurion notified the cabinet and the Knesset.

From the rest of the world, reactions to the electrifying news began coming in at once. The first was from the Argentine government, which transmitted its shocked protest to Jerusalem and demanded the prisoner's immediate return. In response, Ben-Gurion appealed directly to Argentina's President Arturo Frondizi for understanding, but to no avail. The Argentine UN delegate requested a meeting of the Security Council, and the debate on the Eichmann abduction began in late June 1960. Palpably sympathizing with Israel, the American, British, and French representatives sought to devise a formula under which Israel's apology to Argentina might be accepted as appropriate reparation. Eventually they succeeded. In a joint communiqué of August 3, 1960, both governments agreed to regard as closed "the episode that arose out of the action taken by Israeli nationals that infringed fundamental rights of the State of Argentina."

Censure of Israel's abduction and its claims to jurisdiction over Eichmann were not limited to Argentina. Jurists of international standing in many different countries fell out over the issue. Yet their misgivings by and large did not reflect official policy. Except for Argentina, no other country, neither West nor East Germany, neither the Soviet Union nor other European nations that had been the victims of Eichmann's wartime activities, officially demanded the prisoner's extradition. In a Bonn radio interview, Adenauer commented tersely: "Eichmann is no German citizen and we have no obligation toward Eichmann." Theodor Heuss, the former German president, who was visiting Israel at the time Eichmann's capture was announced, instinctively voiced the line that the Bundesrepublik would adopt officially: "[Eichmann] did enormous evil and caused untold suffering all over Europe. . . . I have every confidence that the Government of Israel will handle the Eichmann case correctly and justly." Willy Brandt, West Berlin's Social Democratic mayor, added: "Criminals must be brought to justice, and Eichmann is a criminal."

Indeed, the Bundesrepublik proved entirely cooperative in Israel's efforts to prepare its case against the prisoner, supplying literally thousands of documents on Eichmann's role in the Final Solution. As the trial date approached, in the spring of 1961, Israel permitted

Eichmann to select his counsel from any nation of his preference. At his half-brother's suggestion, he chose Robert Servatius, a West German attorney, unblemished by Nazi associations, with extensive experience in defending war criminals. Israel agreed to pay Servatius's thirty-thousand-dollar fee, and allowed him to bring assistant counsel with him.

The trial began on April 1, 1961, in a remodeled Jerusalem community center. Hundreds of police ringed the building. Those admitted to the makeshift courtroom included over six hundred foreign correspondents, whose presence attested to the vast international interest evoked by the unprecedented spectacle of a leading Nazi criminal on trial in a Jewish nation. The three judges of the special session were all members of Israel's supreme court. Two had themselves been born and educated in Germany. The prosecutor, Gideon Hausner, Israel's attorney general, although Polish-born, also was fluent in German. The principal charges against Eichmann fell under the category of "Crimes against the Jewish People." The prisoner was accused of causing the death of millions of Jews in his role as a leading administrator of the Final Solution, of responsibility for the annihilation of Jews at the hands of SS killer teams in the Soviet Union, and in concentration, labor, and death camps throughout Europe. Defense attorney Servatius then offered three demurrers: The judges should be disqualified by reason of their preconceived opinions; Israel possessed no jurisdiction over Eichmann, inasmuch as he had been abducted from Argentina; Israel's Nazi and Nazi Collaborators' Crimes Law had been enacted post factum, years after the Holocaust.

The judges gave short shrift to these objections. They were obliged to be fair but hardly neutral; otherwise no decent citizen would ever be able to try a criminal. As for Eichmann's abduction, the manner in which a defendant was brought within a state's jurisdiction was irrelevant to the state's competence to try him. The post factum defense was similarly rejected. Murder (let alone mass murder) had been a crime since the dawn of civilization—as the Nuremberg Court had recognized in 1945–46. The atrocities had been perpetrated before Israel's birth, to be sure; but all the Great Powers had since recognized Israel not only as the legal successor to the British mandate but as the successor to murdered Jewry.

Attorney General Hausner's initial oration, on April 17, was high drama at last. It continued for eight hours and three sessions, tracing the course of Nazi antisemitism and wartime massacres throughout Europe, and Eichmann's role in the killings. Subsequently Eichmann's entire statement, recorded in prison, six volumes of it, was offered in evidence. The prosecution also submitted vast quantities of its own documentation, then presented scores of Jewish (and occasional non-Jewish) witnesses to testify on their own ordeal and that of other Jews during the Holocaust. In his defense, Eichmann and his lawyers continued endlessly to minimize his own role. While Attorney General Hausner, in turn, did not contradict the wide diffusion of Nazi guilt, he would not allow Eichmann to fade away in the process. He kept the prisoner under cross-examination for two weeks, and in that time Eichmann's image as a "victim of orders" was demolished.

On August 14, 1961, after 114 sessions, the proceedings ended. The court then adjourned for four months and reassembled on December 11 to pronounce judgment. Eichmann was convicted on fifteen counts of the indictment. "Together with others," he had committed crimes against the Jewish people: by "causing the killing of millions of Jews under conditions . . . likely to lead to their physical destruction"; by causing [them] serious bodily and mental harm"; and by "directing that births be banned and pregnancies interrupted among Jewish women" in Theresienstadt concentration camp. On December 15 Eichmann was sentenced to death. Defense attorney Servatius immediately appealed the verdict, and the case reached the supreme court in March of 1962. This time the hearings were completed in six sessions. On May 29 the judges sustained the lower-court verdict. Eichmann's appeal for mercy to the president of the state was refused. He was hanged at midnight on May 31, 1962.

On several occasions during the course of the trial, Adenauer in Bonn had rather poignantly addressed his people and the world, insisting that contemporary Germany in no sense had been involved in Nazi crimes. But the chancellor also addressed the Israeli leadership directly. While expressing confidence in their fairness, he reminded them of his efforts to make amends, and then added: "Goodwill must be mutual." Ben-Gurion was listening. He knew what was expected of him, all the more at a time when his government was in the process of negotiating the new German loan. Thus, in an interview with a German reporter on August 7, 1961, the prime minister duly reiterated his conviction: "My views about present-day Germany have not changed. There is no longer a Nazi Germany. On the Israeli side, there is readiness for close and normal relations and full cooperation." Moreover, to ensure that nothing should subvert the new rapprochement, Ben-Gurion intervened personally to dissuade Attorney General Hausner from summoning a number of important German public figures as witnesses. One of these was Hans

Glöbke, a former state secretary in the Chancellor's Office, who earlier had been forced to resign upon revelation of his association with the Nazi government. Years later Franz-Josef Strauss, who served as minister of defense in the Adenauer government, acknowledged that there also had been a link between this Israeli concession and the delivery of certain German weapons to Israel (pp. 138–41).

For its choice as "official observer" at the trial, meanwhile, the German foreign ministry had selected Baron Gerhard von Preuschen, an experienced lawyer-diplomat and a distinguished liberal. Preuschen brought with him a large contingent of officials and technical staff from the Bundesrepublik's foreign, press, and information ministries—evidence of Bonn's concern that the German past would be churned up again. Sharing that fear were a number of "authentic" former Nazis. Aware that Eichmann was privy to a trove of information on war criminals still in hiding abroad or underground in Germany itself, these elements were intent on silencing him. Anonymous letters addressed to Eichmann (invariably intercepted by the Israeli authorities) suggested that he should commit suicide. Some letters contained razor blades. And on several occasions ex-Nazis, bearing professional credentials as "textile engineer" or "chartered accountant," managed actually to win entrance to Israel and even to the trial, where they glared balefully at the prisoner in the dock. Israel's Shin Bet (internal security service) soon uncovered their true identities. Retribution was surgical. Cryptic references periodically appeared in the Israeli press to German textile engineers or chartered accountants killed in "road accidents." Neither Bonn nor Jerusalem saw a need for additional comment.

At the same time the scores of German journalists, representing every major newspaper in the Bundesrepublik, found private Israelis at first coolly interested in their presence, but not necessarily hostile. The experience moved them. And so, even more, did the trial's extensive chronicle of the Final Solution. Newspaper readers and television watchers in the Bundesrepublik reacted no less emotionally. In earlier years, a majority of Germans had avoided coming to grips with the sheer enormity of the Holocaust. They had been preoccupied, rather, with the magnitude of Germany's defeat, destruction, and subsequent reconstruction. But now, in late August 1961, a German opinion poll disclosed that 26 percent of its respondents had read every single one of the daily dispatches written about the trial. Indeed, no other event since the end of the war had so riveted public attention in West Germany. Almost without exception, German readers and viewers had been impressed by the trial's dignity and fairness. The Israeli judges had scrupulously avoided polemics of any kind, and assuredly any reference to the German people of the postwar period. Thus, when Eichmann's death sentence was pronounced, in December 1961, few in Germany expressed reservations. Virtually every public figure, every political leader, every major newspaper editorial, expressed satisfaction with both the verdict and the sentence. Throughout the Bundesrepublik, the refrain was identical: "Justice has been done."

Yet, even as the German public at large followed every detail of the unfolding trial, young people began asking embarrassing questions, and a public debate soon opened on the extent to which their parents had been "aware" of Nazi crimes. A flood of letters to German newspapers turned repeatedly to the question: How many Eichmanns are still hiding among us? How much did the German people know? How many millions of Germans were aware of the Nazi atrocities but passively acquiesced in them? As Munich's *Deutsche Woche* editorialized on May 31, 1961:

> Nobody knew? In Jerusalem this [fiction] has been blown away like a straw in the wind. . . . All the officialdom of the ministries knew. . . . [The] widely disseminated thesis is that the army was not implicated. Now it is proved that [the army] set the pace of the extermination. . . . Another official version . . . was that only a few hand-picked SS men did the job. It is now clearly established that every single link in the long chain of administration not only knew but had its assigned share in the criminal acts. . . . Methodically the Jerusalem trial examines the events of the last thirty years. . . . The emerging facts are not confined to a new assessment of the past, but penetrate deeply into our present.

The impact of the Bundesrepublik's media coverage transcended self-examination and belated self-accusation. Through prolonged exposure to the trial, the German population in effect "discovered" Israel. The Jewish state henceforth could be regarded not simply as a refuge for persecuted Jews but as a country like any other, a republic that had developed its own structure, institutions, and characteristics. By the early 1960s it became the fashion in Germany to admire Israel, to be fascinated by its achievements, to praise a nation that had undergone so many rigors and vicissitudes, but that still could function as a "normal" state. German newspapers now began urging citizens to travel to Israel. In fact, the suggestion hardly was needed. The trickle of visits by German political eminences soon was transcended by a stream of private German tourists. In 1962, the German share of Israel's tourist trade comprised barely 3.6 percent. In 1963 it rose to 5 percent; in 1964, to 9 percent. In absolute num͏ure by then reached thirteen thousand.

An early element among the visitors was you͏any of whom were followers of Aktion Sühnezeichen—͏enance. The movement was founded in the wake of the͏trial by a group of German pastors, who demanded that͏ be "accepted" by all German youth. Led by writers, ͏d other intellectuals, together with its original nucleus of͏, Aktion Sühnezeichen encouraged acts of contrition ran͏ unpaid labor for Jewish institutions in the Bundesrepublik͏r social-service institutions in Israel itself. In response to t͏ German youths almost immediately began arriving in gro͏eral hundreds during the spring and summer months to ͏raeli kibbutzim and in senior citizens' and orphan hon͏ted with reserve at first, the volunteers gradually encounter͏ openness among their Israeli counterparts. By 1963 and 19͏ was evidence at long last of a genuine warming of human͏ on among German and Israeli young people alike. The augu͏the future appeared cautiously hopeful.

TRAUMA
F DIPLOMATIC
ECONCILIATION

R CRIMES AND GERMAN MERCENARIES

ormalization of German-Israeli relations might have nued uninterruptedly but for the persistence of a haunt-gacy, and its exacerbation by *Realpolitik*. Throughout the 19 Bundesrepublik appeared diligently to be prosecuting its bac suspected Nazi war criminals. To that end, in 1958, justice m of Germany's individual Länder organized the Central Office Pursuit of Nazi Crimes Committed Outside Germany. Establi Ludwigsburg, and directed by a highly respected jurist, Dr. Er üle, the Central Office coordinated all accumulated evidenc ate prosecution. Yet, by 1964, even after the Eichmann trial, the 's tolerance for these proceedings had begun to wane, and judg tended lately to impose reduced or even nominal sentences or icted defendants. The issue of war crimes in any case presumab uld soon become moot. The twenty-year statute of limitation murder prosecutions was due to expire in May of the following the anniversary of Nazi Germany's surrender.

By the nn of 1964, however, it became evident that the Bundesrepubli d failed to take into account the reaction of other nations, th whose citizens had endured the worst torments of Nazi rule. Amor hese protests, Israel's were the most vehement. On numerous c sions Jerusalem had appealed privately to Bonn for cancellation the statute of limitations on Nazi crimes. The response inv ably took the form of a legalistic disclaimer. To function as a vi democracy, it explained, the Bundesrepublik was obliged to r ect international norms of criminal jurisprudence. Finally, in O ober 1964, Prime Minister Eshkol went public in his demand that e German authorities reconsider their position, and the Knesset p ed a resolution endorsing his appeal.

By then the accumulation of these protests had evoked considerable international attention. Given pause, Chancellor Ludwig Erhard somewhat hesitantly began entertaining various proposals for extending the statute of limitations (Adenauer, then in retirement, preferred a flat abolition). But with a national election imminent, no German political party was willing to test public forbearance on the issue, and in November 1964 Erhard announced that the statute of limitations would stand. By the following May, he added, 99 percent of all Nazi criminals would have been either tried or remanded for prosecution.

The Israelis did not accept that figure. Neither did associations of veterans and former refugees in Western and Eastern Europe. These now began flooding Bonn with new material on Nazi criminals who thus far had escaped prosecution. In February 1965, moreover, the Social Democrats joined with recalcitrant elements of Erhard's own Christian Democratic Union to force a Bundestag debate on the question. Soon a government consensus developed. On March 25, the Bundestag voted to extend the statute of limitations another four years, to September 1969. The cutoff date signified the twentieth anniversary of the Bundestag's establishment. Although the compromise was a disappointment to Israel, it defused at least one of the residual sources of German-Israeli tension.

By then a much graver crisis had burgeoned to imperil normalization of relations between the two governments. For nearly two years this one would be regarded as a matter of Israel's fundamental security. In February 1963 a man describing himself as an Austrian business executive visited the office of Heidi Görke, a young lawyer in Freiberg, Germany. The visitor, Otto Joklik, informed Fräulein Görke that her father, Professor Paul Görke, a physicist then employed in Egypt, was at work on a project to develop ballistic rockets. Their intended target was the State of Israel. Unless she dissuaded her father from continuing this activity, warned Joklik, serious consequences might befall him—and his family. Several days later Joklik telephoned the young woman again. Repeating his threat, he instructed her to meet him on March 2 at a hotel in nearby Basel, Switzerland. Fräulein Görke then contacted the local Freiberg police. Upon hearing her story, they immediately alerted Swiss federal police headquarters in Bern. At the latter's suggestion, Fräulein Görke kept the rendezvous in Basel. Joklik appeared on schedule, accompanied by an Israeli, Yosef Ben-Gal. Repeating his original threat, Joklik then launched into a detailed account of Professor Görke's activities in a nation, Egypt, that had long been committed to Israel's destruction.

The role of German citizens in Egypt's military services actually was far from new. It had begun in the immediate postwar years, when numerous ex-Wehrmacht officers had fled to Arab countries, principally to Egypt, where they found employment as army instructors. By 1951 Egypt's German "colony" achieved a new dimension when General Wilhelm Fahrmbacher, an artillery specialist, arrived in Cairo with some forty additional Wehrmacht veterans. These too were appointed to different branches of the Egyptian army. They proved so useful that, upon King Farouk's abdication in July 1952, the revolutionary government offered them promotions and even broader responsibilities. Soon they were joined by several dozen German technicians, including fifteen jet-aircraft specialists who were immediately appointed to replace the British technicians then working in Egypt's de Havilland assembly plants. In ensuing years other arriving Germans joined Egypt's army research centers and ordnance factories, and the ballistics section of the Helwan munitions works.

For Egypt's President Nasser, intent on expanding his nation's military-industrial base, it was the manufacture of jet aircraft that soon became a priority. Although the Soviets after 1955 had supplied their own equipment in massive quantities, Egypt's payments obligations in bartered cotton were hardly trivial. It was in 1955, therefore, that Marshal Abd al-Hakim Amer, Egypt's armed forces commander, summoned to his office General Mahmoud Khalil, a senior intelligence officer. Nasser had decided to create a new section of the armed forces, Amer explained, "the Bureau of Special Military Programs," for the local manufacture of jet fighters and advanced rocketry. Under Amer's personal direction, the bureau would be allocated an unlimited budget. Khalil's task was to recruit skilled scientists and technicians. Germans were regarded as the best available. Although some of them were known to be working in other countries, most still remained in Germany; and in the Bundesrepublik the manufacture of military aircraft or rockets was prohibited. These "redundant" experts consequently might be eager to sell their talents to Egypt.

On General Khalil's instructions, "help wanted" announcements subsequently began appearing in German newspapers and technical journals. One of the first replies came from Ferdinand Brandner, a renowned aero-engine specialist who had failed lately to secure meaningful employment in Germany. Without delay Khalil signed Brandner up, assigning him the task of recruiting other former colleagues. Eventually Brandner assembled some two hundred. Under his direction the German newcomers set about building a jet-engine factory in Heliopolis, a suburb of Cairo. Equipment would be needed.

Hassan Kamil, a wealthy Egyptian businessman living in Switzerland, was enlisted as the program's key purchasing agent. Kamil in turn organized two "front" companies in Switzerland, MECO (Mechanical Corporation) and MTP (Motors, Turbines, and Pumps), to acquire the needed supplies and recruit specialists for assembling them. Kamil and Brandner themselves directed these companies. MECO's subsidiary in Egypt was directed by Nazi Germany's most famous aircraft designer, Willy Messerschmitt. Recruited personally by Brandner, Messerschmitt sensed an opportunity to complete a project he had earlier sought—and failed—to launch in Spain. It was a high-powered fighter, to be known as the He-300.

By 1960 a substantial community of skilled and experienced German military-scientific veterans was hard at work developing a new range of weaponry for Israel's most formidable enemy. They were well paid and comfortably housed. Indeed, an entire floor of the luxurious Shepheard's Hotel was continually reserved for Messerschmitt. Despite the heavy cost to the Egyptian treasury, Nasser's regime anticipated good value for its money. In fact, the He-300 eventually would prove to be an underperformer that did not so much as reach serial production. Yet its prototype model at least participated in the great military parade of July 23, 1961, during the anniversary celebration of the 1952 Colonels' Revolution. It was this event that first alerted the Israeli public to a frightening new dimension of the German role in the Middle East.

THE "UGLY GERMAN" REDUX

Egyptian military ambitions soared well beyond the production of "conventional" weaponry. In the spring of 1952, several months before the overthrow of King Farouk, Dr. Wilhelm Voss arrived in Cairo. Voss had held important wartime executive positions in Germany's Hermann Göring munitions works and in Czechoslovakia's Skoda armaments works. In Egypt, after the Colonels' Revolution, the new government engaged him to direct the manufacture of small-caliber tactical rockets. Voss in turn began recruiting rocket specialists among his former contacts. One of these was Rolf Engel, who assumed direction of CERVA, an Egyptian firm organized specifically for rocket manufacture. Another was Professor Paul Görke (Heidi Görke's father), an electronics-guidance expert who had worked for the Nazi V-2 rocket program at Peenemünde, and who currently was employed in France's *Véronique* rocket project. Görke too now agreed to join Voss's team.

Yet in those early years of the Nasser regime, Egypt's rocket effort made only halting progress. Voss, Görke, and several of their associates eventually returned to Europe, and by 1955 Nasser and Marshal Amer evidently had abandoned the notion of equipping their army with tactical rocketry. CERVA itself was disbanded. Israel's military intelligence experts, monitoring these Egyptian developments, began to breathe more easily. Yet, in the ensuing two years, Marshal Amer and General Khalil rethought and revived the rocket program, this time placing emphasis on longer-range, strategic missiles; and in 1961 Görke was persuaded to return to Egypt, to share in the enlarged ballistics venture. The catalyst for this sudden shift was Israel itself. In July 1961 scientists in the Israeli defense ministry launched the Shavit II, a solid-fuel rocket that soared to a height of sixty miles. Proclaimed an "experimental rocket" for "meteorological research," the device plainly was intended for noncivilian purposes, and the announcement of its subsequent launch was intended as a less than oblique warning to the Arabs. Its more enduring consequence, however, was to revive Egypt's own rocket program.

The man initially recruited to help direct the Nasser government's new ballistics endeavor was Dr. Eugen Sänger, then by far the most eminent of Germany's rocket authorities. He too had served in a senior capacity during the wartime Peenemünde project. After Germany's surrender, in common with numerous other German military scientists, Sänger had fled the country, and, like Görke, had joined the *Véronique* project. Returning to Germany in 1954, Sänger then was engaged by the Stuttgart Research Institute, an enterprise funded by a combination of major German industrial firms, technical colleges, and the state government of Baden-Württemberg, and committed to the development of civilian aircraft and meteorological rockets. But these were limited tasks, for the Allies had barred the Bundesrepublik from engaging in military research. In 1960 Sänger accepted a part-time assignment to establish Nasser's ambitious new rocket program. When the West German government nervously queried him on the nature of his work in Egypt, Sänger's response invariably was "meteorological research." Soon, however, the Israeli government drew Bonn's attention to the real purpose of the Egyptian rocket program, and Bonn in turn warned Sänger that he was risking future government support for the Stuttgart Research Institute. In late 1961 he decided finally to return home.

Yet Sänger's closest associate remained on in Cairo to direct "Factory 333," the Egyptian ballistics enterprise. This was Professor Wolfgang Pilz, another veteran of Peenemünde and the *Véronique* project. The work continued without interruption. Pilz had Görke available to him, after all, as well as Dr. Hans Kleinwächter, still another rocket authority, and Dr. Heinz Krug, also a veteran of Peenemünde and the postwar Stuttgart Research Institute. Krug in fact remained in Germany as manager of the "Intra Trading Company." Operating at first in Stuttgart, then in Munich, where it was lodged in the same Schillerstrasse suite of offices as Egypt's national airline, Intra served as the rocket enterprise's purchasing agent in Germany.

From the late 1950s, Israeli military intelligence was well informed about these scientists and their work. With the help of an espionage agent, Wolfgang Lutz, whom they had planted in Egypt, the Israelis even managed to compile a detailed map of the secret military and rocket factories in the Cairo suburb of Helwan. By July 1962, they had also discovered that Factory 333 was proceeding to the development of strategic rockets, and on the twenty-first of that month had successfully test-launched four of them. Within days these missiles were put on public display in Cairo. It was July 23, the anniversary of King Farouk's abdication, and amid the glittering parade of military hardware were twenty flag-draped rockets of two classes that Nasser proudly titled *al-Zafir* (the Victor) and *al-Kahir* (the Conqueror). The former was declared to have a range of 175 miles; the latter, 350. Nasser boasted openly now that *al-Kahir* could reach "any target south of Beirut." Tel Aviv of course was the likeliest of those targets.

The shock to the Israeli people was grave. Pressed by Isser Harel, by then chief of Israel's combined security-intelligence board, Foreign Minister Golda Meir now began querying Bonn on the extensive participation of German scientists in this ominous rocket program. The official response was a mixture of embarrassment and reassurance. The constitution forbade interference with the freedom of movement of any of the Bundesrepublik's citizens, it explained; no legal restraints could be imposed on Germans who chose to work in foreign countries. In any case, Bonn noted, Krug, Pilz, Görke, and their associates had not been privy to the latest Great-Power developments in military rocketry, and they presented no danger to Israel. But Isser Harel was not reassured. His own sources rated the Germans as highly competent, and thus Bonn could not be allowed to escape its moral obligations to terminate their activity. He pressed the argument on Ben-Gurion himself.

The prime minister was reluctant to create a diplomatic crisis with the Bundesrepublik. Well aware of Israel's extensive dependence upon German financial and diplomatic support—even upon its military support (p. 141)—he asked Shimon Peres to intercede quietly with Defense Minister Franz-Josef Strauss, a trusted friend. Peres's query to Strauss was eloquent: Could the Bundesrepublik really allow its citizens to share in a venture so potentially lethal to Israel, and at a time when it was embarking on a new era in its relations with the Jewish people? The aftermath of the Eichmann trial, after all, hardly was a propitious moment for the Bundesrepublik to reopen old wounds. With equal discretion, Strauss expressed his fullest understanding of Israel's concern, but adverted again to his government's inability to restrict individuals' freedom of movement. Another trusted German friend, Professor Franz Böhm, visiting Israel on the tenth anniversary of the Treaty of Luxembourg, made the same point to Foreign Minister Golda Meir.

Like Isser Harel, Mrs. Meir had never shared Ben-Gurion's faith in German "repentance." In an abrasive midsummer confrontation with the prime minister, she urged that Harel be permitted to adopt his "own" methods of dealing with German scientists in Egypt. Despite grave misgivings, Ben-Gurion finally agreed. Harel for his part needed little encouragement to handle matters in his "own" way. Lithuanian-born, he had lost most of his family in the Holocaust. In 1958 he had become director of the Mossad, and subsequently chairman of Israel's Security Board, embracing its military, internal, and overseas intelligence services. It was Harel who had personally supervised the abduction of Adolf Eichmann, and who directed numerous overseas "terminations" of Arab spymasters. He was quite prepared now to use the same clandestine techniques in dealing with the hated Germans.

Thus, in late July 1962, Hassan Kamil, the Swiss-Egyptian director of MECO and MTP, engaged a private jet to carry him from his vacation retreat in Schleswig-Holstein to Düsseldorf. At the last minute, however, Kamil was obliged to remain behind, and his wife flew off without him. En route the plane mysteriously crashed, killing her. The following September, Heinz Krug departed his Intra office in Munich with a dark-skinned stranger. Two days later police recovered Krug's abandoned automobile, but he himself was never found. In Cairo two months later, Wolfgang Pilz's secretary, a German woman, opened a parcel addressed to her employer. It exploded, blinding and mutilating her. The next day another parcel was addressed to the German-staffed "research institute" in Cairo. An Egyptian employee opened the package and it too exploded, killing him and four other local functionaries. Additional parcel bombs arrived in Cairo during the next two days, all addressed to German recipients. It was assumed that Israel was behind the mailings. One day in February 1963, Hans

Kleinwächter, who had returned from Cairo to Germany for a short visit, drove home from his laboratory in Lörrach. En route he was waylaid by another automobile and shot at—although the bullet missed.

And finally, on March 2, 1963, during the Basel rendezvous with Heidi Görke, Swiss federal police arrested Otto Joklik and Yosef Ben-Gal, his Israeli companion. Only then did the full story emerge of the purpose behind Israel's intimidation campaign. The previous summer Isser Harel had become increasingly concerned that the Egyptians might seek to apply atomic or chemical materials to their rocket warheads. Several German chemists lately had joined the "Factory 333" project, among them Dr. Hans Eisele, a former concentration-camp physician. Ostensibly functioning as Ferdinand Brandner's medical officer, Eisele was precisely the sort of person who was willing and able to develop bacteriological weapons.

At almost the same time, through Israeli civilians attached to the Purchasing Mission in Cologne, Mossad agents were alerted that one Otto Joklik, an Austrian-born ex-Wehrmacht officer, had returned from Cairo to report that German scientists in Egypt appeared to be working on a "poor man's atomic bomb." The device would be laced with cobalt 60 and strontium 90, both capable of poisoning the atmosphere for months. To the Israelis, Joklik insisted that he had been directed to supply Wolfgang Pilz and his colleagues with large quantities of these elements. Could Joklik's account be believed? The man appeared to be genuinely remorseful. In any case, the danger could not be ignored. Harel decided then that Joklik should be used to seek out potential weak links in the German rocket team. With a daughter in Germany, Paul Görke was regarded as one of these.

It was consequently in Basel that Joklik and Yosef Ben-Gal made their move—and were intercepted. The two were jailed, charged with attempted coercion, and in June 1963 put on trial in Zurich. In their defense their lawyer then shrewdly decided to reveal the plot not against the Görkes but against Israel. Before a courtroom packed with journalists, Joklik and Ben-Gal were allowed to elaborate on the prospect of cobalt-armed rockets descending upon the Jewish state. Joklik produced detailed evidence of the threat, including purchase orders signed by Görke and Pilz for rocket mechanisms and gyroscopes. Even the Swiss prosecutor was shaken. Acknowledging that the defendants had acted with "honorable intent," he asked for a bare three-month sentence. The judges gave them two months and then released them for time already served.

The Israeli government's response to the episode was ambivalent.

The previous winter Ben-Gurion had ordered an end to the under-cover Mossad operations; they were provoking too much resentment in Bonn, he insisted. Nevertheless, against the prime minister's wishes, Harel leaked information on the German scientists to the Israeli press, and the ensuing newspaper accounts produced grave dis-quiet. Many Israelis now heaped scorn on Ben-Gurion for his repeated allusions to "another Germany." Shortly after the arrest of Joklik and Ben-Gal, the prime minister reluctantly authorized Golda Meir to confirm before the Knesset that German nationals were indeed working in Egypt on the development of atomic, biological, and chemical weapons. Mrs. Meir then called upon the Bundesrepub-lik to prohibit its citizens from accepting military-related employ-ment in behalf of Israel's enemies. Phrased in diplomatic language, the foreign minister's statement was comparatively restrained. Not so the ensuing Knesset debate. In its manifestation of anti-German dis-trust, the argument became impassioned, even demagogic. This time, too, not a single member even of Ben-Gurion's Mapai party defended the prime minister against charges of laxity. The next day, March 21, 1963, the legislators unanimously issued a resolution declaring that "[t]he German people cannot deny its responsibility for this contin-ued criminal activity," and demanding that the German government immediately put a stop to it.

In Bonn the Erhard cabinet reacted in some distemper. Two days after the Knesset resolution, a spokesman for the Chancellor's Office insisted that not more than eleven German scientists were working in Egypt, and that the numbers of Austrian, Swiss, and Spanish nationals employed in Nasser's rocket program were much larger. The Bun-desrepublik would not violate its constitution, the spokesman contin-ued, by denying its citizens the right to work wherever they chose. Privately, then, Chancellor Erhard sent word to Ben-Gurion that Israel's unrestrained anti-German campaign might even endanger a secret weapons deal between the two countries (pp. 138–41). A week later, Erhard dispatched his state secretary, Volkmar Hopf, to confer with the prime minister in Jerusalem, and to underscore the message.

Ben-Gurion took the warning seriously. He then asked General Meir Amit, chief of military intelligence, for a candid assessment of the Egyptian missile program. Within forty-eight hours Amit informed the prime minister that his sources had uncovered no evi-dence that the Germans in Egypt were engaged in the development of either chemical or bacteriological weapons, and almost certainly not of nuclear warheads. Immediately Ben-Gurion summoned Harel to his office to accuse the intelligence chairman of instigating public panic, and to demand that the press campaign against German scientists be toned down. The tension between the two men became palpable. On March 25, Harel submitted his resignation.

The following week, out of office, Harel supplied the press with a graphic account of the horrors allegedly under development in Egypt. Menachem Begin and the Cherut party then vehemently pressed the issue in the Knesset, demanding a full-blown public debate. Forced onto the defensive, Ben-Gurion rather wearily responded: "Our grave concern over [Nasser's] designs . . . to destroy Israel and the assistance he is receiving from German and other scientists and technicians should not throw us off our balance . . . for there are certain things that cannot be spoken of here." Uninformed of these "other things" (p. 141), the Knesset was not reassured. Public and political anguish over the role of German scientists in Egypt, and Ben-Gurion's efforts to protect Israel's relations with the new Germany, soon opened a grave fissure within the ruling Mapai party. Golda Meir quarreled bitterly with the prime minister over the issue. By the late spring of 1963, Ben-Gurion already was dispirited and exhausted as a consequence of other, interfactional crises within his party. In June, he unexpectedly announced his own resignation and stepped down, this time for good.

Meanwhile the Erhard government in Bonn was urgently seeking a legal method of stopping the German scientists. The challenge was difficult. Whatever the profound moral debt to Israel felt by all German politicians, they were bound by no less compelling an obligation to their own constitution, with its iron-clad guarantees of personal freedom. Well into 1964 every draft bill restricting that freedom did not so much as pass a first reading. Addressing the Bundestag in September 1964, Chancellor Erhard had to acknowledge that he saw no hope for passage of an effective bill. Thereupon, in his own address to the Knesset the following month, Prime Minister Levi Eshkol, who had succeeded Ben-Gurion in office, deplored the apparent inability of "a great state to find legal and concrete means to express its declared negative attitude towards the activities of the scientists. . . . We have the right . . . to express . . . the hope that the idea of Germans no longer doing anything to harm the Jewish people . . . would have become deeply rooted in the minds and consciousness of the entire German people. . . ." Yet the best response Chancellor Erhard could provide, just three days later, was to explain to the Bundestag: "Prime Minister Eshkol has recognized that the activities of this kind have been widely condemned throughout Germany. . . . I should like to add that we shall leave no stone unturned to eliminate the possibility of the Israeli people feeling threatened by Germans." But whatever stone was turned, it did not appear to take legislative form. Ben-Gurion's years of pioneering overtures toward the Bundestag now appeared in serious danger of collapse.

By the autumn of 1964, in fact, the Erhard government had set about exploring a new approach to the rocket scientists issue. This was one of quiet intimidation. Bonn now began cutting off subsidies to the various local institutes and research programs in which the absconding scientists originally had worked—and to which, someday, they might wish to return. Conversely, government funds were provided for alternate institutes and projects, often on more attractive financial terms than the temporary openings in Egypt. By early 1965, as a result, Krug, Brandner, Görke, and most of the other German advisers were out of Egypt, either back in Germany or engaged in programs in Latin America or other regions. Even Prime Minister Eshkol at last was reassured. In May 1965, as he and Erhard exchanged letters to confirm their intention of entering into diplomatic relations (p. 149), the German chancellor promised Eshkol to support legal measures against anyone seeking to "encourage" Germans to take up such "underground" activities abroad. Significantly, Eshkol himself decided not to focus his efforts any longer on the issue of the German scientists. Well before May 1965, the bruised legacy of resentment and distrust in both capitals had become enmeshed in an even more complex "underground" relationship.

THE BUNDESREPUBLIK AS ARMORER

In late June 1959 the German newsmagazine *Der Spiegel* reported that the Bundeswehr, the West German army, had contracted to purchase several thousand Israeli-manufactured Uzi assault rifles. The weapon had proved its worth in the recent Sinai war, and was competitively priced. In the Israeli Knesset, however, the propriety of the sale was immediately questioned. Again, it was the usual combination of Communists and right-wingers that anathematized the very notion of delivering weapons to a potential "Fourth Reich." Although their initial call for a no-confidence vote in the government was easily defeated, the issue would not die. Belated misgivings about the sale were voiced by the leftist Mapam and Achdut HaAvodah ministers in Ben-Gurion's coalition cabinet. On July 4, 1959, a second Knesset no-confidence vote was raised. It too was defeated, but this time by a much narrower margin. Furious, Ben-Gurion demanded that his cabinet defectors resign immediately. When they refused, he promptly sought to cobble together a new, tighter coalition government, but failed. Subsequently he was obliged to coexist with the Mapam and Achdut HaAvodah ministers on a caretaker basis until scheduled parliamentary elections took place five months later. Notwithstanding their economic dealings with the Bundesrepublik, it was evident that Israelis regarded the sale of military equipment to the Germans—of all peoples—as somehow beyond the moral pale.

Ironically, the public and even a majority of the Knesset remained unaware that the principal flow of munitions by then was not from Israel to Germany but the other way around. Like the Uzi sale to the Bundeswehr, Israel's acquisition of German equipment began as a simple business transaction. In late 1955 Israel's arms-purchasing mission in Paris negotiated the delivery of German spare parts for French armored personnel carriers. Earlier those parts had been acquired from French suppliers. Now it proved more economical simply to buy them direct from the German manufacturer. Yet, within the next two years, Ben-Gurion gave closer attention to a distinctly wider relationship. Even in the aftermath of the Sinai Campaign, the prime minister was unwilling to depend exclusively on France for assurance of military equipment. He had long since abandoned any notion of Britain's reliability. As for the United States, the Eisenhower administration from the outset had adopted an adversarial position toward Israel, and Ben-Gurion would take no chances on Washington.

Together with Shimon Peres, the prime minister was intrigued by the notion of exploring an arms relationship with the Bundesrepublik. As in the case of so many other developing ties with West Germany, moral obligation would serve as its basis. In the autumn of 1957, at Peres's request, France's defense minister, Jacques Chaban-Delmas, extended feelers on Israel's behalf to his German counterpart, Franz-Josef Strauss. Strauss was intrigued, and agreed to receive an Israeli mission. To evade the Knesset ban against official visits on German soil (except for the Cologne purchasing mission), the meeting would have to be secret. Thus, in December 1957, Peres, accompanied by Asher Ben-Natan, the director of Israel's arms-purchasing mission in Europe, and by General Chaim Laskov, Israel's chief of staff, flew initially to Paris, then continued by automobile through a brutal snowstorm directly to Strauss's private home in Roth, Bavaria.

Discussions lasted five hours. Peres outlined his government's "moral" case. This was the Bundesrepublik's historic obligation to help ensure Israel's military as well as economic survival. Yet Peres also laid out a compelling strategic inducement. He noted that

Moscow's efforts to penetrate the Middle East had transformed Israel into a barrier against Soviet expansion. As effectively as any European nation, Israel was guarding the Mediterranean "back door" against the Russians; and more than any European nation, Israel had acquired firsthand combat experience against Soviet weaponry. Indeed, some of that captured equipment could be made available to NATO. The conference wound up after midnight, and Peres later recalled his summation to Strauss: "We told him that the United States was helping us with funds, but not with weapons; France was helping us with weapons, but not with money. Germany would be taking a far-sighted step . . . if she would help us with weapons without requiring either money or anything else in exchange." Strauss did not cavil. He promised to discuss the matter with Adenauer.

Morality aside, the German defense minister discerned certain pragmatic advantages for his government in supplying military help to Israel. The Bundesrepublik had joined NATO only two years before. Thus far, its armed forces remained heavily dependent on the United States for older, essentially surplus weaponry. But inasmuch as the Germans soon would begin producing modern equipment on their own, it behooved them even now to cultivate a Third World market for obsolescent hardware. It would barely matter if significant quantities of this ordnance were turned over to Israel gratis. The shipments would rapidly clear the defense ministry's inventory and cost little in out-of-pocket expenditure. As Peres had contended, moreover, Israel already had proven its ability to secure the West's "back door" against the Soviets, and could do so even more effectively with additional equipment. These were the arguments Strauss presented to Adenauer. The chancellor accepted them. Where Israel was concerned, modest transfers of surplus weaponry fitted the guarantor role he envisaged for the Bundesrepublik.

The initial consignments, beginning early in 1959, were small-scale and of American manufacture, consisting essentially of such noncombat matériel as trucks, training aircraft, and helicopters. In fact the deliveries were known to Washington, which had to approve any third-party transfers of American equipment. The Eisenhower administration requested only that the arrangements be kept modest and discreet, lest the Arabs get wind of them. Whenever possible, deliveries were made from ports in other countries, in France, Italy, and the Netherlands. There was nothing equivocal, however, in Adenauer's support of the arrangement. He reconfirmed it to Ben-Gurion at the Waldorf-Astoria meeting of March 1960, albeit with the cryptic observation that "[Strauss] is all right, he thinks as I do."

By 1962 the range of equipment was widened to include antiaircraft guns, rockets, armored cars, and howitzers. Most of the hardware still was originally American, but some came from other countries, including ground-support and transport aircraft from France, anti-aircraft guns from Sweden, and two refurbished submarines from Britain, as well as trucks, ambulances, and twelve missile boats on order from Germany itself (p. 189).

As a rule, the deliveries continued to be made indirectly, via third countries, and under false bills of lading. Yet the scope of the agreement could not be disguised altogether. As early as 1961, Israeli officers were being trained in the use of this equipment at German military camps in Bendsburg and Müsterlager. In June of that year, when leaders of several German political parties began querying the Chancellor's Office, Adenauer directed his foreign minister, Heinrich von Brentano, to bring them into the picture. This Brentano did, in meetings with Erich Ollenhauer, chairman of the Social Democrats, and with Erich Mende, chairman of the Free Democrats. Neither man objected to the Israeli connection. Without informing their parliamentary rank and file, they agreed instead to participate in a monitoring committee to review each transaction. At all times Strauss remained the driving force behind the arrangement; and on Strauss's retirement in December 1962, his successor, Kai-Uwe von Hassel, maintained the agreement in letter and spirit. Remarkably, the secret was kept.

In the summer of 1964, a new phase in the arms relationship began, as a direct result of pressure from Washington. A year earlier, the Kennedy administration had lifted the embargo on weapons sales to the Middle East. It authorized a modest delivery to Israel of Hawk antiaircraft batteries. In May 1964 Shimon Peres turned to Washington again, this time requesting substantial numbers of Patton tanks. Yet the Johnson administration hesitated. It had no wish to jeopardize its relations with the Arab world. Instead, when Chancellor Erhard visited the United States a month later, Lyndon Johnson suggested as an alternative that the Bundesrepublik turn over to Israel some 150 of the American Pattons then in German arsenals; Washington would pay for the transfer. The chancellor agreed. Once again the transaction was disguised. The Bundesrepublik delivered the tank bodies to Italy, ostensibly for upgrading. In Italy the unarmed Pattons were provided with new American guns and electronic equipment. Only after six additional months in Italian warehouses did shipments begin, direct to Israel.

The Patton transfer in fact represented the last major German arms delivery to Israel. In October 1964 the *Frankfurter Rundschau* broke the story of the German-Israeli arms relationship. Neither government at first acknowledged the report. Under repeated questioning, however, both from the Bundestag and from the Egyptian foreign ministry, the Chancellor's Office conceded that there had been intermittent "minor" transfers of military equipment. At this point, the Bundestag deputies, subdued at first, grew increasingly incensed. Ironically, it was the Social Democrats, Israel's warmest supporters in Germany, who expressed sharpest criticism at weapons deliveries to "areas of military tension." Yet these reservations surfaced even in the cabinet, where Gerhard Schröder, now foreign minister, led the opposition to further arms shipments to Israel. Chancellor Erhard himself was ambivalent. Although as friendly to Israel as Adenauer had been, he hesitated to force his will on his cabinet colleagues.

Following these developments with concern, Israel's Prime Minister Eshkol in January 1965 instructed Felix Shinnar, director of the Israeli purchasing mission and his nation's de facto diplomatic emissary to Bonn, to entreat the Erhard government not to capitulate to "pro-Arab pressures." Within the week, Shinnar secured a meeting with the chancellor. Erhard by then had come up with a compromise proposal. It was to reverse the recent triangular Patton-tank agreement. Inasmuch as 90 of the 150 Pattons had not yet been shipped out of Italy, Bonn would arrange for their return to Germany but compensate Israel financially for their value—thus enabling the Israelis to purchase the tanks directly from the United States or from other suppliers. Shinnar reacted well to the proposal. But when he transmitted it to Eshkol, the latter angrily vetoed it. Bonn could not be allowed to abandon its commitments that easily, the Israeli prime minister insisted.

It soon became apparent that Erhard possessed no leeway even for a compromise solution. In ensuing weeks, spokesmen for all the Bundesrepublik's political parties agreed that Germany, of all nations, had no business playing the role of weapons provisioner to any country, not even to Israel. Nor was the nation's ugly legacy of militarism the only factor in this consensus. Relations with the Arab world had to be considered. On February 11, 1965, repeatedly dunned by Cairo, Erhard felt obliged to assure Egyptian Prime Minister Ali Sabri that the Bundesrepublik would prohibit all future arms deliveries to "areas of tension." Four days later Erhard announced his decision in the Bundestag. In reaction, that same day, a shocked Eshkol addressed the Knesset. "I cannot fail to point out," he declared indignantly, "the flagrant contrast between [Bonn's] haste in taking action to halt arms dispatches to 'areas of tension' and the sluggishness it has displayed . . . in withdrawing its scientists from Egypt." The Knesset then passed its own resolution, all but unanimously rejecting money as a substitute for weapons.

Israel's protests were unavailing. Economic considerations now were powerfully influencing German policy. In the immediate aftermath of the Treaty of Luxembourg, fearing retaliation by the Arabs, Bonn had dispatched emissaries to their respective governments, offering substantial investment and credit terms (p. 47). Costly as these infusions were, they paid off. Soon one Arab nation after another entered into industrial and commercial deals with the Bundesrepublik. German contractors built Arab harbor facilities, metallurgical factories, bridges, and roads, and sold a widening variety of industrial products, from hospital to food-processing equipment. German trade fairs soon became perennials in Egypt and other Arab countries. German banks opened branches in virtually every large Arab city, as did German chambers of commerce. As early as 1956, Arab nations were consuming fully 30 percent of German exports beyond Europe, and nine years later 24 percent of German exports worldwide. Thus, while the Bundesrepublik had forthrightly extended itself to Israel through reparations, restitutions, and generous loan arrangements, it drew the line now on commitments that threatened its widening access to the indispensable Arab market—and to equally indispensable Arab oil supplies.

Of even graver concern to Bonn, however, was the new and even more extensive quid pro quo Israel was demanding for "accepting" cancellation of German arms deliveries. By 1965, this commitment was neither military nor economic, but diplomatic.

AN IMBROGLIO OF DIPLOMATIC RECOGNITION

In the late winter of 1953, as the Treaty of Luxembourg underwent debate in the Bundestag, Konrad Adenauer ventured the hope that ratification of the document would lead "to the normalization of relations between the Bundesrepublik and the State of Israel." The prospect seemed remote. All but exhausted by the ordeal of negotiating both with the Germans and with his own domestic political opposition, Ben-Gurion was unprepared to contemplate further steps toward "normalization." Then, only three years later, he changed his mind. By mid-decade the Bundesrepublik's palpable economic muscularity, and its emerging potential as Israel's access-way to Europe, persuaded Ben-Gurion and Foreign Minister Moshe Sharett that the issue of diplomatic relations was at least worth exploring.

In March 1956, feelers were duly sent out to Bonn on the possibility of an institutionalized relationship. Replying several weeks later, Foreign Minister von Brentano agreed "in principle to establish an agency in Israel that would correspond approximately to the Israeli [Purchasing] Mission in Cologne." The tepid circumspection of the response quite shocked the Israeli government. Why Brentano's sudden caution? Surely the growth of German exports to the Arab world could not have been the only factor? The Treaty of Luxembourg had not inhibited the Bundesrepublik's surging Middle Eastern commerce, after all. Bonn's hesitation in fact was influenced by an even more pragmatic consideration of *Realpolitik*. This was the so-called "Hallstein Doctrine."

In late 1955, the Adenauer government had agreed reluctantly to establish diplomatic relations with Moscow. However inevitable, in view of the Soviet Union's role as a superpower, the decision was a painful one. Committed to the paradigm of an undivided Germany, Bonn until then had refused to exchange ambassadors with any government that maintained diplomatic ties with the Deutsche Demokratische Republik—Communist East Germany. It was consequently vital to ensure that the impending Bonn-Moscow exchange not be regarded as a precedent. To abort that danger, Adenauer instructed Professor Walter Hallstein, deputy director of the foreign ministry, to warn other nations that official contacts with the East German regime would be regarded "as an unfriendly act calculated to aggravate the division of Germany." On the other hand, if the Bundesrepublik now should establish its own diplomatic relations with Israel, would not the Arab governments retaliate by officially recognizing East Germany?

They would. Early in 1956, the Arab League sent word to the Adenauer government that a West German diplomatic exchange with Israel would similarly be regarded as an "unfriendly act," one that "could remove our inhibitions" against recognizing the Deutsche Demokratische Republik. The Arabs had essentially turned the Hallstein Doctrine against Bonn. Thus, in May 1956, conferring in Istanbul with the assembled West German ambassadors to Arab capitals, Hallstein accepted their unanimous evaluation that a full diplomatic exchange with Israel would not be worth the risk. The issue of German reunification henceforth would take priority over all other considerations, even over the "special relationship" with Israel.

Bonn's response plainly was a disappointment for Ben-Gurion. Yet the prime minister shared the view of Moshe Dayan and Shimon Peres that the setback should not be exaggerated or regarded as more than temporary. For the time being the government would concentrate on economic, "practical" cooperation with the Bundesrepublik. In ensuing years Ben-Gurion lost no opportunity to remind his nation that the Germans had remained faithful to their reparations obligations. As a member of the new European Economic Community, moreover, the Bundesrepublik was of vital importance for Israel's economic future. The prime minister could make no mention of the secret weapons deal, but this too fortified his determination to cultivate German goodwill. Indeed, his forbearance seemed to be rewarded in the Bundesrepublik itself, and not alone in weapons transfers but in a concomitant German disillusionment with Gamal Abd al-Nasser. The Egyptian leader's intimate relationship with the Soviet Union had long been a source of growing concern to Bonn. In January 1958, Nasser had welcomed the Deutsche Demokratische Republik's prime minister, Otto Grotewohl, thereby making Egypt the first "non-aligned" nation to receive a high East German dignitary. Three years later, when the East Germans were permitted to open a consulate general in Cairo, Bonn in its displeasure recalled its ambassador from Egypt "for consultations."

By 1961, the Hallstein Doctrine was becoming a constraint on Bonn rather more than on the Arabs. The latter apparently would deal with whomever they pleased. Even Washington appeared bored by the policy, as the new Kennedy administration sought out opportunities for détente with Moscow—and with Moscow's satellites. Meanwhile, in the Bundesrepublik itself, editorial and political impatience was growing with the "quarantine" imposed on Israel, of all nations. As always the Social Democrats criticized the government's stance with particular vigor; yet they found numerous supporters among the Free Democrats and Christian Democrats. By the early 1960s even the cabinet no longer used the Hallstein Doctrine as the rationale for this diplomatic anomaly. It resorted instead to such platitudes as the danger of "increasing tensions in the Middle East."

Then, in late 1964, as rumors of the arms deliveries circulated—and with it dire Arab warnings of retaliation—Herbert Wehner, Social Democratic leader in the Bundestag, proposed a new formula. It envisaged an immediate termination of the weapons deal, coupled with an equally prompt establishment of "clean diplomatic relations with Israel, not a game of hide-and-seek." Wehner's proposal drew hearty support across all party lines. And still Chancellor Erhard and his cabinet ministers dithered in uncertainty and confusion. To exploit that hesitation, Nasser decided to act preemptively, to ensure that Bonn well understood the potential implications of continued arms transfers. On January 26, 1965, the Egyptian president announced that he had invited Walter Ulbricht, East Germany's Communist party leader, for an official visit. Within hours Georg Federer, the Bundesrepublik's ambassador in Cairo, rushed fuming into Nasser's office to protest, and to warn of a possible cutback in West German economic aid. Nasser remained unperturbed. He anticipated better loan terms soon from Eastern Europe.

The Erhard government now found itself enmeshed in a serious dilemma. If it canceled the arms deal with Israel, Nasser might yet put off the threatened Ulbricht visit to Egypt. But what of Israeli outrage? Would the Israelis be satisfied simply with a generous financial compensation for canceled deliveries? On February 15 Eshkol gave his answer. It was a categorical refusal to accept any financial substitute for the promised weaponry (p. 142). The Israeli Knesset then passed its resolution, 54 to 9, endorsing Eshkol's position. Pained by this reaction, Erhard two days later informed the Bundestag that he would have expected "greater understanding" from Israel about the special problems of a divided country like Germany.

Yet the chancellor also had harsh words for the Egyptian government. "We have always proved by our deeds that we were serious about preserving our friendship with the Arabs," he declared. "We therefore have a right to ask what proof there is of Egyptian friendship. Those who treat Ulbricht as the head of a sovereign state make a deal with those who split the German nation." Nasser continued unfazed by the implied warning. The Ulbricht visit would proceed on schedule, he affirmed. Erhard now faced an avalanche of ridicule. The Social Democratic Press Service characterized his policy as a "diplomatic Stalingrad." *Die Zeit*, a newspaper closely associated with the Free Democrats, expressed puzzlement that the chancellor had not terminated German arms deliveries long before Cairo began applying pressure. He could then have established diplomatic relations with Israel immediately as a gesture of Middle Eastern equivalence and national self-respect. The conservative *Handelsblatt* observed that "now apparently we have as good as lost the Middle Eastern game on both sides." It was an accurate assessment.

Between February 24 and March 2, 1965, the deluge of scorn appeared further vindicated when the Ulbricht visit to Cairo took place, replete with a full-dress Egyptian welcome of ceremonial pageantry, banquets, and public tours. Was this not the moment, argued Erhard's critics, for the Bundesrepublik to act the Great Power, to declare the Hallstein Doctrine breached, and to retaliate by severing relations with Cairo? Still the chancellor hesitated. Eventually it was Franz-Josef Strauss and his colleagues in the Christian Social Union (the Bavarian wing of Erhard's Christian Democratic Union) who forced the issue. Together with the Social Democrats and key elements within the Free Democrats, they persuaded Erhard that there remained only one way out of the shameful imbroglio. It was to establish diplomatic relations with Israel. Accordingly, on February 24, overruling Foreign Minister Schröder and the remaining naysayers, Erhard confirmed that decision in principle. To lay the groundwork for its implementation, he would send his closest political adviser, Dr. Kurt Birrenbach, to Israel for discussions with Eshkol.

THE DIPLOMACY OF "NORMALIZATION"

Birrenbach arrived in Jerusalem on March 7, 1965. His initial meetings with Eshkol, with Foreign Minister Meir, and with other senior Israeli officials were cordial. Both sides understood that the issue of diplomatic relations was essentially resolved. Yet complications remained. The Israelis insisted on fulfillment of the weapons deal, including delivery of the remaining Patton tanks. As Shimon Peres explained, his defense ministry had based its military planning on the availability of specific quantities of German-adapted equipment, and none other could appropriately meet the army's needs. Here Birrenbach held firm. His instructions were unequivocal: There would be no further German weapons.

Three additional days of occasionally tense discussion followed, until the outline of a compromise began to emerge. It was the one originally proposed by Erhard and rejected by Eshkol. The United States, which had manufactured the Pattons, would bypass the German conduit and sell the material directly to Israel. Bonn would pay. In effect the proposal envisaged a reversal of the earlier role, in which the Americans had paid for tanks supplied from Germany. The formula was palatable to the Israelis this time, of course, because it would be coupled with diplomatic relations. After further refinements, the German and Israeli governments then submitted their formula to Washington. Discerning possibilities in it, the Johnson administration promptly dispatched Special Ambassador Averell Harriman to Jerusalem to explore and eventually endorse the arrangement. The Pentagon would transfer to Israel ninety of its own stock of Pattons, the quantity Bonn originally had agreed to provide. The Bundesrepublik in turn would reimburse Washington for the tanks in the amount of $35 million.

Negotiations on other issues, conducted directly between Birrenbach and the Israelis, required an additional nine days. Eshkol and his colleagues insisted that the Bundesrepublik act more vigorously against German scientists in Egypt. Birrenbach in turn assured the prime minister that Bonn was offering powerful financial inducements to lure the scientists back, and that, of the senior rocket officials, only Pilz then remained in Egypt (and soon he too would be back). Eshkol eventually accepted this assurance. The prime minister also demanded a commitment for an early exchange of ambassadors, lest Arab pressure force a change of heart in Bonn. He got that, too. At last, on March 16, with the full spectrum of agreements in hand, Eshkol appeared before the Knesset to seek its authorization for a painful moment of diplomatic truth.

In his statement the prime minister cited Bonn's pledges, and its willingness to fulfill a generous economic loan program. Although details of the commitment were not spelled out, it was a deliberately vague allusion to the Adenauer–Ben-Gurion understanding, reached at the Waldorf-Astoria conference five years before. Eshkol noted, too, that the Bundesrepublik was in a position to ease Israel's relationship with the European Economic Community. His concluding words could as easily have been Ben-Gurion's: "We have the sacred duty to assure a safe place for the State in the family of nations. . . . I am sure that, when weighing emotions and reason, the desire to strengthen the State and its prestige will be decisive." It was. This time there were no violent outbursts in the Knesset. The resolution passed easily, by 66 to 29—the negative votes consisting again of Begin's Cherut and the leftist Mapam, with 25 abstentions.

The next day, March 17, welcoming the Knesset's decision, Ludwig Erhard expressed his "deep satisfaction that the Israeli people, its government and parliament have accepted the hand stretched out by us." Even at this last moment, however, all did not go smoothly. Foreign Minister Schröder still preferred to delay a formal exchange of ambassadors. He cited the danger that Moslem nations even as far away as Indonesia might retaliate by recognizing the Deutsche Demokratische Republik. Erhard agreed. At his orders Birrenbach informed Eshkol that a number of "financial adjustments" still had to be resolved, that an exchange of ambassadors was by no means "around the corner."

In their exasperation, there were many, even within Eshkol's Labor party, who suspected by then that the Bundesrepublik might yet find ways of evading its commitments. Foreign Minister Meir was one of these. She listened coolly as Birrenbach, who had returned on April 6 from consultations in Bonn, now asked for a complete news blackout on negotiations, in order to "allow the evacuation of German citizens" from Arab countries. While agreeing to the request, the foreign minister countered with a demand for additional funds to complete the tank deal. Birrenbach refused. Neither would he budge on Mrs. Meir's appeal for a total abrogation of West Germany's statute of limitations on war criminals. The Bundestag's latest compromise, of a four-year extension of the statute, was not negotiable. Mrs. Meir finally backed down on both issues. In return, Birrenbach dropped his qualifications of "financial adjustments."

Several additional weeks were required for—essentially technical—clarifications and refinements. At last, on May 12, Erhard and Eshkol exchanged letters, formally agreeing to establish diplomatic relations. By then Israel's press and public received the news with a relief that fell distinctly short of enthusiasm. In the Bundesrepublik, by contrast, the full range of the political spectrum greeted the announcement warmly. German newspapers hailed the decision with unanimous approval, often with exultant front-page headlines. Editorials alluded repeatedly to the "vindication of German honor." It was a crippled vindication in any case. On that same May 12, the government of Iraq severed diplomatic relations with Bonn. Within hours nine other Arab states followed, including Egypt and Algeria. Plainly it was the Arabs who had turned the Hallstein Doctrine around, using it against the Bundesrepublik.

Even Fritz Schröder sensed that the net effect of the entire clumsy episode was to leave a residue of suspicion among Arabs and Israelis alike. Two months earlier, on March 4, the foreign minister had suggested to the cabinet that it might prove worthwhile for the Bundesrepublik simply to follow its own best interests, even at the price of having two German ambassadors—one from Bonn, one from East Berlin—in certain foreign capitals. In fact, this was the long-held view of the Social Democrats, who had argued that Bonn should cease basing its foreign policy on a mythological German unity. Only four years later, in 1969, coming in as chancellor, Willy Brandt would act on this revised approach, launching a pragmatic and ultimately more effective *Ostpolitik*.

On August 19, 1965, the newly designated West German ambassador to Israel, Dr. Rolf Pauls, drove up from Tel Aviv to Jerusalem to present his credentials to President Zalman Shazar. Pauls brought

with him considerable knowledge of Jewish affairs. He had participated in the end stage of the Luxembourg Treaty preparations, serving as personal assistant to Walter Hallstein (then state secretary).
Later he had been posted to Washington as the Bundesrepublik's
"counselor for political affairs," a euphemism for his role as liaison to
the American Jewish community. But earlier, during the war, Pauls
also had served as a Wehrmacht officer on the Russian front, where he
lost an arm in combat. Upon learning of his background, Mrs. Meir
had raised with Bonn the question of Pauls's military service, and the
appropriateness of his appointment. Coldly rebuffed, the foreign
minister eventually dropped her objections.

As the ambassador-designate arrived in Jerusalem, he encountered
a gauntlet of demonstrators, some hurling bottles at his limousine.
Even after Pauls safely entered the presidential mansion, the sound of
shouting could be heard outside. The ensuing ceremony of presenta-
tion was brief and formal. In his speech, delivered in German, Pauls
dutifully lamented the Nazi past and looked forward to a new beginning. Responding in Hebrew, President Shazar, tense and unsmiling
as he stood beside Golda Meir and senior foreign ministry officials,
similarly evoked the haunting legacy of the Holocaust. Shazar would
not permit his remarks to be translated into German. In the garden
outside, a military band played the Israeli and German national
anthems, and Pauls then returned to his embassy in Tel Aviv.

Ironically, Bonn also had reacted cautiously before giving belated
approval to Israel's choice as its first ambassador to the Bundesrepublik, Asher Ben-Natan. The Austrian-born Ben-Natan (né Arthur
Pier) had long been associated with the secret German arms deliveries, most recently as director-general of the Israeli defense ministry,
and it was specifically these transactions that had caused the Bundesrepublik its latest embarrassment. In future years, the handsome
and dignified Ben-Natan in fact would play an important role in
developing and improving German-Israeli relations. But after presenting his credentials to Bundesrepublik President Heinrich Lübke,
the new ambassador understood that his first official gesture on German soil could not be a pro forma genuflection to an anticipated
future harmony. Rather, he laid a wreath beneath the Cologne Synagogue inscription that memorialized Jewish victims of the Final Solution, then participated in a religious service of commemoration inside.
Throughout the Bundesrepublik every major newspaper, every television channel, carried extensive accounts of the historic event.

Was Ben-Gurion's prophecy for German-Israeli relations on the
verge of fulfillment? Interviewed two years earlier at his desert retreat

of Sde Boker, the former prime minister spoke candidly of the issues
at stake:

> [O]nly those who live completely in the past . . . can believe that
> Hitler's Germany may be resurrected. . . . [Although Germany]
> is definitely a rising power . . . [i]t is clear that the great major-
> ity of the German people prefer to remain in the democratic
> camp. . . . To us, it cannot be unimportant whether West Ger-
> many is for or against Israel. . . . An unfriendly Germany might
> endanger Israel's relations with other peoples of Western
> Europe, and could also have an undesirable influence on the
> United States. It is therefore doubly important for Israel to pro-
> mote closer relations with [West] Germany.

More than any other man, the old prophet had launched his nation
on the course of reconciliation; and more than any other nation, it
was the Bundesrepublik that ultimately would secure Israel its long-
cherished goal of access to an integrated Europe.

VII A WIDENED SOVIET
WINDOW ON THE
MEDITERRANEAN

Notwithstanding the battlefield humiliation suffered by their Egyptian client, the Soviet leadership at no time gave serious thought to direct intervention in the 1956 Sinai-Suez war. Only after Nasser's repeated appeals was Prime Minister Nikolai Bulganin prepared to issue his menacing rocket threats against the Western Allies and Israel. It was in any case American, not Soviet, pressure that terminated the Anglo-French invasion of Suez, and that impelled Israel's eventual withdrawal from the Sinai. Only after Middle East hostilities had effectively ended were Moscow's ominous warnings forthcoming. Gratuitous by then, they functioned at most as a smokescreen for inaction in the war itself, and for the concurrent Soviet suppression of the Hungarian uprising.

As the price for their access to Egypt's Mediterranean littoral, however, the Russians in ensuing years felt obliged to offer Nasser rather more tangible compensation. It took the form of 500 new combat aircraft, 1,200 tanks, and 1,500 artillery pieces, as well as vast quantities of support vehicles and ammunition. The deliveries were impressive in quality as well as quantity. They included MiG-19 and MiG-21 interceptors, TU-16 heavy bombers, and T-55 tanks—advanced equipment that had not been made available even to Moscow's Warsaw Pact allies. The resupply effort was paralleled by equally substantial shipments of military hardware to the new leftist regime in Syria (pp. 154–5).

There was reason for this exertion. Even more than in earlier years, the Kremlin's Mediterranean strategy was animated by genuine fear of the United States Sixth Fleet. This mighty weapon of American "imperialism" by the early 1960s had developed enough missile strength to reach every Soviet target from Kazakhstan to the Baltic coast. Beyond its striking power, the sheer intimidating force of the armada, cruising just south of the USSR's "soft underbelly," was capable of encouraging separatist unrest among the Moslem populations of the Caucasus and the Crimea. For Khrushchev, Bulganin, and their colleagues, it was vital to "leapfrog" this awesome Western presence by exploiting their own targets of opportunity in the Arab world. To achieve that goal, in turn, military hardware, economic investment, and diplomatic support remained the Soviet leadership's weapons of choice.

Their principal client of choice, during the post-Sinai years, remained Gamal Abd al-Nasser. In the summer of 1958, the Egyptian president all but singlehandedly torpedoed the Baghdad Pact by inciting a political coup that claimed the lives of Iraq's young king Feisal II and its pro-Western prime minister, Nuri es-Saïd. With this "northern tier" confederation removed, Moscow thereafter could further "neutralize" the Sixth Fleet by allocating substantial quantities of weaponry to Algeria, Tunisia, and Morocco, and to Sudan and Yemen. By the mid-1960s, ensured of "appropriate" governments in these nations, the Soviet emplacement in the Mediterranean appeared to be solidly, even irreversibly, established.

In developing their Middle Eastern strategy, the Soviets also periodically conjured up war scares as useful propaganda weapons. Thus, in 1957, long-standing tensions between Turkey and Syria over the port region of Hatay (Alexandretta) reached a crisis. Although the confrontation was entirely unrelated to Israel, the Soviet press issued accusations that "Israel is preparing aggression against Syria with the help of the United States," and darkly "suggested" that the Ben-Gurion government "abandon its policy of intimidation." Tensions subsided only when Washington issued its own "suggestion" that the Soviets back down. Over the years, Moscow turned its Israeli war-scare faucet on and off at will. The device was crude but not ineffective, and after a bit of muscle flexing, the Israeli scarecrow would disappear and the Arabs would be grateful to Moscow for having saved them from a nonexistent threat. Eventually the Soviet game would prove less than fail-safe.

Nevertheless, during this same period between 1956 and 1967, the Kremlin in its functional dealings with the Jewish state evinced a certain pragmatic forbearance. Rarely did it loose the kind of menacing diatribes against Israel or Zionism that had characterized the last, terror-racked phase of the Stalin era or of the Sinai-Suez war. In 1963 Levi Eshkol succeeded David Ben-Gurion as Israel's prime minister. A convivial and affable man, Eshkol preferred the soft-spoken approach in both domestic politics and foreign affairs. Only a year later the impetuous Nikita Khrushchev was replaced as Soviet leader by the cautious, low-keyed tandem of Leonid Brezhnev and Aleksei Kosygin. Sensing an opportunity for "moderate" discourse, Eshkol then made a point of conferring frequently with Soviet Ambassador Leonid Chuvakhin, chatting with him easily in Russian, assuring him that Israel would play no part in Great-Power rivalries. Between 1964 and 1966, a reciprocal if limited tourism developed, accompanied by a series of Soviet-Israeli cultural exchanges. In October 1964 an agreement was negotiated on the disposition of "Red" church properties in Jerusalem (p. 61). Israel paid $1.5 million in hard currency and $3 million in goods for several vacant buildings owned by the Russian Orthodox Church. Eshkol was determined to press on in these gestures. In 1966 the urbane Abba Eban replaced the flinty Golda Meir as foreign minister, and pleased Moscow by expressing his hope that the Soviets would participate in any Arab-Israeli peace process.

For their part, the Soviets then welcomed any opportunity to drive a wedge between Israel and the Western camp. Relaxation of tensions with Israel might even help foster détente with the United States, at a time of growing Sino-Soviet rivalry. Thus, in 1965 and early 1966, Moscow reduced the scale of its anti-Israel propaganda, while Jerusalem in turn eased its campaign on behalf of the Soviet Jewish minority (p. 258). For the first time, *Pravda* alluded to the heroic role of Jews who had fought in the Red Army against the Germans. In September 1965, when Katriel Katz presented his credentials as Israel's new ambassador to Moscow, the event received extensive and not unfriendly coverage in the Soviet press. In the winter of 1965–66, the Kremlin leadership intimated that they might yet be interested in sponsoring an Arab-Israeli "Tashkent," along the lines of the recent Soviet-brokered peace agreement between India and Pakistan. As late as 1966, even as East European weaponry flowed to Egypt and Syria, Moscow discouraged the Arab governments from indulging in any notion of a renewed and possibly uncontrollable war against Israel.

SUDDEN THUNDER IN THE MEDITERRANEAN

It was the sudden escalation of tensions along the Syrian-Israeli frontier that impelled a renewed crisis in Soviet-Israeli relations. Violence along this northern border no longer could be related exclusively to territorialist claims and counterclaims. Much of it reflected the unique nature of the Syrian Ba'athist regime, whose principal members were Alawites, members of an Islamic subcommunity notably divergent from mainstream Islam. The regime had been in power since February 1966, when a cabal of Alawite officers staged a military coup under the leadership of Colonel Salah Jadid. Lacking a strong popular base for its rule, the new regime was as politically insecure as its predecessor, and accordingly felt obliged to prove its nationalist bona fides by posturing as the most grimly chauvinist regime in the Middle East. Its diatribes in support of the Viet Cong, the Maoists, and the Guevarists, and against the United States, were violent and even psychotic. Above all else, Jadid and his colleagues focused their animus on Israel, the Arab world's universally accepted bête noire.

Gamal Abd al-Nasser, on the other hand, regarded this escalating campaign of Ba'athist militance with a distinct lack of enthusiasm. The Egyptian president was by no means certain of his ability to win a war if the Syrians drew his nation into a full-scale confrontation with Israel. Indeed, his 1964 defense treaty with Syria was proved a dead letter only three years later, on April 7, 1967, when a flight of Israeli jets penetrated Syrian air space and downed six MiGs. The Egyptian army did not budge. Rather, Nasser dispatched his prime minister to Damascus in early May to warn that "our agreement for mutual defense will apply only in the event of a general attack on Syria by Israel. No merely local incident will cause us to intervene." It was the intercession not of Syria, but of the Soviet Union, that forced the Egyptian president's hand.

The intensification of Soviet efforts on behalf of the Arabs, and notably on behalf of Syria, reflected Moscow's acute concern over the demise of "anti-imperialist" regimes elsewhere. It was in this period of the mid-1960s, ironically, at the apogee of Soviet influence in the southern Mediterranean, that the downfall of Ahmed Ben Bella in Algeria was followed by the overthrow of Ahmed Sukarno in Indonesia and of Kwame Nkrumah in Ghana. Rightist elements lately had seized power in the former Belgian Congo. In Greece a newly installed military junta was stamping out leftist opposition. To the Kremlin it appeared that Washington was manipulating events behind the scenes. More ominously, Chinese emissaries were descending on Arab capitals with competitive offers of weapons, technology, and economic aid. Caught between these western and eastern dangers, Communist Party Chairman Leonid Brezhnev envisaged only one response. It was to continue to outbid all others in support of the Arab "national liberation" movement.

Thus, in 1966 Soviet Marshal Andrei Grechko signed a new defense agreement with Nasser. Under its terms, the Russians were extended naval facilities at Egypt's Mediterranean ports of Mersa

Matruh and Sidi Barani, at the Red Sea port of Quseir, and at three Red Sea fishing villages. Three airports similarly were placed at the Soviets' disposal. In return for these concessions, Moscow undertook to increase its shipments of arms and technicians to Egypt. In May 1966 Prime Minister Kosygin arrived in Cairo to pledge his government's support for Egypt's struggle against "imperialism." That year, too, a series of windfalls appeared likely to transform Russia's cautious infiltration of the Middle East into a galloping conquest. The first was London's announcement of its intention to withdraw all British military forces from Aden by 1968. With the Egyptians already ensconced in southern Yemen, the way now appeared open for a Soviet move into the Persian Gulf. Moreover, with Syria under Salah Jadid evidently in the process of becoming the first radical leftist state in the Arab world, the Soviets were certain that they had access to a Mediterranean base even more dependable than Egypt. Their technicians immediately began operating Syrian electronic and monitoring equipment, and within six months transformed the country into an intelligence clearinghouse and relay center for Soviet military and diplomatic personnel on both sides of the Mediterranean, and as far east as the Persian Gulf.

Israeli foreign and defense ministry officials followed these developments with grave concern. They understood the potential for a major confrontation with Syria, now that Moscow was lending Jadid its support. As early as May 1966, Soviet Deputy Foreign Minister Vladimir Semyonov summoned Ambassador Katriel Katz to his office to warn against Israeli "troop concentrations on the Syrian border." A second warning came in late July 1966 from Nikolai Federenko, the Soviet ambassador to the United Nations, who informed an incredulous Security Council that Israel was assembling a quarter-million-man force along the Syrian frontier, and that "an imposing squadron of the United States Sixth Fleet has appeared at Beirut and a British squadron has dropped anchor in Haifa." And then, in early April 1967, Israel's direst concerns about Soviet intervention appeared justified, following the recent Israeli-Syrian air battle.

In Moscow, on April 7, a group of senior army officers visited the Supreme Soviet. Citing the gravity of the Israeli-Syrian aerial incidents, they voiced objections to Prime Minister Kosygin's announced intention of appointing a civilian, Dimitri Ustinov, as defense minister to succeed Marshal Rodion Malinovsky, who had died the previous month. They demanded instead the appointment of a military man, the more aggressive Marshal Andrei Grechko—Brezhnev's protégé. After three days, the Supreme Soviet capitulated and agreed to appoint Grechko. Subsequently, on April 23, Brezhnev felt able to strike a more belligerent tone, declaiming before a press conference: "By what right does the American Sixth Fleet patrol the Mediterranean . . . ? The moment has come to demand the withdrawal of the Sixth Fleet from the Mediterranean."

By then the Soviets had markedly raised the level of intimidation against Israel. In New York, a week after the Israeli-Syrian air battle, Soviet UN Ambassador Federenko cautioned Israeli Foreign Minister Abba Eban: "You seem to be celebrating your victory of April 7, but . . . before long you will regret your success." Two weeks later, Deputy Foreign Minister Jakob Malik bluntly warned Israel's Ambassador Katz that the Israelis were "endangering the very existence of their state." It was the most ominous threat since the Sinai Campaign of 1956. The deteriorating Syrian-Israeli border situation already was electric with danger. Palestinian guerrillas were crossing the frontier into Israel with greater frequency, each time accompanied by larger numbers of Syrian regular army troops. In Jerusalem, on April 14, Soviet Ambassador Chuvakhin complained to Prime Minister Eshkol about "heavy concentrations of Israeli forces on the Syrian border." Eshkol immediately offered to drive Chuvakhin to the border to see for himself that the information was false.

And finally, on May 11, Soviet foreign ministry officials informed a visiting Egyptian parliamentary group that at least "eleven Israeli brigades" were concentrated along the Syrian border. It was questionable if the Soviets actually believed that Israel intended to attack Syria's formidable topographical defenses. Moreover, Israel's Independence Day celebrations were in the offing, and it was not the time for a large-scale military operation. But even a fake ultimatum, and Israeli nonaction, would reinforce the pro-Soviet government in Damascus. By then Eshkol had issued his own repeated warnings of Israel's right to "act in self-defense" against Syrian military provocations. Whereupon, on May 12, 1967, the Soviets took their most calamitous misstep since the onset of their penetration of the Middle East. They brought Nasser directly into the picture.

It was on that day that Dimitri Podyedyev, the Soviet ambassador in Cairo, wired Moscow: "Today we passed on to the Egyptian authorities information concerning the massing of Israeli troops on the northern frontier for a surprise attack on Syria." The "information" was fake. It was based on an actual Israeli position paper that was fully ten years old. Produced by Yuval Ne'eman, assistant director of Israeli military intelligence, the document had been written in 1957 to cover all possible situations of Arab-Israel confrontation, and evidently had been secretly transmitted to the Russians by the spy Israel Beer (p. 69). The Soviets needed merely to update it, then present it to the Egyptians as "evidence" of Israel's current plans for striking preemptively against the Syrians. But Sami Sharaf, Nasser's personal intelligence chief, regarded the memorandum as authentic. With this "information" in hand, Nasser decided finally to act in behalf of his Arab ally. If the Russians asked him to help shore up the Ba'athist regime in Syria, he could hardly refuse.

Rather than dispatch troops to Syrian soil, however, Nasser on May 15 dispatched two armored divisions across the Suez Canal and into western Sinai. Once these troops were in place, the Egyptian president unexpectedly pulled a coup de théâtre—one that astounded the Soviets no less than the rest of the world. He ordered the 3,400-man UNEF force patrolling the Gaza-Israeli frontier to redeploy in encampments within the Strip itself. In response, U Thant, the Burmese secretary-general of the United Nations, made the first in a series of disastrous blunders. He rejected any "half-measures." Either the UNEF carried out its patrol mission without restrictions, he insisted, or it would be withdrawn from Gaza altogether. U Thant was certain that Nasser was uninterested in having these troops evacuated, and that he would back down. But the secretary-general was wrong. On May 17, Nasser trumped U Thant's ultimatum. He ordered a complete UNEF evacuation from the Gaza Strip. At this point, without calling an emergency meeting of the Security Council, and under pressure from India, which supplied the principal UNEF contingent, U Thant complied all but reflexively, withdrawing the United Nations force. Emboldened then by the lack of international diplomatic resistance, Nasser that same day also ordered evacuation of the tiny UNEF contingent at Sharm es-Sheikh, guarding the Strait of Tiran. And again U Thant capitulated. The UNEF troops were evacuated forthwith, and with their departure collapsed the world body's single most impressive peacekeeping achievement. Three Egyptian divisions now began fanning out through the Sinai Peninsula. In turn, Syria's Jadid regime promptly mobilized fifty cadet battalions, while three Iraqi brigades moved out to the frontier of Jordan. The governments of Kuwait, Yemen, and Algeria then announced their own intention to dispatch troops for confrontation with Israel.

To his own astonishment, Nasser had won a brilliant political victory by scarcely raising his little finger. Once again he had emerged as the unchallenged leader of the Arab world. Now he would have to act the part. Accordingly, on May 21, the Egyptian president issued a chilling announcement: "The Strait of Tiran is part of our territorial waters. No Israeli ship will ever navigate it again. We also forbid the shipment of strategic materials to Israel on non-Israeli vessels." The threat to Israel was mortal. Tiran and the Gulf of Aqaba represented Israel's gateway to Africa and Asia, the outlet for which it had fought its 1956 Sinai Campaign. Now this vital passage was to be closed off.

Worse yet, the United Nations had revealed its ineffectuality in dealing with the crisis. As the Security Council met, from May 29 to June 4, its various delegates appeared unwilling to take a stand, beyond urging all parties to "avoid hostilities" and "exercise restraint." From May 15 on, the Western Powers similarly failed to reach agreement on an international naval force capable of guaranteeing passage through the Strait of Tiran (p. 106). And the United States, leader of the Free World, was hopelessly mired in its own Vietnam war. Israel stood alone, and acutely vulnerable to Egyptian and Syrian forces vastly replenished by Moscow. Other Arab countries were now adding their weight to Egyptian and Syrian combat strength.

If, however, the Soviets bore heavy responsibility for igniting the long fuse, they were by no means interested in a full-scale Middle Eastern war, and its attendant risks of confrontation with the United States. In Moscow there was only astonishment that Nasser had moved so rapidly in driving the Israelis into a corner. Thus, in the predawn of May 27, Nasser was awakened by an urgent note from Soviet Prime Minister Kosygin, requesting the Egyptian president to exercise restraint. Publicly, the Soviets felt obliged to affirm their support of the Arab cause. Yet their one and single official comment on the Middle Eastern crisis, issued three days earlier, on May 24, declared: "Any attack on the Arabs will be met by the united strength of the Arab countries . . . [and] the strong opposition . . . [of the Soviet Union]. . . . It is the firm belief of the Soviet Government that the [Arab] peoples have no interest in kindling a military conflict in the Middle East." Moscow's endorsement of peace, rather than of Nasser's political position—for example, his blockade of the Strait of Tiran—and the qualification that the Soviets would respond to an Israeli attack only with "strong opposition," suggested that the Russians were adopting a cautionary stance. The same implicit restraint was evident in the pledge to do "everything in [Soviet] power to prevent a violation of peace."

At almost the same time that Kosygin's note was delivered to Nasser, Levi Eshkol was pulled from bed in Jerusalem at the insistence of Ambassador Chuvakhin, who had come to hand-deliver a—similarly qualified—warning from Kosygin. "We are concerned," the message stated, "that, however complicated the situation on Israel's borders with Syria and [Egypt] may be, it is necessary to find ways to settle the conflict by nonbelligerent means." Eshkol waited until June 2 before responding, and then forthrightly insisted on Israel's legal right of free navigation. For the Israelis it was plainly the Arab threat, not Soviet bluster, that had to be taken with greater seriousness. All diplomatic efforts by then had failed to lift the Egyptian blockade, and there appeared no alternative to a swift and decisive preemptive attack. But first a ruse was needed. On June 3, General Moshe Dayan, Israel's newly appointed defense minister, informed a press conference that "[a]t this moment, we are . . . in a position of being . . . too late to react with force . . . and too early to come to any final conclusion about the diplomatic efforts applied to this matter." Immediately, Ambassador Chuvakhin in Tel Aviv cabled Moscow that Israel was unlikely to start hostilities for at least two weeks, if at all. It was a prognosis that would destroy his career.

Other, even more sophisticated sources of information were available to Moscow, and they also failed. The Soviet and other East European embassies in Israel were fully staffed with intelligence personnel. While many of these agents were persuaded that Israel would attack sooner or later, not one predicted accurately when or where. Neither did "objective" electronic monitoring facilities serve Moscow any better. The Soviets operated three disguised fishing boats off Israel's coast, all assisted by flotillas of helicopters based on two minicarriers, the *Leningrad* and the *Moscow*. Each surveillance vessel was loaded with electronic gear capable of intercepting Israeli radio and telephone conversations. On board were Hebrew-speaking operators. And for all of them, diplomats and intelligence agents alike, the day and hour of Israel's move remained impenetrable.

A SECOND SOVIET DEBACLE IN THE MIDDLE EAST

At 7:10 a.m. on June 5, the Israeli air force launched its preemptive attack on Egyptian air bases. Within the space of three hours, Israel's pilots smashed the best-equipped of those bases and turned 300 of Nasser's 340 combat planes into flaming wrecks. The Israelis were free now to concentrate on their land offensive. This began the same morning. Two and a half days afterward, by late afternoon of June 7, all of the Sinai was in Israel's hands, and the Egyptian army in the peninsula was in flight. The havoc was fearful. In its combined land and air operation, Israel had destroyed or captured eight hundred Egyptian tanks. Devastation on this scale exceeded the destruction of

Nazi armor at al-Alamein twenty-five years earlier. Egypt's war machine, the crucial link in the Arab chain of steel, was broken.

Other links were similarly to be shattered. On the morning of June 5, in a critical miscalculation, Jordan's King Hussein authorized his army to move into Jerusalem's demilitarized zone and begin shelling the Jewish sectors of the city. The Israelis responded decisively. In fighting that continued into June 6, units of their army seized control of the Jerusalem mountain ridge, then swooped down on the rest of the Palestinian West Bank, easily overrunning its principal towns, including the Arab Old City of Jerusalem, with its ancient Jewish quarter and Western Wall. It was on June 6, too, that a Syrian armored infantry company launched a series of attacks on three small Israeli frontier communities. Although these assaults were easily repelled, the Israelis needed little further inducement to repay a nation whose border incendiarism had precipitated the current war.

For the moment, priority was given to the Egyptian and Hashemite fronts. But at 3:00 a.m. on June 9, once the Egyptian and Jordanian cease-fires had come into effect (pp. 162–3), Defense Minister Dayan issued the order to move against Syria. The task was formidable. The Golan Heights, from which the Syrians intermittently had rained their artillery shells on Israel's northern farm settlements, was a perpendicular dragon's nest of apparently impregnable fortifications. Nevertheless, at high noon on June 9, in the glare of the burning sun, the Israelis set out to ascend the heights. The struggle was an inferno, but after a day of close-quarter fighting, Israel's forces succeeded in ensconcing themselves on the Golan plateau. By afternoon of June 10, their armored units had cracked the main Syrian fortifications, and were racing inland. Thus it was, in less than six days, that the entire Arab chain was in ruins. Israel's triumph was complete.

As in 1956, Soviet reaction to the Middle Eastern catastrophe was an amalgam of verbal bluster and military restraint. For Washington, the priority was to ensure that restraint. At the outbreak of war, when President Lyndon Johnson cabled Moscow appealing for a strict hands-off approach by all the Great Powers, he elicited a seemingly favorable response. A return phone call from Prime Minister Kosygin on the "hot line" accepted the American president's approach, and proposed that Moscow and Washington jointly seek an immediate cease-fire through the UN Security Council. Shortly afterward, as news of the Egyptian debacle belatedly reached him, Kosygin telexed a second message to Johnson, accusing Israel of "criminal aggression." The Arab governments, he added, could be certain of Moscow's "absolute support." But once again his diatribe was vague, and not yet coupled with specific threats of intervention.

Lyndon Johnson would run no risks. By the evening of June 5 he had learned of Israel's spectacular air and early land victories. Intent on deterring a Soviet effort to reverse the situation, he ordered the United States Sixth Fleet to proceed toward the fighting zone. Within minutes the huge armada was moving under full steam toward the Sinai coast, registering on the radar of Soviet vessels in the area. The warning was taken seriously. Early the next morning, when Egyptian Ambassador Mohammed Ghaleb called on Kosygin to seek active military help, the Soviet prime minister's response was blunt. His government would support the Arab nations diplomatically, he replied, but under no circumstances would it intervene militarily. Indeed, during the course of the war, the Soviets did not so much as resupply the Egyptians or Syrians. As Kosygin had made clear, his government's help during the hostilities would be exclusively diplomatic.

Even on this front, Moscow's intercession proved of limited value. On the evening of June 5, Soviet Ambassador Federenko at the United Nations demanded a Security Council resolution ordering a cease-fire and a withdrawal by all belligerents (that is, Israel) from occupied territory. Thereupon Arthur Goldberg, the United States ambassador, proposed a straightforward cease-fire without reference to evacuation. The Arabs, still anticipating victory, rejected Goldberg's proposal. Visibly confused, Federenko then asked the Security Council to postpone its deliberations until the next day. This was a serious blunder, for each passing hour added to Israel's military successes. On June 6, moreover, Kosygin cabled Lyndon Johnson, once again demanding a Security Council resolution for a cease-fire and evacuation. The president was not forthcoming. The Soviets plainly had failed to grasp the magnitude of the Arab defeat. Their objective remained Israeli withdrawal, not an immediate cease-fire at any cost. But on the morning of June 7, Egypt's UN Ambassador Muhammad al-Kony informed the Security Council that his government would indeed accept a cease-fire without conditions. Grudgingly, then, Federenko concurred in the resolution, which was duly passed, and subsequently accepted by Israel.

Thus far the Soviets had operated within the framework of United Nations diplomacy. But their threshold of restraint was severely tested when their Syrian protégé faced a near-total military collapse less than forty miles from Damascus. In the late afternoon of June 9, the Syrian delegate to the United Nations announced his government's compliance with the Security Council cease-fire resolution. Israel's delegate then assured the Council that his government, too, would abide by the resolution. But it soon became apparent that the Israeli army was continuing its offensive, with the intention of seizing the entirety of the Golan plateau. In Jerusalem the following morning, Soviet Ambassador Chuvakhin stormed into Israeli Foreign Minister Eban's office to read a note that had just arrived from Moscow. It was harsh.

The previous day, reacting to the Middle East crisis, leaders of the Communist satellite regimes had gathered urgently in Moscow to adopt a collective stance. Chuvakhin's note reflected that position, but also the Communist bloc's rather transparent effort to substitute diplomatic belligerence for military intervention. "[I]n light of the continued aggression by Israel against the Arab states," it declared, "and the flagrant breach of the Security Council's resolutions, the USSR government has adopted a decision to break diplomatic relations with Israel." With the exception of Romania, each of the satellite governments followed in tandem. The diplomatic rupture proved no less ill-advised than Moscow's original role in precipitating the crisis. As Abba Eban later noted, "the immediate effect of Moscow's decision was to exclude the Soviet Union from any future participation in Middle Eastern dialogue, thus awarding the United States an unearned victory in the competition for influence in the Middle East."

In New York on June 10, palpably terrified that the Syrian regime might collapse altogether, Soviet Ambassador Federenko warned the UN Security Council that "other measures" would be taken unless Israeli forces halted their military advance across the Golan plateau. At 8:00 a.m. Washington time that same day, Prime Minister Kosygin telephoned Lyndon Johnson over the "hot line," demanding that the Israelis be stopped forthwith. Later that morning, two additional messages arrived from Kosygin, and their tone was increasingly ominous, with veiled hints of "further Soviet measures." The president then made a crucial decision. He ordered the Sixth Fleet, already approaching the Egyptian littoral, to dispatch two task forces specifically in the direction of the Syrian coast. Immediately the aircraft carriers *Saratoga* and *America* headed northeastward, together with their destroyer escorts and some two hundred planes. Nevertheless, in a cautionary move that same morning, Secretary of State Dean Rusk pressed the Israelis, "in the strongest possible terms," to accept the cease-fire forthwith. They did. By then, their pincers had closed on the Golan. The Six-Day War ended officially at 6:30 p.m. Israel time on June 10.

In ensuing days, Federenko in the Security Council intensified his efforts to reverse Arab losses. Characteristically, his weapon of choice remained verbal intimidation. Unless the Israelis withdrew unconditionally to the 1949 armistice lines, he warned, it would be "necessary to seek other ways and means to ensure that the United Nations does its duty." The threat hardly unsettled the other Great Powers, however, least of all the United States. When the Security Council vote was taken on Federenko's draft resolution, only the Soviet Union, together with Bulgaria, India, and Mali, supported the operative paragraph "condemning" Israel. Its second paragraph, calling for withdrawal behind the armistice lines, obtained only six votes of the necessary nine. Thereupon Federenko requested an emergency meeting of the General Assembly. It was the technique the United States and other nations had adopted in 1956 to circumvent the Anglo-French veto in the Security Council.

When the Assembly convened on June 19, the Soviet-bloc governments left no doubt of the importance they attributed to its proceedings. From Moscow, Prime Minister Kosygin himself arrived at the head of a sixty-man entourage that included Foreign Minister Gromyko and other diplomats. They were supported by formidable delegations from the other Communist-bloc nations, most of these also led by their prime ministers. In his opening speech to the Assembly, Kosygin began in a tone of deceptive moderation. He acknowledged Israel's right to exist, even the need to ensure "peace and security in the Middle East." But then, shifting to the offensive, the prime minister once again demanded condemnation of Israel and total Israeli withdrawal from occupied Arab territory. And when Abba Eban, who had arrived from Jerusalem to state Israel's case, ascended the rostrum to rebut Kosygin's demand, the Soviet prime minister and other Communist delegates joined the Arabs in departing the hall.

Throughout the next two weeks, Kosygin's efforts failed either to achieve Israeli withdrawal or to win United Nations support. The General Assembly turned back all Soviet draft resolutions seeking either condemnation or evacuation. In ensuing months, moreover, between June and November 1967, draft condemnations of Israel were rejected six times; demands for withdrawal, four times. Israel manifestly had won its greatest diplomatic victory since the original November 1947 General Assembly partition resolution. It was Washington's victory as well. A nation friendly to the United States had spared Washington the need of a rescue effort, triumphed against Moscow's Arab clients, and thereby strengthened the American diplomatic position in the Middle East. Lyndon Johnson was prepared to reciprocate. His UN ambassador, Arthur Goldberg, pressed for a Security Council resolution supporting "negotiated [Arab-Israel] arrangements," and assurance of "national security against terror, destruction, and war." As the Israelis gratefully noted, the American position of 1967 contrasted vividly with the adversarial stance Washington had adopted after the 1956 Suez-Sinai War, when Eisenhower and Dulles had demanded full, unconditional Israeli withdrawal from occupied territory.

In ensuing weeks, Israel's bargaining position in the UN General Assembly was fortified not merely by United States support but by Soviet economic vulnerability. During the Six-Day War the Suez Canal had been blocked by sunken Egyptian and other vessels. Suez was a major trade route for Soviet ships departing Black Sea ports for Asia and Africa. A quick solution to the Middle Eastern impasse would have permitted clearance of the canal and its reopening. At a reception for the Algerian and Iraqi foreign ministers in July 1967, therefore, Leonid Brezhnev almost plaintively sought a moderation of Arab intransigence, even invoking the example of Lenin in 1918, who had agreed to the Brest-Litovsk Treaty for the sake of a tactical "breathing space." By then the Arabs grasped the Soviets' unwillingness to maintain an indefinite state of Middle Eastern war. They were sobered.

Eventually, both the American and Soviet UN delegations inched toward a draft resolution that would incorporate two vital principles: Israeli withdrawal and the Jewish state's right to exist in peace and security. An additional glimmer of hope appeared in October, when First Deputy Foreign Minister V. V. Kuznetsov, a known moderate, was appointed to succeed the hard-line Federenko at the United Nations. Even then agreement eluded both sides until, suddenly, events in the Middle East itself took a critical new turn. On October 21, Egyptian missiles sank the Israeli destroyer *Eilat*, cruising off the Mediterranean coast; three days afterward, the Israelis retaliated by shelling and destroying Suez City's major oil installations. At this point the UN Security Council intensified its peace-seeking efforts. On November 18, finally, a compromise draft was hammered out, a document acceptable both to the Soviets and Americans, although rather less to the Arabs and Israelis. The formula was approved by the Security Council on November 22 as Resolution 242 (p. 179). The

Middle East crisis now apparently ebbed, and with it Soviet-American tensions in the region.

A RENEWAL OF COMMUNIST "ANTI-ZIONISM"

Throughout Eastern Europe, there were ambivalent reactions to the Jewish state's recent military triumph. These tended to reflect internal political developments. In Budapest, the Communist leader, Janos Kadar, Moscow's hand-picked choice to rule postrevolutionary Hungary, was prepared to tolerate the nation's liberal elements, provided they offered no further overt resistance to his regime. At his direction, antisemitism, whether or not disguised as "anti-Zionism," was dropped as government policy. Indeed, Kadar periodically alluded to the wartime suffering of the Jews, even to the right of Israel to exist as a Jewish homeland. "Thus, we are against the imperialist policy [of Israel] and not against the Jewish people," he emphasized, somewhat embarrassedly, in June 1967, when he was obliged to follow Moscow's lead in breaking relations with Israel. "Nor are we against the State of Israel." By Communist standards, anti-Israel criticism remained moderate in Hungary.

Yet the unthreatened, even placid circumstances of Hungary's eighty thousand, essentially middle-class Jews were not altogether consonant with those of other Jewish populations in Eastern Europe. In Poland the "thaw" in Communist police terrorism that followed the death of Stalin in March 1953 unleashed an upsurge of nativist rage against the Communist regime, and most vindictively against the party's Jewish component. And with the accession in 1956 of a more thoroughly Polonized Communist Central Committee, the new party chairman, Wladyslaw Gomulka, allowed it to be known that those Jews who "wished" to leave for Israel were free to do so. Gomulka's purpose was hardly benign. He wanted Jewish employment positions and housing for "authentic" Poles. Nevertheless, his offer was compelling. Some thirty-three thousand Jews streamed out of Poland between 1956 and 1958 and journeyed directly to Israel. Only twenty-seven thousand remained.

The Middle East crisis of 1967 produced an even more striking ambivalence in Poland's public and private reaction. On the one hand, there was much subliminal admiration for Israel's battlefield performance, its ability to dispose of Arab armies equipped and trained by the Soviet Union. Indeed, the commander of the Polish air force and two other senior officers were removed from their positions for refusing to hew to the party's anti-Israel line. But soon afterward, domestic

Polish political rivalries again fastened on "anti-Zionism" as a useful weapon. Facing a party and popular revolt against his heavy-handed leadership, Gomulka in 1968 sought to trump his political rivals in competitive xenophobia, once more by "inviting" the nation's remnant Jewry to depart for Israel. Some ten thousand did.

In Czechoslovakia, too, whose fourteen thousand surviving Jews had begun to breathe more freely after the death of Stalin, the 1967 Middle East war triggered a cruel throwback to the antisemitic terror of the early 1950s. For Antonin Novotny, the Communist party chairman, a revived campaign of "anti-Zionism" functioned as a classic diversion. Liberal unrest was gestating more vigorously in Czechoslovakia than in any of the other East European nations. Accordingly, by midsummer of 1967, following Moscow's lead, the anti-Jewish onslaught was revived, with "spontaneous" demonstrations and incendiary media assaults against "Zionist unreliables and fifth columnists." Except for the absence of trials and executions, the post-1953 liberalization appeared to be reversed altogether.

Ironically, the onslaught also signified the last spasm of the Novotny regime itself. Later in the year, after a series of intra-presidium crises, Alexander Dubcek, the Communist chairman of Slovakia, and a committed moderate, was installed as party first secretary. Dubcek immediately set about democratizing the government, emphasizing "socialism with a human face." By early 1968, the nation's "Prague Spring" had become in effect a quiet revolution. For the Jews, in fact, it signified a repudiation of antisemitism—and of "anti-Zionism" as a euphemism for antisemitism.

The "Prague Spring" was an unacceptable provocation for Moscow. Once again, the pendulum swung. On August 20, 1968, the Soviets ordered a direct military assault on the Czech capital, this time employing the Warsaw Pact armies of East Germany, Bulgaria, Hungary, and Poland. Dubcek and his fellow reformers were arrested. By no coincidence, the invasion was synchronized with a full-scale "anti-Zionist" offensive mounted simultaneously in the capitals of the other Soviet-bloc nations. Within Czechoslovakia itself, a reinstalled hardline administration almost immediately issued a farrago of accusations against Czech Jewry and the entire "spiderweb of Israeli aggression." Indeed, all the well-familiar canards of the earlier Slansky treason trials were worked overtime, not least of all the "conspiratorial" relationship attributed to the CIA, the Joint Distribution Committee, and international Zionism.

The ongoing upheavals in Eastern Europe left the Jewish world at large in a state of confusion and continual reassessment of the role of

Israel in their lives. Indeed, by the late 1960s, it began to appear that the establishment of a Jewish state, intended as a solution for diaspora vulnerability, had solved only part of the problem. In Israel itself, those Jews who were "superfluous" elsewhere unquestionably had found a guaranteed asylum. Yet it was becoming equally apparent that the little republic's very existence, and assuredly its unanticipated muscularity, had provided the Communist empire with an official pretext for the manipulation of a classic phobia under an only faintly more cosmetic euphemism.

FROM SURROGACY TO FRONTAL CONFRONTATION

Out of the debacle of the Six-Day War, the Soviet Union's one substantive achievement on behalf of its Arab clients was an intensified rearmament program for Egypt and Syria. In the aftermath of the cease-fires, and throughout June and July 1967, a series of giant Antonov cargo planes shuttled from Soviet bases to Egyptian and Syrian airfields, bringing unprecedented quantities of planes, tanks, artillery, and other equipment, while additional matériel came by sea. Within a half year, some 90 percent of Egypt's war losses, and almost 100 percent of Syria's, had been replaced, this time virtually free of charge. And within two years, by mid-1969, the Soviets had provided Egypt alone with at least 600 of its latest model tanks, 300 equally modern aircraft, and some 150 batteries of sophisticated new SAM-2 and SAM-3 antiaircraft rockets. It was a formidable arsenal. More significantly, it was accompanied by thousands of additional military personnel, who now assumed wider responsibility for training within the Egyptian armed forces, from division to brigade and even to battalion level. Meanwhile, in the immediate aftermath of the war, Nasser asked General Gyorgy Zakharov, commander of the Soviet military engineering corps, to accept responsibility for constructing a defense line along the western length of the Suez Canal. This Zakharov did, designing an intricate and powerful new system of fortifications. With the task completed by November 1968, Nasser could breathe more easily. Integral—trans-Sinai—Egypt no longer appeared vulnerable to further Israeli moves.

At the same time, throughout 1968, the Soviet government also sought to recoup its prestige as a major player in the Middle East by proclaiming its support of Swedish diplomat Gunnar Jarring, who had been appointed to mediate Arab-Israeli peace efforts under the terms of UN Resolution 242 (p. 178). As early as January 1968, Moscow revealed its own peace scenario, first to Jarring, then to

Washington. By no means harshly one-sided, the formula accepted the legitimacy of open navigation through both the Suez Canal and the Strait of Tiran, as well as the recognition of secure Middle Eastern frontiers, and the transformation of truces and armistices into permanent peace. To be sure, the Soviets added qualifications that were unacceptable to the Israeli government. These envisaged early Israeli withdrawal from Arab territory before any final peace treaties were negotiated, the relinquishment of East Jerusalem, and a "Big Four" guarantee of Israel's safety—a thinly disguised format for institutionalizing a Soviet presence in the region. Nevertheless, Moscow plainly was serious in its efforts to defuse the volatile Middle East impasse. In July 1968, when Nasser visited the Soviet capital to press for still additional infusions of weaponry, Brezhnev and Kosygin conditioned their approval on Nasser's promise to undertake no strategic military moves against Israel without first consulting them. There could be no further impulsive adventurism of the kind that had produced the recent disaster.

Yet it was also assurance of Soviet support that allowed the Egyptian president at least incrementally to widen the scale of conflict along the Suez Canal. The Israelis could not be allowed to cling fast to the waterway without paying a heavy price. By autumn of 1968, fully 150,000 Egyptian troops had been packed into the west embankment's fortifications. On October 27 their artillery suddenly launched a nine-hour shelling of the eastern shore, inflicting some fifty Israeli casualties. From then on, Nasser left no doubt that the cease-fire of June 7, 1967, was inoperative, that Egypt thenceforth would rely on its massive numerical and artillery superiority to wage a "war of attrition" against the enemy. The Israelis, with their limited demographic resources, presumably would be unable to sustain extensive manpower losses.

In turn, to confront the new danger, Israeli Chief of Staff Chaim Bar-Lev set his army engineers to work constructing a fortification network along their own, eastern stretch of the canal. Completed in March 1969 at great effort and expense, the "Bar-Lev Line" provided a certain shelter against Egypt's pulverizing barrages. Yet it could not end them. To mitigate the sheer weight of these salvos, Israel's air force then was hurled into a series of increasingly heavy raids on Egyptian artillery and antiaircraft defenses along the waterway. On September 9, 1969, exploiting the twenty-five-mile-wide "corridor" its planes had blown in Egyptian defenses, Israeli armor crossed the canal, traveling some thirty miles into integral Egypt, destroying twelve Egyptian outposts and warning stations and inflicting more than one hundred military casualties. The scope of the widened conflict soon proved terrifying to Egyptian civilians in the canal cities. Hundreds of thousands of them began to flee, pouring into Cairo, overwhelming the capital's housing resources and public services. Subsequently, on January 7, 1970, in the first of a series of "deep-penetration" raids, Israeli planes bombed fifty miles west of the canal; and two weeks later, their fighter-bombers struck only twelve miles from Cairo itself. Thereupon, in a panic, with his capital naked to Israeli attack, Nasser flew secretly to Moscow to plead for additional Soviet military and technical personnel.

Until January 1970 the Kremlin leadership had remained unwilling to become directly involved in the Middle Eastern conflict. Only a month before, United States Secretary of State William Rogers had offered a formula under which Israel would evacuate all Arab lands in return for a binding Arab pledge of peace. Moscow had reacted cautiously but not negatively. It was Israel's Prime Minister Golda Meir—successor to Levi Eshkol upon the latter's death in March 1969—who shot the proposal down. Much to the discomfiture of the Soviets, then, so did Nasser. Nevertheless, in January 1970 the Russians came up with a formula of their own. Like the Rogers plan, their scheme envisaged an Israeli withdrawal from occupied territory, but it made no demand for full evacuation until at least a de facto peace agreement could be put in place. The proposal also finessed the Soviet role in a peacekeeping force by suggesting instead a permanent UNEF presence along demilitarized frontiers. On January 31 Prime Minister Kosygin dispatched the plan to President Richard Nixon in Washington, urging that Israel be pressed to accept it, and at all costs to cease its deep-penetration air raids on Egypt. Nixon refused, because Israel refused. Prime Minister Meir was adamant that issues of territorial accommodation would have to be negotiated directly between the belligerents.

Faced with this obduracy, Moscow concluded that Nasser's urgent appeal for help deserved an affirmative response. The holes in Egypt's defenses would be repaired. From February 1970 to May 1971, the Soviets delivered to Egypt two hundred new SAM-3 missile batteries, and one hundred MiG-21 fighters, the most advanced in the Soviet arsenal. Comprising three squadrons, the MiGs this time were manned by Soviet crews. Altogether, by mid-1970 some fifteen thousand Soviet personnel had been stationed in Egypt. No such force ever before had been assigned to a non–Warsaw Pact country, not even to Cuba. It was prefigured, on January 31, 1970, by Aleksei Kosygin's ominous pronouncement that "the Soviet Union would be forced to see to it that the Arab states have the means . . . [by which] a due rebuff can be made to the arrogant aggressor."

Israel's Defense Minister Dayan took the warning seriously. On February 25 he got word back to the Russians that Israel's air force would indeed halt its raids into the Egyptian heartland if the Soviets would stay clear of the canal battle zone. The offer was ignored. Rather, on April 18 two Israeli Phantoms flying just west of the canal encountered eight MiG-21s. Although the decals on the planes were Egyptian, the voices Israeli radios picked up on the enemy wavelength spoke Russian. The Phantoms then beat a hasty retreat under thick cloud cover. Apprised of the incident, Dayan ordered an immediate halt to deep-penetration raids. On May 4 Prime Minister Meir announced publicly that Israel's armed forces would make every effort to avoid direct engagement with Soviet military personnel.

In fact, Israel's restraint proved counterproductive. Spared the threat of deep-penetration air raids, the Egyptians, and Soviets, enjoyed a breathing space to extend their Suez missile emplacements. The Israelis soon felt the impact of this heavy concentration. During April and May 1970, Egyptian artillery salvos killed sixty-four of their troops and wounded twice that many. And in June and July, when Israeli planes intensified their bombardment of Egyptian positions on the canal, they encountered a much deadlier curtain of antiaircraft fire. Seven of their planes were shot down. Worse was to come. On July 25 Israeli Skyhawks overflying the canal's southern entrance at the Gulf of Suez were jumped by six MiG-21s. Again, radio communication indicated that the pilots were Russians. Although the Israelis managed to break free, it was evident that the Soviets were forcing a confrontation over the Canal Zone itself. In that case, there appeared no alternative but to accept the challenge head-on. Without Israeli air superiority over the waterway, the Bar-Lev Line would become untenable.

On July 30 four Israeli Phantoms overflew the canal. Sixteen Russian-piloted MiGs immediately rose in pursuit. Four Israeli Mirages flying at a still-higher altitude then pounced on the MiGs, downing four of them. The remaining Soviet interceptors promptly broke off contact. News of the humiliation sent shock waves through the Soviet military establishment. Two days after the episode, Marshal Pavel Katkov, commander of the Soviet air force, flew into Cairo to appraise personally the consequences of the dogfight. His initial reaction was to approve a counterambush for the Israelis. Dummy missile batteries were installed near the site of the recent air battle. When Israeli jets attacked it, a flight of awaiting Soviet MiGs downed two of them. Thus it was, by August 1970, that the War of Attrition was developing into a head-on Soviet-Israeli confrontation. No less than the Israelis, the Russians and Americans understood the acute gravity of the situation. Direct Soviet involvement in a Middle Eastern war ran the risk of an equivalent American reaction.

For some weeks even before the July–August 1970 crisis, Secretary of State Rogers had been circulating a plan for a cease-fire. Unlike its predecessor, this "Second Rogers Plan" avoided such nonstarters as an "interim" Israeli withdrawal or a "de facto" Arab commitment to peace. It proposed simply a cease-fire in place for three months. During that limited period UN Mediator Gunnar Jarring would renew his diplomatic mission, seeking a broader accommodation between Israel and its Arab neighbors. Moscow responded favorably. Its Egyptian protégés were desperately in need of a breather. Two years into the War of Attrition, they had suffered fifteen thousand casualties and witnessed the virtual depopulation of their canal cities. On June 29 Nasser departed for Moscow, where he acknowledged that his nation's morale had all but collapsed. The following July 23, then, with Soviet approval, the Egyptian president announced his willingness to accept a cease-fire.

Prime Minister Golda Meir was hesitant. Characteristically, she distrusted any formula short of a directly negotiated, permanent peace. But Israel by late July had sustained three thousand military casualties of its own, and each day added to the hemorrhage of the nation's young men. The danger now of an escalating confrontation with the Soviets was particularly threatening. At the same time, vigorously endorsing his secretary of state's formula, President Nixon assured Prime Minister Meir that he was prepared to sell Israel additional Phantom jets—the most modern fighter-bombers in the world, and a critical replacement for the embargoed French Mirages (p. 186). It was a compelling inducement. Before accepting it, however, Mrs. Meir insisted that a key provision of a three-month cease-fire must be a "standstill" in weaponry, that is, assurance that the Egyptians and Russians would not use the interregnum to move additional SAM missiles forward to the canal area. Upon conferring with the Soviets, Secretary of State Rogers gave that assurance. The prime minister then announced her government's agreement. The cease-fire came into effect on August 7, 1970.

Almost immediately Israeli intelligence learned that the Egyptians were violating the missile standstill commitment; and three weeks later the American CIA confirmed Israel's finding. In her outrage, Mrs. Meir then threatened to repudiate the cease-fire. It was to deter this move that the Nixon administration promised to ensure Israel's military edge by opening the pipeline even wider for Phantom jets. After further consultations, the Israelis grudgingly agreed to stay their hand. Although the missile advance at Suez continued, so did the cease-fire. Indeed, it continued even beyond the three-month deadline, for on September 28, 1970, Egypt's President Nasser died of a massive heart attack. His successor, Anwar al-Sadat, preoccupied with consolidating his political base, evinced little apparent interest in renewing the conflict. Silence reigned along the canal at last.

Had the Soviets come out the losers in the War of Attrition, as they had in the Six-Day War? Not likely. Their influence appeared far more extensive in Egypt by the summer of 1970 than at any time in the twenty-five-year relationship between the two countries. Thousands of Soviet instructors were training Egyptian personnel. Thousands of Soviet technicians were servicing Egypt's newly provided Soviet military equipment. Several hundred Soviet pilots were flying reconnaissance missions that had little to do with the Arab-Israeli conflict but much to do with surveillance of the U.S. Sixth Fleet. The port of Alexandria and all its extensive facilities, plus other Mediterranean harbors, now were available for the Soviet navy.

In the process, too, of shoring up Egypt's fragile economy, the Soviet bloc by 1970 was absorbing fully 38 percent of Egypt's exports, while Soviet-bloc products accounted for the near totality of Egypt's industrial imports. Altogether, the industrial sector of the Egyptian economy was shot through with Soviet-bloc experts and advisers. One sector of Cairo's fashionable Zamalek neighborhood was known simply as "the Russian quarter." A sizable downtown movie theater, the Odeon, specialized exclusively in Soviet films. The largest bookstore in town, the Dar al-Sharq, was given over entirely to Marxist literature and Soviet technical works. Gamal Abd al-Nasser had made his reputation by "liberating" Egypt from the British imperial presence. Yet, in the decade and a half since concluding the 1954 Anglo-Egyptian Heads of Agreement (p. 23), the president had handed over his nation's most critical military and economic infrastructure to still another, and conceivably even more formidable, imperial presence.

VIII   1967: A TRANSPOSITION OF WESTERN ALLIANCES

A REASSESSMENT IN LONDON

The reaction of West Europeans to the 1967 Middle Eastern trauma offered a dramatic contrast to the confusion and contumely of the 1956 crisis. This time Israel's case was open and shut, and sympathy for the Jewish state was overwhelming. Britain's response was characteristic. For some years even after the tactical Suez-Sinai alliance, the Macmillan government had remained wary in its relations with Israel, and cautiously "even-handed" in its pronouncements on Middle Eastern issues. But now, with public tolerance for Nasser's adventurism long since exhausted, editorials of support for the Israelis appeared in the *Times*, the *Observer*, the *Guardian*, the *Economist*, and other influential newspapers and journals. It was a goodwill that emanated no less from the highest official quarters. Even earlier, in 1964, when Britain elected its first Labor cabinet in thirteen years, Prime Minister Harold Wilson had underscored his government's revised approach to the Arab-Israel confrontation by inviting Levi Eshkol for an official visit and receiving the Israeli leader, a fellow Socialist, with visible warmth. The cordiality was personal no less than political. Wilson had many friends among British Jews, and his son had spent a number of months working on an Israeli kibbutz. He genuinely wished Israel well.

On May 18, 1967, therefore, upon learning that Nasser had evicted UNEF troops from Gaza and Sharm es-Sheikh, Wilson publicly and vigorously condemned the move. Yet the prime minister was not an impulsive man. In notes to Lyndon Johnson and to France's Foreign Minister Couve de Murville, he observed that Egyptian occupation of Sharm es-Sheikh was not yet tantamount to an actual blockade of the Strait of Tiran. It was thus vital to deter a preemptive Israeli move. Cabling Israel's Foreign Minister Eban, Wilson made his pitch for restraint:

> If it appeared that any attempt to interfere with the passage of ships through the waterway were likely to be made, we should promote and secure free passage. We stand by this statement. We think it important, however, that attention should be concentrated on free passage and not on the shore positions.

But on May 23 Nasser took the fatal step of announcing closure of the strait to Israel-bound shipping. "In contrast to [the circumstances] in 1956 when France and Britain were at her side," he proclaimed, "Israel this time is without the support of any European Power." The Egyptian president was not altogether correct. Wilson promptly called an emergency cabinet meeting and declared his intention of lending Israel every possible support. His ministerial colleagues unanimously endorsed his stance, even Foreign Secretary George Brown, who rarely had taken Israel's side against the Arab "Third World." Thus, in Washington, when Lyndon Johnson's initial strategy in the crisis was to explore a reactivation of the 1950 Tripartite Declaration, Wilson and Brown rejected the proposal. The Tripartite Declaration involved a commitment to maintain the frontiers not only of Israel but also of Egypt, they noted, and Britain and Israel themselves had dispensed with that commitment in the Sinai-Suez invasion of 1956. Neither government was in a credible position to reinvoke it now.

On the other hand, in March 1957 Britain had joined the world's other principal maritime powers in an unambiguous commitment to enforce freedom of navigation through the Strait of Tiran. Accordingly, more than ten years later, on May 23, 1967, Wilson emphasized that "it [is] in this spirit that we should act now." He would participate with the United States and other maritime nations in organizing a naval force to keep open, or reopen, the Gulf of Aqaba to the shipping of all countries. "The declared purpose of the operation," the prime minister explained to his cabinet colleagues, "would be to assert maritime rights rather than specifically to assist Israel, and it would be unlikely to have any serious effect on our relations with the Arab states generally."

The statement was revealing. Even as friendly a government as Wilson's was unprepared to be seen acting specifically in Israel's interests. Abba Eban grasped the distinction from the outset. On the late afternoon of May 24, the Israeli foreign minister departed Paris for London in his urgent round of Western capitals (p. 180). On arriving at Heathrow Airport, he proceeded immediately to 10 Downing Street. Wilson received him with great warmth, exhibiting (in Eban's recollection) a "decent respect" for the gravity of Israel's situation. The prime minister recently had been in touch with Paris, and he assured Eban now that he was unimpressed with de Gaulle's vision of a Four-Power conference that would include the Russians. The Soviet Union was part of the problem, Wilson acknowledged, not of its solution.

Eban then emphasized Israel's determination to resist the blockade. His only current purpose was to learn whether the maritime powers intended to fulfill their 1957 commitment. Wilson's response was almost as forthright. He and his cabinet just that morning had agreed that Britain would join with others in an international flotilla to open the Strait of Tiran. In fact, he already had dispatched Minister of State George Thompson and Admiral E. L. T. Henderson to Washington to discuss a plan of common action with the Americans, one of "nuts and bolts." But the prime minister did not specify whether an international naval flotilla would serve as escort for Israeli shipping or exclusively for the vessels of other maritime nations. Neither would he guarantee that such a naval force could even be organized. First and foremost, Eban sensed, Wilson was determined to forestall precipitous Israeli action—and only secondly to guarantee "unlimited" (that is, Israeli) free access to the Gulf of Aqaba. On that ambiguous note, the meeting ended. Eban flew on to Washington.

At the White House, Eban received from Lyndon Johnson essentially the same assurances of goodwill, the same commitment to an international flotilla, and the same warning—this one far more explicit than Wilson's—that "Israel will be alone only if it acts alone." The foreign minister returned to Jerusalem. In London, meanwhile, Wilson and his Foreign Office advisers diligently pressed ahead on the flotilla project, while Thompson and Henderson in Washington sought to coordinate this agenda with the American government. The British also made clear that they were uninterested in an exclusively Anglo-American force. To gain international credence and simultaneously to diffuse Arab criticism, the flotilla would have to be multinational in the broadest sense. It was a formidable challenge. Indeed, it soon proved an impossible one. The Russians manifestly had a vested interest in blocking the scheme. De Gaulle was opposed to any proposal not based on a Four-Power conference. As for the other maritime nations, only Australia, New Zealand, and the Netherlands expressed willingness to commit naval vessels and risk Arab obloquy. But in the end, participation ultimately depended upon Lyndon Johnson's ability to provide the backbone of the task force, and Johnson's initiative in turn depended on Congress. With American forces already mired in Vietnam, Congress was resistant.

Wilson followed these developments with a sinking heart. By the last days of May, he was reduced to canvassing other governments in the hope at least of assuring a multilateral declaration if not a naval armada. In that effort, at least, the prime minister enjoyed warm support from all factions in Parliament. May 31 saw a full day's debate in the House of Commons on the Middle Eastern crisis. Edward Heath, leader of the Conservative opposition, and Alec Douglas-Home, the Conservatives' "shadow" foreign secretary, both invoked the "Munich" metaphor in assuring Wilson and Brown of "the full support of this side of the House." Otherwise, as Wilson acknowledged later, "we would not be able to guarantee freedom of passage for an Israeli ship passing through [the Strait of Tiran], short of providing [it] with a naval escort; this was certainly not our intention." For the prime minister, as for Lyndon Johnson, the solution was an international force or nothing. On June 2 Wilson flew to Washington to meet with the president. The two leaders spent the entire next morning reviewing all alternatives. Yet one of these options could not be American participation in a naval armada. Congress would not support it. Britain in turn could not act without the United States and the other principal maritime powers. On the night of June 3–4, the prime minister returned to London.

In the early morning of June 5, he was awakened to learn that war had broken out in the Middle East. Minutes later, a telegram arrived at 10 Downing Street from Aleksei Kosygin in Moscow, urging an immediate cease-fire and withdrawal of Israeli forces. Not likely. Here at least, Wilson's reaction, like Johnson's, was to ensure that Israel be spared punishment for acting on its own to defend its security. The prime minister telexed Johnson forthwith, suggesting that the UN Security Council request a Middle East cease-fire—nothing more. The president agreed. Afterward Wilson and his cabinet followed with tense gratification Israel's unfolding military triumph. The priority henceforth was to monitor the Soviet reaction. It came in the form of a verbal blast on the night of June 7–8, and again on June 9 (p. 163), as Israeli forces crushed Syrian resistance on the Golan Heights. Wilson allowed a day and a half to pass to ensure that Israel's victory in the north was complete. Only then, on June 10, did he respond to Moscow, equably favoring a cease-fire. At the same time the prime minister cabled Eshkol in Jerusalem, urging the Israeli leader not to run the risk of Soviet intervention. "I can assure you," he stated, "that [we] will work for a thorough examination of everything necessary for a constructive arrangement that will take account of [Israel's] legitimate interests."

Wilson was in earnest. By then he had been deluged by cables from leaders of the Afro-Asian members of the Commonwealth, pleading for him to use his influence "in quest of the restoration of the Arab territories." The prime minister fended them off. It was a stance he adopted with de Gaulle, as well, politely but firmly rejecting the French president's request for "Big Four" action to compel unilateral Israeli withdrawal. Yet, by the same token, Britain was unprepared to offer Israel carte blanche to keep its winnings. On June 21, addressing the UN General Assembly in New York, British Foreign Secretary Brown maintained his opposition to unilateral Israeli withdrawal, but added the reproof that no nation should be permitted to secure "territorial aggrandizement" by war.

As the summer wore on, and the Security Council erratically grappled with a formula to resolve the Middle East standoff, it was Britain's ambassador to the Security Council, Lord Caradon (Hugh Foote), who emerged as the West's most skilled and tenacious negotiator. A former governor of Cyprus, widely experienced in dealings with that island's volatile Greek and Turkish populations, Caradon brought an incisive imagination to his discussions with the "nonaligned" ambassadors. At all times, of course, he was advocating the balanced approach favored by Wilson and Brown. Thus, meeting repeatedly with Abba Eban and with Gideon Rafael, Israel's ambassador to the United Nations, Caradon emphasized that London and Washington were in fullest accord on Israel's right to security guarantees before making a move for withdrawal. But he cautioned the Israelis that any UN draft resolution omitting a reference to the "nonadmissibility of the acquisition of territory by force" would fail to get through the Security Council.

The draft Caradon then presented to Eban and Rafael on November 18 included the "nonadmissibility" stipulation, as well as a clause mandating "withdrawal of Israeli armed forces from territories occupied in the recent conflict." Yet the draft linked these demands with "termination of all claims or states of belligerency, and respect for and acknowledgement of the sovereignty, territorial integrity and political independence of every State in the [Middle East] and their right to live in peace within secure and recognized boundaries free from threats or acts of force." The document also provided for a special United Nations representative to "promote agreement and assist efforts to achieve a peaceful and accepted settlement." It was an ingenious compromise. The Israelis sensed immediately that it did not oblige them to withdraw their forces specifically to the prewar armistice lines of June 4. In fact several resolutions calling for such a return already had been defeated in both the Security Council and the General Assembly. And when the Indian and Arab delegations, almost at the last moment, pressed for a clause demanding evacuation of "the" territories—implying *all* territories—Caradon refused to include the definite article. Thereupon, returning to Jerusalem, Eban recommended that the cabinet accept Caradon's draft. It did. So did the Security Council on November 22. With the reluctant acquiescence of the Soviet Union, its members approved the draft as Resolution 242.

In achieving a diplomatic victory that was light-years removed from the condemnation of 1956, Israel doubtless owed most to the support provided by Lyndon Johnson and by UN Ambassador Arthur Goldberg. But it was Caradon's matchless negotiating skills that steered Israel's military triumph to international approbation. Behind Caradon, in turn, Harold Wilson had sent the decisive signal that Israel was to be regarded as a legitimate and abiding presence in the Middle Eastern firmament. The man was no Anthony Eden. Far from proposing an attenuation of the Jewish state's frontiers as Britain's quid pro quo for Arab friendship, the prime minister in effect was reversing the equation, demanding recognition of Israel's territorial integrity as Arab payment for British goodwill.

A BACK OF THE HAND FROM PARIS

> De Gaulle undoubtedly is the greatest European statesman today.... He has tremendous natural leadership. He is as fearless in politics as he was in war. He has a dazzlingly original and analytical mind.... He has grandeur of style and, like Churchill, a profound sense of history and destiny.

It was David Ben-Gurion speaking, in a journalist's interview of early 1964. While hardly unaware of recent tremors in French policy toward his country, the former prime minister could not have anticipated the sea change soon to occur in French-Israeli relations. As late as February 1966, while on a visit to Paris, Foreign Minister Abba Eban was assured that deliveries of French military equipment to Israel would continue on schedule. In the summer of that year, the Israeli government signed a new agreement for the purchase of fifty French Mirage Vs (p. 114), the latest version of a world-class interceptor that would include numerous improvements suggested by the Israeli air force.

It was the May–June 1967 crisis that became the litmus test of Israel's relationship with its "friend and ally." As Nasser suddenly

evicted United Nations troops from Gaza, then announced his blockade of the Strait of Tiran, Paris this time reacted with a distinct lack of
urgency. In veiled asides to the press, French foreign ministry officials
even intimated that there were "juridical obscurities" about Israel's
maritime rights. These media accounts resonated ominously in Jerusalem. Was there a gleam of light behind the impenetrable cloud?
Foreign Minister Abba Eban was determined to find out. In the
predawn hours of May 24, he flew off to Paris, landing at Orly Airport
at 7:00 a.m. Together with Walter Eytan, Israel's ambassador to
France, Eban was rushed under police escort directly to the Élysée
Palace. Foreign Minister Couve de Murville was waiting to usher the
Israelis into de Gaulle's office. Even before greetings were exchanged,
however, the French president declaimed urgently: "Do not make
war!" After the introductions, he continued: "At any rate, do not
shoot first! . . . The Four Powers must be left to resolve the dispute.
France will influence the Soviet Union toward an attitude favorable
to peace."

Under tight composure, Eban then made Israel's case. Laying particular stress on the blockade, he reminded de Gaulle that in 1957
France had joined Britain, the United States, and other maritime
nations in supporting Israeli rights in the Gulf of Aqaba, including
Israel's right to defend itself against blockade. Israel was now prepared to wage war to defend that right, Eban continued, but first
wished to know where France stood, to determine if there might be a
"harmonization of policies" between the two governments. Yet de
Gaulle, unmoved, merely repeated his admonition: Israel must not
make war. Was not Nasser's blockade an act of war? Eban riposted.
Evidently not. For de Gaulle, an act of war meant firing the first shot.
He acknowledged that France's declaration of 1957 was correct
juridically, but it was a commitment that had reflected the "particular
heat" of Sinai-Suez.

The president continued: "Today it must be understood that there
are no Western solutions"; the Soviet Union would have to be associated in a "concerted effort by the Four." When Eban then observed
that the Soviet Union itself shared responsibility for the present crisis, de Gaulle remained implacable. Moscow would accept Israeli passage in the Gulf of Aqaba, he insisted; but time was needed for France
to concert Four-Power action to enable ships to pass through the
Strait—and also, presumably, to allow France to project itself back to
a state of diplomatic equivalence with the two superpowers. The
interview proved a dialogue of the deaf. As it ended, the French minister of information, Georges Gorse, already was summarizing to

reporters the conclusions reached in the morning's emergency cabinet session (just before the Eban–de Gaulle meeting). When asked what France's attitude would be if Egypt were to fire on an Israeli vessel in the Strait of Tiran, Gorse replied that, in view of the current tension, the appearance of an Israeli vessel in the Strait would be a "provocative act."

Yet it soon became evident that France's government policy was distinctly at odds with the nation's popular mood. From late May onward an ad hoc "Comité de Solidarité Français avec Israël" was organizing pro-Israel demonstrations in Paris, Strasbourg, Marseilles, Nice, and other cities. One rally, in the capital on June 2, brought an estimated seventy thousand people to the Avenue Wagram, outside the Israeli embassy. Passing automobiles sounded their horns three times, evoking the syllables of "Is-ra-ël." Except for *Le Temps* and *Le Monde*, the austere eminences of French journalism, the country's most widely read newspapers editorialized in behalf of Israel. Between June and September 1967, public opinion polls revealed that sympathy for the Jewish state reached 68 percent, with barely 18 percent registered for the Arabs. Was there yet a chance that de Gaulle was listening?

On the morning of June 2, Israel's Prime Minister Eshkol dispatched a last, forlorn appeal for understanding to the French president. It went unrequited. Later that day, a cabinet meeting at the Élysée Palace was followed by a presidential declaration. France considered that each of the Middle Eastern states had the right to exist, it stated, but none had the right to begin hostilities; only a meeting of the four "Great Powers" could resolve the problem of navigation in the Gulf of Aqaba, as well as the problem of "the Arab refugees"—a new genuflection to "equivalence" on the Middle East crisis. But de Gaulle's diplomatic initiative, like Eban's, was an exercise in futility. Moscow displayed no interest whatever in a "Great-Power" summit. In Washington, President Lyndon Johnson's reaction to the Four-Power proposal was a mocking query: "Which are the other two?" There remained still another way, however, for de Gaulle to influence Middle Eastern events. That same afternoon of June 2, he ordered an immediate cessation of French weapons shipments to the Middle East—in effect, to Israel.

Since the onset of the crisis in mid-May, Israeli passenger and air force transports had been flying into France around the clock to load up with military equipment. French munitions manufacturers and defense ministry officials warmly cooperated in the effort, cutting through all red tape, clearing every Israeli request within hours. At

the instructions of Defense Minister Pierre Messmer, military airfields were made available to the Israelis. Yet by June 2, the French
press was giving increased attention to the heavy traffic of Israeli Boe-
ings and Nords, and the rushed delivery of military equipment, particularly from the Sud-Aviation Company, manufacturer of Israel's
Mirage aircraft and its spare parts. It was at this point that de Gaulle
issued his order to end deliveries. In turn, upon learning of the ban,
Yochanan Meroz, Israel's minister plenipotentiary in Paris, rushed to
the office of Claude Lebel, director of the foreign ministry's Middle
East department, to protest. Not without embarrassment, Lebel
assured Meroz that the suspension would be "temporary and even
very temporary." On June 4, Prime Minister Georges Pompidou intimated to Meroz that the embargo would be put into effect slowly and
selectively.

Pompidou was not dissembling. Importuned by Defense Minister
Messmer, the premier managed to delay activation of the embargo
for forty-eight hours. Messmer in turn ordered French military personnel to help load the Israeli planes. Eventually, selective deliveries
of French equipment to Israel would continue both in the days immediately before and for nearly a year after the Six-Day War. They
comprised spare parts for matériel already shipped, including radar,
helicopters, support vehicles, even quantities of rockets earlier contracted for. The fifty Mirage Vs were placed on hold, to be sure, but
the manufacture of these aircraft in any case had not been completed.
Meanwhile, on June 4, Israel's Ambassador Walter Eytan arrived at
the Élysée Palace to discuss the embargo with the presidential chef de
cabinet. To Eytan's surprise, de Gaulle himself emerged from his
office and invited the ambassador to remain for a personal talk.

During the conversation, the president warned that Israel must not
rely on the United States. Washington might be supportive at first, he
conceded, but its friendship soon would cool if war broke out and if
the Suez Canal and oil shipments were blocked. For the first time,
then, de Gaulle acknowledged openly that his nation's interests had
shifted since the Franco-Israeli honeymoon of 1956–57. The issue of
Algeria had been resolved, he explained, and France consequently was
able, and obliged, to develop closer relations with the Arab world. Yet
the president remained confident that French-Arab friendship also
could serve Israel's interests; at least there would be one power to
which both sides would be prepared to give heed.

Until that moment, Eytan had listened without comment. But now
he ventured an interjection of his own. If France intended to press

Israel not to launch a war, he suggested, an arms embargo might well engender "an attitude of desperation," and thus make war even more probable. Without addressing the point directly, de Gaulle simply alluded once again to the importance of a Four-Power conference. In fact Eytan's warning was prescient. The arms embargo proved entirely counterproductive to de Gaulle's objective. As the ambassador telexed a report of his conversation to Jerusalem, the Israeli cabinet now sensed a new dimension of urgency. At a time when Soviet arms were pouring into Egypt and Syria, a ban on French equipment would distend the Middle East arms equilibrium even further—and possibly fatally.

A day afterward, war broke out in the Middle East. In France, public opinion remained overwhelmingly sympathetic to Israel. On June 5 yet another mass rally took place outside the Israeli embassy, this one comprising some one hundred thousand people. That day, too, three Gaullist deputies, Joël Le Tac, Pierre Clostermann, and Robert-André Vivien, departed for Israel, in tandem with other, non-Gaullist deputies, to demonstrate their solidarity with the Jewish state. The government's public reaction meanwhile was one of thunderous silence. On June 6 de Gaulle exchanged private messages with Soviet Prime Minister Kosygin, repeating his appeal for a Four-Power conference and urging a Security Council resolution for an immediate cease-fire and withdrawal of Israeli troops. But Kosygin remained as uninterested in a summit conference as he had before the war; and by June 7, it became evident that a plain and simple cease-fire, unlinked to Israeli withdrawal, was the best the Arabs and their patrons could achieve. Accordingly, on June 9, de Gaulle too was obliged to concur in the Security Council's demand for a cease-fire in place.

THE DIPLOMACY OF RETRIBUTION

Ten days later, on June 19, Harold Wilson flew to Paris for personal discussions with the French president. He found de Gaulle in a state of depression. His cherished scenario of a Four-Power conference had been spurned. Once more, his vision of France projected into the big league of superpowers had come to naught. Yet again, the Soviet Union and the United States were deciding everything between themselves. Britain, too, would be a loser, de Gaulle warned the prime minister. "Someday the West will thank me for this [evenhanded] policy of mine," he insisted, "for France now . . . [will] be the only Western power to have any influence with the Arab governments."

The president ensured that his directives reflected his strategy. In
ensuing weeks, throughout the June and July sessions of the UN
Security Council, France's delegate voted steadfastly in favor of Communist and Third World resolutions demanding Israeli withdrawal
from occupied Arab territories, together with a halt to the annexation
of East Jerusalem, and an immediate return of displaced West Bank
Arabs. On June 21, in the first of a series of press conferences, de
Gaulle insisted that France "cannot acknowledge any territorial
changes achieved by military action," and deprecated Israel's appeal
for direct negotiations with its Arab enemies. Only a Four-Power
conference could impose a just solution on Arabs and Israelis, he
declared. Yet, with every passing day, it was becoming clearer that the
president was flogging a dead horse.

De Gaulle's frustration and bitterness doubtless accounted as well
for the single most bizarre press conference of his public career. It
occurred on November 27, five days after the UN Security Council
had issued Resolution 242, thereby dashing the French president's
last hopes for Israeli withdrawal and a Four-Power conference.
Acknowledging Jewish courage and energy in building Israel, and the
goodwill France bore Israel during the Jewish state's early years, de
Gaulle then turned harshly critical. After the Suez-Sinai campaign of
1956, he noted, "we watched the emergence of a State of Israel that
was warlike and set on expansion . . . [and the] recent vexatious affair
of Aqaba was to offer a pretext to those who had been longing for
war." France had warned Israel not to attack, but "France's voice was
not heeded. . . . Now, in the territories [Israel] has captured, she is
organizing an occupation which can only be accompanied by oppression, repression, and expulsion."

It was not merely the vindictive tone of the president's censure that
drew attention, or even the rapidity with which Israel had been transformed from an "ally" into an aggressor and oppressor. Adverting to
the circumstances of Israel's birth, de Gaulle observed:

> Some even feared that the Jews, scattered hitherto but remain-
> ing what they had always been, that is, an elite people, self-
> assured and domineering, might, once they were reunited,
> turn . . . [their] hopes [of] "Next Year in Jerusalem" into a burn-
> ing ambition of conquest. In spite of the wave of ill feeling . . .
> which [the Jews] had . . . aroused in certain countries and at cer-
> tain times, a considerable capital of interest and even sympathy
> [remained]. . . . That is why . . . many countries, and France
> among them, looked with satisfaction on the establishment of

their state . . . while at the same time wanting them to reach a peaceful modus vivendi with their neighbors through the use of a little modesty.

The remarks aroused headlines in the French press and outrage among Jews in both Israel and France. From his desert retirement in Sde Boker, even Ben-Gurion on December 6 felt impelled to send the president an eleven-page letter expressing his dismay. De Gaulle himself soon realized that he had stirred up a hornet's nest. Professing to have been misunderstood, he accepted his advisers' counsel to "clarify" his meaning, and invited France's Chief Rabbi Jacob Kaplan to explain that his, the president's, use of the terms "elite" and "domineering" had been intended not as pejoratives but as compliments. Yet de Gaulle remained obdurate in his refusal to accept Israel's conquests as a fait accompli. His earlier explanation to Harold Wilson on June 19 had been succinct and forthright. "France must align itself with the Arabs. . . . It has vital interests with the tens of millions of Arabs."

In fact, those interests transcended the Middle East. They mandated international recognition of France's stature as a Great Power, an equal player with Britain, the Soviet Union, and above all the United States in addressing critical issues of world security. De Gaulle's resentment influenced his policy of global *grandeur* in every phase—his withdrawal of France from the NATO command, his decision to build France's own nuclear *force de frappe*, and his later rejection of Britain's membership in the Common Market. By no coincidence, the president's diatribe of November 27 had ended with a backhanded swipe at America's "hateful war . . . in Vietnam."

The price Israel paid for Gaullist *grandeur* remained less diplomatic than military. The French embargo on "heavy-item" battle hardware—principally aircraft and artillery—continued intact. At first, the restrictions did not significantly affect Israel's qualitative edge over its vanquished enemies. Spare parts and "low-offensive-capacity" equipment in any case evaded de Gaulle's embargo. It was the issue of the pending fifty Mirage V interceptors that remained crucial. Their manufacture was scheduled for completion in April 1969. Determined to maintain its lien on these vital craft, Israel scrupulously met its payment installments throughout 1967 and 1968; and the fate of the Mirages consequently remained in doubt until late 1968. But then Israel itself supplied de Gaulle with his pretext for closing off the military pipeline altogether.

In 1968 a chain reaction of Palestinian airjackings and assaults on El Al, Israel's national airline, and, later, on transports belonging to other airlines with service to Israel, culminated in December 1968 when two Arabs machine-gunned an El Al plane on the runway at Athens airport. An Israeli passenger was killed. This time Israel's reaction was massive. As in the case of several earlier terrorist attacks, Lebanon had functioned as the guerrillas' staging base. The hijackers had been recruited and trained there. Accordingly, on December 28, the Israelis launched a helicopter-borne commando raid on Beirut airport, destroying thirteen planes—virtually the entire fleet—of Lebanon's national carrier, Air Liban. In its unprecedented dimensions, the attack evoked comparably harsh international criticism, and a UN Security Council resolution of condemnation.

But nowhere was shock greater than in France. Tiny Lebanon was a country with historic French associations. Its government had taken great pains to avoid direct confrontation with Israel. For de Gaulle the episode presented an intolerable personal no less than diplomatic provocation. Immediately he ordered France's Ambassador François Huré recalled from Israel. A week later, on January 3, 1969, the president imposed a total embargo on all weapons destined for Israel—on all equipment, large or small, including all spare parts on order or paid for. The crucial issue of the Mirages now was resolved decisively: They would not be available to Israel under any circumstances. The blow was a severe one to the French military aircraft industry. Israel in recent years had been providing some 20 percent of its income. But for the Jewish state, the consequences clearly were far more unsettling. Until that moment the French embargo ostensibly had applied to the Middle East in general, to Israel and its Arab adversaries alike. But now Israel alone was singled out. By implication the French weapons pipeline might now be opened to the Arab nations. Indeed, queried on this point, de Gaulle remained ominously noncommittal. On January 13, moreover, he dispatched Minister of Information Gorse to Lebanon to reaffirm France's traditional and historic friendship for that country. The gesture was decisive. Once de Gaulle openly cast France's lot with the Arabs, it became evident that Israel's final lingering hope of moderating the president's adversarial stance had expired.

On the other hand, it was a stance uniquely identified with Charles de Gaulle himself. In the spring of 1969, a combination of trade union and radical student factions launched into violent demonstrations against the Gaullist government, which they regarded as ossified and reactionary. The president managed to overcome the threat, even to win a hurriedly scheduled parliamentary election. Nevertheless, he remained baffled and discountenanced by the challenge to his authority. To reaffirm his leadership, he mounted still another test at the polls, submitting a pair of—relatively minor—constitutional amendments to a popular referendum. Yet by then, the French public apparently had had enough of the Great Man. On April 27, 1969, the president's amendments were soundly defeated. That same night, he silently abandoned his office.

Could de Gaulle's party and government system survive without his personal leadership? It appeared that both would, although with some modification. Indeed, his supporters actually turned to a former Gaullist prime minister, Georges Pompidou, as their standard-bearer, and succeeded in electing him president in June 1969. Fifty-eight years old, Pompidou was rather more of a bon vivant and lover of literature than a career politician. Upon assuming the presidency, he evinced greater flexibility than had his predecessor in both domestic and international affairs. Under the direction of his foreign minister, Michel Jobert, the government set about easing tensions with Washington and encouraging Britain's entry into the Common Market. Although France did not rejoin NATO's integrated command, it moved toward a more functional cooperation with its other treaty partners. Witnessing these developments, Israeli foreign ministry specialists were cautiously hopeful that the new president would also adopt a softer tone toward their country.

In earlier years, Pompidou had served as a director of the Rothschild Bank and was known to have remained close to his old patron, Guy de Rothschild. Several of his new cabinet members had evinced sympathy for Israel, and Léo Haman, a Jew, was a close political adviser to the new president. And on Middle Eastern issues, as on those of foreign affairs generally, Pompidou appeared distinctly less frontal than de Gaulle in his approach. At a 1970 presidential reception for the diplomatic corps, he greeted the new Israeli ambassador, Asher Ben-Natan (who had formerly served in Bonn), with a friendly "Shalom." Genuflecting to the Gaullist formula of a Four-Power agreement—a requirement that later he would drop—Pompidou at least did not insist on full Israeli withdrawal from the captured territories. He alluded simply to the advantages of a more "durable" peace for Israel itself, and laid his emphasis on the plight of the Arab refugees, linking their fate to the enforcement of UN Security Council Resolution 242.

The Israelis soon were disenchanted. Pompidou made clear that France's new orientation toward the Arab world would remain intact. The reason had less to do with France's need for *grandeur*, however, or Great-Power equivalence, than with commercial realities. For the new president, an economist by training, the facts spoke for themselves. From 1966 to 1970 French exports to the Moslem world had risen from $921 million to $1.326 billion, a 44 percent increase, the largest achieved in the Middle East by any Western country, not excluding the Bundesrepublik. In Pompidou's and Foreign Minister Jobert's perspective, the economic potential of the Arab world could not be overlooked by any responsible government, and surely not by France, with its near-total dependence on North African and Middle Eastern oil. In earlier shipments to Israel, to be sure, weaponry had proved its unique value to the French economy; and, as a result, the ensuing embargo against the Jewish state inflicted a 37 percent loss in income from armaments exports between June 1967 and June 1968. Afterward, however, these losses soon were made good. As early as June 1970 the acceleration of weapons deliveries to the Third World, and particularly to the Arab world, completely erased the initial, short-term loss. By then, military exports totaled more than one-fourth of all French manufactured exports, and this time Arab nations were by far the largest purchasers. In the government's view, it was critical to maintain this growth against the intimidating sales power of the giant American military-industrial conglomerates.

A CONTEST OF MANEUVER

In the years following de Gaulle's 1967 volte face on the Middle East, Israel was not prepared to twist passively in the wind, allowing its heavy investment in French military equipment to slip away by default. Beyond the Mirage jets, there was another consignment of weaponry whose fate initially remained in limbo. These were naval vessels. In 1962 Wolfgang Lutz, an Israeli spy in Egypt, sent back word that the Soviet Union was about to provide Egypt with a number of powerful, Komar-class missile boats. The threat was a serious one. Israel's own obsolescent little navy comprised barely a dozen torpedo boats, two destroyers, and two submarines. By then, however, Israeli defense ministry officials had concluded that the day of heavy warships in any case was over, for they were fatally vulnerable to land- or sea-based missiles. These officials were aware, too, that the West German naval command had reached essentially the same decision. In 1962 the Bundesrepublik had embarked on construction of the Jaguar, a speedy and highly versatile coastal vessel. For the Israelis a boat of this category could be fitted with their own recently developed Gabriel missile, an exceptionally accurate sea-skimmer capable of evading enemy radar. In that same year, therefore, Shimon Peres won the Adenauer government's agreement to provide Israel with twelve of these craft, to be named "Sa'ar."

Two years later, in December 1964, as the first of the Sa'ars moved toward construction at a Kiel shipyard, rumors of the secret German-Israeli military agreement leaked to the press. The relationship had to be ended (p. 142), and with it, the Sa'ar project. Yet, rather than abandon their investment, the Israelis sought out experienced shipyards in other countries that might be prepared to build the vessels under license. Eventually one was located, in Cherbourg, France. It was a private firm, Constructions Mécaniques de Normandie, and its owner, Félix Amiot, was delighted to acquire the commission at a time of slumping business. Work on the Sa'ars accordingly began in 1965. At the direction of Rear Admiral Mordechai Limon, chief of Israel's naval purchasing mission in France, a contingent of some forty Israeli engineers and naval officers arrived in Cherbourg to monitor construction. Eventually, with their families, the number of Israelis in Cherbourg would reach two hundred.

The first of the vessels was launched in April 1967. It was subjected to ten thousand miles of punishing sea tests, and subsequently numerous improvements were added. The Israelis were more than satisfied with the boat. Indeed, Admiral Limon persuaded his government to double the order of Sa'ars, from twelve to twenty-four. Although the initial price of $2.5 million each also would double as new electronics were added, and only twelve actually were constructed, the contract still would prove to be the most successful in Israeli military history. Before the Six-Day War, three of the Sa'ars had departed for Israel, although not in time for combat action. Even after de Gaulle's initial embargo of June 2, 1967, work on the project continued. French naval and marine officials in Cherbourg simply ignored the ban, routinely assuring the defense ministry in Paris that only civilian projects were on order in Félix Amiot's shipyard. Cherbourg's municipal authorities, grateful for the lucrative Sa'ar contract, willingly collaborated in the charade. By December 1968, three additional missile boats had completed their tests and cruised off to Israel.

Yet it was also in late December 1968 that Israeli commandos destroyed the Lebanese airline and evoked the wrath of Charles de Gaulle. Within days, Admiral Limon in Paris learned from a private contact in the French defense ministry that the president now was about to impose an airtight embargo. At the informant's "suggestion," the Israelis in Cherbourg hurriedly set about dispatching any of the vessels capable of sailing. Only two of the boats were—Sa'ar 6 and Sa'ar 7. Even these had not yet undergone their preliminary sea tests.

Nevertheless, Captain Hadar Kimche, Israel's Sa'ar project manager in Cherbourg, ordered his crews to prepare the vessels for immediate departure. At 5:00 a.m., on Friday, January 4, 1969, the two Sa'ars inched their way out of the harbor, ostensibly for "breaking-in" tests. They never returned. Refueled at sea, they navigated the three-thousand-mile journey in rough winter waters to Israel. Meanwhile, on Monday, January 7, upon learning of the escape, the French defense ministry upbraided Admiral Limon. Blandly, the Israeli purchasing director insisted that news of the embargo had arrived only after the weekend. Local officials in Cherbourg "corroborated" the story. But the French government was having none of it. It ordered all Israeli personnel out of Félix Amiot's shipyard.

Amiot, and the citizens of Cherbourg, still were not prepared to forgo their golden goose. They continued to work on the five remaining Sa'ar vessels, accepting Israeli payments, trusting that a way still might be found for delivery. Yet the challenge this time would be much more difficult. A special contingent of French naval officials kept the boats under tight surveillance. Diplomacy no longer appeared to be an option for Israel; the new Pompidou government evidently intended to maintain de Gaulle's embargo. Even then, however, Israel's defense ministry was unwilling to abandon the Sa'ar project. The future of Israel's entire naval defense was at stake. All training and logistics had been structured around the vessels, and they were tantalizingly near completion.

In the end, Defense Minister Moshe Dayan agreed that a ruse was the only remaining alternative. He summoned Admiral Limon back to Israel, and a strategy was devised. It was for the shipyard to entertain offers from "other buyers." Informed of the scheme, Félix Amiot willingly cooperated. Soon afterward, in November 1969, the shipyard owner was visited by a potential buyer, one Martin Siem, ostensibly a director of the Norwegian shipping company Starboat & Weil. The company, Siem explained, was interested in the Sa'ars for oil exploration off the coast of Alaska. He was prepared to meet Amiot's price, but he needed the boats immediately. Thereupon Amiot sought his government's approval. The deal would solve a painful diplomatic impasse, he emphasized, and prove economically useful to France. Two weeks later, an interministerial defense committee gave its consent.

This was careless. Starboat & Weil had been incorporated in Panama only a few days before Siem's arrival in Cherbourg. Siem was indeed a Norwegian, but he was also a partner in the Israeli shipping company Maritime Fruit Carriers, Ltd., and assuredly he was planning no oil explorations off the Alaskan coast. Neither did the French government trouble to investigate the group of blond, blue-eyed "Norwegian" sailors who arrived to prepare the boats for departure. They were Israeli naval personnel. Working around the clock, the newcomers collaborated with Amiot's work crews in rushing the five vessels to completion. The departure date was carefully selected. It was December 24. On Christmas Eve, French naval and customs officials in Cherbourg were likely to be reduced to a skeleton force. They would have little cause for vigilance, in any case. For that festive evening, it was learned, elaborate reservations had been made for the "Norwegian" sailors at a Paris restaurant.

In the early darkness of December 24, additional oil tanks were hurriedly lashed to the Sa'ars for refueling at sea. The Israeli crews then climbed on board and inched the five boats out of Cherbourg's treacherous eastern inlet to the open sea. It was not until late Christmas Day that France's defense ministry got word of the escape. Informed at his country home, Pompidou was astounded—and mortified. Foreign Minister Maurice Schumann then put in an urgent telephone call to Israeli Ambassador Walter Eytan at the latter's Paris residence. He was informed that Eytan was in Switzerland, "visiting friends," and that his location was "unknown." Summoning Israel's press attaché, Schumann raged for nearly an hour. If the boats turned up in Israel, he warned, "the consequences will be grave indeed for your country."

The little vessels were having a difficult enough time as it was. The winter seas gave them a fearful buffeting. Refueling en route was a perilous operation. Two of the boats nearly foundered in the Bay of Biscay. French naval aircraft shadowed them continually. European news agencies meanwhile covered the episode with breathless excitement—and barely suppressed admiration. When the first Sa'ar entered the Strait of Gibraltar, the British coastal station flashed it a "Bon Voyage." And as the vessels plied their way across the Mediterranean, it became evident that there was little France could do to stop them. On December 31 Pompidou convened a working lunch with Prime Minister Jacques Chaban-Delmas, Defense Minister Michel Debré, and Foreign Minister Schumann. They agreed that the entire episode should be played down to avoid even further international derision. A government press release then declared that the vessels had been sold to a civilian company, and their destination accordingly was no longer a matter for official concern.

That same December 31, the five Sa'ars reached Haifa, nudging up to the wharves on their last reserves of fuel. A cheering crowd awaited them. Indeed, the entire nation was exultant. With all twelve vessels in its possession, Israel at last had a navy appropriate to its needs. Three years later, during the Yom Kippur War, the missile boats ravaged the Egyptian and Syrian coasts, destroying Arab oil installations and sinking nineteen Arab naval craft, including ten Soviet-manufactured Komars, without themselves sustaining a single loss.

Georges Pompidou was not inclined to forget that Israel had humiliated him before the world. Two weeks after the escape episode, he exacted his revenge. In return for oil, France would sell the government of Libya—Muammar Qadafi's Libya—110 Mirage V jets. The consignment would include the 50 Miragв bought and paid for by Israel. All the planes, presumably, would include the numerous refinements Israel's air force advisers had introduced during the production process. In Israel itself, outrage was mixed with horror. The entire Libyan air force did not possess more than eight jet-trained pilots, and manifestly the planes were destined for Qadafi's friend and ally, Gamal Abd al-Nasser. In Paris, on January 29, 1970, a huge protest meeting was conducted at the Sports Palace. Two months later, Pompidou paid a state visit to the United States. One of the cities on his agenda was Chicago. Emerging from his limousine in front of the Palmer House Hotel, the president and his wife were spat upon by a crowd of young American Jews. Shocked and embarrassed, President Richard Nixon immediately flew to Chicago to join the Pompidous at the banquet in their honor.

The protests availed Israel little. The embargo remained airtight. France's goodwill appeared to be ancient history. Diplomatic relations between the two governments were minimal and glacial. In ensuing years the Pompidou government became a vigorous critic of Israel's occupation policies in the Arab-inhabited West Bank and remained notably silent when Arab guerrilla violence took Israeli civilian lives. The number of lectureships in Hebrew at French universities declined from twelve in 1967 to two in 1972. In Israel, English once again moved ahead of French as the optional "second language" in state high schools. Although at no time did recriminations between the two nations approach the frontal antagonism of the recent Soviet-Israeli relationship, frigidity from an ally was more painful than hostility from an enemy. As Foreign Minister Eban observed in 1970, "It is the France we once cherished that has wounded us in our very cultural essence."

Which of the Great Powers, then, continued resolute in its commitment to a still-beleaguered little nation? Among the world's authentic heavyweights, only two remained dependably at Israel's side. One of these had developed into a trusted friend but was six thousand miles distant, and not European. And the other, emerging as the Continent's industrial powerhouse, was archetypically European but remained foreclosed by its poisoned history from ever becoming more than a suspect patron of convenience.

IX   ISRAEL IN THE
EUROPEAN
CONSCIENCE

A SYNERGY OF CIVILIZATIONS

It was the dream of Theodor Herzl, founder of modern Zionism, that his envisioned *Judenstaat* ultimately would develop into a paradigm of all that was humane and ennobling in European civilization. Herzl was not without his critics. Preeminent among them were the "Hebraists," devotees of the ancestral tradition, for whom a Jewish homeland represented the opportunity first and foremost to develop a specifically Hebraic culture. Nevertheless, once statehood was achieved in 1948, it was Herzl's original vision of eclecticism that appeared the likelier to be fulfilled. If not a paradigm, Israel emerged at least as a microcosm of the pre-Holocaust European experience. As late as 1975, eleven of Israel's twenty-four daily newspapers were published in European languages. From the outset of independence, the Jewish nation's "civic" culture was rooted in the pre-state legacy of British jurisprudence and public administration. In the realm of "private" culture, European immigrants comprised the principal reservoir of instructors in Israel's public school systems and of teaching scholars in Israel's growing network of universities.

Among the latter, in turn, the decisive European influence on Israeli science was provided by the German-Jewish refugees of the 1930s, those who swiftly added their talents to the fledgling Hebrew University and Haifa Technion. Fifty years later, owing largely to that initial jump start, Israel ranked first in the world in scientific publications per capita. It was Central European Jews who established the Palestine Philharmonic Orchestra and a host of smaller instrumental groups, and who laid the basis of the State of Israel's densely sophisticated musical culture. It was from France and Germany that Israeli artists first adapted the modes of expressionism and abstractionism, even as the nation's architects borrowed initially and extensively from Germany's Bauhaus School. As far back as the 1920s, meanwhile, East

European immigrants brought with them the pioneering theatrical techniques of Konstantin Stanislavsky and the Moscow Art Theater.

Israeli literature provided a more ambivalent picture. In the pre-state era, poetry and prose tended to draw from the classically Hebraic traditions of Russian Zionism. After 1948, however, and well into the 1950s, the "Palmach Generation" of young Israeli patriots focused self-consciously on the development of a "national identity," and the rejection of both European and European Jewish antecedents. It was a divorce in turn that concerned Binyamin Harshav, Natan Zach, and Gershon Shaked, all recent graduates of the Hebrew University's comparative literature program, and all soon to become eminent literary critics. Translating and vigorously interpreting the "high modernism" of such writers as Eliot, Auden, Rilke, and Kafka, the young critics revived and decisively sold the case for European humanism. In the 1960s, moreover, as Israel's economic circumstances improved, cultural relations with Europe intensified. European orchestral, operatic, and theatrical groups, as well as exhibitions of European artists, were booked and gratefully welcomed by Israeli audiences. However belatedly, a renewal of ties with a revived and liberalizing Europe once again was projected as a legitimate, even indispensable objective for a nation whose physical and military isolation remained an existential threat, and whose cultural identity was under challenge by the arrival of hundreds of thousands of undereducated North African and Middle Eastern immigrants.

Did the Europeans, in turn, accept Israel as a legitimate extension of their own civilization? Throughout its early decades, the image of the Jewish state as a gallant little outpost of Western-style democracy and humanism appealed to those with guilt-stricken consciences, most specifically in the Bundesrepublik. That image was fostered by perennial "interpreters" of Israel in the German vernacular, writers and academicians such as Manfred Wolffsohn and Hendryk Broder in Germany, and Moshe Zimmermann and (Hungarian-born) Ephraim Kishon in Israel. Accepting the Jerusalem Prize for Literature in 1988, the renowned Czech writer Milan Kundera expressed the view that

> . . . the great Jewish figures, exiled from their lands of origin and thus lifted above nationalist passions, have always shown an exceptional feeling for a . . . Europe conceived not as territory but as culture. Even after Europe so tragically failed them, the Jews nevertheless kept faith with that European cosmopolitanism. Thus it is that Israel . . . strikes me as the true heart of Europe—a strange heart, located outside the body.

The impression of Israel as a transplant of European culture in the Middle East was widely shared among European intellectuals at large.

And witnessing the palpable muscularity of Israeli science, of Israeli scholarship, literature, music, and theater, Europe was prepared to respond in a network of cooperative relationships. Throughout the 1960s and 1970s, private French sources continued to sponsor and fund a host of Israeli-French research seminars and joint projects in computer science and biotechnology. Israeli universities shared in exchanges of professors and postdoctoral researchers with Britain's Royal Society, Sweden's Royal Academy, and the European Laboratory for Nuclear Research. Israel's leading scientists were elected as members of virtually all European multinational scientific organizations—of physicists, chemists, biochemists, microbiologists. Israeli artists were tendered exhibitions in the principal cities of Europe. By the 1980s Israeli musicians were performing in the major European concert halls, sharing the stage with the Continent's most prestigious symphony orchestras, occasionally becoming conductors in a number of European cities. Altogether, for European scientists, scholars, artists, and musicians, for European curators and impresarios, there was never a question that the Israelis belonged in their midst.

A PAPAL SUSPICION

Would Israel be accepted as "respectable" by Europe's oldest and most venerated bastion of religioecclesiastical authority? Well into the twentieth century, the Vatican's decrees and bans still exerted far-reaching moral and even political influence in the Roman Catholic world. To the Zionists, with their aspirations focused on the Holy Land, on terrain historically drenched in eschatological associations, Rome's favor or disfavor was a matter to be taken with great seriousness. In January 1904 Theodor Herzl initially sought that goodwill in a personal interview with Pope Pius X. He did not get far. The pontiff opposed the very notion of a collective return of Jews to Zion so long as they did not accept Jesus as their savior.

More than a decade would pass before the Zionists ventured a renewal of contacts with the Vatican. But in World War I the Palestine issue became the object of Great-Power ambitions. In May 1917 the Zionist diplomat Nahum Sokolow was granted an audience with Pope Benedict XV. In contrast to his predecessor, this pontiff appeared not unsympathetic, even declaring that the return of the Jews to Palestine was a providential event that was consonant with God's will— although Benedict insisted that a "reserved" zone for the Holy Places (later identified with Jerusalem, Bethlehem, Nazareth, Tiberias, and Jericho) "for us is of extraordinary importance." Sokolow gave every assurance, and the pope concluded: "Yes, yes, I do hope that we shall be good neighbors."

The Vatican's approbation remained cautious and selective, however. In December 1917 the entire Catholic press hailed British General Edmund Allenby's capture of Jerusalem from the Turks as a triumph for Christianity. It was simply the postwar prospect of a Jewish enclave in the Holy Land that evoked growing papal reservations. Once the Paris Peace Conference began in early 1919, Benedict XV, who had evidently had a change of heart since his talk with Nahum Sokolow two years earlier, told a secret Vatican consistory on March 10 that "it would be for us and all Christians a bitter grief if the unchurched were . . . placed in a privileged and prominent position." Although the pontiff was resigned to a British mandate, he preferred that it extend no official status to the Jews. Pius XI, who succeeded Benedict in 1922, shared his predecessor's concerns. These were exacerbated when lurid reports of "Zionist imperialism" arrived from Monsignor Luigi Barlassini, the Latin Patriarch of Jerusalem.

"Zionist imperialism" in fact was only one feature of the Vatican's evaluation of the Jewish people. Throughout the 1920s and 1930s, during a period of acute ideological strife in Europe, papal suspicions of the Jews, in and out of Palestine, resurfaced dramatically and invidiously. In 1929 *L'Osservatore Romano*, the official organ of the papacy, editorialized with the headline: "The Jewish Danger Threatening the Entire World." In 1936 the Jesuit paper *Civiltà Cattolica* insisted that "the Jews constitute a serious and permanent danger to Christianity," and a year later began publishing charges of Jewish ritual murder. A Jewish presence in the Holy Land assuredly was to be regarded as inimical to Church interests. In 1937 the Vatican urged that Jewish refugees be settled in the United States, not Palestine. When the British White Paper of May 1939 foreclosed Jewish immigration to Palestine, Rome expressed its approval.

By 1939, too, Eugenio Pacelli had ascended the papal throne as Pius XII. Pacelli's silence during the ensuing Holocaust has been extensively documented. Less well known was the implacability of his opposition to the Jewish National Home, even as an asylum for refugees. In May 1943 Luigi Cardinal Maglioni, the Vatican secretary of state, issued an explicit warning against the "unsettling" dangers of the Zionist enclave in the Holy Land. As late as April 1945, even with the magnitude of the Jewish tragedy more fully revealed, the Vatican would not reverse its position. In that month, Moshe Shertok (later

Sharett), the Jewish Agency's political director, was received by Pius XII. When Shertok sought to assure the pontiff that a Jewish government in Palestine would guarantee fullest protection for the Christian holy places, he evoked only courteous noncommittal.

By war's end, American and European opinion was palpably shifting in favor of a Jewish homeland. The Vatican no longer felt able then to challenge Zionist claims head-on, and specifically at a time when it required Washington's support in the struggle against communism. Instead, maintaining a stance of discreet reserve, Rome focused on the minimalist goal of security for Palestine's Christian holy places. And in August 1947, when the United Nations Special Committee on Palestine issued its majority report in favor of partition, the Vatican tacitly accepted the committee's recommendation of a ten-year UN trusteeship for Jerusalem as apparently the least objectionable formula available. In turn, encountering no formal opposition from Rome, the governments of a number of Latin American and other Catholic nations felt free to vote for partition.

Nevertheless, unsettled by the declaration of Israeli independence, *L'Osservatore Romano* in May 1948 could not withhold a last, back-handed swipe at the Jews. Zionism was a militantly secular movement, it insisted, and Christianity alone regarded the Holy Land as integral to its very theology. Afterward the outbreak of war in Palestine, and specifically the bitter struggle for Jerusalem, became a source of growing alarm to the papacy. On May 30 the Latin Patriarchate of Jerusalem accused Israel of violating

> the sanctity of our churches, convents, and institutions. We therefore appeal to all those in power and to the civilized world to compel the Jews to respect the Holy Places and the religious institutions and to desist from making them into military bases and targets.

Several of the charges were legitimate. Both Hashemite and Israeli forces were breaking into church buildings for access to protected firing sites. On June 2, addressing the College of Cardinals, Pius XII voiced his shock that "the Christian world would allow the devastation of the Holy Places. . . . May it be God's will that the peril of this horrifying scourge be finally dissipated." The imputation was barely disguised that the Jews were responsible for "the scourge." In later weeks Rome vigorously endorsed Count Folke Bernadotte's recommendation to incorporate Jerusalem into a United Nations–administered *corpus separatum* (as the original partition plan had required). In

April 1949 Pius XII issued an encyclical, *Redemptoris Nostri*, openly calling for the internationalization of all Christian holy sites throughout Palestine, including Jerusalem "and its surroundings."

Thereafter, in the ensuing armistice negotiations and Palestine Conciliation Commission hearings of 1948–49, it was the fate of Jerusalem that obsessed the Vatican beyond any other single feature of the Palestine settlement. Ironically, the military division of Jerusalem between Israel and Transjordan by then had become a fait accompli, one that both sides were determined to institutionalize politically. So long as the Jerusalem issue remained a subject of United Nations debate, however, Rome would continue to press its case. There appeared a certain anomaly in this campaign. Although thirty of the thirty-four principal Christian churches and shrines in the Jerusalem-Bethlehem area had fallen under Hashemite rule, the Vatican was uninterested in exerting pressure on the Transjordanian government. Moslem preeminence in the Middle East was an established fact of life, and the Church had long since managed to coexist with it. But who could predict the way the mystical genius of Jerusalem would evolve under Jewish rule? Judaism's historic links with the Holy City were older than either Christianity's or Islam's. Would not Israel exploit that historic nexus to the Church's ideological disadvantage?

Yet, in the end, papal diplomacy was influenced by *Realpolitik* even more than by spiritual concerns. For centuries, an intense rivalry had festered between Orthodox and Latins in the Holy City. In 1847 the Vatican established its Latin Patriarchate in Jerusalem, signifying a new and more urgent proprietary concern for Roman Catholic interests there. Even then, the Latins remained outnumbered by the Orthodox, and the asymmetry continued well into the World War II era. But in the United Nations afterward, the Orthodox for the first time possessed no spokesmen at all, except for Greece; the Soviet empire had swallowed up their constituencies. By contrast, the Latins were represented by a substantial bloc of delegations. With this new diplomatic advantage, the Church was in a unique position to protect its bridgehead in Jerusalem by defining the United Nations role in a *corpus separatum*. These were the considerations Pius XII had in mind when he issued his encyclical *Redemptoris Nostri* of April 1949.

Even as Catholic opinion worldwide responded in varying measure to the pope's appeal, the Palestine Conciliation Committee in September 1949 recommended its own compromise plan to the United Nations. It was for the holy places alone to become the responsibility of a UN commissioner. Here at last the Israeli and Hashemite governments discerned a certain room for accommodation. Much to their surprise, however, it was Australia's Foreign Minister Herbert Evatt, a warm supporter of partition, who now became the champion of a *corpus separatum*. Once again the reasons were political. National elections were pending then in Australia, and the Catholic vote in that nation was powerful. So it was also in France. Thus, while the Australian resolution was opposed by such Protestant countries as Sweden, Denmark, Norway, the Netherlands, and Britain (supporting its Hashemite client), the UN General Assembly in December 1949 voted in favor of the original *corpus separatum* formula. Even the Soviet-bloc delegations now supported the plan. Their aim plainly was to embarrass King Abdullah and his British patrons.

Israel's reaction to the vote was swift and emphatic. On December 13 the Knesset unanimously approved Prime Minister Ben-Gurion's proposal that the legislature be moved to Jerusalem. Indeed, less than three weeks later, on January 1, 1950, the Israeli government was transferred in its entirety to Jerusalem's New—Jewish—City, except for the ministries of defense, police, and foreign affairs (the latter two were transferred later). That same day, across the border, King Abdullah issued his own decree, conferring Hashemite citizenship on the population of the West Bank, including the inhabitants of Arab Jerusalem. By then the UN General Assembly did not trouble to react, either in condemnation or in support of any further resolutions on Jerusalem. For Rome too, then, the issue of a *corpus separatum* remained one more of principle than of practical aspiration.

A CAUTIOUS PAPAL ACCOMMODATION

Nevertheless, well into the 1950s, Vatican suspicions of Israel remained apparently implacable. For the Holy See, the Jewish state with its Labor government was irredeemably "atheist," "Socialist," and hence "pro-Communist." It was a view fortified by the hard evidence of Soviet support for Israel in its early years, and by the massive influx of Jews from Eastern Europe. At the same time, the presence of tens of thousands of Palestinians vegetating in a network of refugee camps threatened to destabilize the surrounding Arab governments, even to foster Communist penetration among traditionally conservative Moslem societies. Year in and year out, Rome sustained a tripartite campaign not only for an internationalized Jerusalem, but for a repatriation of Palestinian Arabs to their homes, and for an Israel reduced to the frontiers envisaged in the original partition resolution.

"There is no change whatsoever in the Vatican's position," lamented Israel's Foreign Minister Sharett in a diary entry of November 10, 1953. "On the contrary, it is even more rigid and intransigent. The Vatican insists, and it is not ready to accept any compromise, on the promulgation of [these] three associated principles."

From the mid-1950s on, however, the Latin Patriarchate and the Catholic Apostolic Mission in Jerusalem managed to develop a certain functional relationship with the Israeli government. By then the Vatican had accepted Washington's warning that there existed graver dangers to stability in the Middle East—and hence to Catholic interests in the Middle East—than even a secular, "Socialist" Jewish state. Preeminent among these was Nasserist radicalism. Far more than Israel, the Egyptian president's militant campaign of "anti-imperialism" appeared to function as a stalking horse for the Soviet Union in the Mediterranean.

Perhaps even more fundamentally, Israel's 1956 Sinai victory evoked a certain thoughtful reappraisal in Catholic circles. It was not irrelevant that the triumph had been achieved in conjunction with France. A significant minority within France's own Catholic hierarchy, led by Jean Cardinal Daniélou, by the brave Resistance veteran Monsignor Daniel Pézer, and by Father Yves Congar, editor of *Le Croix*, the organ of progressive Catholicism in France, applauded the establishment of Israel as an act of moral justice. The stance reflected both the historic tradition of French ultramontanism and possibly retroactive shame at the Church's role in the wartime Vichy regime. Beyond France, the Mediterranean Colloquium, established by Florence's Mayor Giorgio La Pira as an ongoing sounding board for liberal Catholic intellectuals and political leaders, advocated Israel's right to live in peace and security.

By no coincidence, the new forbearance became particularly notable during the pontificate of Angelo Roncalli. Assuming office in 1958 as John XXIII, the "good pope" reigned until 1963. These were the years that encompassed the Eichmann trial, and as the full story emerged of Vatican passivity during the Holocaust, Rome found itself on the moral defensive. Renowned in any case for his humanity, Pope John was prepared to make overtures to the Jews, even to Israel. As early as 1959, he invested Israel's ambassador to Italy with the Grand Cross of Sylvester, a meaningful gesture after the Curia's earlier unwillingness so much as to make official reference to the Jewish state.

Otherwise the pontiff chose to express his goodwill by authorizing the Second Lateran Council, scheduled for 1962, to reevaluate the historic Catholic charge of deicide against the Jews. At John XXIII's instruction, a special committee under the chairmanship of Augustin Cardinal Bea, leader of the progressive element in the Vatican, worked in intimate consultation with a network of international Jewish organizations. The committee's proceedings were completed only in October 1965, two years after Pope John's death. Taking the form of a *Schema* on the Jews, the document rejected the notion that the Crucifixion could "be attributed without distinction to all Jews then alive, or to the Jews today," and thus "deplore[d] on religious grounds any display of anti-Jewish hatred or persecution."

During the nearly three years of the committee's deliberations, its Jewish interlocutors had sought also to elicit a pro-Israel statement. But here they encountered the vehement opposition of Arab Christian leaders. Even the good-hearted Cardinal Bea rejected efforts to interpret the *Schema* as a legitimization of Israel. "We are not talking about Zionists," he emphasized, "or the political State of Israel, but about the followers of the Mosaic religion, wherever in the world they may dwell." Yet the fact that Zionists and even Israeli representatives belonged to such consultative organizations as the World Jewish Congress, and negotiated with the Church over various drafts of the *Schema*, gave Israel enhanced credibility in Catholic public circles. Following publication of the *Schema*, moreover, Rome established a National Secretariat for Catholic-Jewish Relations. The body's purpose was to conduct training seminars, conferences, and workshops for Catholic teachers, and many of these projects too were cosponsored by Jewish organizations that invariably were pro-Zionist. So it was that a network of Israel-oriented lobbies began developing in and around the Church.

In January 1964 Pope Paul VI, who had succeeded John XXIII upon the latter's death the year before, embarked on a pilgrimage to Christian shrines in the Holy Land. Although the journey was described as nonpolitical, it was significant that the pontiff carefully avoided any reference to the State of Israel. And during the course of his visit Paul could not avoid a brief ceremonial meeting with Israel's President Zalman Shazar at a Jordanian-Israeli border crossing. In following years, contacts widened between Church leaders and Israeli officials, in both Jerusalem and Rome. On several occasions Israel's ambassadors to Italy were granted brief papal audiences. Even the Vatican's tone and language toward Israel gradually softened. By the mid-1960s the outlines of pragmatic rapprochement between the Roman Church and the Jewish state were becoming at least faintly discernible.

AN ECONOMIC *CORDON SANITAIRE*

There were other, distinctly less spiritual manifestations of Israel's lingering "unacceptability." Economic isolation in the long run proved by far the most painful. From 1949 on, Egypt blocked the Suez Canal not only to Israeli ships but to selected cargoes carried by vessels of other nations bound for the Jewish state. Although occasionally challenged by both Israel and foreign governments, the ban was never lifted, either in the aftermath of the 1956 war or following the 1967 war. The closure of Suez in and of itself was less than crippling to the Israeli economy. Rather, it was a wider economic boycott that exerted a more invidious, longer-lived impact. The quarantine was launched in 1951, when the Arab League organized a Central Boycott Office in Damascus, with branch offices in other member states. Initially the proscription on economic dealings with Israel was intended for the Arab countries themselves. Little time passed, however, before the boycott was extended to other nations.

The ban was imposed first and foremost on non-Israeli vessels that stopped at Israel's ports. The Central Boycott Office maintained a detailed blacklist of these transgressors, and over the next three decades more than six hundred ships fell under the ban. Henceforth, they were denied access to any Arab port. Shipping companies soon learned to adapt to these regulations by allocating certain vessels— often under charter or fake registrations—exclusively to the Israel run. But in 1953 the Central Boycott Office extended its restrictions to foreign airliners stopping in Israel. No plane flying to or from Israel was allowed to continue over Arab airspace to any other destination, Arab or non-Arab. Most Western airliners were obliged to terminate their eastern schedules at Israel's Lod Airport, then return directly to their home bases. Ticket prices reflected this economic dysfunctionalism.

In practice, every overseas Arab embassy and consulate operated as a branch of the Central Boycott Office. These branches in turn played a crucial role in developing a new, "secondary" boycott on Israel. The technique was to gather data on foreign companies, even to circulate questionnaires among them, to determine which were doing business with Israel; which maintained factories, plants, or agencies in Israel; and which sold Israeli patents, copyrights, or trademarks or purchased shares in Israeli enterprises. Once included on the office's blacklist, a foreign company was promptly denied access to the Arab market. It was a price few businesses were willing to pay. To circumvent the boycott Israeli companies were obliged to make their purchases or sales through dummy agencies. The price in extra commissions was high. Indeed, of all the Arab world's arsenal of weapons against the Jewish state, this secondary economic boycott proved by far the most effective. No nation, no company, however large or powerful, was exempt from its operation.

On signing the 1953 Treaty of Luxembourg, the Bundesrepublik became a logical early target. Yet there was never a chance that Konrad Adenauer would submit to Arab pressures. "It would be shameful indeed," the chancellor declared, "if we were to waver in our decision only because of being threatened with economic disadvantages. There are higher values than good business deals." But Adenauer was speaking for his government, not for private German businesses. Under German law these were entitled to make their own decisions. While a number of German corporations defied the ban, no fewer than two hundred complied over the ensuing three decades, and these included such heavyweights as Telefunken, BASF, and Siemens.

From its outset in 1951 the boycott operated with even greater effect in Britain, the nation with which Israel had developed its most extensive trade connections since the earliest years of the Palestine mandate. These now shriveled drastically. Like Bonn, London refused officially to participate in the quarantine. Yet a nation with Britain's historic dependence on Arab goodwill could hardly bar individual companies from pursuing their own opportunities in the Middle East. From 1951 on, a substantial majority of Britain's larger companies sooner or later capitulated to the boycott, and these included such giants as Shell, British Petroleum, and the largest number of banks and insurance firms. The ban also extended to companies owned or partly owned by Jews. In a particularly notorious episode, the Central Boycott Office in 1963 coerced the Norwich Union Insurance Society into dropping Lord Mancroft, a Jew and a former minister in the Macmillan government, from its board of directors.

In France, too, even at the apogee of the French-Israeli honeymoon, hundreds of companies were surrendering to boycott pressures. In 1957 the Renault automobile company agreed to sublicense assembly rights for its Dauphine model to an Israeli company. Two years later, threatened by the Central Boycott Office, Renault summarily canceled the contract. The interdiction against firms with Jewish ownership or part ownership also was applied in France. Finally, in June 1977, under heavy pressure from the Carter administration in the United States, the French National Assembly passed a mild form of antiboycott legislation. Known as the Loi Générale sur Diverses

Dispositions Economiques et Financières, it forbade compliance with inquiries relating to "national origin or membership or nonmembership in a particular ethnic group, race, or religion." But a year later Prime Minister Raymond Barre issued a decree that seriously undermined the Loi Générale; and in May 1980 the Giscard d'Estaing government specified that any commercial transaction relating to energy, agriculture, minerals, transportation, machine and consumer goods—in effect, everything—was to be excluded from the 1977 law.

Meanwhile, even nations warmly disposed toward Israel—the Netherlands, Denmark, Belgium, Norway, among them—were helpless to block private businesses from exercising their own discretion in buying or selling in the Middle East. The boycott's ramifications penetrated every corner of the European economy. At no time did the Arab campaign choke off Israel's international trade. But the damage was heavy. An Israeli finance ministry report covering the period 1972–83 estimated that as a consequence of Arab economic warfare, the nation in these years had lost more than $6 billion in exports.

AN ONGOING GERMAN LIFELINE

In May 1966 Konrad Adenauer, now two years into retirement, accepted Israel's long-standing invitation to visit the Jewish state. After receiving an honorary doctorate from the Weizmann Institute of Science, the former chancellor was escorted through the country, then tendered a banquet by Prime Minister Levi Eshkol. At this point, toasting his guest, the plain-spoken Eshkol almost singlehandedly dissipated the *Stimmung* of goodwill by adverting repeatedly to the Holocaust, and warning that "the reparations agreement, which you signed in the name of your people, is not atonement. There is no atonement for annihilation." Adenauer was offended. Declining to raise his own glass, he responded tersely: "I can only say that we have done everything possible to . . . overcome this time of horror . . . [b]ut if goodwill is not recognized, nothing good can come of it." At a later reception, however, Nahum Goldmann defused the tension by offering the former chancellor a warm and gracious tribute; and on May 9, the last day of his visit, Adenauer was brought by helicopter to visit David Ben-Gurion at the retired prime minister's desert retreat in Sde Boker. The two old men closeted themselves in Ben-Gurion's cottage for two hours. As Adenauer prepared to leave, they wordlessly clutched each other's hands for a long moment. Upon returning to Germany, the former chancellor issued a statement: "My impressions . . . [of] Israel have strengthened my conviction that we must never desert this struggling state. . . . To those who think that restitutions should end . . . I want to say that one cannot put figures to a moral obligation or pay it off, penny by penny."

Adenauer's forbearance was not always matched by other German public figures. That same year Rolf Pauls, the Bundesrepublik's first ambassador to Israel, felt it appropriate to issue his own warning that goodwill had to be "reciprocal." Several months earlier, Jerusalem had announced its recognition of the Oder-Neisse frontier as Germany's eastern border. Although many Western governments similarly had accepted the reality of an enlarged Poland and a territorially attenuated Germany, few had done so formally. The Erhard government was not pleased. In June 1966, therefore, a month after the Adenauer visit, speaking at the opening of a German trade exhibit in Tel Aviv, Ambassador Pauls declared bluntly: "It is with great concern that we observe how, for reasons of political advantage or out of selfish motives, the sufferings of the past are constantly stirred up. . . . Those forces which are hostile to present-day Germany do a bad service to their own country by their agitation." The Bundesrepublik no longer was obliged to prove itself, Pauls insisted. It already occupied a respected place in the world and required no further dispensation from any people. In Bonn the Erhard government confirmed that it stood behind its ambassador's remarks. The Israeli government, taken by surprise, opted for silence. But the question was mooted in the press of both nations: Was the German-Israeli rapprochement, achieved only after years of complex, painstaking negotiations, now in jeopardy?

In fact German public goodwill remained as widely diffused as ever. The directors of German museums, galleries, and trade fairs extended themselves to promote displays of Israeli art and Israeli products. German universities underwrote generous scholarships for Israeli students. German Länder and private benefactors established libraries in Israel and stocked them with books and journals. In 1966, the Hamburg publishing tycoon Axel Springer contributed DM4 million to the Israel Museum. And in the acid test of the 1967 Six-Day War, German solicitude proved overwhelming. Indeed, as the crisis erupted into hostilities on June 5, Kurt-Georg Kiesinger, who the year before had succeeded Ludwig Erhard as Christian Democratic leader and chancellor, defined Bonn's policy as nonintervention rather than "neutrality." Neutrality, stated Kiesinger, implied indifference, which was far from the German mood. Addressing the Bundestag, Foreign Minister Willy Brandt, who had brought the Social Democrats into Kiesinger's coalition government, endorsed the chancellor's stance, insisting that "our nonintervention . . . cannot mean moral indifference or indolence of heart." The government put its policy where its emotions lay. Although maintaining its ban on weapons exports to the Middle East, Bonn rushed quantities of non-military goods to Israel. These included twenty thousand gas masks taken from civil defense stocks.

The German public's concern for the Jewish state meanwhile was overwhelming. The day war broke out, the German Trade Union Council asked its members to engage in demonstrations "to reestab-lish the state of peace and to safeguard the existence of Israel." Three days before the war, a similar request, initiated by Adolf Arndt, a Social Democratic member of the Bundestag, was signed by hundreds of the nation's most prominent citizens. "We urge all who bear public responsibility in our state," it declared, ". . . not to stand silently aside but to . . . stand by the Israeli people, morally and by peaceful means." The full text of the appeal was carried gratis in most of the Bundesre-publik's leading newspapers. Torchlight demonstrations in support of Israel were conducted in virtually all the larger cities. At the request of the Federal Association of Protestant Churches, ecumenical prayer services were held for Israel in the Bundesrepublik's Catholic and Protestant churches alike. On June 5, too, the Trade Union Federa-tion decided to invest DM3 million in Israel Bonds "as a visible expression of solidarity. . . ." The Berlin Senate donated DM100,000 for the shipment of medicines to Israel. The Municipality of Frank-furt made a flat contribution of DM30,000. Innumerable other col-lections and contributions were dispatched by private organizations and even private individuals. In Bonn some one thousand doctors and nurses volunteered their services to the Israeli embassy for work in Israel.

For their part, the Israeli people reacted to the wave of German friendship and support with surprise and gratification. Ambassador Asher Ben-Natan, who had been deluged by thousands of letters of sympathy and admiration, commented at a press conference on June 2, 1967, that the upsurge of goodwill "was a positive and important experience in the eyes of many Israelis." Six months later, on Decem-ber 24, as a gesture of reciprocity, Israel's state radio for the first time added German to the six languages in which it traditionally broadcast coverage of the Christmas Eve midnight mass from Bethlehem.

The euphoria of pro-Israel feeling could not be sustained indefi-nitely, no more in Germany than elsewhere in the world. Within two years after the war, the heartrending plight of tens of thousands of Palestinian refugees was given wide coverage in the German media, and particularly in the Social Democratic press, whose younger generation of readers almost reflexively sympathized with the underdogs of the world. It was also in 1969 that a new election gave the Social Democrats sufficient electoral strength to abandon their "Grand Coalition" with Kiesinger's Christian Democrats, and to negotiate a political alliance with the Free Democrats. As Willy Brandt assumed the chancellorship the Bundesrepublik now had its first Socialist government, one that did not share its predecessors' obsession with German unification. Rather, Brandt focused on the improvement of "human" relations with Communist East Germany and the rest of the Communist bloc, and with leftist regimes throughout the Third World—not excluding the Arab world.

There was never a question of the new chancellor's commitment to Israel's security and well-being. Yet Brandt was equally committed by then to a "normalization" of relations between the two states. Even as foreign minister, before the crisis of the Six-Day War, he had tentatively adopted this new approach. "I am not in favor of making a hair shirt into one's national costume," he had declared. As the Israelis feared, Brandt as chancellor placed his emphasis now on a "balanced" policy in the Middle East conflict. The Arab governments reacted well to the altered approach. After a seven-year hiatus, they agreed in 1972 to restore their diplomatic ties with Bonn.

Altogether, the year 1972 prefigured a new *frisson* in German-Israeli relations. It was symbolized in the Munich Olympics massacre of eleven Israeli athletes at the hands of Palestinian terrorists (pp. 233–5). Beyond its horror at their deaths, Israel reacted ambivalently to the behavior of the German authorities. On the one hand, there was respect that Bonn at least had refused the terrorists' demand for safe passage out of the country. But two months later, three surviving guerrillas who had been captured at the time of the attack were flown to Zagreb, Yugoslavia, whence they "escaped" to North Africa and eventually to Syria. Plainly the "escape" was Bonn's contrived payoff for twenty German civilian hostages whom other Palestinian guerrillas recently had seized on a hijacked Lufthansa airliner—an episode that itself may have been jointly contrived. Expressing Israel's mood of outrage, Prime Minister Golda Meir denounced the exchange as "a disgraceful act . . . an affront to human intelligence." Israeli press comment was scathing.

To make amends, Brandt decided then to fly to Israel in June 1973. His official visit, ostensibly to accept an honorary degree from the Weizmann Institute, was the first by a German chancellor while in office. He was received everywhere with courtesy, and by Prime Minister Golda Meir, an old Socialist comrade, with renewed warmth. In turn, Brandt promised to defend Israel's economic interests within the European Community, and affirmed that German-Israeli relations "must be seen against the somber background of the Nazi terror. That is what we mean when we say that our normal relations are of a special character." For the moment, with this redefinition of "normalization," the Israelis breathed somewhat easier.

SCIENTIFIC PARTNERSHIP, ECONOMIC PATRONAGE

It was not a coincidence that both Adenauer and Brandt embarked on their visits as honorees of the Weizmann Institute of Science in Rehovot. As early as the 1960s, Israel and the Bundesrepublik had been exchanging research scholars and university students, as well as opera, dance, and theatrical companies. Yet it was in the realm of science that the two nations achieved their most extensive cooperation. In 1957 the Weizmann Institute convened an international conference in physics. Among those invited was Professor Hans Jensen of Heidelberg, a Nobel Prize laureate and the first German scientist to be invited to Israel. Impressed by the quality of scientific research in the Jewish state, Jensen on his return home encouraged other German scientists to establish relationships with their Israeli counterparts.

One of those who liked the idea was Dr. Wolfgang Gentner, within the year to become director of the Max Planck Society, a major research organization funded jointly by a selection of German industrial firms and universities and Bonn's federal ministry of science. Gentner explored the possibility of German-Israeli cooperation with Dr. Amos de Shalit, research director of the Weizmann Institute, and with Dr. Josef Cohn, a German-born physicist and one of the institute's most eminent scholars. In 1959 a meeting was arranged for Cohn with Chancellor Adenauer. Straightforwardly, Cohn requested Adenauer's help in funding German-Israeli scientific cooperation, which he described as a natural extension of the historic role once played by Jews in German science. The chancellor was moved. Afterward he requested the Max Planck Society to explore ways of farming out a number of its projects to the Weizmann Institute. Bonn would share in the expense. The following year, Adenauer delivered this commitment as a "present" to Ben-Gurion when the two statesmen met in New York.

By 1960 the Max Planck Society duly began dispatching its younger scientists on visits to Rehovot, bringing with them suggested projects.

Once their Israeli colleagues accepted the proposals, money was forth-coming from the Bundesrepublik. With the infusion of funds, the Weizmann Institute in turn was better able to subsidize its faculty and to acquire important scientific equipment for its laboratories. More-over, as the ambit of the cooperative ventures widened throughout the 1960s, the Max Planck Society established a special subsidiary, the Minerva Foundation, which henceforth became the principal coordi-nating agency for all the various grants and exchanges. During the 1970s the program was enlarged beyond the Weizmann Institute to include other Israeli universities and institutes. At the recommenda-tion, too, of the Minerva Foundation's joint German-Israeli evaluation committee, Israeli scientists were brought over to the Bundesrepublik for longer research stays.

As the Israel-based programs grew in scope and duration, they led ultimately to the establishment of professorial chairs and research centers. By 1998 thirty-seven such permanent "Minerva" chairs and centers were operating in Israel, while the number of individual pro-jects supported within the Minerva framework reached sixteen hun-dred. And, meanwhile, other public and private German foundations similarly endowed Israeli research. These included the German-Israel Foundation, jointly funded by the governments of both coun-tries, and ad hoc programs underwritten by the Bundesrepublik's ministry of science and technology. Altogether, between 1960 and 1998, more than DM200 million was spent in Israel to subsidize pro-jects and exchanges in the fields of biotechnology, medical research, water technology, environmental research, agricultural and materials science, and laser research. This was largesse second only to the con-tributions provided by the United States government and private American donors, and by far the largest undertaking ever supported by the Bundesrepublik outside Germany itself.

At the same time German funds were reaching Israel in the form of a more conventional, government-to-government loan. It was in January 1966, just as German reparations payments were phased out, that the final legal and financial details were completed on the DM2 billion—approximately $500 million—loan agreement reached between Adenauer and Ben-Gurion in their 1960 Waldorf-Astoria meeting (pp. 118–19). The negotiations had been complex and painstaking. Bonn had approved the figure on the assumption that the money would be applied to specific projects, each to be approved by the Bundesrepublik in the amount of DM160 million ($37.5 million) annually, with payments to be spaced out over twenty-five years at a bargain-basement interest rate of 3 percent, with the first repayments not to be due until seven years into the loan. Much of the aid would be allocated for housing and industrial development in the Negev, with about 30 percent to finance small and medium-size businesses. Once the first loan installments began to arrive, too, they paved the way for additional investments in the form of Israel Bond purchases by individual German Länder, municipalities, banks, insurance companies, and other public and private agencies. The German Trade Union Federation alone invested $1.3 million in Koor, an industrial complex owned by Israel's counterpart labor federation, and added to this investment year by year. German banks lent funds to private Israeli companies at rates often much less profitable than those prevailing in the Bundesrepublik itself.

For all their functional usefulness, however, and the tangible evidence they provided of German goodwill, these infusions did not offer the self-sustaining economic relationship that Israel would have preferred. As late as 1960, Israeli exports to Germany were limited essentially to citrus fruits, textiles, handicrafts, and books, as well as several thousand Uzi assault rifles. The annual value of these shipments was a negligible $21 million. By 1993, to be sure, exports had climbed impressively, to $774 million. Yet the figure was misleading. In these same thirty-three years, Israel's imports from Germany, which stood at $72 million in 1960, skyrocketed to $2.5 billion. Indeed, by then only the United States exceeded Germany in the value of its exports to Israel. For a still-underdeveloped little nation, it appeared that only one alternative remained for meaningful economic growth: It was via the European Economic Community—the Common Market. And here, too, as Ben-Gurion had anticipated, the Bundesrepublik's support would prove indispensable.

IN QUEST OF EUROPE

Established by the Treaty of Rome in 1957 as the crowning achievement of Western Europe's postwar economic recovery, the European Economic Community was by no means simply a customs union, or even a free-trade area operating behind a common external tariff. For its six initial members, the EEC imposed a uniform set of rules intended to promote cooperative agricultural policies, to jump-start fledgling industries, and to equalize social welfare costs in a way that would nurture the Community's weaker members to viability. What, then, would be the impact of this awakening economic giant on nonmembers? It was to explore that uncharted terrain that Israel's government almost immediately embarked on an intensive study of a possible relationship with the new European trading confederation. Access to the Common Market, after all, with its geographical proximity and its potential for Israeli exports, could transcend such bread-and-butter issues as balances of payments. It might well signify political no less than economic liberation from Arab strangulation.

Thus, in October 1958, Prime Minister Ben-Gurion instructed Gideon Rafael, his newly appointed ambassador to Belgium, to focus his diplomatic efforts principally on the EEC Commission in Brussels. Rafael rose to the challenge with alacrity. Indeed, he became only the third nonmember "observer" to the commission, after the representatives of Britain and Ireland. A year and a half later Ben-Gurion himself met with Dr. Walter Hallstein, president of the commission, to emphasize his nation's compelling, all but existential need for some form of associate membership. Hallstein was sympathetic and cooperative. As it happened, he and his colleagues already had discerned a format in which Israel logically could be accommodated.

Under its formal provisions the Treaty of Rome limited EEC membership to European countries. But the Community's six charter members had always envisaged a future "dotted-line" relationship with the non-European nations of the Mediterranean Basin. Within the ensuing decade, these countries of North Africa and the Middle East would absorb fully 12 percent of the EEC's exports, and provide Europe with 62 percent of their own exports—most of it in the form of oil and gas—and virtually all of Europe's migrant laborers. From the outset the network of mutual economic interdependence was further enhanced by historical, cultural, and even (in the case of France) political affiliations. As Hallstein often declared: "We are not only in business; we are in politics." Without exception, Europe's statesmen favored the promotion of trade links as a means of fostering political stability in the Mediterranean. To that end, as early as 1961, the EEC Council of Ministers authorized the commission's technocrats to study a possible institutional relationship with the Mediterranean "poor cousins." And Israel, too, then, became an object of EEC evaluation. Negotiations between the commission's study teams and Israeli representatives continued uninterrupted from early 1962 to late 1964.

In the end, however, the fate of Israel's application depended less upon the recommendations of technocrats than upon the goodwill, even the sponsorship, of the Community's charter members. Thus Belgium itself, which served as headquarters both of the Common Market and of NATO, and as the earliest postwar champion of economic integration, became a likely target for Israeli diplomacy. It was still an uncertain target. During the 1947 struggle for partition, Belgium tended to follow the lead of Britain, its historical protector, in cultivating the Arab export market. Only at the last moment, and largely through the personal influence of Foreign Minister Paul-Henri Spaak, a pro-Zionist, was Belgium's vote cast for Jewish (and Arab) statehood. Favoring an internationalized Jerusalem, moreover, the Brussels government waited until January 1949 before extending *de facto* recognition to Israel, and held off *de jure* recognition for another year.

Yet, in the 1956 Middle Eastern crisis, no such equivocation characterized Belgian policy. Foreign Minister Spaak then was among the most outspoken of Western statesmen in condemning Nasser's nationalization of Suez. During the ensuing Sinai-Suez war and its diplomatic aftermath, Belgium refused to join the UN General Assembly in censuring any of the three allies. And on Israel's ensuing quest for a relationship with the Common Market, Belgium proved entirely sympathetic. Campaigning behind the scenes in Israel's behalf, Spaak won the unanimous support of the Benelux trading consortium.

Even with this approbation, however, and that of the Bundesrepublik, the maximum the Community appeared willing to offer a small, non-European nation like Israel was a tightly limited commercial agreement. Jointly formulated in 1964 by the EEC Commission's technocrats and by Sergio Minerbi, Israel's resident economist in Brussels, the accord reduced the EEC's duties essentially on such historic Israeli staples as grapefruit, avocados, and plywood. The deal was a modest one. Yet its significance lay in its future promise. The document confirmed that Israel would share in whichever duty reductions might later be extended to other Mediterranean nations, including such European nations as Italy or Spain (should Spain be admitted to the Common Market), or even to France's protégés in North Africa. For the Jewish state, it was a meaningful foot in the European door.

Within three years, in fact, Israel was in a position to test European goodwill—and at its very apogee, in June 1967, during the immediate aftermath of the Six-Day War. Never was admiration for the little Zionist republic more widespread. To exploit that wellspring, the Eshkol government decided to move swiftly. It submitted its formal application for associate membership to the EEC Commission. And with equal dispatch the commission endorsed and enthusiastically transmitted Israel's application to the EEC Council of Ministers. The matter thenceforth rested with the individual governments of the six founding members. By then, however, one of those members, France, had turned coldly against Israel. There was no longer a chance of winning de Gaulle's approval. As a consequence, under EEC rules, which required unanimity among the Council of Ministers, Israel's request for membership was tabled.

THE FRUITS OF PERSEVERANCE

Jerusalem dared not flag in its efforts to circumvent French opposition. By 1967 the EEC had become the largest trading bloc in the world, accounting for more than 40 percent of all international imports and exports. No Mediterranean government could ignore that surging market. Thus Spain, as well as Morocco, Tunisia, Cyprus, and Malta, now applied for a preferential relationship. Here was Israel's opportunity—and that of its supporters. In addition to the Bundesrepublik and Belgium, there was a third nation on whose sponsorship Israel could depend with near-reflexive certitude. This was the Netherlands, whose historic friendship to the Jews extended back at least four centuries, and whose support of partition in 1947 was immediate and unqualified. The Hague's recognition of Israel, to be sure, did not take *de jure* form until January 1950. The Moslem loyalties of the vast Dutch East Indian empire had to be respected. Nor was Holland immune to Arab boycott pressure. Royal Dutch Shell divested its interests in the Haifa oil refineries. Phillips closed its electronics plant in Netanya in 1957. Several of the Netherlands' leading banks consented to accept checks and letters of credit stamped "not negotiable in Israel." These and other acts of surrender to Arab intimidation continued well into the 1970s.

Yet of all European nations, the Netherlands alone matched the Bundesrepublik in the vigor of its opposition to the Arab secondary boycott. In 1957, while acknowledging his government's helplessness to interfere with the free choices of private businesses, Foreign Minister Willem Drees entreated all citizens, individually and collectively, to resist boycott pressures. His appeal was endorsed by the Netherlands Association of Employees (the nation's largest trade-union federation) and by other pluralistic organizations. The Dutch Reformed Church and the Association of Catholic Bishops refused to issue baptismal certificates to businessmen seeking visas from Arab nations. The government-owned Netherlands Bank in 1961 denied export-credit insurance for any shipments to the Arab world based on anti-Israel or anti-Jewish declarations. In 1978, when a Jewish group documented an extensive ongoing business compliance with the boy-cott, and a special parliamentary committee confirmed its findings, Parliament swiftly approved a bill to outlaw religious or racial dis-crimination in business transactions. In 1981 still another parliamen-tary law obliged all private companies to report any boycott requests to a special "Foreign Boycott Assessment Committee," which in turn would recommend "corrective" measures to the government. No other member of the European Community, not even the Bundes-republik, went as far.

Of greatest relevance to Israel was the palpable empathy of the Dutch people. For this Calvinist nation, which traditionally charac-terized Jews as "people of the Book," the birth of a Jewish state was hardly less than a fulfillment of biblical prophecy. As a small nation, too, the Dutch could relate to the vulnerability of a beleaguered little country of refugees. Thus, during the crisis of the Six-Day War, Dutch support for Israel was intensely emotional. Prayer services for Israel's welfare were conducted in every Dutch church, Catholic and Protestant alike. And once the magnitude of Israel's triumph became evident, the nation all but exploded in public relief and joy. The Netherlands government soon afterward gave tangible expression to that goodwill. When the East European bloc severed diplomatic rela-tions with Israel, it was the Netherlands embassy in Moscow that unhesitantly agreed to care for Israel's interests, and later to issue Israeli visas for Soviet Jews seeking emigration (p. 335). In the United Nations, Foreign Minister Joseph Luns vigorously supported the diplomacy that produced Security Council Resolution 242.

In the effulgence of its solicitude, the Netherlands accordingly became a natural patron in Israel's quest for a relationship with the Common Market. During the preliminary negotiations of the late 1950s and early 1960s, it was the Dutch, together with the Germans, who fought Israel's battle with every artifice of persuasion and tough bargaining. One of the uncertain factors in this effort was Italy, which feared the competition of Israeli citrus fruits. Yet the Italians also favored a modest EEC relationship with Iran, with which they had developed profitable trade links. To exploit that connection, the Dutch and Germans pressed for an equivalent Italian flexibility toward Israel, and eventually secured their quid pro quo. And now, in the aftermath of the Six-Day War, the Netherlands and the Bun-desrepublik led the campaign for wider Israeli access to the Common Market. In 1968, during the EEC committee hearings on other Mediterranean applications, Foreign Minister Luns made clear that a

preferential Community agreement with Spain, and with France's
Algerian, Tunisian, and Moroccan protégés, required parity treatment for Israel.

Predictably resisting the notion of linkage, French Foreign Minister Maurice Schumann urged a more cautious approach to Arab sensibilities. But the Dutch were not having it, any more than the West
Germans. If France was seeking a favored relationship for its North
African wards, and for a Spain still ruled by a discredited Fascist
regime, it would have to accept a trade-off. Finally, in the late spring
of 1970, Schumann acquiesced in a wider "Mediterranean" approach
to the EEC. Preferential agreements would be extended to Israel and
also to Spain, Morocco, Tunisia, and Algeria—and eventually to any
Arab nation seeking a "parallel" relationship in the future. On that
understanding, in July 1970, the EEC signed its second treaty with
Israel, and then a simultaneous, concomitant agreement with Spain.
Several months later, Tunisia and Morocco entered into the identical
configuration.

The July 1970 pact still fell short of the associate membership
Israel consistently had sought. Nevertheless, the treaty represented
an important step beyond the initial 1964 accord. Under its provisions a limited number of Israeli products henceforth would be
admitted into the Common Market on a reduced-duties basis, in
some instances by as much as 50 percent—well beyond the 1964
accord. Among the selected items were citrus fruits, avocados, fresh
vegetables, and fruit preserves, all delectables that would prove valuable hard-currency earners in central and northern European countries. The arrangement manifestly was a good one for the Jewish
state. Indeed, to Israel's Foreign Minister Eban, the 1970 treaty, if
offering the Jewish state less than associate membership in the EEC,
at least represented an important second stage toward acceptance as a
favored junior partner of the West. "We were on our way to Europe,"
Eban recalled exultantly.

THE CHALLENGE OF MODERNIZATION

In 1971, two years after Charles de Gaulle's departure from the
French presidency, the successor Pompidou government finally con-
sented to Britain's membership in the EEC. Britain's accession in
turn was linked to a package deal that included Ireland and Denmark.
Thus, by January 1, 1973, the Community's original Six had become
Nine. Yet the enlargement was a source of serious concern to Israel.

Historically committed to free trade in agricultural products, Britain for more than half a century had offered the single largest market for citrus fruit from Palestine and—later—Israel. But now, under EEC rules, the British would be obliged to raise their tariffs to match the higher ones of the Common Market. For Israel, as a result, it was critical that its own 1970 treaty with the EEC be revised to adapt to Britain's membership in an enlarged trading confederation. The earlier pact in any case had always been envisaged as a temporary way station toward a more extensive Israeli relationship with Europe. Would it not be appropriate now, argued Foreign Minister Eban, to devise a more thoroughgoing, even-handed partnership?

The EEC Council of Ministers acknowledged the logic of Israel's case. Pressed by German Chancellor Willy Brandt, even France's Foreign Minister Schumann recognized that the new Mediterranean "globalization" mandated a revision of the 1970 pact. The quid pro quo, of course, would be a negotiation of comparable revisions with Greece, Spain, Morocco, Algeria, and Tunisia, and later with the Middle Eastern Arab nations. Negotiations with the Israelis consequently began in the autumn of 1973. Interrupted by the Yom Kippur War, they were not concluded until December 1974, and the agreement was not signed until May 1975. But that signature produced a landmark transformation of Israel's relationship with the Continent. Far wider in scope than its 1970 predecessor, the new pact at last gave the Jewish state access to the EEC as an associate member in all but name. Duties were reduced by 70 to 90 percent on an even more extensive range of Israeli agricultural products, thereby allowing them entry to the Continent on terms not inferior to those previously available in Britain—and equivalent to those soon to be available to Spain, Greece, and the Maghreb countries.

Was there a poison pill in the accord? Israel's economy had shifted dramatically from its earlier emphasis on citriculture. Altogether, by 1975, the products of farms and orchards accounted for less than 20 percent of the little nation's export income. Rather, Israel was well on its way to becoming a light-industrial producer of irrigation equipment, of textiles, communications and medical electronics, and military hardware. To be sure, the Common Market henceforth would permit Israel's industrial exports virtual free entry. Indeed, by July 1977, EEC customs duties on these products would be eliminated entirely. Yet Israel then would be obliged to eliminate its own protective barriers against Common Market industrial goods. The process would not be instantaneous. In a gesture unmatched even to such full-fledged European associate members as Greece or Spain, the EEC Commission granted Israel a twelve-year grace period for lowering its tariffs on European industrial imports. Free trade would not become an authentically two-way relationship until 1987. Nevertheless, Israel's de facto associate membership in the Common Market would also prove a two-way gamble. On the one hand, the Community would emerge as Israel's largest commercial partner. On the other, Israel's own market then would be opened wide to the influx of European industrial and agricultural products alike. Would the gamble not be a dangerous, possibly losing one for Israel's fledgling economy?

In signing the 1975 treaty, Israel's Foreign Minister Yigal Allon was by no means oblivious to the risk, indeed, the virtual certainty, of a trade imbalance that would continue for years. Yet Allon, himself the product of one of Israel's Socialist parties, was prepared to accept that gamble. In the long run, the impact of free competition with European industry could only produce a rationalizing effect on the single most promising component of Israel's own economy—high-tech, high-skill, science-based industry. This was the segment that exploited the nation's unusually large pool of educated native and immigrant labor. In earlier decades Israel had endlessly protected and subsidized its industry, and consequently had distorted its potential capacity for change. But now, on the level playing field of the Common Market, the nation's factories and workshops would be forced to adapt to international competition. It spoke much for Allon and the leadership of the Labor party, no less than for Israel's right-wing successor governments, that they were prepared to accept that challenge. Plainly, they had grasped the consequences of refusal to sign on to the 1975 treaty. Israel's trading position almost certainly would have deteriorated much further, and possibly irretrievably, as additional countries joined the Common Market (the number has since grown to fifteen), and as still others negotiated comparable preferential trade deals with the Community.

More fundamentally yet, Israel's government leaders, like those of the EEC nations, recognized from the outset that association with the Community was above all a political declaration. In its very emphasis on European integration, after all, the EEC from its inception was intended as a political as much as an economic community. The objective had been underscored as far back as 1957 by Jean Monnet, the father of European integration. "Politicians," he declared, "are seldom impressed by political arguments. They tend to be more easily persuaded by economics and statistics." In 1971 Shimon Peres made the same point in his book *David's Sling:* "This approach—starting to deal with a political subject from the economic end—can also apply to the Middle East." It was Peres's argument that Israel was culturally, economically, even geographically closer to Turkey, Greece, Italy, and France than to Yemen, Saudi Arabia, or the other Gulf States. In 1964, and more definitively in 1970 and 1975, Europe for its part had accepted the full implications of that proximity, and had responded to it with sensitivity both to Israel's existential needs and to the pragmatic requirements of Mediterranean stability.

X A SURROGATE BATTLEFIELD

S pain, imbued with its universal Christian spirit of love for all the races on earth, contributed to the rescue of Jews, and acted more for spiritual than for merely legal or political reasons." Issued by Francisco Franco in 1949 as a belated claim on Western goodwill, the declamation was a fake. Fascist Spain's wartime asylum to Jews was grudging and expedient, limited essentially to thirty thousand Vichy refugees holding transit visas for Portuguese steamship lines. An additional thousand Jewish refugees, lacking those documents, endured starvation conditions in Spanish internment camps. Even in the early postwar years, Spain's approach to the Jews was ambivalent. The nation's press and pulpit continued to disseminate anti-Jewish propaganda. Yet, bowing to pressures from Washington, the Franco government concurrently authorized freedom of private worship. By the 1970s the right of public worship similarly had been granted, and some thirteen thousand Jews had taken up residence in Spain, where they conducted their business and communal activities without disturbance.

In these same decades the relationship between Spain and Israel continued equally ambivalent. Intent on succeeding Benito Mussolini as "protector of Islam," Franco acquiesced in the Arab League's diplomatic and economic quarantine against Israel. At the same time, however, eager to cultivate Western and liberal goodwill, Madrid cooperated with the Jewish Agency by lending its transit facilities to the migration of Moroccan Jews to Israel. Additionally, during the 1956 and 1967 Middle Eastern wars, the Spanish government extended consular protection to several hundred "Sephardim" of Egypt, who then were able safely to depart that country. By 1975, on Franco's death, Israel was prepared to reciprocate. It dropped its opposition to Spain's membership in the United Nations.

Until the 1970s, in the same ambivalent pattern, even as trade, tourist, and shipping contacts developed steadily between the two countries, Spain remained the single Western nation to deny the Jewish state official recognition. Then, with Spain's reversion to a constitutional monarchy in 1976 under Juan Carlos de Borbón, Israel looked forward to a full normalization. The prospects appeared hopeful. In meetings with Jewish representatives the young king made numerous friendly references to Israel. But once again Israel's expectation of diplomatic relations remained premature. The Arab nations intensified their pressure on Madrid, threatening curtailment in oil supplies and cancellation of an impending $450 million loan to the Spanish government. Shelving all plans to establish official ties with Israel, Prime Minister Adolfo González Suárez then arranged instead for King Juan Carlos to embark on a series of goodwill visits to Arab countries. In 1977 the Palestine Liberation Organization was allowed to open an information bureau in Madrid, and in 1979 the Suárez government tendered Yasser Arafat his first official reception in a Western capital.

If Israel negotiated a diplomatic opening in the Iberian Peninsula, it was achieved only beyond the Mediterranean, along the Atlantic frontier. Unlike Spain, Portugal's most important nexus of overseas relationships lay not with Moslem North Africa but with the mighty United States. During the tenure of the autocratic Prime Minister António de Oliveira Salazar, who governed until 1968, and of his successor, Marcello Caetano, Lisbon hesitated to establish formal relations with the Zionist republic. Yet the Caetano government permitted American planes to use its Azores refueling facilities during the 1973 Yom Kippur War airlift to Israel. And with the accession to power of Mario Soares's Socialists in 1976, the friendships that Israel's Laborites had developed with their Portuguese colleagues in the Socialist International bore immediate fruit. The two countries promptly exchanged ambassadors. Thereafter, sharing Israel's reliance upon American patronage, the Lisbon government remained impervious to Arab pressures. Its relations with the Jewish state continued to develop equably.

A MOSLEM EASTERN CONNECTION

Rather less predictable was the functional association that Israel eventually developed with its easternmost Mediterranean neighbor. This was Turkey, a nation not renowned for genial treatment of its own minorities. During World War II some ten thousand Jewish businessmen (and other thousands of Greeks and Armenians) had been ruined by the *Varlik Vergesi*, Ankara's palpably xenophobic capital levy on "war profiteers." After the war, it seemed equally unlikely that the Zionists could have anticipated "normal" discourse with a Moslem nation, even one whose government was as committedly secular as Turkey's. Thus, in the United Nations, the Turkish delegate voted against partition in 1947—although less for pro-Arab sympathies than in hope of Britain remaining on in Palestine as a buffer against Soviet penetration.

In March 1949, however, once Britain itself and other Western nations had established diplomatic relations with Israel, President Ismet Inonu's government extended its own cautious *de facto* recognition, and in December even opened a legation in Jerusalem. Israel in turn assigned one of its most experienced Middle East professionals to the Turkish capital. This was Eliahu Sasson. Born in Damascus, Sasson only recently had helped negotiate the secret peace treaty with Transjordan's King Abdullah (p. 20). He intended now to use the Ankara billet as a listening post for developments in the Arab world. Moreover, committed in those early years to a policy of nonalignment, Israel also regarded its links with Turkey—an American ally—as a means of strengthening its pro-Western ties without formally abandoning its neutralist stance.

At the outset the strategy appeared less than successful. Reflexively anti-Russian, the Turks did not trust Israel's Labor government and its unwillingness to criticize Soviet foreign policy. The Ankara post might have remained a consignment to permanent frustration had it not been for Israel's decision in 1950 to condemn North Korean aggression (p. 62). After 1952, too, Egypt's new colonels' regime evoked grave distrust in Turkish military and government circles. Relations between Israel and Turkey accordingly began to warm. By 1953 the two countries' armed forces were in frequent consultation on regional defense issues, and their bilateral commerce grew steadily. Turkey soon provided half of Israel's wheat and all of its cotton requirements, and in turn purchased substantial quantities of Israeli pharmaceuticals, electrical appliances, tires, fertilizers, and cement and other building materials.

By the same token, the Jewish Agency office in Istanbul was allowed free rein in organizing the emigration to Israel of some forty-five thousand Turkish Jews. These were essentially the nation's poorer, "redundant" Jewish citizens, often those who had been hard hit by the wartime *Varlik Vergesi* levy, and who feared possible future eruptions of Turkish xenophobia. Fortunately, that chauvinism remained subdued in the postwar period. By the 1960s Turkish government leaders had become respectful of their tough and dynamic Israeli neighbor, with its close ties to the United States. Israel for its part neglected no opportunity to cultivate Turkish goodwill. The Hebrew University organized a symposium commemorating five hundred years of Turkish rule in Constantinople (Istanbul). The Jewish National Fund planted a forest on Mount Carmel in memory of Kemal Ataturk. Turkey even was allowed to function as the unofficial protector of Moslem property in Jerusalem. Perhaps most significant, Israel was among the states that lobbied Latin American ambassadors in support of Turkey's request for membership on the UN Security Council, and then similarly petitioned Washington on behalf of Turkey's application to NATO. At Ankara's request, the Israeli government discreetly urged American Jewish organizations to be "understanding" of Turkey's position on the Cyprus issue. Altogether, it was the Israeli pipeline to the United States, either directly to the White House or indirectly through American Jewish connections, that served as Israel's principal leverage with the Ankara government.

Yet at no time could the Turks remain indifferent to the diplomatic weight of Arab and Moslem countries in the United Nations and other international forums. Thus they requested Jerusalem to be discreet in its references to contacts between the two nations. Israel's foreign ministry cooperated, as did the Israeli press. Indeed, the government censor was vigilant in muting public criticism of Turkish policy or "image." It was uncertain at first if Ankara was prepared to reciprocate this goodwill. In 1955, much to Israel's concern, Turkey joined the Baghdad Pact, together with Iraq, Iran, and Pakistan. In a worst-case scenario, the Turks could have been drawn into a common military confrontation against Israel. As matters developed, however, Israel's concerns were unwarranted. Notwithstanding the pact's alleged "northern-tier" protection against the Soviet Union, Ankara remained chronically suspicious of the Arabs. Syria then was pressing its territorial claims on Hatay, a port region that the French mandatory government in Syria had ceded to the Turks in 1939. Egypt was supporting Greek territorial claims on Cyprus. And in the summer of 1958, Nasserist forces overthrew the pro-Western government of Iraq, dooming the Baghdad Pact altogether.

In July 1958, concerned over the Nasserist threat to Middle Eastern stability, and responding to persistent Israeli initiatives, Turkish Foreign Minister Fatin Rustum Zurlu sent word to Jerusalem of his interest in a "peripheral" compact with Israel, which also would include Iran and Ethiopia. Prime Minister Ben-Gurion's reaction was enthusiastic. Initially, the Israeli leader felt obliged to secure Washington's approval for the proposed alliance. Once the Eisenhower administration gave its benediction, however, Ben-Gurion departed secretly for Ankara on August 28, together with Foreign Minister Golda Meir and Reuven Shiloah, his security adviser. In the Turkish capital, the Israelis conferred with Prime Minister Adnan Menderes and Foreign Minister Zurlu, and within hours reached agreement on areas of cooperation. Israel would provide specialized technology for Turkish military needs. Both governments would share intelligence on Middle Eastern strategic developments. Each would act on the other's diplomatic behalf in Washington, where Turkey also would support Israel's appeal for advanced American jet fighters and tanks. Subsequently, Iran and Ethiopia shared in the "peripheral alliance."

The arrangement never was official or even public. For the Turks, national pride would not have permitted acknowledgment that a little people like the Jews, traditionally regarded as a powerless, commercial minority, should now be dealing with Turkey as a military-diplomatic equal. In any case, the relationship was not carved in stone. Israel's spectacular triumph in the 1967 War put the Turks in an awkward position. Privately they were impressed, even awed, by the Jewish state's military proficiency. Regarding it as impolitic, however, to acquiesce in Israel's occupation of the Palestinian West Bank, the Turkish government supported every Arab draft resolution for United Nations condemnation. The shift also coincided with Ankara's intensified diplomatic campaign to win Arab support on the Cyprus issue. Throughout the 1970s Turkey thus maintained an uncharacteristically chill stance toward Israel. Bilateral relations were further strained in 1980 with Menachem Begin's decision to proclaim "united" Jerusalem as Israel's capital. For the first time since 1959, the Turks downgraded their diplomatic representation in Israel to a second secretary.

Possibly the strain between the two governments would have continued indefinitely had the Arabs reciprocated Turkish goodwill. But not a single Arab nation withdrew its support from Greece on the Cyprus issue. Moreover, the Palestinian terrorist campaign on Israelis and Jews abroad ultimately spilled over onto Turkish soil. In September 1986, two Palestinian Arabs burst into Istanbul's stately Neve Shalom synagogue during Rosh HaShanah services, and raked its sanctuary with automatic fire. Twenty-two worshippers were killed. There had been earlier Arab assaults on Israeli diplomats in Turkey, but this latest atrocity, committed against local Jews—Turkish nationals—was too much for a sovereign government. Several months later, Ankara decided to exchange ambassadors with Israel.

In the ensuing decade, trade between the two countries sextupled. Some 250,000 Israeli tourists were visiting Turkey each year. In 1996 and 1997, the two governments again negotiated a series of military cooperation agreements. These in fact were discreetly fostered by Washington. Intent on strengthening the defenses of a valued NATO partner, the State Department preferred not to expose Congress to anti-Turkish pressures from the Greek-American and Armenian-American lobbies. It was a simpler matter to operate through the Israeli conduit. Israel would sell Turkey extensive quantities of its locally manufactured weaponry, and would upgrade Turkey's aging American-manufactured air force equipment. Joint Turkish-Israeli air and naval maneuvers were projected in the eastern Mediterranean. Unlike the earlier 1958 understanding, neither side this time bothered to veil its cooperation. By the late 1990s, after all, the dangers that evoked their partnership were themselves less than clandestine. Syria, Israel's perennial enemy, was lending its support to a widening Kurdish insurrection against Turkish rule. More ominously for Israel and Turkey alike, a potential nuclear threat to both countries was looming up over the Persian Gulf.

AN AEGEAN IMPLACABILITY

In ancient times, their cultures were synergistic; in modern times, antipathetic. The long-standing conflict between Judaism and Byzantium provided an appropriate backdrop for Greek domestic anti-semitism in the post–World War I years, and Greek diplomatic hostility in the post–World War II years. From the moment the Palestine issue reached the United Nations in 1947, Athens vigorously opposed partition; and during the ensuing 1948–49 Palestine war, its support of the Arab cause was flagrant and even collaborative. The Greek government banned passage through its territory of volunteers or "contraband" matériel destined for Israel, although not for concomitant support to the Arab nations. For several years even after Israel's birth, Israeli citizens on foreign airliners were not so much as allowed to leave their planes during stopovers at Athens Airport.

Yet it was counterproductive for Greece to withhold diplomatic recognition of Israel altogether. The Orthodox Church's extensive network of institutions in Jerusalem required the presence of a Greek consul general in the Holy City. Israel, in turn, eager to foster those official contacts, was prepared to guarantee Greek Orthodox access to Christian shrines against encroachments by the Latins; while, for its part, the Orthodox Patriarchate entered an expedient alliance with Israel in opposing a *corpus separatum* for Jerusalem. Except for the Jerusalem relationship, however, formal contacts between the two governments remained minimal. Refusing to countenance an ambassadorial exchange with the Jewish state, the Greeks permitted Israel no more than a legation in Athens, and, at that, accredited the Israeli emissary simply as a "diplomatic representative." In its coverage of the Arab-Israeli impasse, the Greek press hewed unremittingly to the Arab line.

The animus reflected classic self-interest. The Greek diaspora in the Arab world was extensive. In Egypt alone, the Greek-speaking population totaled at least 140,000, with a third that number dispersed throughout other Arab nations. For Athens, these kinsmen were regarded as hostages to an "appropriate" stance on Middle Eastern affairs. Equally vulnerable was Greece's maritime industry, the nation's largest foreign-currency earner. More than the carriers of any other nation, Greek shippers relied on the Arab oil traffic, an income source they dared not jeopardize. Finally, and most decisively, the envenomed Cyprus issue determined Greece's Middle Eastern policy with all the certitude of a mathematical law. For Athens, assurance of support from the powerful Arab bloc in the United Nations demanded a reciprocal endorsement of Arab claims against Israel. No Greek political party, whether of the right or the left, was willing to tamper with that formula.

The Israeli government learned early on, as a result, that attempts to cultivate Greek understanding, or at least forbearance, were wasted effort. Even Nasser's harshly xenophobic laws of 1956–57, a series of property confiscations and punitive taxes that soon reduced Egypt's Greek population to less than 30,000, would not shake Athens's stance on Israel. Whether on the issues of Arab-Israeli border violence, Palestinian refugees, or the status of Jerusalem, Greek support for the Arabs was reflexive. By the mid-1950s Israel had come to regard Greece as a de facto member of the Arab League, and hardly worth consulting any longer, let alone cultivating. Diplomatic contacts between the two nations remained perfunctory, year after year. Trade between them was negligible.

Meanwhile, endlessly traumatized by the Cyprus issue, the Greek political system during the 1960s and 1970s underwent a wrenching transformation. In 1967 a cabal of army colonels seized power, and held it for the next seven years in an effort to press through *enosis*, a union of Cyprus with the Greek mainland. Yet all the colonels achieved for their effort was international isolation and a Turkish invasion of northern Cyprus in 1974. Discredited, the military regime was overthrown several months later. Its successor in office, the New Democratic party, itself quite rightist, gingerly sought to negotiate Greece back into the good graces of the West. That move, too, evoked little public enthusiasm. In 1981 the New Democrats lost a national election to PASOK, the Socialist party. Under the leadership of Andreas Papandreou, a fiery doctrinaire leftist, Athens adopted a resentful attitude toward NATO and the European Community, both of which it regarded as under "imperialist" American influence.

By the same token, no "puppet" of "American imperialism" was as vulnerable to Papandreou's inflammatory rhetoric as Israel, whose post-1967 occupation of the Palestinian West Bank now was equated with Turkey's 1974 occupation of northern Cyprus. On his first day in office, in April 1981, Papandreou invited Yasser Arafat to visit him in Athens. Subsequently a PLO representative shared with Israel's emissary the identical subambassadorial status in the Greek capital. In the United Nations, as in the European Community, the Papandreou government functioned as the West's most dependable and uncompromising spokesman for the Palestinian cause. It was accordingly Israel's invasion of Lebanon, in June 1982, that allowed the PASOK cabinet a unique opportunity to claim the moral high ground. On television Papandreou indicted Israel as a "murderer" of women and children. Thereafter some one hundred thousand demonstrators converged on the Israeli diplomatic mission, led by Papandreou's wife, Margaret, and Minister of Culture Melina Mercouri (a film actress married to a Jew). The crowd was deterred from violence only by the presence of the United States embassy, close by. In August the Papandreou government provided a flotilla of Greek vessels to evacuate PLO troops from Lebanon.

A CONTINENTAL VULNERABILITY

Well before the summer of 1982, it was specifically these PLO irregulars who lent a unique element of volatility to the Arab-Israel conflict. The Arab nations' shattering defeat in the Six-Day War had left their governments temporarily discredited as champions of the anti-Israel crusade. In their stead it was the Palestine Liberation Organization, functioning as a loose affiliation of guerrilla brotherhoods, that emerged in subsequent years as a dynamic new instrument of resistance to "Zionist imperialism." In the captured West Bank, to be sure,

Israeli security forces easily suppressed isolated outbursts of Palestinian violence. It was rather beyond its own enlarged frontiers that the Jewish state proved unexpectedly vulnerable.

On July 22, 1968, an El Al flight en route from Rome to Tel Aviv was hijacked by two Arab passengers. These were later revealed to be members of the PFLP—the Popular Front for the Liberation of Palestine—a leftist PLO faction. The terrorists forced the crew to fly the plane to Algiers. There twelve Israeli male passengers were held hostage for fifteen Palestinians incarcerated in Israeli prisons, and a $5 million ransom. After thirty-nine days Jerusalem agreed to the exchange and the payment. The capitulation was a bitter pill for the Israeli government. Manifestly its enemies had discovered the nation's Achilles' heel: It was extraterritorial.

The July 1968 hijacking in fact soon triggered a chain reaction of new terrorist assaults on El Al, then on other airlines with service to Israel, and ultimately on Israeli civilians in Europe. At Athens Airport on December 26, 1968, a trio of PFLP terrorists loosed a spray of automatic-weapons fire at a crowd of passengers waiting to board an El Al flight. Two Israelis were struck, one fatally. At this point, aware that PFLP training bases were concentrated in Lebanon, the Eshkol government two days later launched its devastating commando raid on Beirut Airport, blowing up thirteen passenger jets of Lebanon's national airline. Western reaction was not forbearing. The UN Security Council vigorously condemned Israel. De Gaulle found his pretext for canceling the Mirage fighter contract (p. 186). Sobered, the Israeli government then decided that future acts of retaliation would be directed exclusively against the guerrillas themselves, albeit in their Lebanese strongholds.

But over the ensuing months, air force or occasional commando raids against these nests failed to deter terrorist attacks against Israelis abroad. In February 1969 Palestinian guerrillas fired at an El Al plane loading passengers at the Zurich airport. A crew member was killed. In August 1969 a TWA plane en route from Rome to Tel Aviv was hijacked and diverted to Damascus, where four Israeli male passengers were imprisoned. They were released only four months later, in exchange for Syrian infiltrators held in Israeli prisons. In November of the same year, an Arab terrorist threw grenades at the El Al office in Athens, wounding fourteen people and killing a Greek infant. Shortly afterward, three Arab guerrillas fired at passengers waiting to board an El Al flight at Munich Airport. An Israeli was killed, and another, Hannah Meron, one of Israel's most respected actresses, lost a leg. In February 1970 terrorists planted a bomb on a Swissair plane destined for Tel Aviv. The jet blew up in midair, and sixteen Israelis were among its forty-seven victims.

The mayhem continued. On September 2, 1970, Palestinian guerrillas hijacked an El Al plane en route from Amsterdam to New York. In this case the airliner's crew managed to subdue the two attackers, killing the man and wounding his female companion. The plane made an emergency descent in London. As the plane rolled to a stop at Heathrow Airport, an urgent message arrived from the Israeli foreign ministry, ordering the El Al captain to take off immediately for Tel Aviv; Israeli intelligence wished to interrogate the surviving hijacker, Leila Khaled. It was the British police who intervened, refusing to allow the plane to depart until they took the young woman into their own custody. Whereupon, four days later, regarding Britain and the Western democracies as accomplices of the Israelis, other teams of Palestinian terrorists hijacked three additional passenger jets, belonging to BOAC, TWA, and Swissair, and forced their crews to land at an abandoned desert airstrip near Zerqa, Jordan. There 310 passengers became hostages to be exchanged for some 200 Palestinian prisoners in Israel, as well as for Leila Khaled in Britain, and for a dozen other Arab terrorists held in Switzerland and Germany. Unless the prisoners were released within seventy-two hours, warned the hijackers, all the planes would be blown up, together with their passengers and crews.

The British, Swiss, and German governments were prepared to comply. Not so Israel's Prime Minister Golda Meir. After seventy-two hours of sphinxlike silence from Jerusalem, the Palestinians at Zerqa began to waver. Jordan's King Hussein also had warned that he was prepared to use force against them, and his troops appeared to be closing the ring around the captive airliners. Unnerved, the terrorists then evacuated the passengers, blew up the planes, and carried off the hostages to isolated holding pens. Still Israel held firm. In the end the hijackers wilted, accepting as their quid pro quo the release exclusively of Arab prisoners in European prisons.

As it happened, the hijacking episode represented a final provocation for Jordan's King Hussein, whose authority for months had been threatened by a virtual PLO quasi-government functioning on Hashemite territory. On September 16, 1970, he ordered his army to move against these PLO encampments and installations, and during the ensuing weeklong assault the entire PLO infrastructure in Jordan was crushed. In the mêlée, possibly as many as two thousand Palestinians were slaughtered, many of them innocent refugees. For Yasser Arafat and his confederation of Palestinian guerrillas, the debacle would be characterized as "Black September." And "Black September," in turn, would become the talisman of an enlarged and intensified campaign of retribution against both Jordan and Israel.

Thus, in May 1972, an elite PLO shock contingent, "Black September," managed to hijack a Sabena airliner shortly after its takeoff from Brussels en route for Tel Aviv. With consummate audacity, the four terrorists—two men and two women—ordered the crew to continue its scheduled flight to Israel. Upon landing at Lod Airport, the hijackers threatened to blow up the plane with its ninety-three passengers unless a group of Palestinians in Israeli prisons were released and brought directly to the plane, which would then fly on to Cairo. The Israeli reaction was characteristic. Within hours their commandos stormed and recaptured the aircraft. Although one passenger was killed, both male Palestinians were shot dead and the two women hijackers were taken prisoner. Under interrogation, the latter provided Israeli intelligence with vital information on the composition and modus operandi of the Black September strike force. It became clear then that Europe had been targeted as the principal battleground for guerrilla operations against Israel.

A EUROPEAN KILLING GROUND

In the ensuing months of 1972–73, an unfolding series of terrorist attacks confirmed these intelligence findings. A letter bomb killed the Israeli agricultural attaché in London. Bombs exploded at the Israeli embassies in Brussels and The Hague, although without fatalities. In Brussels, grenades were thrown at an El Al office, injuring four Belgians. In each instance the Popular Front for the Liberation of Palestine claimed responsibility. Israeli newspapers and political commentators in their anguish began to speculate that the Israeli people apparently were becoming as vulnerable again as Jews always had been in the years before 1948. If the reaction was overwrought, the statistics nevertheless were ominous. In 1971 foreign operations counted for only 3 percent of all guerrilla attacks against Israel. In 1972 the figure rose to 12 percent. By 1973 it reached 30 percent. Western Europe plainly was superseding the Middle East in the phantom war between the PLO and Israel. Worse yet, no European government seemed willing to impose heavy punishment on convicted Arab killers. Rather, it was revealed later that Lufthansa had entered into detailed negotiations with several Arab guerrilla organizations to ensure the safety of its flights; even as France's Pompidou government negotiated a "gentleman's agreement" with the PLO federation to refrain from assaults on Air France flights.

By the early 1970s, several factors evidently had transformed Western Europe into an ideal staging base for Israel's enemies. For one thing, large communities of Palestinians and other Arabs lived in these countries, as students, workers, or transient businessmen. They provided convenient "hinterlands" for terrorist groups. Western Europe also offered PLO killers geographic proximity and compactness, and excellent transportation facilities that permitted rapid cross-border movement. Democratic and "open," the Continent also was substantially immune to surveillance or interference with private conspiratorial activities. It offered an abundance of targets, as well, in the network of Israeli diplomatic and commercial offices, of local Jewish business and communal institutions. Finally West European governments and populations alike wished above all to be left alone to pursue the tangible blessings of improved living standards. The security of Israelis or of other Jews on their soil doubtless was not a matter of indifference to them; but neither was it their central preoccupation.

Inevitably, it was Israel's intelligence services that had to bear the heaviest burden of protecting the nation's citizens and institutions in Europe. Yet, as late as 1972, none of Israel's shrewdest counterterrorism specialists grasped the magnitude or audacity of the Black September component in the Palestinian guerrilla campaign—or of Europe's pusillanimity in coping with the violence in its midst. Only in the late summer of that year was the lesson conclusively driven home. The agent of its instruction was Ali Hassan Salameh, a guerrilla chieftain of extraordinary daring and ruthlessness. Salameh came by his talents naturally. In the 1930s his father, Hassan Salameh, a Palestinian villager, was renowned as a brutal extortionist who eventually transferred his lust for violence to the cause of Arab nationalism. During the Palestine War of 1947–48, Hassan Salameh became one of the Arabs' most effective commandos, specializing in the murder of Jewish civilians. Israeli military forces launched an urgent hunt for him, and in May 1948 cornered and killed him.

The son, Ali Hassan Salameh, was taken by relatives to Lebanon, where he lived comfortably on his late father's banked extortions. In 1967, enraged by Israel's pulverizing recent victory, the younger Salameh became an ardent volunteer in Fatah, Yasser Arafat's personal faction within the PLO. Rising swiftly in Arafat's esteem, he soon became commander of Fatah's military wing. Then, in the aftermath of the September 1970 massacre of Palestinians in Jordan, Salameh and Arafat together created the Black September unit as an instrument of revenge against the "enemies of the Palestinian people." As chief of Black September operations, Salameh promptly embarked on his mission with a ferocity and dynamism that transcended even his late father's.

Black September's first "hit" was the murder of Jordanian Prime Minister Wasfi al-Tel in Cairo in November 1971. Three weeks later, the unit struck again, machine-gunning the limousine of the Jordanian ambassador in London (although failing to kill him). Other assaults followed in rapid succession: a firebomb attack on the Jordanian embassy in Paris, another on a Jordanian airliner in Cairo, the hijacking of a Jordanian plane to Algeria, the assassination of five suspected Jordanian secret service agents in Bonn. At first Israeli intelligence paid only marginal attention to Black September, assuming that its principal targets would continue to be Hashemite. But the May 1972 Sabena airliner hijacking to Lod Airport gravely shook that assumption. And when the Shin Bet, Israel's internal security service, interrogated the surviving Arab terrorists, and determined that Ali Hassan Salameh was the brains of the operation, it began to grasp that it was facing its most ruthless adversary.

Salameh was continually expanding his resources. In ensuing months he negotiated a partnership with other guerrilla cabals: with George Habash's Popular Front for the Liberation of Palestine, then with such non-Arab terrorist outfits as Germany's Baader-Meinhof Gang, the Japanese Red Army, Iran's Liberation Front, and Turkey's People's Liberation Army. Each shared with the others its intelligence information, its training techniques, its "safe" houses in various European cities. It was with these groups too that Black September plotted a move to avenge the Sabena airliner failure. The initial blow fell only two and a half weeks later, on May 30, 1972, when Air France Flight 132 arrived at Israel's Lod Airport after a stopover in Rome. It was then that three disembarking passengers, members of the Japanese Red Army, opened their hand luggage, pulled out Czech submachine guns, and coolly slaughtered twenty-six people and wounded seventy-two others in the terminal before Israeli police wounded and captured them. Ironically, most of the victims were Puerto Ricans, who had arrived as pilgrims to visit the Holy Land's Christian shrines. But even the Lod Airport massacre, although unprecedented in scope and carnage, was but a prelude to Salameh's single most audacious bid for revenge and world attention.

A MOMENT OF TRUTH IN MUNICH

On August 23, 1972, a Palestinian couple, bearing Algerian passports, landed in Cologne, Germany. Their hand baggage went unsearched. It contained eight assault rifles, ten grenades, six pistols, and twenty-one boxes of ammunition. The couple then rented an automobile and drove to Munich. As the site of the international Olympics, scheduled to begin on September 1, the Bavarian capital was a logical tourist magnet that summer of 1972. Once in Munich, the Arabs transferred their luggage to the local Black September commander, Muhammad Massalha. With Massalha were seven other Palestinians who had shared training with him in Lebanon. Their current objective was nothing less than the capture of Israel's entire Olympic team.

In previous weeks the guerrillas had studied the layout of the "Olympic Village," the living and training compound allocated for the scores of visiting athletic teams. The plan was to infiltrate the enclave, break into the apartments allocated to the Israelis, take the athletes hostage, and demand in exchange 234 Arab guerrillas imprisoned in Israel, as well as two leaders of the Baader-Meinhof Gang who recently had been captured by the German police. If the thirty-six-hour deadline was met, captors, hostages, and prisoners alike then would be flown to an Arab country in three separate airplanes, where the transfer would take place. The date set for the operation was September 5. Several days earlier, Ali Hassan Salameh flew to Communist East Germany, taking up his "command post" in a rented East Berlin apartment.

The attack on September 5 unfolded like clockwork. Donning ski masks, Massalha and his seven fellow guerrillas climbed the fence into the Olympic Village, made their way to the targeted building on Connellystrasse 31, and swiftly ascended to the complex of third-floor lodgings where the Israeli athletes were housed. There the Palestinians succeeded in blasting open one of the apartment doors with gunfire. The Israeli wrestling team was inside. Some of the athletes managed to jump through windows and escape, but two were killed and nine captured. Thereupon Massalha appeared at an open window and threw out a typed "declaration" containing his group's demands. Within minutes the building had been surrounded by a massive police cordon. Alerted in Bonn, Chancellor Willy Brandt now confronted his worst nightmare: a possible new massacre of Jews on German soil. Immediately he instructed his interior minister,

Hans-Dietrich Genscher, to fly to Munich and seek to negotiate a peaceful solution. At the same time, Brandt telephoned Prime Minister Golda Meir in Jerusalem, inviting the Israeli government's cooperation. The chancellor hardly was surprised that Mrs. Meir rejected any notion of capitulating to the terrorists' demands. Instead she dispatched Mossad director Zvi Zamir to Munich on an executive jet, together with a team of Arabic-speaking agents.

Stalling for time, the German authorities engaged in tedious negotiations with the terrorists. As Zamir anticipated, Ali Hassan Salameh had authorized Massalha to extend his deadline several times. All the while, over Israel's objections, Brandt allowed the Olympic Games to continue—in surrealistic counterpoint to the deadly game being played out on Connellystrasse. Meanwhile, television coverage brought the unfolding Munich kidnapping drama to hundreds of millions of viewers all over the world, precisely as Salameh had hoped. As the third deadline approached at noon on September 8, Zamir won Mrs. Meir's approval for a possible solution, one that was immediately approved in Bonn. It was an agreement to exchange the nine Israelis for an equivalent group of German volunteers—Interior Minister Genscher and Bavarian *Land* Minister Bruno Merck among them—who would then be flown with the kidnappers to Cairo. After two or three months, once formal connection with the abduction was "dissipated," Israel would liberate some fifty Palestinians from its prisons. The terms were communicated to Massalha. On his own, he approved them. Departure was scheduled for 10:30 p.m. that same September 8.

In fact the "compromise" was a ruse. Neither Brandt nor Golda Meir intended to honor it. The terrorists would be seized before they left German soil. But Zamir, the Mossad director, had expected the police to launch their assault on the Palestinians the moment they departed the apartment building. Instead, the German scenario was to rescue the hostages only after they had been carried by two helicopters from the Olympic Village to the neighboring air force base of Fürstenfeldbrück. Once the Arabs descended from the helicopters and continued by foot to the bus assigned to drive them to an awaiting Lufthansa jet, they would be picked off by police snipers.

Matters did not work out as planned. Upon landing at Fürstenfeldbrück, Massalha smelled a rat: The distance to the waiting bus was suspiciously long. He ordered the other seven terrorists to remain in the helicopters with the hostages. For the police sharpshooters, waiting on the roof of the terminal, it was then or never. They opened fire, killing Massalha and wounding one of his companions. Thereupon the other Palestinians fired long bursts into their Israeli hostages, killing them all. One of the terrorists also threw a grenade at the second helicopter, blowing it up. As a result, by the time police reinforcements arrived, the clumsy ambush had left all nine Israelis dead, together with Massalha, five of the seven terrorists, and one German policeman.

It was not until midnight that the tragic facts reached Israel. Abba Eban, the foreign minister, recalled later:

> The terrible symbolism of the murder of Israelis in the city associated with the Hitler curse cast a pall of indignant fury over Israel. . . . There ensued a period of coolness in German-Israeli relations. We had been fully in accord with the basic decision of the Brandt government to deal firmly with the terrorists, but we could not fail to be enraged by the clumsy failure in the execution of the plan.

The bitterness left in Israeli mouths became gall only three weeks later. Bonn freed the two Palestinians who had been captured alive during the Munich rescue operation, flying them off to Benghazi, Libya, whence they were transported to Damascus and a hero's welcome. Subsequently they were "exchanged" for a Lufthansa plane that had been "hijacked" over the Mediterranean. In its fury at this palpable German-Arab collusion, Israel briefly recalled its ambassador to Bonn for "consultations."

Lionized by the Arab world, Ali Hassan Salameh returned from East Berlin to be embraced by Arafat as "my son." Afterward, heady with victory, Salameh ordered an intensification of his terror campaign. Letter bombs were mailed out to Israeli diplomats in Europe, as well as to eminent European Jewish industrialists, businessmen, and community leaders. Several of the devices exploded, wounding either their targeted victims or unsuspecting postal workers. Nor did the terrorists hesitate to strike at the Mossad itself. On September 10, 1972, only two days after the Munich massacre, an alleged Arab informer telephoned the Israeli embassy in Brussels, asking to speak to Zadok Ophir. Ophir was an undercover Mossad officer. Somehow the Arab had penetrated his identity, and now lured him to a meeting at a Brussels café with the promise of information about Black September. As Ophir arrived, he was shot four times (miraculously he survived), and the "informant" escaped. In Paris, five weeks later, three Arab guerrillas shot a Syrian radio reporter to death. The Syrian, Khader Kanou, was an authentic informer for the Mossad, and now he too paid.

AN OVERSEAS COUNTEROFFENSIVE

Israel soon faced a crisis that was ghettoizing its population, in effect vitiating the core objective of national sovereignty—a government's protection of its citizens. In 1956 and 1967, when the threat was military, the solution was to strike back at the enemies' military infrastructure across neighboring Middle Eastern frontiers. But in this case, was the parallelism to counterattack the terrorist infrastructure in Europe? Foreign Minister Eban had reservations. There was no need to roil Western governments, he argued, specifically at a time when access to the European Common Market was a priority goal for Israel. Prime Minister Golda Meir was not insensible to this logic. It had influenced Israel's decision to reject earlier schemes for assassinating Nasser, or even Arafat. Yet there were precedents for retaliating against nonpolitical figures. Israel in the 1950s had put on its death list two Egyptian colonels, Mustafa Hafez and Salah Mustafa, who had authorized guerrilla killings of Israeli civilians. In the early 1960s, for that matter, the Mossad had launched assassination attempts against German scientists working for Egypt (pp. 134–5). Were the reasons not equally compelling to seek out Arab terrorists in Europe? This was the argument of Zvi Zamir and of other Israeli intelligence advisers. In the end, Mrs. Meir agreed.

Under Zamir's direction, a secret committee was established, "Committee X," with the mandate of identifying, targeting, and eliminating those responsible for the latest string of murders against Israeli civilians overseas, and specifically for the Munich Olympics massacre. Zamir in turn appointed a veteran operative, Michael Harari, chief of Mossad headquarters in Paris, to hand-pick the assassination squads. Before these agents moved, however, each proposed act of "termination" would have to be reviewed and specifically authorized by Committee X, and ultimately by the prime minister.

Less than two weeks passed before the first operation was approved. The intended victim was Walid Zwaiter. Posing as a translator for the Libyan embassy in Rome, Zwaiter in fact was a Palestinian who directed Black September's key operational base in Europe. Rome suited the terrorists' purposes almost ideally. Its Fiumicino Airport was nearly as inefficient as Athens's in its haphazard security precautions. Terrorists easily smuggled weapons in and out of Fiumicino's terminals. The El Al flight diverted to Algiers in 1968 had taken off from Fiumicino, as had several hijacked European and American planes. Most recently the Japanese killers responsible for the Lod Airport massacre had boarded their Air France flight at Fiumicino. Walid Zwaiter had been deeply involved in these projects. Harari's agents then began studying the man's apartment building, evaluating the neighborhood traffic pattern. Zwaiter in turn, suspecting he was in jeopardy, took elaborate precautions, altering his schedule and surrounding himself with armed guards. But on October 16, returning home in mid-evening, he was shot dead at the entrance to his apartment. Before the night was over, the four Israeli hit men had left Italy.

Zwaiter's assassination in turn set off tremors of alarm in Paris, where lived Dr. Mahmoud Hamshari, the PLO's "director of information" in Europe. Projecting an aura of moderation, Hamshari actually was the second-ranking Black September operative in Europe, and his apartment served as an advance base, weapons depot, and communications center. Hamshari also was alert enough to take greater security precautions after Zwaiter's death, always avoiding precise appointments or meeting places. Nevertheless, on December 8, 1973, Mossad agents succeeded in gaining entry to Hamshari's apartment during his absence. Upon his return home in the early evening, his telephone rang. Picking up the receiver, Hamshari set off a concealed bomb—and perished.

The "executions" continued, all of them personally reviewed and approved by Committee X, by Defense Minister Dayan, and ultimately by Prime Minister Meir. It soon became evident to the Black September leadership that none of their members was safe. Thus Nicosia had long been a favored Black September staging ground, and its resident director, Hussein Abd al-Qir, was a senior figure in the organization. It was Qir who personally selected the agents to be trained in the Soviet Union by a renowned master of "unconventional" warfare, Colonel Anatoly Vassiliev. Three weeks after Hamshari's death in Paris, two men holding British passports arrived in Nicosia. Several days later, Qir returned to his hotel room and retired for the evening. When he turned off his lights, one of the "Englishmen" standing in an alley outside pressed a switch. Qir's bed promptly exploded, together with its occupant.

In Beirut, evaluating the attrition of his top men, Ali Hassan Salameh recognized that Black September needed a dramatic countercoup in the sinister underground war. Accordingly, in March 1973, he and his colleagues devised a major body blow. It was to hijack a commercial aircraft in Europe, fly it to Tripoli, Libya, load it with explosives, and then have it flown to Tel Aviv by a suicide commando. Coordinator of the operation would be Dr. Basil al-Qubaissi, a professor at the American University of Beirut who recently had arrived in Paris to fill the vacuum left by the assassinated Mahmoud Hamshari. But this operation also was aborted. The Mossad got word of it through an informer. On April 6 two Israeli agents sauntered by Qubaissi's apartment building as he was returning from his office and calmly shot him to death. In Cyprus the very next day, a new Black September agent, who had been sent to replace the assassinated Hussein Abd al-Qir, returned to his Nicosia hotel room, turned on the light, and died in an explosion—exactly as had his predecessor.

Even as they picked off Black September's senior operatives, Michael Harari and his team were endlessly frustrated by their inability to track down Ali Hassan Salameh himself. The man's instinct for self-protection continually defied every Israeli effort to set a trap. As a result, in April 1973, Prime Minister Meir approved Committee X's plan for a climactic blow. This one would be launched directly at Black September headquarters in Beirut. By then, painstaking intelligence work had identified the terrorist nerve center as an apartment building on Beirut's rue Verdun. On April 7, the operation began. It was a joint Mossad-army offensive. Posing as European businessmen and bearing false passports, a half dozen Mossad agents arrived separately from different European cities and registered in separate hotels. Renting automobiles, they drove through and carefully studied the targeted neighborhood. The following night two Israeli missile boats and two patrol vessels disembarked thirty commandos at a deserted beach outside Beirut. The "businessmen" awaited them with a small fleet of automobiles, and the full entourage then converged by differing routes on Black September headquarters.

As they entered the building, the commandos moved with precision toward selected apartments. Blowing open the doors with grenades, they used automatic weapons to rake the occupants' bedrooms. There was some resistance on the upper floors, but this was swiftly overcome. After forty minutes of room-to-room "combat," the commandos withdrew, evacuated the building's women and children, then dynamited the entire edifice. Remarkably, there was no interference from the Lebanese police, who assumed that the fighting was yet another intramural battle between Palestinian guerrilla factions—and they had learned to steer clear of these elements. The entire assault team then was picked up by three Israeli helicopters, landing in the very center of Beirut. Flown off to the waiting vessels, the commandos were carried back to Haifa. Altogether two Israelis had been killed, four wounded. Three Palestinian family members and two Lebanese civilian passersby also had been killed. But the operation otherwise was a spectacular success. Three senior Fatah leaders had been slain, together with fifteen other guerrilla members of varying echelons. Indeed, of the entire Black September command then in Beirut, only Ali Hassan Salameh had escaped. He had retired for the night to another house down the block on rue Verdun.

Still others of Salameh's lieutenants continued at risk. One of the most important of these, Zaïd Muchassi, served as Black September division chief in Athens, where the Israelis had long kept him under surveillance. While in his hotel room on the night of April 9, listening to a radio news program, Muchassi learned of the Beirut raid. Shocked, he rushed outside to buy a newspaper. Upon his return, two waiting Israelis shot him dead. A month later, as Yasser Arafat and Ali Hassan Salameh were evaluating their recent shattering losses, the Israelis struck yet again. During the Beirut raid they had carried off many of Black September's files. These revealed the name of a top guerrilla operative in London. The man was located, and "turned." For a handsome payoff he agreed to supply information on other surviving Black September agents.

One of the most innovative of the latter was an Algerian, Mohammed Boudia, a veteran of his own country's earlier nationalist uprising. In the 1960s Boudia had been recruited by KGB agents for additional training in the Soviet Union. Near the end of the decade, settling in Paris, Boudia soon became an active participant in numerous PFLP–Black September operations in Europe, ranging from arms-smuggling to hijackings. By 1971 he functioned as Salameh's chief of operations in France. In May 1973, a group of Mossad agents arrived in Paris to track Boudia down. It was not a simple task. A former theater manager, Boudia was a master of disguises. But with information gleaned from arrested accomplices in Israel, the Mossad eventually determined his location. On June 28, 1973, Boudia climbed into his automobile, turned on the ignition, and was blown to bits.

Well before these spring–summer operations, Committee X had moved decisively to a multifarious offensive in the underground war. Like the Palestinian organizations, its armory also included letter bombs, pistol ambushes, and explosive devices. Nor were psychological weapons ignored. The Mossad began running premonitory obituaries of suspected terrorists in local European Arab newspapers, and dispatching warning letters to other suspects, providing intimate details of their private and sexual lives. The apparent omniscience with which the Mossad foiled plots against Israeli targets also proved unnerving to Salameh and his surviving collaborators. An early case in point, in January 1973, was Black September's audacious plan to kill Prime Minister Golda Meir upon her arrival in Rome for an audience with Pope Paul VI. Mrs. Meir's aircraft would be shot down as it descended at Fiumicino Airport. The Mossad learned of the plot from an Arab informer in London. Drawn up by Salameh himself, it envisaged the use of Soviet-made Strella missiles, shoulder-launched weapons that were capable of homing in on the exhaust heat of jet engines. Fatah had acquired these missiles at its training camp in Yugoslavia and had smuggled them into Italy by sea. Currently three of the weapons were cached in a "safe" apartment in Rome.

Three weeks remained before the prime minister's visit. Pursuing every lead, the Mossad still was unable to locate the "safe" apartment. The Italian police were alerted, and diligently assigned scores of additional men near Fiumicino's runways. Yet no missiles were found. On the day of Mrs. Meir's scheduled arrival, the Mossad unit was consumed with unbearable tension. Indeed, the prime minister's El Al jet actually was on its final descent when one of the agents, scouting a perimeter highway in his automobile, suddenly noticed an anomaly in a food-concession cart by the side of the road. There were three stacks poking out of its roof, but only one was smoking. The Israeli did a sharp U-turn on the road and crashed his automobile directly into the cart, turning it over and pinning two of its five occupants beneath it (one of them died). Climbing out, the Israeli confirmed that the men were all Arabs, and that there were missiles inside. The surviving plotters were arrested.

The entire audacious enterprise had been intended as Salameh's masterstroke, the most audacious coup since the Munich Olympics massacre. But once again the Black September chieftain had been outmaneuvered, and had lost still another vital cell of intensely committed and highly trained agents. And by the spring of 1973, Salameh's principal operatives in Rome, Paris, Athens, Nicosia, and even in Beirut, had been liquidated.

A TESTING OF EUROPEAN FORBEARANCE

At no time, however, was Salameh prepared to abandon his offensive. In tandem with Israel's counterblows, the Black September underground war continued. Thus, in January 1973 a senior Mossad agent in Madrid, Baruch Cohen, was lured to a meeting at a streetcorner café by one of his Arab "informers." There he was ambushed by Black September gunmen and shot dead. In March, Palestinian guerrillas killed an Israeli businessman in Cyprus; in April, an Italian employee of El Al in Rome. On April 9, only a day after the Israeli commando raid on Beirut, the Palestinians had come within minutes of wiping out the Israeli ambassador and his family in Nicosia. At the Vienna airport a week later, also at the last minute, sky marshals intercepted a trio of guerrillas as they prepared to blow up an El Al jet. On July 1, three days after the assassination of Mohammed Boudia in Paris, a Palestinian waylaid Israel's air attaché in Washington, shooting him dead outside his suburban home. In August two Palestinians attacked a TWA plane in Athens just as it landed on a flight from Tel Aviv, killing five passengers and wounding four. The shootings and bombings continued into 1974. In September of that year, Arab terrorists threw a hand grenade at the El Al office in Paris, killing two passersby and wounding twelve. In December, another group of Palestinians machine-gunned the corridor near the El Al ticketing area at Rome's Fiumicino Airport, killing thirty-two passengers and injuring forty. For every senior Palestinian terrorist the Mossad liquidated, the retribution on Israeli, Jewish, and European civilian victims continued, apparently unabated.

Beyond the timorousness of many Western governments, a second, continental factor bedeviled Israel's struggle to ensure the safety of its nationals overseas. Europeans traditionally had adopted a double standard toward the Jews. In the prewar era, their rightist elements had stigmatized Jews as a retrograde people, from whom nothing good could be expected. But with the postwar revelations of the Holocaust, followed by the rise of Israel, and the Jewish state's underdog military victories over the Arab armies, Europe tended to embrace a maximalist view of the Israelis as "new" Jews, paragons of all that was gallant, decent, honorable, and moral in the human condition. Belatedly and subliminally, Europe in effect was imposing on Israel a categorical imperative that its own peoples earlier had forfeited. Now, however, the Israelis were engaging not in a "clean" war against their enemies, but in a Mafia-like underground campaign whose implacable ruthlessness appeared to narrow the qualitative distinction between them and the Palestinian guerrillas.

That distinction appeared to be eradicated completely, moreover, when innocent civilians fell victim to Israeli "counterterrorists." On April 12, 1973, only three and a half days after the spectacular Israeli commando operation against Black September headquarters in Beirut, a Libyan commercial passenger plane en route from Benghazi to Cairo lost its bearings in an enveloping sandstorm and veered into Israeli airspace. Anticipating a desperate guerrilla retaliation for the Beirut disaster, Israel's defense ministry ordered air force jets into action. The interceptors shot the airliner down, killing 105 of its 111 passengers. The world was aghast. Occasional civilians had gotten into the line of fire of earlier Israeli bombings and shootings in Europe and Beirut. But this latest transgression was regarded as unworthy of a civilized nation.

In fact, by then the Golda Meir government was seriously reconsidering its counterterrorism campaign. Except for Ali Hassan Salameh himself, the Black September command had been all but shattered. At the same time, Israel's own clandestine operations in Europe were becoming costly in both lives and public opinion. This had been Abba Eban's contention all along, and even Zvi Zamir and the Mossad leadership now gave the argument heed. It gained further urgency a few months later.

In July 1974 Michael Harari, the Committee X director in Paris, was evaluating reports that Ali Hassan Salameh had been spotted in Germany, en route to Scandinavia. There was speculation that the guerrilla chieftain had arrived to direct a possible kidnapping operation against the Israeli ambassador in Stockholm. Harari then dispatched a special three-man team to the Swedish capital. There the Mossad agents received a coded message from Harari, ordering them to proceed on to Oslo, where further evidence had surfaced of Salameh's presence. In Oslo, the Israelis were joined by a special Mossad hit team of six men and two women. And there further inquiries led them to Lillehammer, a modest summer resort in central Norway. By late July, a dozen Mossad agents were swarming through Lillehammer, seeking out their man. Finally they detected an Arab who appeared to match their dated photographs of Salameh. Tracking the suspect down the street, they cornered him at a bus stop and riddled him with bullets.

The Israelis had not prepared their escape route with care. Minutes later, two of the women and one of the men were caught. Under police interrogation the women broke, providing extensive details about their operation, including the names and addresses of their accomplices—even their other Mossad contacts in Europe. Worse yet for Israel's reputation, the slain Arab turned out to be not Ali Hassan Salameh but a poor Moroccan waiter who had been living in Lillehammer for four years with his Norwegian wife. The Israeli defendants were tried, convicted, and sentenced to prison (although for surprisingly short terms). News of the debacle profoundly shocked the Israeli people. Beyond sorrow for the human tragedy inflicted on an innocent man and his family, there was awareness that the entire Mossad infrastructure in Europe had been compromised. Agents who had been exposed had to be recalled, "safe" houses abandoned, telephone numbers changed, operational methods altered. In Israel, Mrs.

Meir instructed a dejected Zvi Zamir to abandon any future search for Salameh on European soil.

In the end, however, it was less the Lillehammer catastrophe that dictated the phase-out of Mossad operations in Europe than a belated reassessment of the Middle Eastern source of the nation's peril. From 1973 onward Palestinian guerrillas proved increasingly adept in striking at Israelis in their own homeland. Crossing over from Lebanon, they attacked homes, schools, buses; took civilians hostage; murdered women and children. One attack came by sea, when a dinghy unloaded terrorists just outside Tel Aviv. By 1975 guerrilla bombs were going off in Jewish Jerusalem, killing scores of civilians. And yet, ironically, it was once again in Europe that Palestinian guerrillas inflicted their gravest blow on integral Israel—and fully ten months before Lillehammer. On September 28, 1973, three armed Arabs slipped aboard a Soviet train carrying Jewish émigrés to Vienna. As the train entered Austrian territory, the guerrillas seized five Jews and a customs official as hostages, then demanded air passage to an Arab capital.

In fact they got more than they asked for. Fearful lest his country become a battleground for the Arab-Israeli vendetta, Austrian Chancellor Bruno Kreisky ordered closure of the transit center in which the Jewish Agency housed and classified Soviet Jews before flying them off to Israel (p. 294). Thereupon Prime Minister Golda Meir rushed to Vienna in a last-minute effort to change Kreisky's mind. She failed. Upon returning to Jerusalem, Mrs. Meir summoned a cabinet meeting on October 3. Its main order of business was to discuss the Kreisky episode—rather than intelligence reports of the concentration of Arab armies along Israel's borders. It was three days before the Jewish High Holy Day of Yom Kippur.

RELINQUISHING THE CONTINENTAL BATTLEFIELD

If Black September's leadership was badly shredded, there were not lacking other Palestinian guerrilla factions to continue the grim surrogate war. Between 1968 and 1980 these elements launched some eighty attacks on Israeli and Jewish targets outside the Middle East, sixty-six of them in Western Europe. There were peaks and valleys of activity. A certain lull followed the Yom Kippur War. In 1975, with the outbreak of wide-ranging civil strife in Lebanon, the guerrillas for the next three years focused their energies on the internecine Moslem-Christian fratricide. Yet, even during this "interregnum," there were occasional assaults on Israelis abroad. At the Istanbul air terminal in August 1976, two PFLP gunmen opened fire at passengers waiting to board an El Al flight to Tel Aviv, killing four people and wounding twenty-six.

By 1978 the momentum of violence picked up again. The ongoing magnitude of the guerrilla threat could be gauged by a single year, 1980, in operations that were planned although often foiled. In January, Palestinian terrorists blew up part of the Mount Royal Hotel in London, the residence of several Israeli diplomatic staffers. In March another terrorist assassinated a Spanish lawyer in Madrid, whom he had misidentified as a local Jewish leader. In April, inspecting baggage intended for an El Al airliner in Zurich, security agents detected and disarmed a suitcase bomb wired to an altimeter. In July, acting on a tip, police in Copenhagen arrested a group of terrorists preparing an attack on an El Al crew. In July also, a Palestinian was arrested before he could hurl his grenades at El Al passengers in the Brussels airport. On July 27 a grenade attack on a Jewish school in Antwerp left one child dead and thirteen wounded. And in Paris on October 3, a bomb exploded outside a synagogue on rue Copernic, killing four people and injuring thirteen. Although never found, the perpetrators almost certainly were Arab guerrillas.

The violence continued, every second or third month, year by year, its consequences occasionally far-reaching. Thus in London, on June 3, 1982, a Palestinian shot and gravely wounded the Israeli ambassador, Shlomo Argov. The assailant was caught, and within hours police tracked down and arrested three of the man's Arab colleagues, together with substantial quantities of weapons. In their ensuing trial, it became clear that three of the defendants belonged to the Palestine National Liberation Movement. Far from being connected with Yasser Arafat, the PNLM's leader, Sabri al-Banna (a.k.a. Abu Nidal), was bitterly opposed to Arafat's leadership. Indeed, his objective in plotting Argov's assassination was to provoke the Israelis into an attack on the PLO in Lebanon. He succeeded. Three days after the attempt on the ambassador's life, Prime Minister Menachem Begin seized on the episode as his long-awaited pretext for launching Israel's army into southern Lebanon. The invasion soon aroused more international condemnation than the Jewish state had encountered in the thirty-four years of its independence. Assuredly the campaign did little for the security of Israelis abroad. In the course of the war, a Lebanese woman living in Paris shot and killed Israel's consul general, and the PNLM bombed a crowded Jewish restaurant in the French capital, killing three patrons and wounding seven.

If Menachem Begin's reaction to Palestinian terrorism was ill-judged and exploitative, it nevertheless reflected a fundamental policy decision, adopted by the predecessor Labor government eight years earlier. This was to abandon all further violation of the sovereignty or sensibilities of West European countries and henceforth to strike back against terrorists within the Middle East or, at the outer limit, at terrorist enclaves in Moslem North Africa. At all times it was Ali Hassan Salameh who remained preeminent among those targets. If the Mossad had been burned in earlier efforts to terminate the archterrorist abroad, it awaited a likelier opportunity closer to home. In 1978, at long last, it found its chance.

That year Salameh married a Lebanese beauty, a former Miss Universe. In accordance with traditional Moslem practice, he did not divorce his first wife. Instead, living in Beirut, Salameh traveled between the home of his original family and his current wife's apartment near Black September headquarters on rue Verdun. His schedule, increasingly predictable, was duly noted. The observer was one Penelope Chambers, an English spinster who lived in an apartment not far from Salameh's beauteous second wife. Chambers was a Mossad agent. In January 1979 she planted a small tracking radio transmitter under Salameh's automobile. Two weeks later, Salameh and his bodyguards drove past a parked Volkswagen at the corner of rue Verdun and rue Madame Curie. Either Chambers or another Mossad agent pressed a button, and the Volkswagen exploded. Salameh, his bodyguards, and several passersby were blown to bits. A weeping Arafat attended his protégé's funeral, together with fifty thousand other mourners.

If the last of Black September's hierarchy had been disposed of and the Munich Olympics massacre avenged, Israel still had another, critical objective to fulfill. It was to strike decisively at Arafat's PLO headquarters. By autumn of 1982 these no longer were in Beirut. The guerrilla confederation had been driven from the city during Israel's 1982 invasion of Lebanon. Since then Arafat had set up shop in a suburb of Tunis. Relying on classified United States satellite data provided by an American spy, Jonathan Pollard, Israeli intelligence had been able to identify the precise location of the PLO complex. As in the case of the Entebbe rescue operation, the air force was called into action. On October 1, 1985, a flight of Israeli F-15 jets set out for Tunis. The distance was 1,140 miles, and air-to-air refueling was required in both directions. Nevertheless the aircraft reached their target and completely destroyed it. At least sixty PLO personnel were killed, another sixty wounded. Arafat himself barely escaped with his life. All the aircraft returned safely.

And still the Israelis were not through—no more than were their Palestinian adversaries. In March 1988 Khalil al-Wazir, chief of the PLO military branch, launched a raid from the Egyptian Sinai that killed three Israeli tourists in a bus. Known by the sobriquet Abu Jihad, Wazir was a key Arafat aide. His guerrilla operations over the years had been almost as far-reaching as Salameh's. Determined to eliminate him, the Mossad was obliged to plot a follow-up strike against PLO headquarters outside Tunis. This time the attack would come not by aerial bombardment but by commandos disembarked by sea. As in the earlier Beirut raid of April 9, 1973, both Mossad and military personnel were involved.

On the morning of April 12, 1988, three Mossad agents flew into Tunis from Europe. Arabic speakers, using false Lebanese passports, the two men and one woman posed as tourists. It was they who pinpointed the location of Wazir's villa in the suburb of Hamman a-Shatt. Three days later, an Israeli missile boat disembarked a squad of thirty commandos by dinghies at a nearby beach. Following the Beirut precedent, the three civilians awaited them with rented vehicles. Overhead, cruising in a civilian lane due south of Sicily, an Israeli air force Boeing directed the operation by radio. On board were Chief of Staff Dan Shomron, his deputy, General Ehud Barak, and General Amnon Lipkin-Shahak, director of military intelligence. At about 1:00 a.m. on April 16, two automobiles parked outside Wazir's villa. Eight Israeli commandos, dressed in civilian clothing, climbed out, carrying Uzi assault rifles equipped with silencers. Moments later, they were joined by the rest of the commando team. Approaching the villa they shot the guard, then broke open the door. Wazir by then had rushed out of his bedroom. He was cut down instantly. All the Israelis then returned to the beach, rejoined their waiting patrol boats, and departed safely by sea.

In its lethal precision, the operation shook Arafat seriously. By then the PLO chairman doubtless recognized that he had all but lost his underground war. Morale among his PLO colleagues was eroding rapidly, and Arafat sensed his personal vulnerability to an assassination attempt whenever the Israelis chose to strike. Assuredly that awareness was not the only, or even the decisive, factor that induced him to begin scaling down his guerrilla campaign. With the *intifada* and Israeli suppression paralyzing the West Bank, diplomatic pressures for a nonmilitary solution were building equally in Europe, in the United States, in Israel, and in Palestine itself. But once Israel's military-security apparatus had focused on the Middle Eastern nerve center of guerrilla operations, and honed its tactics in counterterror warfare as impressively as in Europe, the handwriting was on the wall. Another approach to the Palestine issue would have to be explored.

ITALY'S MOMENT OF RECOGNITION

Conceivably, that strategic alteration might have been adopted well before the late 1980s, had European governments chosen to respond forthrightly to guerrilla transgressions on their own terrain. Several did. It was pro-Israel bias that influenced Norway's rather mild reaction to the Lillehammer murder, and the Netherlands' and Denmark's quiet police cooperation with the Mossad in monitoring Palestinian movements in their own countries. But most of Europe's governments declined to respond with vigor. Blatant pro-Arab partisanship determined the willingness of Greece and France to repatriate Arab terrorists. Preoccupation with airline safety accounted for years of clandestine Swiss and West German blackmail payoffs to the PLO. In the case of Austria, the closure of the Jewish Agency transit center was intended as a prophylactic move for territorial immunity.

Nowhere, however, was the balancing act between principle and expediency more poignant than in Italy. The nation's wartime record on behalf of European Jewry was humane, even noble, and hardly less so in the postwar transmigration of refugee Jews to Palestine. Although Italy's cabinets of the next decades were largely dominated by the centrist Christian Democrats, loosely associated with the Vatican and with the nation's larger business interests, even these governments were not unfriendly toward Israel. In 1947–48, as a defeated Axis power, Italy was excluded from the United Nations vote on partition; but in 1949 it extended *de facto* recognition to Israel, and *de jure* recognition a year later. From 1951 on Italian ambassadors presented their credentials to the president of Israel in Jerusalem (over the reservations of the Vatican). In the 1950s, as Israel pressed for association with the European Economic Community, occasional disagreements and rivalries on issues of Italian-Israeli citrus competition in no sense affected the two countries' fundamentally equable relationship. For the Italians, even for Italian Communists, Israel was accepted as a nation of common European civilization.

But Italy was also a leading player in Mediterranean affairs, and hence could not avoid vulnerability to the aftershocks of the Arab-Israeli conflict. In the years following the Six-Day War, Italian public opinion reflected a characteristic sympathy for the Palestinians as underdogs, and government policy in some measure reflected that compassion. More fundamentally, Arab irredentism in the Middle

East threatened to ramify on toward the Mediterranean littoral of
North Africa, where any crisis might expose Italy to multiple risks.
Less than one hundred miles separated Sicily from Tunisia. Fifteen
thousand Italians lived and worked in the five North African nations.
During the 1980s Libya provided between 25 and 46 percent of Italy's
oil imports. Three-quarters of Italy's gas imports came from Algeria.
The synergy between the Middle East and North Africa could not be
ignored by any of Italy's governments.

In reaction, then, to the Arab oil embargo during the 1973 Yom
Kippur War (pp. 184–7), Italy's relations with Israel suddenly deteriorated. In ensuing years, whether as prime minister or foreign minister,
Giulio Andreotti was a perennial in his nation's Christian Democratic
cabinets. It was thus at Andreotti's initiative that the government
enlarged its relationship with the PLO, authorized the opening of a
PLO office in Rome, and finally invited Yasser Arafat to an official
reception at the presidential palace. By the same token, in the 1970s,
even before the Yom Kippur conflict, the government's attitude toward
guerrilla violence was equivocal and often timorous. It was a stance
that contrasted sharply with the cooperation that in earlier years
had existed between the Italian secret service and the Mossad. Hard-
bitten professional elites, each of these security agencies developed a
warm respect for the other. From the late 1960s on, however, the Italian secret service came directly under the control of the politicians,
and the latter evinced a characteristic sensitivity to Arab goodwill.

The capitulation to guerrilla terrorism became particularly evident
in January 1973, following the aborted Strella missile attack on Golda
Meir's plane at Fiumicino Airport (p. 240). The Israelis had been
impressed by Italian police cooperation during the episode. Yet their
gratification did not endure. Under heavy economic and diplomatic
pressure from Libya's Qadafi, the Italian government released the
prisoners in November of the same year, then arranged for them to be
flown secretly to Benghazi. Other Palestinians who were seized following acts of terrorism against Israelis or other Jews on Italian soil,
or for booby-trapping airliners departing Fiumicino, were dutifully
arrested, tried, and incarcerated. But most served only partial sentences before being repatriated to Arab countries.

It was on October 1, 1985, that Israel's air force launched its devastating bombing raid on Arafat's PLO headquarters in Tunis. In retaliation, only six days later, on October 7, a group of Arab guerrillas
commandeered the Italian cruise ship *Achille Lauro*, en route from
Alexandria to Port Saïd. Five hundred passengers were on board,
most of them American. The terrorists, members of Sabri al-Banna's

Palestine Liberation Front, then radioed an ultimatum to Rome, warning that the civilians would remain hostages until fifty PLF prisoners in Israel were released. There was never a chance that the Israelis would capitulate to the demand. Nor would the United States or Italy ask them to do so. Instead, with full American (and British) support, Rome dispatched a battalion of assault troops to RAF bases in Cyprus and ordered Italian naval units to converge on the *Achille Lauro*.

On the early morning of October 9, the Palestinians radioed a second ultimatum. If their demand were not met by midnight, they warned, they would begin "executing" hostages. Thereupon Prime Minister Bettino Craxi, a Socialist, and Foreign Minister Andreotti, of the Christian Democrats, intensified their efforts to find a peaceful solution. Over the objections of Defense Minister Giovanni Spadolini (a member of the rightist Republican party), Craxi accepted the recommendation of Egypt's President Hosni Mubarak. It was Mubarak's proposal that a senior Palestinian representative be flown to Egypt to act as "mediator" in the crisis. After brief hesitation, the hijackers also concurred. Agreement was reached to allow the notorious PLF chieftain Abu Abas to serve as that mediator, and it was he who was promptly flown into Cairo from Baghdad. Soon afterward, in the course of frenzied telephonic negotiations between Cairo, Rome, Washington, and the *Achille Lauro* hijackers, a deal was reached. Provided the ship were released, with all its passengers unharmed, the four Palestinians would be turned over to Egypt. President Mubarak in turn would guarantee them safe passage to an Arab country of their choice.

On the same afternoon of October 9, the hijackers gave up control of the *Achille Lauro*, and Italian Foreign Minister Andreotti confirmed to Washington that the passengers were all safe. Immediately the four Arabs were turned over to the Egyptian authorities, who prepared to fly them out of the country, together with Abu Abas. It is virtually certain that Mubarak, and probably even Andreotti, already possessed information which they did not share with the United States: Only hours before the vessel was released, the hijackers had cold-bloodedly shot an aged and infirm American Jewish passenger, Leon Klinghoffer, and dumped his body into the sea. On boarding the *Achille Lauro* at 11:00 p.m., American Ambassador Nicholas Veliotis belatedly learned of the tragedy. Furious, he demanded that Cairo turn the hijackers over to American custody forthwith.

Throughout the night and much of the next day, American pressure on Mubarak intensified. Finally, secretly, in the early evening of

October 10, an Egyptian Boeing 737 carrying the four hijackers and Abu Abas departed Cairo for Tunis. When the Tunisian government refused it permission to land, the plane made for Algiers. Once again, landing permission was denied. The Boeing then headed back to Cairo. During the entire odyssey President Mubarak blandly assured Ambassador Veliotis that the hijackers remained in Egyptian custody. But an Israeli intelligence officer, Amiram Nir, had intercepted the airliner's radio transmission and alerted the CIA "point man" monitoring the crisis, Lieutenant Colonel Oliver North. With this information in hand, the Reagan administration promptly instructed carrier jets of the United States Sixth Fleet to intercept the Egyptian airliner. This was done over the Mediterranean, with the fighters ordering the Egyptian crew to follow their "escort" to the American NATO base at Signorelli, Italy.

During these same hours, Prime Minister Craxi and Foreign Minister Andreotti preened in self-congratulation that their diplomacy had won a "great victory," proving that Italy exerted influence with the Arabs, even with their guerrilla organizations. Indeed, only the week before, Craxi had followed the Socialist line in condemning as a "terrorist action" Israel's bombing of PLO headquarters outside Tunis. Andreotti had equated the raid with the wartime Nazi massacre of Jews hiding in the catacombs of Rome. But now, shortly after midnight on October 11, Secretary of State George Shultz reached Andreotti by phone to alert him that the hijackers were en route to Signorelli, and that Washington insisted that they be brought to the United States for trial under the American-Italian extradition treaty.

A grave crisis ensued beween the two countries. Italian troops were alerted to surround the Egyptian Boeing as it landed at Signorelli. Yet the American escort planes turned out to be cargo transports, and these in turn disgorged several hundred Navy commandos, who promptly surrounded the fifty-man Italian contingent. Hours of tense Rome-Washington negotiations followed. In midafternoon, President Reagan telephoned Prime Minister Craxi personally to request the extradition of the terrorists. After another day of back-and-forth discussions, a compromise again was reached. Rome gave its solemn assurance that it would prosecute the terrorists to the full extent of the law, provided they were allowed to remain in Italian custody. Washington then dropped its objections, but on a stringent condition. In truth, Washington—and Israel—were less concerned with the four hijackers than with the éminence grise behind them, Abu Abas, who had accompanied the terrorists on the Egyptian airliner. The United States wanted assurances that Abu Abas would be held in custody and aggressively prosecuted. At this point, however, President Mubarak raised objections. Abu Abas had arrived at Egypt's invitation, Mubarak insisted, and thus was under Egyptian diplomatic protection. To give substance to his protest, Mubarak warned that he would not release the *Achille Lauro* (still in Egyptian waters) to Italy until Abu Abas was released.

Craxi and Andreotti had not reckoned on this complication. If they sought no difficulties with Washington—Israel figured only minimally in their considerations—they also wanted none with Egypt and the Arab world. Repeatedly the two Italians protested to Washington that their commitment to incarceration and prosecution had not applied to Abu Abas. He was under diplomatic protection, they insisted. Upon confirming this Italian stand, Mubarak then released the *Achille Lauro*. Meanwhile, the five Arabs already had been flown in Italian aircraft from Signorelli to Rome, where they were jailed. As the diplomatic standoff continued, the Italian government suddenly took its own steps to resolve it. Before Defense Minister Spadolini could be informed, Prime Minister Craxi had Abu Abas rushed to Fiumicino Airport, escorted onto a Yugoslav airliner, and flown out of the country. In this case, it was not only Israel and the United States that reacted in outrage. Denouncing the premier's "abject capitulation to international terrorism," Spadolini on October 14 pulled his Republican colleagues out of the Craxi cabinet, and the Italian government collapsed.

Eventually, in the immemorial Italian tradition, it was restructured. Craxi induced Spadolini and the Republicans to rejoin the cabinet. But the quid pro quo was a new government platform, adopted by all five member parties. Among its foreign-policy commitments, the program emphasized noncapitulation to blackmail by international terrorists, and stern condemnation of the violence used by Palestinian organizations. In its domestic ramifications, the *Achille Lauro* episode conceivably represented a fractional turning point in Italy's usefulness as a surrogate Palestinian battlefield.

A EUROPEAN REAPPRAISAL

Elsewhere, on the wider European battlefield, guerrilla mayhem continued well into the latter 1980s. Spain functioned as a haven for terrorists of all backgrounds. In October 1984 two Israeli sailors were murdered in Barcelona. The Costa del Sol became a favored site for assassination attempts against Israelis and vacationing European Jews. It was in September 1986 that Arab gunmen slaughtered twenty-two worshippers in Istanbul's Neve Shalom synagogue (p. 224). As always, Greece remained a choice killing ground. In July 1988 three Palestinians opened fire on a Greek cruise ship en route from Paleo Phaleron to Piraeus. Many of the passengers were Jews, and nine were killed, forty-three wounded.

In London, the year before, Nizar Hindawi, a Palestinian working for Syrian intelligence, attempted to blow up an El Al airliner by planting a bomb in his Irish girlfriend's luggage (it was discovered in time at Heathrow Airport). In July 1988 Palestinians shot down an alleged Mossad informer, Naji al-Ali, in a London street. Subsequent police investigation revealed an extensive guerrilla network in England, operating in numerous "safe" houses that functioned as ammunition caches and laboratories for the manufacture of bombs and fake passports. Sobering as the discovery was, Israel drew comfort from Britain's estimable record of cooperation in the struggle against terrorism. Indeed, as early as the 1960s, the Mossad had developed a close relationship with British intelligence. With their own experience of IRA bombings, the British displayed little tolerance for guerrilla atrocities of any kind. On the Continent only the West German, Dutch, and Norwegian intelligence services provided Israel with comparable support.

The Palestinians' underground war continued. Nevertheless, by the late 1980s, statistics revealed a subtle shift in the trajectory of their violence. From 1980 to 1989, there had been 365 terrorist incidents in Europe, inflicting 518 deaths and 1,933 injuries. Yet "only" 51 of these attacks, or 14 percent, were directed specifically against Israelis or Jews. Vendettas among rival Arab factions emerged as a major new source of havoc. The most volatile of these internecine conflicts was waged between Fatah and the Palestine National Liberation Front—in effect, beween Arafat and Sabri al-Banna. Assassinations and counterassassinations between the two factions occurred in Greece, Italy, Austria, Switzerland, France, and Spain. And well beyond the spillover of Middle Eastern warfare, the nations of Europe simultaneously were bedeviled with "native" terrorism: IRA bombings in Britain and Northern Ireland; Basque and Catalonian killings in Spain; in Italy, kidnappings and bombings by "Red Brigades"; and Baader-Meinhof murderousness in Germany. Altogether, by the late 1980s, Europe's threshold of sufferance for guerrilla atrocities was reaching its limit.

Yet if Israelis overseas were marginally less exposed to terrorist violence, the explanation could not be attributed exclusively to a diffusion of guerrilla priorities in Europe, or even to an exhaustion of

European forbearance. In late 1987 it was the outbreak of the *intifada* in the Israel-occupied West Bank that focused guerrilla attention and resources increasingly on Palestine itself. Soon afterward the implosion of Communist Eastern Europe deprived Palestinian resistance groups of valuable terrain for asylum and training. For Yasser Arafat, the evidence of personal vulnerability to Israeli retribution may also have influenced the PLO chairman's strategy. But so too did mounting international condemnation. By the end of the decade the stiffening of European resistance to terrorism was becoming more evident. One of its manifestations was the growing efficiency of "Kionet," a confederation of European antiterrorist intelligence agencies that functioned as a counterpart to Interpol. Israel's Mossad was an active and respected participant in Kionet, this time sharing in the data exchanges of virtually every European government, even those of France and Italy.

The crisis of overseas vulnerability was far from ended, either for Israel or for other nations. In Europe it was simply shifted from targeted guerrilla "safe" houses and bomb laboratories to juridically protected national embassies. Preeminent now were those of Iran, whose commitment to the extirpation of Israel fully matched, and eventually transcended, the PLO's. Nevertheless, by the end of the twentieth century, the focus of violence—of shootings, stabbings, and, increasingly, of suicide bomb attacks—once again had become the Middle East itself. It was familiar terrain, for Israelis and Palestinians alike. Only the approach to its resolution appeared subject to change, from military confrontation to the faintly glimmering possibility of diplomatic accommodation.

A FAILED SOVIET BRIDGEHEAD IN THE MIDDLE EAST

A ROMANIAN "OASIS" IN THE COMMUNIST DESERT

During the early years of Soviet hegemony in Eastern Europe, Romania appeared to fit the Communist pattern of anti-Zionist and antisemitic vindictiveness. Even after Stalin's death in 1953, scores of Romanian Jewish leaders were sentenced to long prison terms, and those who survived were released only during the Khrushchev era after 1956. Yet it was specifically this era of Communist-bloc "thaw" that allowed Romania's party boss, Gheorghe Gheorghiu-Dej, a more flexible stance in foreign policy. So, too, even more fundamentally, did the emergent Sino-Soviet rivalry, and the temporary immunity this intramural schism offered Romania from Soviet retaliation. In July 1958 Bucharest negotiated the departure of Soviet troops from Romanian soil, and four years later announced its intention to follow an "independent Socialist program." Gheorghiu-Dej's death in 1965 did not reverse the new approach. Nicolae Ceausescu, the recently appointed party general secretary (and later his country's president), was determined to explore new links with the West, principally for reasons of trade and economic growth. To that end, swallowing the hoary legend of backstairs Jewish influence, Ceausescu began to examine the possible usefulness of Jewish intermediaries.

Here it was that the Romanian chief rabbi, Moses Rosen, played a central role. As early as 1961, Rosen was allowed to travel to the United States on a goodwill lecture tour of American Jewish federations. In the course of his visit, the chief rabbi dutifully called his listeners' attention to the "fairness" with which Bucharest was treating Romanian Jewry, the extent to which it was "alleviating" all the old constraints on Jewish religious and cultural expression. Rosen was gilding the lily, but Washington no less than American Jewry was listening. Soon afterward, intent on exploiting still another fissure in the Iron Curtain, the State Department granted Romania's minister in Washington "special status," akin to the privileged access enjoyed by the Yugoslav ambassador. Rosen flew home to a hero's welcome.

Subsequently the chief rabbi won Bucharest's approval to reopen dozens of synagogues and Jewish schools. In 1969 the Ceausescu government also permitted the resumption of contacts between Romanian Jewry and such international Jewish organizations as the World Jewish Congress and the Joint Distribution Committee. Once the Joint began pouring millions of dollars into Romanian Jewish institutions, the nation's economy also shared in the largesse. Yet President Ceausescu by then was in search of an even more valuable economic benediction from the United States. It was most-favored-nation trading privileges for Romania. And here too Rosen functioned as a vital intermediary. He returned to Washington to make Romania's case. Reacting with interest, the State Department promised to give the proposal favorable consideration. In turn, reciprocating the chief rabbi's help, Ceausescu offered a recompense of vast significance to the Jews. The compensation this time was relaxation of the ban against departure for Israel.

Even earlier in the decade, exploring a new leeway for itself in international affairs, the Bucharest regime (then under Gheorghiu-Dej) had been developing a more flexible Middle East policy. Abstaining on various Soviet-sponsored condemnations of Israel in the United Nations, the Romanian government also countenanced a selective increase in trade and scientific cooperation with the Jewish state. In the wake of the Six-Day War, moreover, identifying with a small nation that had withstood the might of Soviet weaponry, Ceausescu refused to follow Moscow's lead in severing diplomatic relations with Israel. Rather, soon afterward, arrangements were negotiated for joint Romanian-Israeli industrial enterprises and direct, inexpensive air routes between Romania and Israel. Ceausescu even came to regard himself as something of an "honest broker" between Israel and the Arabs. In May 1972 he tendered Israel's Prime Minister Golda Meir a lavish state reception. Five years later, in autumn 1977, his meetings with Menachem Begin and Anwar al-Sadat helped pave the way for the Egyptian president's historic visit to Jerusalem.

As the specter of Israel gradually was exorcised from Romanian foreign policy, it became a somewhat easier matter to contemplate Jewish emigration there. Even following the initial, postwar emigration (p. 60), no fewer than 220,000 Jews continued to live in Romania, the densest Jewish population in Eastern Europe except for the Soviet Union. In 1958, however, Gheorghiu-Dej first studied the possible

economic advantages of thinning out this substantial minority presence, and thereby of reclaiming Jewish lodgings and job openings for
"integral" Romanians. If relaxed emigration would produce still further dividends in American goodwill, so much the better. To that end,
in September 1958, Bucharest authorized a limited number of exit
visas for Israel. At first some 33,000 Jews managed to leave before
the door was closed again. Jerusalem inadvertently had leaked word
of the emigration, and Arab governments reacted with vehement
protests.

But in 1961, when Bucharest agreed to risk another wave of departures, the emigration was carried out in near-total secrecy. Between
1961 and 1975, no fewer than 160,000 additional Jews left the country. Most of them settled in Israel, where they soon comprised that
nation's second largest bloc of immigrants. Approximately 30,000 of
their kin remained behind, but the number would continue to dimin-
ish by natural attrition and selective departures to less than 10,000 by
1991. By then, too, Bucharest had achieved its cherished goal of
most-favored-nation trading privileges with the United States.

Characteristically, for the leader of a Balkan nation of post-Ottoman
venality, Nicolae Ceausescu also achieved still another important
financial objective. In a secret deal, for which Rabbi Rosen again
served as intermediary, the Romanian dictator in 1965 demanded
Jewish Agency remuneration to his government of up to $3,000 for
each departing Jew (the sum was adjusted to the economic "value" of
the individual emigrant). By some calculations the Jewish Agency
transferred fully $100 million to the Bucharest regime by 1989, the
year of Ceausescu's death. The president was no less covetous in his
quest for recognition as a "world statesman." Here too Israel was prepared to cooperate. Abba Eban recalled: "On each anniversary of
Romanian 'independence,' at a celebratory meeting in Tel Aviv, I or
one of my colleagues would have to praise President Ceausescu's
practice in maintaining contacts across the entire range of the international system, irrespective of Cold War psychology." For Israel,
both the money and the kudos were a cheap price to pay for Romania's diplomatic friendship, and its dividend in the massive immigration of Romanian Jews.

A STIRRING OF SOVIET JEWRY

The relaxation of police repression following Stalin's death in 1953
became apparent not least of all in the vortex of the Communist
empire, in the Soviet Union itself. Political prisoners gradually were

emancipated and rehabilitated, and Soviet cultural life experienced a cautious liberalization. For Soviet Jews, numbering approximately 2,250,000, the immediate consequence of the "thaw" was an end to the Doctors' Plot (p. 66), the release of their own extensive subcommunity of imprisoned victims, and an incremental relaxation of the ban on Jewish cultural activities. Yet even after 1953, other dangers were not long in surfacing for this minority people. During the mid-1950s the new political leadership under Nikita Khrushchev was intent on resolving a troubling demographic phenomenon. It was a disproportionate enlargement of the non-Slavic populations of Soviet Central Asia and the Caucasus. To cope with this unanticipated ethnic challenge to Slavic dominance, Khrushchev and his advisers decided to ensure Slavic political control throughout all Soviet republics, but to compensate the "native" peoples by awarding them a virtual monopoly of second-level technocratic openings in their state bureaucracies, liberal professions, and universities.

These were precisely the slots traditionally held by Jews, the best-educated of the Soviet Union's nationalities. Now the Jews would be replaced. Moreover, in their high-density urban visibility, the Jews were classic targets for local resentments. Nikita Khrushchev would exploit that vulnerability as well. Thereafter, the number of trials for "financial corruption" appeared to be focused almost exclusively on Jews—who invariably were identified as Jews. Widely publicized, the court spectacles provided a useful diversion from Soviet economic shortcomings. For Khrushchev and his colleagues, in any case, the Jews were exploitable not only as traditional objects of folk contumely. They were genuinely suspect as the collective appendage of an international people, most of whose kin lived in the West or in Israel, the West's supreme "outpost" in the Middle East. Either way, they remained a people uniquely vulnerable to a new revival of discrimination.

It is recalled that Israel's effort to develop contacts with Soviet Jewry, orchestrated by Shaul Avigur as Ben-Gurion's intelligence adviser, was administered in Moscow by Nechemia Levanon, who operated under the façade of agricultural attaché at the Israeli embassy (pp. 71–2). In 1958 Levanon was brought home to become director of the entire outreach operation. His place at Israel's embassy in Moscow was taken by Aryeh (Lova) Eliav. Born in Russia, Eliav was a veteran of numerous underground operations, including the postwar Jewish refugee emigration to Palestine. In Moscow now, holding the title of embassy first secretary, Eliav moved vigorously to widen the network of Zionist "cells" among Soviet Jewry. Synagogues often proved useful in the endeavor. Within their premises Eliav and his staff circulated Russian-language literature on Israel, as well as a variety of Israeli mementos, from plastic records of music to miniature bottles of wine. The Israelis also managed to travel throughout the vast reaches of the Soviet Union, meeting with local Jews in one republic after another, distributing information and organizing Hebrew-language study groups.

In Tel Aviv, meanwhile, from an inconspicuous suite of rooms designated "the Liaison Office," Nechemia Levanon was organizing an even wider-ranging campaign in behalf of Soviet Jewry. His arena was the Diaspora. To avoid compromising Israel's fragile relations with Moscow, Levanon devised the euphemism of "Contemporary Jewish Libraries." Whether in Paris, London, Rome, or—later—New York, these propaganda centers were locally directed and bore no official connection with the government of Israel. Yet in each instance their purpose was to disseminate information on the precarious circumstances of Soviet Jews, the marginalization of their vocational and cultural opportunities in the Soviet empire, and to plead the cause of their rights as Soviet citizens.

It was notable, however, that Levanon thus far carefully avoided listing mass emigration as among those rights. No Soviet nationality possessed that option, not in a closed society that had lost twenty-five million of its inhabitants in the war, and that (at least in its "heartland" Slavic republics) could ill afford to lose its Jewish scientists, engineers, and other elite Jewish contributors to the Soviet economy. More important, the en-bloc award of exit *vyzovs* to one nationality would set a dangerous precedent for others, and specifically for the Soviet Moslem populations whose kinsmen lived directly across the USSR's southern frontiers, in Turkey, Iran, and Afghanistan. For this reason the Israeli embassy staff was instructed to remain noncommittal on the emigration issue. A premature campaign for departure conceivably would provoke an upsurge of Stalinist-style retribution.

Yet, as a consequence of Israel's victory in the Six-Day War, the Jews in any case were singled out as targets for the Kremlin's frustration and vindictiveness. Besides the vast military disaster suffered by their Arab clients, the Soviets had lost prestige among their own satellites. It soon became evident that most of the East European peoples distinctly favored Israel, a nation they regarded as a symbol of effective resistance to Soviet power. Even within the USSR itself, Lithuanians, Latvians, Moldavians, and other contentious nationalities similarly exulted at Moscow's discomfiture. Rarely in its history, therefore, did the Soviet leadership react to a foreign-policy debacle with a more explosive outburst of vilification. In July 1967 they launched a high-powered propaganda campaign against Zionism as a "world threat," an "international force" that was to be equated with Jewish communities everywhere, not least within the Soviet Union itself. In a throwback to the Stalin era, the well-worn canards of classical antisemitism were once again to be trotted out and belabored overtime.

In fact, Soviet Jews by then were generating their own reaction to Israel's Six-Day triumph. Like Jews everywhere, they were stirred to their depths. The response was particularly intense among the intensely ethnocentric Jewish populations of the Baltic and Caucasus republics. Their tentative and guarded Zionist revival now burgeoned into a spontaneous and militant emigrationist movement. It was ironically Moscow's severance of diplomatic relations with Israel that offered these activists a certain advantage. The latter could take the decisive step of petitioning for the "right" of emigration without fear any longer of injuring Soviet-Israeli relations. Indeed, with the help of Liaison Office guidelines that were circuitously dispatched to them from Israel, they were able to make an impressive case. Basing it directly on the Soviet constitution, the petitioners alluded to the right of "reunion" with family members abroad—and specifically in Israel. It was from Israel's Liaison Office that documented verifications of these family connections now were forthcoming.

Here it was that Nechemia Levanon's emphasis on strict legality began to pay off. In 1968 the Soviet government responded to the growing wave of emigration petitions by cautiously granting three thousand exit *vyzovs* to Soviet Jews with family members in Israel. The Kremlin was not motivated by considerations of philanthropy, of course, or even of legality. Rather, it hoped to decapitate the leadership of the emigrationist movement by allowing its small nucleus of activists to depart. If this were done, presumably the danger of Zionist infection could be eradicated before spreading from the Baltic and Caucasus republics to the more extensive Jewish populations in the "heartland" republics of Ukraine, Belarus, and Russia itself.

The strategy failed. As thousands of applications flooded the *vyzov* office, the government recognized that it had allowed the camel's nose under the tent. It promptly clamped a lid on all further exit permits. With nothing further to lose, then, the activists set about organizing networks of mutual support groups even within the "heartland" republics, sharing information with their Jewish kinsmen on various legal and diplomatic procedures that might be exploited for emigration. Moreover, borrowing from techniques then in use by the growing *samizdat* dissident movement (itself extensively interpenetrated by Jews), the applicants embarked on a letter-writing campaign to friends and newspapers in the West and Israel, describing the afflictions now meted out to them. In turn, alarmed and infuriated, the Soviet government responded by intensifying its own counteroffensive of harassment and vilification. The "anti-Zionist" campaign even achieved an apotheosis of sorts on March 2, 1970, when the Kremlin proclaimed a nationwide "Day of Protest against Israeli Aggression."

Once begun, however, the emigration campaign would not be checked. Indeed, by 1969, Soviet Jews had developed techniques and generated the momentum for reaching out to Western news media on their own. If the dissident movement, with its *samizdat*, underground literature, was one source of inspiration, so was the irredentism festering among the Communist empire's other heterogeneity of peoples. Baltic Germans, a diffuse element of some two million who had been transplanted far into the Soviet interior during the war, now were launching impassioned protest marches for repatriation. So were a half million Crimean Tatars who also had been deported inland in the course of the war. Even the Mtshtektians, another Turkic people that similarly had been uprooted to Central Asia, were seething in defiance. The groundswell of native protests was not lost on the Jews. Neither was the glare of public attention that had driven the Soviet government into its earlier relaxation of the emigration ban. In its eagerness to defuse tensions with Washington and gain access to American technology (pp. 263–4), Moscow surely would be prepared to pay the price by opening wider the gates of departure.

Of acute concern to the Jewish activists, however, both in the Soviet Union and, increasingly, in the United States, was the Israeli government's public silence on the issue of Jewish emigration, and this at a time when thousands of Soviet Jews were risking their livelihoods and security in reaching out to the Jewish state. But Prime Minister Golda Meir was persuaded that Israel's role behind the emigrationist movement dared not be publicly acknowledged (even though Moscow was entirely aware of it). Too much could be lost by putting the Kremlin's notoriously paranoid leadership on the defensive. More important, the Soviets might be provoked into exploiting the emigration issue to seek concessions from Israel in the Middle East. It was vital for Mrs. Meir to keep the two issues separate. Even when she was vigorously pressed by concerned Knesset members (many of them representing the unrequited Cherut opposition), Mrs. Meir remained adamant. Strict press censorship would be maintained on Soviet Jewish emigration, she insisted.

The prime minister's stance was not sustainable. By the autumn of 1969, American newspapers had picked up the story of the Soviet Jewish emigration campaign, and were using material supplied by American Jewish activists to give it extensive coverage. Reluctantly, then, and with full awareness of the diplomatic risks, Mrs. Meir's office in November announced that the government of Israel thenceforth would take the lead in championing the cause of Soviet Jewish emigration. Within days a Knesset resolution all but unanimously endorsed the new approach.

SOVIET JEWRY IN INTERNATIONAL DIPLOMACY

By the spring of 1970, exultant that the "second front" had been opened, Soviet Jews who earlier had emigrated to Israel began holding collective prayer sessions at Jerusalem's Western Wall. Beyond Israel, Jewish mass rallies in support of the emigration campaign were mounted in various European capitals. Although coordinated by the Liaison Office in Tel Aviv, the demonstrations were heartfelt and passionate. By no coincidence they were launched against the backdrop of escalating Soviet involvement in the War of Attrition along the Suez Canal (pp. 170–2), and of Moscow's intensified anti-Israel propaganda campaign. In turn, with Jewish applications for exit *vyzovs* all but out of control, the Kremlin leaders now were determined to crush the emigration campaign for good.

But once again, their strategy was upset by an unanticipated minority initiative. This one was unplanned by Israel. In December 1969 a group of Soviet Jewish activists, borrowing a tactic then being pioneered by Palestinian guerrillas, devised a plan for hijacking an Aeroflot passenger plane in Leningrad, and flying it to Sweden. In Sweden, the hijackers would release the plane and its crew, then demand sanctuary and the right of departure to Israel. Their purpose, like that of the Palestinians, was to dramatize their struggle for freedom. The scheme was secretly transmitted to the Liaison Office in Israel. Nechemia Levanon in turn hastened to discuss it with Prime Minister Meir. Both agreed that it was "insane," that it was precisely the kind of terrorism that lately had been victimizing Israel. But the warning, sent back to the Jewish conspirators, was disregarded. The date for the abduction was set at June 15, 1970. On that late spring day, posing as a wedding party, a half dozen young Jewish activists walked out of the terminal to board their scheduled Aeroflot flight at Leningrad's Smolny Airport. Before they so much as reached their plane, however, they were seized by waiting KGB agents. The plot evidently had been penetrated. Indeed, an ensuing KGB roundup arrested some 232 other implicated Jews in other cities.

When the first group of defendants was put on trial in the Leningrad district court on December 15, 1970, the state prosecutor charged them with "treason," with conspiracy to commit "large-scale theft of state property," and with "anti-Soviet agitation." In response, the accused denied their intention of harming anyone, and defended their action as their only recourse for emigrating to their "ancestral homeland." Unmoved, the prosecutor launched into an extensive peroration against the "intrigues of international Zionism," and requested the death penalty for the two principal conspirators, Mark Dymshits and Eduard Kuznetsov, as well as heavy sentences for the rest. He got them. On December 24 the judge convicted all the defendants, and sentenced Dymshits and Kuznetsov to death, the others to prison terms ranging from fifteen years to life.

When an account of the proceedings and sentences was smuggled out to Israel and the West, it triggered an international sensation. The Liaison Office in Israel, and its surrogate, the New York–based National Conference on Soviet Jewry, immediately set about organizing petitions and mass demonstrations worldwide. Through the efforts of the Contemporary Jewish Libraries, the governments of twenty-four nations then interceded diplomatically on behalf of the Leningrad defendants. Even the Communist parties of several nations, including those of France and Italy, cabled protests to Moscow. Taken aback, the Kremlin then recognized that it had blundered. Instead of treating the aborted plane hijacking as the widely execrated crime that it was, the Soviet leadership had chosen to transform the trial into a frontal campaign against the emigration movement. Indeed, they had focused world attention on the plight of Soviet Jews even more effectively than had the Liaison Office itself. Within a week of the original verdict, the supreme court of the Russian Federal Republic commuted the death sentences to life imprisonment.

The Leningrad trial, and its successor trial months later, evoked the most extensive condemnation of the USSR since the Soviet-sponsored invasion of Czechoslovakia in August 1968. Orchestrated by the Liaison Office, the avalanche of protests flooded into Moscow. And all the while, Soviet Jews continued deluging their government with emigration petitions and mailing off letters to Western and Israeli correspondents, seeking help in their efforts. By 1971 the numbers of would-be emigrants reached into the tens of thousands, and for the first time included substantial numbers of Jews in the "heartland" Slavic republics. The worst of the Kremlin's fears were realized. The "infection" of emigrationism plainly was spreading to the interior, to the most educated and valuable members of the Soviet economy.

It was a self-inflicted wound, of course. Had the Soviet regime not launched its "cold pogrom" in the 1950s, imposing a harsh numerus clausus on Jewish educational and professional opportunities, the extensively acculturated "heartland" Jews would have been unlikely material for a Zionist renaissance. But with their futures constricted at home, growing numbers of these formerly privileged elements now sensed that their only alternative was emigration. Once they seized on that alternative, they did so with vigor and resourcefulness. Indeed, no other national or religious group pressed its case with comparable fervor. But no other was in as effective a position to do so. Centrally directed by Israel's Liaison Office, often financed by money discreetly transferred by American and other Western Jews, the growing network of "refuseniks" appeared to confirm Moscow's paranoia that Israel and world Jewry were engaged in a far-reaching anti-Soviet conspiracy.

Yet if harsh retribution and intimidation represented one approach to the emigration movement, it could not be the only one. The Kremlin also was prepared to use the carrot as well as the stick. As far back as March 1971, in tandem with its campaign of repression, it quietly began increasing its number of exit visas. By then 15,000 Jews had been allowed to depart for Israel. The number more than doubled in 1973, reaching 34,000. Between January 1968 and June 1973, not less than 53,000 Jews arrived in Israel, and in the peak years of Jewish departure—1972–73—some 43 percent of those applying for emigration were permitted to leave. Simultaneously the Kremlin authorized a limited increase in Soviet-Israeli mutual visits of scientists, scholars, and "peace" delegations. In May 1972, Moscow's Orthodox Patriarch Pimen visited Jerusalem, where he was received by high Israeli officials.

The manipulative chess game reflected Party Chairman Leonid Brezhnev's preoccupation with two key accords, both with the United States. One was the Strategic Arms Limitation Treaty, successfully consummated with the Nixon administration in May 1972. From Brezhnev's perspective, the "SALT I" agreement codified the status of the Soviet Union as a superpower. The second of Brezhnev's aspirations was access to United States technology on a "most-favored-nation" basis, that is, at tariff rates and on credit terms enjoyed by America's oldest and most reliable customers. President Nixon in fact was prepared as early as 1971 to offer Moscow this vital dispensation in the interest of détente. Not so Senator Henry Jackson of Washington, however, who entertained presidential ambitions—and who coveted Jewish financial help in that effort. Early in 1971 Jackson and a number of his Senate colleagues began formulating an amendment to Nixon's proposed most-favored-nation trade treaty with the Soviet Union. Under terms of the draft amendment, cosponsored by Congressman Charles Vanik of Ohio, any nation within the "nonmarket economy" bloc would be denied participation in American credit-and-investment (most-favored-nation) guarantees "unless that country permits its citizens the opportunity to emigrate to the country of their choice."

One "nonmarket" nation, Romania, had of course already met the standards of the Jackson-Vanik "trade-for-freedom" proposal by quietly allowing its Jews to depart for Israel. Yet between Washington and Moscow, the Jackson-Vanik draft set off an extensive effort of diplomatic maneuvering. For their part Nixon and Secretary of State Kissinger were dismayed by the proposed amendment, regarding it as a gratuitous obstacle to normalized relations with the Soviet Union. Under pressure from the senators, however, negotiations between Washington and Moscow, and between Congress and the White House, continued for more than two years, and agreement was reached only in October 1974, in an exchange of letters between Kissinger and Jackson. The accord reflected a parallel understanding that first had been reached between Washington and Moscow. Under its terms, as Kissinger's letter explained to Jackson, the Soviets in effect agreed to cease harassment of Jewish applicants, including special "diploma taxes" imposed on Jews as "repayment" of their free Soviet education. In his reply to Kissinger, Jackson indicated that "we understand that the actual number of emigrants will rise promptly from the 1973 level [of 34,000] to about 60,000," a figure that the Senate henceforth would use as a benchmark. It was an extraordinary feat. In the entire history of the Soviet regime, no such concession had ever been extracted on behalf of any ethnic or religious group.

The most-favored-nation legislation, with its incorporated Jackson-Vanik Amendment, easily passed the Senate on December 13, 1974. Yet all was not over. The pro-Israel lobby in Congress had assumed that American credits to the USSR would be generous enough to induce the Soviets to fulfill their bargain on Jewish emigration. At the last moment before the vote, however, Senator Adlai E. Stevenson III of Illinois added a new qualification, in effect an amendment to the amendment. Its most important feature placed a tight $300 million ceiling in Export-Import Bank credits to the Soviets. The ceiling would not be lifted until the Soviets proved forthcoming not only on emigration but on Middle East arms control and on military force reductions. The Senate routinely passed this qualification. Onerous and humiliating—indeed, unacceptable to Moscow (or possibly to any sovereign government)—the new legislation for all practical purposes canceled out the Jackson-Vanik Amendment.

Thereupon the outraged Kremlin leadership, sensing that the game was not worth the candle, repudiated the trade agreement. Although the document remained on Congress's legislative books, it simply would not be activated. Neither would the Soviet-American "understanding" on Jewish emigration. As it later developed, Israel's painstaking diplomatic effort of two and a half years had by no means gone down the drain. The incontrovertible evidence of Jewish political muscularity had well registered on the Kremlin, and eventually would take its effect (pp. 332–3). But in the short term, Moscow's exasperation with the issue of Jewish emigration would play a role even in Soviet Middle Eastern policy.

A FORECLOSED SOVIET PRESENCE IN EGYPT

Strategic and geopolitical factors manifestly would remain decisive in that policy. The most critical of these was the preservation of Soviet naval and air bases in Egypt and Syria. In May 1971 Moscow had experienced a tremolo of concern when Egypt's President Anwar al-Sadat purged his Marxist rival Ali Sabri. But only weeks afterward, Sadat reassured the Kremlin of his goodwill by signing a new "Soviet-Egyptian Treaty of Friendship and Cooperation," and pledging to seek a further "coordination of positions" with the USSR in foreign affairs. In return the Soviets agreed to provide important new quantities of economic and technological aid to Egypt, and to maintain their training program for the Egyptian armed forces. Soviet weapons deliveries would also continue, although carefully weighted on the side of defensive equipment. In this fashion Moscow limited Egypt's ability to gravitate toward the United States, and simultaneously protected itself against further Egyptian military surprises.

Yet the Kremlin's Middle East specialists failed to discern that the overweening Soviet role in Egyptian public affairs was evoking restiveness among the Egyptian government and people alike. It was a role that prejudiced the nation's influence in Africa, for one thing, by

fostering an ongoing European military presence on African soil.
Within Egypt itself the spectacle of Soviet officers in the streets and
clubs of Cairo and Alexandria, enjoying privileged residential and
travel opportunities, was reviving painful memories of British occupation. Under Sadat, meanwhile, "Socialist" restrictions on the Egyptian
economy were being relaxed, and new inducements offered for private capital formation. In September 1971, the president announced a
new cotton policy, abolishing barter deals with Moscow and thereby
foreclosing the Soviet practice of marketing Egyptian cotton below
the world price; and in 1971–72, Egyptian-Soviet commercial relations altogether visibly declined. In the area of foreign policy, not
least of all, Sadat was embarked on an initiative to improve relations
with Saudi Arabia, a United States ally; and in the summer of 1971 he
dispatched troops to help restore Ja'afar al-Numeiri to power in the
Sudan, following a brief pro-Communist coup in that nation.

Over the ensuing months, proclaiming 1971 to be the "Year of
Decision," Sadat also began pressing the Soviets for augmented military help in anticipation at least of a limited offensive against Israel.
But in November 1971, India launched an invasion of East Pakistan,
and the Soviets felt obliged to divert to their Indian ally important
quantities of equipment originally scheduled for Egypt. Worse yet,
Moscow in that same November presented Washington with a new
blueprint for a Middle Eastern settlement. Based on a proposal
offered by UN Mediator Jarring, it would be a two-stage process
envisaging, initially, a reopening of the Suez Canal, then a full and
formal peace treaty. The notion was as distasteful to Sadat as it was to
Israel's Prime Minister Meir. He had made no commitment to a permanent peace treaty—no more than had Mrs. Meir to full Israeli
withdrawal. Thus, on December 28, Sadat was obliged to inform his
nation that, "without additional Soviet help," Egypt could not go to
war. The acknowledgment was a personal humiliation for the president. In their impatience and exasperation, his people were urging
him to "wage war or conclude peace."

It was in response to these pressures that, in February 1972, Sadat
flew to Moscow for a three-day visit. Meeting with Brezhnev and
Foreign Minister Gromyko, the Egyptian leader made an emotional
appeal for military help in driving the Israelis back from the Suez
Canal Zone. But his hosts were not forthcoming. With their growing
armada off the Egyptian coast, the Soviets finally had reached a certain naval equilibrium with the United States Sixth Fleet. It was
hardly the moment to transform parity into confrontation, and least
of all when Moscow was seeking most-favored-nation trade status

from the United States. Sadat's mission ended in failure. A second visit to Moscow, in late April, proved equally unsuccessful. And afterward, as Sadat had feared, Richard Nixon's May 1972 visit to the Soviet Union produced a carefully orchestrated joint communiqué, making plain that the two sides had failed to reach agreement on the Middle East, and thus would postpone discussions on the issue for a "future occasion." By then Sadat was approaching the limits of his forbearance. Nevertheless, in a final effort to keep the Egyptian-Israeli impasse from being consigned to the diplomatic back burner, he dispatched his minister of defense, Muhammed Sadek, to Moscow with an extensive shopping list. Sadek, too, returned empty-handed.

The Egyptian president had waited long enough. In late June of 1972, he telexed an urgent letter to Brezhnev, seeking an assessment of the Middle East implications of the recent Moscow summit. On July 8 an answer arrived. It was read off to Sadat by Soviet Ambassador Vladimir Vinogradov, and was studiously noncommittal. Coldly, then, Sadat informed Vinogradov that the services of the Soviet military mission in Egypt were "no longer required." Ten days later, when the decision was made public, it was greeted with a virtual explosion of national enthusiasm. Egyptian newspapers vied with each other in congratulating Sadat. Moslem *qadis* delivered sermons of thanksgiving in their mosques. The Soviets were not in a position to object. Unable to stay on by force, they were obliged to allow the process of departure to proceed uneventfully. Within a month the largest numbers of their 15,000 military and civilian personnel were out of Egypt. Returning with them were some one hundred fifty combat aircraft and three hundred SAM batteries, equipment the Russians themselves had operated.

For Israel, in turn, news of the expulsion produced infinite gratification and relief. It appeared certain now that Egypt would be weakened both militarily and diplomatically. Indeed, in Jerusalem all political activity relating to the Middle Eastern conflict was suspended. The Jarring Mission had long since guttered out. Thereafter Israel's principal security concerns would shift from military confrontation in the Middle East to Arab guerrilla terrorism abroad.

A WAR OF JUDGMENT

By contrast, Anwar al-Sadat's objective was exclusively one of military confrontation. His strategy focused on a limited armed offensive, a campaign effective enough at least to drive Israeli forces back from the Suez Canal, and thus to induce the Meir government to negotiate a more permanent withdrawal. To that end the Egyptian president anticipated the military cooperation of Syria, whose Golan Heights lay under Israeli occupation. It was a realistic expectation. In 1969 the Jadid regime was overthrown by a less militant Alawite cabal under the leadership of an air force colonel, Hafez al-Assad. It was under Assad's aegis that the Syrians became more thoroughly equipped for a military offensive than ever before in their history. Indeed, Sadat's eviction of Soviet advisers from Egypt actually had strengthened President Assad's bargaining leverage with Moscow. To protect this alternate Middle Eastern bridgehead, the Soviets agreed to ship Syria unprecedented quantities of military equipment, including three hundred new tanks, three hundred jet fighters, and between four and five hundred late-model SAM-6s. Thus, when Sadat in March 1973 proposed a joint offensive against Israel, Assad felt strong enough to respond favorably.

But in the end, a joint Egyptian-Syrian military campaign would have been unrealistic without Kremlin support. Thus, on October 16, 1972, only three months after expelling the Soviet military mission, Sadat dispatched Prime Minister Aziz Sidqi to Moscow to revive discussions on military supplies. This time the Russians were prepared to listen. Sadat had called their bluff earlier, and the president's arsenal did not lack additional diplomatic weapons. Thus far he had refrained from foreclosing the Soviets' treaty access to Port Saïd and Alexandria. From these harbors Soviet naval forces still maintained their capability to survey the United States Sixth Fleet. It was not an asset they were prepared to risk. Accordingly, Brezhnev and Defense Minister Nikolai Podgorny agreed in principle to offer the Egyptians an incremental new infusion of modern weaponry. With the new equipment the Egyptians presumably could launch an offensive across the canal and achieve a modest bridgehead in Sinai, yet not penetrate deeply enough to threaten Israel's fundamental security—and thereby provoke a Soviet-American confrontation. A limited war might also usefully punish Israel for its embarrassing propaganda campaign on behalf of Soviet Jewry, and possibly even cripple the little state's capacity to absorb an extensive new wave of immigration.

In July 1973, therefore, Moscow began shipping selected quantities of modern equipment to both Egypt and Syria. The weaponry included hardware as sophisticated as Scud surface-to-surface missiles and MiG-23 aircraft. By then the Soviets had been informed of the scheduled date of the offensive—October 6. On September 23 they recalled the last of their military advisers from Syria. On October 3 they launched a reconnaissance satellite from its Turyatom base, and sent it into orbit over the Middle East. Almost at the same time, Soviet vessels berthed in Alexandria and Port Saïd headed out to sea.

In the small hours of October 6, on Yom Kippur, the Jewish Day of Atonement, an Egyptian informant alerted Israel's military intelligence to the forthcoming attack. The report was only partially accurate. It suggested a "modest" offensive, to be launched at sunset. Instead, the assault began at 2:00 p.m., and far from being modest, it commenced in the north with thousands of shells exploding along the Golan Heights. Soon five Syrian divisions began rumbling across the Golan cease-fire line, cracking the Israeli front in two sectors. In the south a firestorm of shells simultaneously descended on Israel's "Bar-Lev Line," along the eastern embankment of the Suez Canal. Here 436 Israeli soldiers in eleven isolated bunkers confronted an assault of five Egyptian divisions and twenty-two infantry, commando, and paratroop brigades.

When the Egyptian barrage reached its crescendo at 2:25 p.m., the first wave of eight thousand Egyptian infantry moved across the waterway in fiberglass boats. Responding, Israeli jets were hurled indiscriminately against these amphibious forces—only to be shot down in large numbers by SAM-6 missile salvos and other antiaircraft weapons. By nightfall, thirty thousand Egyptian infantrymen had overrun the Bar-Lev Line, secured a beachhead throughout the eastern length of the canal, and had begun pushing into Sinai. As Israeli tanks were rushed forward to strike at this vanguard, Egyptian troops lying in ambush fired off hundreds of portable Sagger rockets, scouring Israel's armor, wiping out entire tank crews with each blast. By early afternoon of October 7, eleven pontoon bridges spanned the canal and three hundred Egyptian tanks and five mixed infantry-and-armored divisions had crossed the waterway.

The next day, when the UN Security Council met in emergency session, the United States called for an immediate cease-fire and a return of "all forces" to the original preattack line. But, in response, the Soviet delegate neatly blocked the appeal by insisting on full Israeli withdrawal to the pre-1967 frontiers; while the French and British called only for a cease-fire "in place." At an impasse, the Security Council then dispersed. Meanwhile the Soviets had committed their extensive logistical resources to support of the Arab offensive. Relays of East European vessels unloaded thousands of tons of weapons at the ports of Alexandria and Latakia. From Hungarian air bases a continual relay of Antonov transport planes ferried guns, tanks, SAM rockets, and dismantled jet fighters to Syria and Egypt. Between October 9 and October 22, Soviet flights averaged thirty a day.

Monitoring these developments, Henry Kissinger in Washington concluded that the Soviet-backed offensive had to be challenged. It was vital for the Arabs to grasp that they could never win a victory under Soviet patronage alone. In the secretary of state's calculation, a substantial infusion of American weaponry to Israel conceivably would restore the military balance in the eastern Mediterranean, and thus provide the United States with diplomatic leverage to shape a Middle Eastern settlement. President Nixon agreed. On October 13, at his orders, Phantom jets began flying to Israel via the Azores; while, from military airfields in New Jersey and Delaware, giant C-130 and C-5 transport planes, packed with ordnance, began a round-the-clock airlift. In this manner, between October 14 and November 14, the United States transported 22,000 tons of supplies in 166 flights. Much also came later by sea.

In the first two days of the Arab offensive, meanwhile, between October 6 and October 8, Israel's two outnumbered brigades on the Golan Heights waged a desperate rear-guard battle against a Syrian offensive that threatened to inundate the entirety of northeastern Israel. By dawn of October 9, however, additional tank reinforcements reached the Golan, and the Israelis launched a counterattack. During the next thirty-six hours their armor drove the Syrians back, indeed, well beyond the original 1967 cease-fire line, and even to within twenty-five miles of Damascus. By October 11, Israel's general staff agreed that the army could safely shift its efforts to the Sinai theater.

It was in the south that seventy thousand Egyptian troops had crossed Suez, establishing an unbroken Sinai front six miles in depth. Sadat's commanders then prepared to launch a major second-stage breakthrough. At dawn on October 14, they hurled their full strength eastward, with the principal attack developing toward the Gidi Pass, Israel's key access route into western Sinai. The effort proved disastrous. By the time the firing died down in midafternoon, the Israelis had destroyed some 250 Egyptian tanks and established total control of the field. Within hours, then, the Israeli general staff turned to the offensive, preparing to countercross the Suez Canal.

The operation began in the late afternoon of October 15. Fighting was savage, but throughout the ensuing two days, despite continual Egyptian shelling, the Israelis succeeded in throwing a makeshift bridge across the waterway. By the afternoon of October 17, their first armored columns began crossing over. By the late morning of October 18, their engineers completed a second bridge. Larger supply columns began rolling over, including two armored divisions of three hundred tanks and fifteen thousand troops. Subsequently Israel's invasion force fanned out on the western embankment to destroy SAM batteries along a fifteen-mile stretch of the canal. With Egyptian antiaircraft defenses "punctured" in this region, and Israel's air support once again available, the invading tanks encountered little difficulty in pushing south along the waterway. By the evening of October 17, in fact, the pattern of the war had decisively changed.

Apprised of these developments, and fearing a repetition of the 1967 disaster, the Soviets as early as October 12 began alerting Cairo that the Israelis were regrouping. And on October 15, once Soviet satellites transmitted photographs of the Israeli countercrossing, Prime Minister Aleksei Kosygin flew into Cairo for personal discussions with Sadat. During the next three days Kosygin outlined to Sadat a plan to end both the current hostilities and the Arab-Israel impasse altogether. Its terms envisaged a cease-fire in place, an Israeli withdrawal to pre-1967 boundaries with only "minor" changes, and an international peace conference to negotiate a final settlement—which in turn would be "guaranteed" by the Soviet Union and the United States. Sadat was recalcitrant. Israel would have to withdraw unreservedly and permanently behind the pre-1967 lines, he insisted, nothing less. Only on the last day of discussions, October 18, as Israeli divisions thrust deeper into integral Egypt, did the president grasp his army's critical situation. On conferring with his military advisers, Sadat at last grudgingly agreed to Kosygin's formula. The Soviet prime minister then departed for home.

A RENEWAL OF GREAT-POWER CONFRONTATION

Moscow's ensuing move was to secure American cooperation. On October 19, Anatoly Dobrynin, the Soviet ambassador in Washington, transmitted President Leonid Brezhnev's personal message to Henry Kissinger. It requested the secretary's immediate presence in Moscow for "urgent" discussions. With the threat of unilateral Soviet intervention against Israel now palpable, Richard Nixon authorized Kissinger to depart forthwith, and to take with him a presidential "power of attorney" for resolving the Middle Eastern crisis. Kissinger flew out of Washington that night. The moment his jet landed in Moscow in the early evening of October 20, the Soviets rushed him into conference.

By then additional Israeli bridges had gone up across the canal, and the Egyptian military situation had deteriorated irretrievably. Aware of his bargaining strength, Kissinger promptly laid down his own conditions for ending the war. A cease-fire in place would have to be linked subsequently to a UN Security Council resolution mandating direct, face-to-face peace negotiations between Arabs and Israelis. In fact, the Kissinger scenario did not vary in any significant respect from the formula Kosygin had pressed on Sadat. The two sides swiftly reached a meeting of minds.

From the United States embassy, Kissinger then telephoned the proposal directly to Golda Meir in Israel. Explaining to the prime minister that his recommendation had the approval equally of Nixon, Brezhnev, and Sadat, he underscored its advantages. Under the terms of the impending Security Council cease-fire resolution, as the Americans and Soviets would draft it, Israeli troops would be allowed to maintain their current positions. Afterward, for the first time, the Egyptians would negotiate directly with the Israelis, although under the aegis of an international, Geneva, peace conference. Kissinger also reminded Mrs. Meir that even Security Council Resolution 242, which ended the 1967 Six-Day War, had not explicitly committed the Arabs to a face-to-face "negotiating" process, but rather had appointed a mediator. The new proposal thus represented a significant concession to Israel.

Mrs. Meir listened carefully and reacted cautiously. Upon discussing Kissinger's offer with her cabinet afterward, she encountered harsh resistance from several of her ministerial colleagues. Following its recent painful sacrifices in manpower, they pointed out, Israel's army at last stood on the threshold of total victory. Egyptian forces in the Sinai were facing annihilation. Surely this was the moment to teach Sadat a decisive lesson. And who could believe any good would come from a peace conference in which the Soviet Union would serve as cosponsor? Nevertheless, following hours of vehement predawn debate, the cabinet finally accepted Kissinger's formula.

At this point, the Soviet and United States governments requested and obtained an emergency Security Council meeting for October 22. The assembled delegates in turn promptly approved the Soviet-American appeal for a cease-fire in place. The resolution—338—called for the parties "to start immediately after the cease-fire the implementation of Security Council Resolution 242 [of 1967] in all of its parts." It further stipulated that, "immediately and concurrently" with the cease-fire, negotiations should commence between Egypt and Israel under "appropriate auspices," with the aim of establishing a "just and durable" peace in the Middle East. Israel then joined Egypt in accepting the cease-fire the same day, October 22. Syria's acceptance came two days later.

Throughout the night of October 22–23, Egyptian infantry on the canal's eastern embankment ignored the deadline, striking repeatedly at Israeli tank emplacements. The Israelis in turn were determined to close the single remaining access route from the canal's western embankment to the beleaguered Egyptian Third Army on the eastern, Sinai, shore of the waterway. Well into October 23 Israeli armored units continued moving across pontoon bridges, slashing along the western embankment to bestride the principal road connections to Cairo. At midmorning on October 23, informed of these ominous developments, Sadat loosed a panic-stricken appeal for Soviet intercession. Moscow responded with a tough ultimatum to Washington. If the Israelis did not withdraw immediately to the October 22 cease-fire line, it warned, the Soviet Union would inflict "the most serious consequences" on them. Kissinger, by then back in Washington, took the threat seriously. He pressed the Israelis to comply. That afternoon the secretary of state and Soviet Ambassador Dobrynin jointly formulated the text for a second cease-fire resolution. It was passed unanimously by the Security Council that same evening as Resolution 339.

And still the fighting continued. On the morning of October 24 Israeli forces turned back a Red Cross convoy en route to the entrapped Egyptians. Thoroughly unnerved by then, Sadat cabled Moscow and Washington, imploring both governments to organize a joint force to police a Suez cease-fire. Here it was, for the third time in less than two decades, that the Arab-Israeli imbroglio brought the Soviet Union and Israel—and possibly now the United States—to the threshold of confrontation. Moscow endorsed Sadat's appeal. Although favoring a cease-fire, Kissinger in turn flatly rejected the very notion of Soviet participation in a Middle East "police force." It was a stance on which American policy had remained consistent for thirty-five years, and it was not about to change now. But neither were the Soviets willing passively to endure yet another debacle in the region, at least without engaging in their customary tactic of verbal intimidation. On the evening of October 24, Brezhnev dispatched a personal message to Nixon, demanding that Soviet and American contingents be flown immediately to Egypt. "I will say it straight," Brezhnev warned, "that if you find it impossible to act together with us in this matter, we would be faced with the urgent necessity to consider the question of taking appropriate steps unilaterally."

Richard Nixon did not quail before this challenge to the Middle Eastern balance of power. Soviet bluster was an old story to the Americans. Rather, he ordered all United States military commands placed on alert, even on nuclear alert. An additional aircraft carrier was dispatched to the Mediterranean. Soviet monitoring stations picked up these movements—and the crisis was immediately resolved. On October 25 Brezhnev withdrew his demand for a Soviet-American peacekeeping expedition. Subsequently he accepted Kissinger's proposal for a United Nations force that would exclude troops of the Great Powers. So did the Security Council, which that same afternoon of the twenty-fifth dispatched to Egypt the first contingent of a 7,500-man UNEF force ("borrowed" from Austrian, Finnish, and Swedish units among the UN peacekeepers in Cyprus). The troops were assigned to patrol the anomalous, jigsawed series of battle zones along the Suez front.

Even then the fighting drew to a close only slowly. On October 26, in a final, despairing effort to improve its position, the entrapped Egyptian Third Army mounted an attack on Israeli pontoon bridges over the canal. It was thrown back. At last, with both sides prepared for compromise, Kissinger in Washington was able to negotiate with the Israeli and Egyptian ambassadors directly. Together they devised a formula under which a Red Cross convoy would be allowed to bring medical and food supplies through Israeli lines to the besieged Egyptians. Afterward, to negotiate the details, senior officers from both sides met under United Nations auspices on October 27 at a clearing on the Suez–Cairo highway. This was Kilometer 101, inside Israeli-occupied territory west of the canal. The discussions were businesslike and successful. The following day Israeli troops allowed one hundred Red Cross trucks to pass through to Egyptian lines. In return, Cairo permitted the Red Cross to visit Israeli prisoners of war. It was clear by then that hostilities would not be resumed. The most brutal of the four conflicts between Egypt and Israel had ended. So too, as events unfolded, had the diplomatic bargaining power of the Soviet Union in the Middle East.

A SOVIET NONPRESENCE

By early November 1973, Egyptian and Israeli negotiators at Kilometer 101 reached further agreement on a permanent supply corridor for the Egyptian Third Army, and on a full exchange of prisoners. Encouraged by their initial understanding, both sides then continued their discussions in an effort to achieve a wider military disengagement between the two armies, each ensconced precariously behind the other's lines. But no further progress was made, and by early December the Kilometer 101 talks were suspended. The issue of disengagement would be taken up at a higher, diplomatic level. At this point Henry Kissinger departed for an extensive Middle Eastern swing. The secretary of state was determined at all costs to sustain the diplomatic momentum, to nudge the belligerents into his envisaged Geneva peace conference later in the month. He got nowhere with the Syrians. The Assad government refused so much as to furnish a list of Israeli POWs. On other fronts, however, the secretary's efforts achieved a certain limited success.

During visits to Cairo, Jerusalem, and Amman (the Hashemites, although not involved in the recent war, were included in this diplomacy under UN Resolutions 242 and 338), Kissinger achieved a tripartite recommitment to a peace conference. Thus, on December 22, 1973, the foreign ministers of Egypt, Jordan, Israel, the United States, and the Soviet Union gathered at Geneva's Palais des Nations. The atmosphere was cold, with Egyptians and Israelis exchanging terse accusations. The following day, by prearrangement, the conference "temporarily" adjourned, with the understanding that Egypt and Israel would continue talks at the military level for a disengagement of forces as the next stage toward peace. It had been a short "conference," but there appeared every likelihood that discussions would resume later at Geneva.

That hope went unrequited. The Egyptians evinced no interest in resuming purely military discussions at Kilometer 101, or further direct negotiations of any kind with the Israelis. They preferred instead to rely on the intermediary efforts of the United States. Henry Kissinger had saved their Third Army from disaster, after all. Possibly the secretary of state might yet achieve the kind of settlement that Sadat's generals had failed to win on the battlefield. Thereupon the Israelis were confronted with a painful choice. On the one hand, the opportunity for face-to-face negotiations had been a key inducement for the Meir government's original decision to accept a cease-fire, and subsequently to open a corridor to the Egyptian Third Army. On the other hand, little progress had been made through direct negotiations, either at Kilometer 101 or at Geneva. Even less could be anticipated at a renewed conclave attended by hostile Soviet and Arab foreign ministers. Thus, after only minimal hesitation, the Israeli cabinet made the choice for indirect negotiations. Mrs. Meir and her colleagues preferred not to risk additional loss of life.

The decision soon produced tangible results. Shuttling in the presidential jet between Egypt and Israel, the secretary of state rapidly narrowed the differences between the two sides. By January 17, 1974, he had brokered an agreement. Its military feature obliged the Israelis to withdraw twelve miles into the Sinai Peninsula. Sadat, for his part, agreed to limit the Egyptian military presence in Sinai to a symbolic twelve thousand troops in a restricted geographical zone, with a middle—buffer—zone to be occupied by United Nations troops. The Geneva Peace Conference, which had opened to fanfare only a month earlier, played no part whatever in the disengagement agreement.

And neither, manifestly, did the Soviet Union. It was significant that the other key feature of the agreement lay in the series of "private" communications exclusively from President Nixon to Sadat and Golda Meir, which the latter two then countersigned. In this fashion the Egyptian president agreed to set about clearing the Suez Canal and rebuilding the canal cities, thereby in effect making them hostages to peace. Nonmilitary cargoes to and from Israel would be allowed passage through the canal, although not in Israeli vessels. Nixon's letter to Mrs. Meir in turn confirmed that the United States would maintain aerial reconnaissance of the disengagement area, and would help meet Israel's military equipment requirements "on a continuing and long-term basis." From beginning to end, the Soviet Union had been excluded from this diplomacy.

By the spring of 1974, moreover, even Syria's President Hafez al-Assad was prepared to accept American mediation. The Russians could offer his nation weapons and more fighting, but not assurance of returned territory. It was evident that only the United States enjoyed the leverage with Israel to do better. In late April, Kissinger departed again for the Middle East. Continuing without pause over the next thirty-two days, this last shuttle effort was the most arduous in the secretary's experience. But at last, on May 31, an agreement was reached for the Syrian-Israeli front. It established a new and binding cease-fire, a minimal withdrawal of Israeli forces on the Golan slightly west of the prewar cease-fire line, with a demilitarized buffer zone to separate the two armies. As in the case of the Egyptian-Israeli understanding, the Soviets had played no role in the negotiations.

Nor did they in the final, "Sinai II," Egyptian-Israeli disengagement negotiations. Upon completing his Syrian mission, Kissinger sounded out Cairo and Jerusalem on the possibility of enlarging their accord of several months earlier. Both governments concurred. In Israel, by then, Yitzchak Rabin had succeeded Golda Meir as prime minister, but he fully shared Mrs. Meir's pragmatism. For him, too, the American route to functional peace, rather than a Geneva conference, seemed the likelier one, even if it finessed the issue of direct talks with the Egyptians. Accordingly, in June 1974, triangular negotiations were resumed, this time in Washington, where Israeli and Egyptian representatives dealt with Kissinger and other State Department officials. The talks did not go easily, for they took place during the Watergate crisis that bedeviled the last months of the Nixon administration. But Kissinger was a tireless intercessor, and after a final shuttle visit to Israel and Egypt fully a year later, in August 1975, he achieved his second-stage disengagement agreement.

"Sinai II" was initialed by Sadat and Rabin on September 1, 1975. The Israelis agreed to pull back an additional twenty miles in Sinai, yet with safeguards that precluded any substantial weakening of their defensive posture. Once again the United States provided the inspectors and the sophisticated electronic equipment to monitor the demilitarized zones. More important, the new Ford administration in Washington agreed to guarantee Israel's oil supplies and an uninterrupted flow of modern weapons systems, together with grants and loans totaling $3 billion annually for the ensuing five years. Egypt also would receive American weaponry and some $2 billion in American financial aid.

It was unimaginable that the Soviets could have matched these inducements, or exerted a comparable leverage either on Egypt or Israel. For Sadat, intent on moving his nation's economy off its chronic war footing, the United States connection offered nothing less than a lifeline. Indeed, to gain access to it, almost immediately following the 1973 conflict, he had restored the diplomatic relations with Washington that Nasser had severed during the Six-Day War. And, as Sadat hoped, American businessmen soon began testing the quality of his government's promised new moderation. David Rockefeller and other prominent corporation executives arrived in Cairo to investigate possible investment opportunities. Meanwhile, throughout 1974 and early 1975, as Moscow pressed him to return to Geneva, the Egyptian president remained evasive. His decision in June 1975 to open the Suez Canal, and thus to facilitate the movement of Western shipping, deeply angered the Soviet leadership. In January 1976, finally, an exasperated Leonid Brezhnev canceled his scheduled visit to Cairo. Soviet commentators by then had launched a furious editorial campaign against the Egyptian government's rapprochement with the United States, its "obsequious dependence" on Western private capital.

For his part, Sadat was quite prepared to accept the logical implications of his new diplomatic orientation. On March 14, 1976, he asked his People's Assembly to cancel the 1971 Soviet-Egyptian Treaty of Friendship and Cooperation. The "request" was immediately approved. In his speech to the assembly that day, the president explained that the Soviets had consistently opposed the "trend toward peace which [had] taken shape" since the October 1973 War. They had opposed Egypt's new "open-door" policy of a freer economy, the nation's "sovereign right" to carry out its own social and political changes. Worse yet, they had refused to reschedule Egypt's debt payments, even to overhaul Egypt's Soviet-built aircraft or to provide spare parts. For a brief while longer, Sadat allowed the Soviet fleet continued access to Egyptian ports. But on April 4, 1976, responding to the "public will," the president canceled those naval privileges as well. It was at this point that the Soviet investment in Egypt, launched with a spectacular weapons deal twenty-one years earlier, and maintained thereafter with a limitless outlay of economic, diplomatic, and military patronage, expired in a farrago of mutual acrimony.

THE DIPLOMACY OF FUTILITY

If the Soviet Union's ability to monitor the U.S. Sixth Fleet was seriously weakened by foreclosure of its Egyptian bases, there still remained a precarious foothold in Syria. To protect it, the Soviets continued to provide the Assad regime with generous quantities of weaponry. In a break with tradition, they decided also to embrace Damascus's traditional support of the Palestinian cause. Before the war, fearing the precedent that guerrilla terrorism might set for its own contentious nationalities, Moscow had been cool to Arafat and the PLO. It preferred to depend on more conventional bilateral relations with Arab governments.

But as Sadat and even Assad relied increasingly on Kissinger's mediation, the Soviets at last began to advocate recognition of Palestinian "national" rights. In visits to Moscow in July 1974 and February 1975, Yasser Arafat was greeted personally, and warmly, by Brezhnev, Kosygin, and Gromyko. Indeed the Soviet leaders for the first time spoke of the need for a Palestinian "state," and for a PLO delegation at a revived Geneva peace conference. In November 1975 the Soviet delegate joined the Afro-Asian bloc in supporting a UN General Assembly resolution terming Zionism a form of racism.

Even then the Russians managed to keep a line open to Israel. Before and immediately after the Yom Kippur War, they countenanced intermittent exchanges of Soviet and Israeli cultural and sports delegations (p. 263). In his opening address at the Geneva Peace Conference in December 1973, Andrei Gromyko adopted a moderate tone—as had Kosygin at the United Nations in June 1967—noting again that Moscow had always favored the independence and even the security of Israel. Gromyko then invited Israel's Foreign Minister Eban to the Soviet embassy for a lengthy private talk. Although no progress was made on the Middle Eastern crisis, the tenor of the discussion at least was equable. In fact, Moscow's bicephalous diplomacy was animated by its hope of reviving the Geneva format, and thus of remaining a "player" in the Middle East. By the same token, a "carrot" to the Israelis might yet defuse the Jewish lobby's opposition to Soviet most-favored-nation trading opportunities in the United States.

In January 1975 Israel's new foreign minister, Yigal Allon, and Anatoly Dobrynin, the Soviet ambassador to the United States, exploited a "chance encounter" to discuss these issues in New York, during a short meeting that laid the basis for lengthier conversations the following April in Washington between Dobrynin and Israel's Ambassador Simcha Dinitz. The two diplomats held five secret meetings at the Soviet embassy over the ensuing two months. Although most of these related to the issue of Jewish emigration and the "Stevenson Amendment" (p. 265), Dobrynin adverted periodically to Geneva. On Jerusalem's instructions, Dinitz took a firm line. There seemed little advantage in a revived international conference under Soviet cosponsorship, he suggested, if Moscow refused even to maintain diplomatic relations with Israel. Those ties would first have to be restored. Foreign Minister Allon reconfirmed that stance in September 1975, during meetings with Andrei Gromyko at the United Nations in New York. The Soviet foreign minister was unprepared to accept this condition. Moscow dared not jeopardize its increasingly precarious ties with the Arab world.

Even then, Soviet-Israeli contacts were not interrupted. Both earlier and later, they were sustained through other channels, through German and French diplomats, through British Prime Minister Harold Wilson and Dutch Foreign Minister Joseph Luns. In May 1975 the Soviet journal *International Affairs* pressed the Arabs to accept a political settlement with Israel, insisting that conditions now were favorable. That same month Romanian President Ceausescu visited Cairo to entreat the Egyptians to return to Geneva. But despite all the frenetic diplomatic movement, neither the Israelis nor the Egyptians seemed interested in a resuscitated Geneva conference, with its prospect of revived Soviet participation in Middle Eastern affairs.

Meanwhile, the United States Congress, whose good offices were required for the dispensation of trade privileges, continued to monitor Soviet behavior with suspicion. Moscow's role in the Yom Kippur War offered cause enough for distrust. The legislators were not in a hurry to revise the Stevenson Amendment, with its unforgiving $300-million credit ceiling on Soviet purchases of American products. To dissipate those reservations, the Soviets at first maintained their cautiously forbearing approach to Jewish emigration. In 1973 they authorized the departure of 34,000 Jews, the highest figure ever recorded—including 4,200 who left for Israel in October, even as the Yom Kippur War raged. In 1974 the figure sank back to 21,000, and in 1975 to 13,000. But in 1976, to gauge the attitude of the incoming Carter administration, the Soviets permitted a fractional increase, to 14,000, and in 1977 to 16,000.

By the same token, as late as 1977, the Kremlin discerned a flickering opportunity to remain a player in the Middle East. The incoming Carter administration shared Moscow's preference for a revived Geneva conference, although specifically one that would produce an internationally recognized Palestinian "entity" in the West Bank and Gaza. The Soviet response was encouraging. Indeed, in May 1977, Leonid Brezhnev made his most conciliatory offer to Israel thus far. It was a mirror image of the Carter peace plan. Acknowledging that details could be negotiated in Geneva, the Soviet president suggested that Israel commit itself to withdraw from Arab-occupied territories gradually, in two stages, with all suitable provisions to be made for demilitarized zones and Big-Four guarantees at every stage of the process. Brezhnev even declared his support for Israeli maritime rights in the Strait of Tiran and in the Suez Canal. He affirmed, too, that each participant, Arab and Israeli, would have the right to approve or veto any Big Power proposal at Geneva. For all its self-interest the Brezhnev proposal struck President Carter and his advisors as a significant commitment to moderation. Like the Americans, the Soviets appeared genuinely intent upon defusing the Middle Eastern time bomb. In October 1977, therefore, Washington and Moscow issued a joint statement. The Kissinger-style step-by-step approach had reached its limits, they declared. In its place the two governments proposed a reconvened Geneva conference. At Geneva at last, a comprehensive Middle Eastern settlement would be formulated.

But in fact Anwar al-Sadat had never favored the prospect of a renewed Geneva conference, no more in 1977 than in 1974. He wanted no part of a Soviet presence at any stage of negotiations. Neither did Yitzchak Rabin in Israel, or his successor, Menachem Begin, who assumed the prime ministry following the Israeli election of May

1977. To be sure, neither Middle Eastern government was prepared to issue a flat repudiation of the Geneva proposal. One did not cavalierly offend an American president. In November 1977, however, Anwar al-Sadat revealed his own, dramatically simple, alternative route to peace. It would run not through Geneva but through Jerusalem. From that moment on, the Soviet factor became altogether irrelevant, indeed moribund, in the relationship between Israel and the largest and most powerful of its traditional Arab enemies.

XII A CONTINENTAL CHILL

A YOM KIPPUR ISOLATION

In 1969, troubled by superpower domination of international affairs, the European Economic Community explored the likelihood of redefining itself as a straightforward "European Community," a confederative player in the fullest ambit of international affairs. Until then Charles de Gaulle had attempted unrelentingly to superimpose his own parochial vision of French *grandeur* on Europe's anticipated role as an independent "third force." But with the general's resignation as president of France in 1969, and with Britain, Ireland, and Denmark soon to join the Common Market, was the time not opportune for the EEC nations to move into the wider arena of political cooperation? In early 1970 their respective governments provided an answer by endorsing the "Davignon Report," the blueprint produced by the EEC's Council of Ministers, advocating across-the-board policy coordination as a European Community on vital issues of international stability and security.

Among those issues, surely, none was more critical, not even the wider East-West schism, than the Arab-Israeli impasse, a ticking time bomb that in 1956 and 1967 had paralyzed the Suez Canal and seemingly threatened to engulf Europe itself in a Great-Power confrontation. Moreover, by the new decade, even Israel's closest European friends expressed reservations over the Jewish state's apparent inflexibility in the occupied territories. Thus, in January 1971 Joseph Luns, the Netherlands foreign minister, criticized "all" the parties to the Middle East conflict for "not wanting to make concessions." Foreign Minister Pa Harmel of Belgium repeatedly entreated Israel to "give up all expansionist plans," as did Italy's Prime Minister Aldo Moro. Under the Conservative government of Edward Heath, Britain resumed its traditional sensitivity to Arab oil resources and financial power.

At no time was there full coordination of policy within the emergent European Community. But in May 1971 the EC achieved enough of a consensus to issue its first pronunciamento on foreign affairs. Known as the "Schumann Paper" (after its author, French Foreign Minister Maurice Schumann), the statement recommended: progressive Israeli withdrawal from the occupied territories, with only minor border changes; free choice for Arab refugees either to return to their homes or to accept repatriation and indemnification; support for the Jarring mission. Roughly consistent with UN Security Council Resolution 242, the document signified no dramatic shift in the European position against Israel. But the subtle change in atmospherics concerned the Golda Meir government.

It was the Yom Kippur War of 1973 that disclosed the ultimate fragility of Israel's painstakingly negotiated relationship with Europe. The Continent's industrial economies by then had become too heavily dependent on the goodwill of the Arab world to allow a policy of tacit forbearance. In France the Pompidou government's pro-Arab bias was defined by Foreign Minister Jobert's caustic observation: "Can you call it unexpected aggression for someone to try to repossess his own land?" In Britain the reaction of the Heath cabinet was even more of a shocker to the Israelis, for it produced an immediate suspension of arms supplies to the Middle East. Israel's main battle tank was the British-manufactured Centurion, and the embargo blocked all further deliveries of this armor, including spare parts contracted and paid for. More painful yet, London denied American planes access to landing and refueling facilities at RAF bases in Cyprus. Over the years, Britain and Israel had developed a correct, even equable relationship that had all but erased the painful early memories of refugee blockade, underground terrorism, or Whitehall-inspired scenarios for attenuating Israel's borders. Yet for Israel, now twenty-five years into statehood, distrust of British *Realpolitik* flared up anew.

Disillusionment arose from still another source. This was the West German Bundesrepublik. Only five months before the Yom Kippur War, Chancellor Willy Brandt had visited Israel, and the palpable evidence of his goodwill did much to alleviate resentment of German ineptitude and insensitivity during the 1972 Munich Olympics massacre. But once the war began, the Israelis faced a new crisis of ambivalent friendship. In supplying emergency shipments of weaponry, the United States had intended to draw upon the equipment stored in its complex of NATO bases in Germany. Bonn soon found itself in a quandary. The previous year, after a seven-year hiatus, it had managed to resume diplomatic relations with the Arab governments (p. 208). Determined afterward to avoid jeopardizing these revived ties, the Bundesrepublik refused use of its airfields for the American resupply effort to Israel.

In fact, the Brandt government initially had allowed American and even Israeli vessels access to German maritime ports for reprovisioning the Jewish state, asking only that the shipments be kept secret. There was never a question of Bonn's goodwill to Israel. As Willy Brandt privately observed to his cabinet on the third day of the Middle East conflict: "It would be terrible if Israel were knocked to the ground! What a disastrous effect this would have on our own people!" But two and a half weeks into the war, news of the Bundesrepublik's role in the American deliveries leaked to the German press, and the Arab governments immediately weighed in with protests. Brandt and Foreign Minister Walter Scheel then saw no alternative but to deny the United States further use of the Bundesrepublik's port facilities. The decision actually was taken on October 25, two days after the Egyptian-Israeli cease-fire was announced, and thus exerted only limited influence on Israel's fighting capacity. Months later, too, when the facts became known of Brandt's initial acquiescence in sea deliveries, the Israeli people were somewhat mollified. But in October 1973 their bitterness was vocal and unrestrained.

Realpolitik played a comparable role in the European Community's diplomatic equivocation throughout the Yom Kippur War, and its widening political estrangement from Israel. For one thing, the Middle East crisis appeared yet again to have thrust the United States and the Soviet Union onto a terrifying collision course. However brief and exaggerated, it was a danger the Europeans were intent on avoiding at almost any future cost. Meanwhile, a peril hardly less invidious was that of energy starvation. Western Europe imported 65 percent of its oil from the Middle East and North Africa. To exploit the Continent's economic vulnerability, Egypt's President Sadat had cemented his ties with Saudi Arabia and other Gulf nations before the war. His diplomacy paid off now. As fighting began, the oil ministers of the Arab OPEC nations gathered in Kuwait on October 17 and swiftly agreed to reduce their oil consignments to the West by 5 percent a month, and possibly more later, "depending on the Middle East situation." The ministers then established categories for the various purchasing nations, linking their oil "quotas" to their support of the Arab cause. Under these OPEC guidelines, then, France was virtually exempted from the ban. Conversely, a total embargo was imposed on both the United States and the Netherlands.

Arab grievances against Washington were an old story. In the case of the Netherlands, however, the punishment evinced indignation both at The Hague's discreet statement of sympathy for Israel at the outset of the war, and at the longer-standing Dutch tradition of support for the Jewish state. That tradition actually had undergone a certain modification in recent years. Since the 1967 war, the Dutch had expressed growing concern at Israel's settlements policy in Arab-inhabited territory. Although Foreign Minister Luns had carefully withheld support for Palestinian self-determination, he also favored the developing EC emphasis on Palestinian "rights" as an indispensable element of any peace settlement. Nevertheless, when the Arabs launched their Yom Kippur offensive, the Dutch rallied again in support of the Jews. On October 9, 1973, their government officially condemned the Arab resort to violence and called for a return of the Egyptian and Syrian armies to the June 10, 1967, cease-fire line. The stance represented a final provocation to the Arabs, and evoked their OPEC decision of October 17.

In an attempt to ease the pressure on the Dutch, the major Western oil companies were prepared to ship the Netherlands a proportion of the supplies that had been allocated to other members of the European Community. But the formula immediately encountered opposition. France prohibited the diversion of even the minutest quantity of its own scheduled consignments. Britain also wavered. Initially Foreign Secretary Alec Douglas-Home proposed an Order-in-Council to block any tampering with his nation's oil allocation. It was only The Hague's anguished reminder of its loyal support of Britain's application for membership in the Common Market, coupled with the discreet intercession of Germany's Foreign Minister Scheel, that persuaded Douglas-Home to reverse himself. Over French objections, the oil companies then divided their supplies equitably among all their European consumers. Under this arrangement the Netherlands managed to survive the embargo, and by November to operate at 63 percent of its prewar oil capacity.

But when a second Arab OPEC meeting took place in Kuwait on December 9, 1973, and the Arab ministers decided to apply the next reduction in deliveries to all countries—friendly, neutral, or hostile alike—it became clear that the war simply had offered the Gulf oil nations their pretext for cutting production and raising prices. Thus, at yet a third Arab OPEC meeting on December 23, the ministers agreed to raise oil prices to $11.65 a barrel—a staggering 360 percent increase from the $2.59 price of October 1, 1973. Money, therefore, was the key, and politics only a secondary factor. Either way, the oil shock was grave enough to send Europe into panic. As early as the first OPEC cutback, on October 17, the British, Italians, and Germans immediately introduced tight controls on fuel. Following the second cutback in fuel consumption on December 9, Britain soon reduced its factory work schedule to four days a week. Italy's ocean liners were kept in port.

Meanwhile, in early November, France's Pompidou government discerned in the emerging oil crisis an opportunity to lead Western Europe in its own pro-Arab direction. At Pompidou's initiative, the European Nine convened two emergency summit conferences, the first in Brussels on November 6, the second in Copenhagen on December 14. In Brussels, to placate the Arabs, the Community representatives—even the Dutch and Germans—agreed to endorse a Franco-British text that went much further than the Schumann Report of 1971. Urging a "just and lasting peace" based on UN Security Council Resolution 242, their declaration now also recommended that a settlement ensure "the legitimate rights of the Palestinians" and an Israeli withdrawal from occupied lands. In a further genuflection to the Arabs, the statement offered two additional proposals that the Israelis had long regarded as inimical: that Arab-Israeli negotiations take place within the framework of the United Nations; and that a peace settlement include "international guarantees," a concept that implied either United Nations or Soviet participation. The second meeting of the EC foreign ministers, in Copenhagen on December 14, essentially reinforced the Brussels Declaration. Yet, in still another departure from earlier norms, the EC this time invited five Arab ministers to attend the conference as "observers." Their presence signified the beginning of a "Euro-Arab Dialogue," whose ostensible purpose was to develop closer "understanding and cooperation" between the European Community and the Arab world.

Eventually, in March 1974, the Arab OPEC nations ended their oil cutback, even the embargo on the Netherlands and the United States. None of the underlying Arab-Israel political issues actually had been resolved, but Henry Kissinger by then had successfully negotiated the Sinai military disengagements, and the Arabs accepted resumption of full oil production as their quid pro quo. The cost of their oil was another matter, however. Neither the Brussels nor the Copenhagen Declaration eased the OPEC oil price escalations. Rather, by 1975, the price of oil imports into Western Europe would rise to $20.00 a barrel. After a brief period of stabilization in the latter 1970s, a second oil crisis developed in 1979, with the overthrow of the shah in Iran and establishment of the Islamic Republic in that country. By then the total cost of oil imports on the world market rose to a surrealistic $65 billion. Henry Kissinger's efforts, meanwhile, to coordinate Western oil policy fell flat. For the European Community it was not the time to be held hostage to American leadership, which was suspect in Arab eyes. Better to follow the French lead, accept the Arab agenda, and exert pressure on Israel to accommodate the "legitimate needs of the Palestinians." So it was, with EC policy reflecting the vicissitudes of the oil market no less than concern for Middle Eastern stability, that Israel's long courtship of Europe was placed in its gravest jeopardy.

THE PALESTINE FACTOR

In April 1974 Georges Pompidou died. He was succeeded as president of France by Valéry Giscard d'Estaing, chairman of the Independent Republican party. Although a non-Gaullist, Giscard remained committed to his predecessor's vision of France as leader of a self-assertive Europe. Would that vision offer leeway for an equitable Middle East settlement? In earlier years Giscard frequently had assured his many Jewish friends of his sympathy for Israel. Upon taking office, moreover, he lifted the embargo on selective quantities of antimissile and antitank equipment for the Jewish state. In 1975 his foreign minister, Jean Sauvagnargues, paid a visit to Israel, where he reaffirmed to Prime Minister Yitzchak Rabin his government's understanding of Israel's need for "safe and recognized" frontiers. That same year, Paris also vigorously condemned the UN General Assembly's resolution equating Zionism with racism.

But these protestations of friendship turned out to be cosmetic. It was under Giscard's leadership that France concentrated upon exploiting the petrodollar-bloated Arab market. Between 1974 and 1978, the value of French weapons exports rose from 4.8 billion to 8.4 billion francs, and the bulk of this equipment was delivered to the Gulf oil states. It was similarly the Giscard government that now took the initiative in emphasizing the Palestine factor as the key to Middle Eastern peace. In October 1974 France supported a United Nations resolution inviting the PLO to share in the General Assembly's scheduled debate on the Palestine issue. The decision led to Arafat's famous pistol-packing appearance before the world body, as well as the ensuing General Assembly decision to allow the PLO observer status. In November 1974 Giscard informed a press conference that "[t]he Palestinians are . . . an entity, a people. . . . [and] the natural aspiration of any people is a homeland." A year later, visiting Tunis in November 1975, the French president affirmed that a *"patrie indépen-*

dante" was a legitimate Palestinian objective. That same month France authorized the PLO to open an information office in Paris. Five months later yet, on the eve of departure for a state visit to Saudi Arabia, Giscard declared that he favored recognition of the PLO as "sole representative" of the Palestinian people. Except for Greece, none of the other EC members had been willing to go that far.

By mid-decade, however, as soaring oil prices brought the Community to its knees, even Israel's most dependable friends—Germany, the Netherlands, Denmark—were prepared to accept France's initiative in adopting a pro-Palestinian stance. Thus, in November 1975, the Nine supported a UN General Assembly resolution advocating a Palestinian homeland, and in ensuing years called repeatedly for acknowledgment of Palestinian "rights." In June 1977, at a gathering of the EC Council of Ministers in London, Giscard arrived personally to make the case for a new policy declaration on the Israel-Arab conflict. The issue was critical, for only a month earlier Menachem Begin had been elected prime minister of Israel, and a more aggressive annexationist campaign was anticipated for the West Bank. Accordingly the EC this time issued a unanimous, unequivocal appeal for the realization of Palestinian "national identity"—a phrase it had not used before—and for "representatives of the Palestinian people" (in effect the PLO) to share in all future negotiations. The Israelis were stunned.

But so, in turn, were the Europeans, only four months later, upon Anwar al-Sadat's dramatic November 1977 visit to Jerusalem. In the aftermath of the diplomatic bombshell, even the French evinced an uncharacteristic forbearance. Cautiously the Nine waited, through the end of 1977, through the spring, summer, and autumn of 1978, as the peace process underwent its tortuous ordeal in bilateral Egyptian-Israeli meetings, then in trilateral discussions with the United States at Camp David. Sadat himself meanwhile requested the Community to exercise restraint, to allow Washington to broker the peace. The Europeans were mystified, therefore, in March 1979, when the Egyptian president consented to a treaty that the Palestinians insisted left them with less than half a loaf. Afterward, as it became increasingly apparent that Egyptian-Israeli negotiations on Palestine were at an impasse, the Europeans broke their silence. In December 1979 France once again defended the "legitimacy of a Palestinian homeland"; while Britain, Italy, and the Netherlands spoke of the Palestinian people's right to a "national identity," and offered to help fund a self-governing enterprise. The Europeans' patience with Washington's mediation clearly had worn thin.

Their concern was intensified by the Arab world's execration of Sadat for his "sellout." It was the oil and the vast purchasing power of the Arab Gulf nations, after all, not of Egypt, that Europe coveted. Moreover, the goodwill of the OPEC governments achieved a renewed importance in 1979, with the establishment of the Khomeini regime in Iran. As the ayatollahs' hatred of the West was translated into interrupted oil supplies and quantum price increases, the Germans, Italians, and Benelux nations were obliged to increase their oil imports from the Gulf Arab states and from Libya and Algeria. By no coincidence, the Europeans also became increasingly outspoken in their criticism of the Egyptian-Israeli treaty's shortcomings, and in support of Palestinian "national identity."

It was thus during the autumn of 1979 that the Community agreed to develop a relationship with the Palestine Liberation Organization. To that end, in November 1979 Giscard invited Yasser Arafat for an official visit to France. The news infuriated Meir Rosenne, Israel's ambassador to Paris. During a television interview he all but exploded: "I refuse to believe that the land of the Declaration of the Rights of Man would invite a terrorist. Would France invite Hitler?" It was inauspicious commentary from a professional diplomat. The next day, Sion de Leusse, director-general of the French foreign ministry, summoned Rosenne for an acrimonious meeting, accusing him of having "outraged" France. But the ambassador would not back down. Thereafter he remained virtually a nonperson in French official circles. At the annual presidential New Year's reception for foreign ambassadors, Giscard d'Estaing ignored him.

The diplomatic chill was an omen of worse to come for Israel. Indeed, it emanated from every European quarter. In February 1980, touring the Gulf states, Britain's Foreign Secretary Lord Peter Carrington affirmed that a "dialogue" with the PLO had become necessary to ensure the Palestinians' "self-determination." Concurrently Naboth Van Dijl, a senior Dutch foreign ministry official, held formal talks with Abd al-Hassan al-Maizer, a member of the PLO Executive Committee. It appeared a matter only of months before Europe redefined its relationship with a Palestinian federation that once had been identified exclusively with guerrilla violence.

The Israelis' anxiety deepened in April 1980, when the Council of Europe, a nonofficial but prestigious collection of European parliamentarians, issued a resolution favoring "mutual recognition" between Israelis and Palestinians. At a meeting in Naples soon afterward, the EC foreign ministers similarly reached consensus that the Camp David process was "fatally flawed." It was time now for Europe to offer its own collective recommendation on the Palestine issue. An ensuing EC conference was scheduled for Venice in June 1980. In advance, fearing a possible disruption of its own Middle Eastern diplomacy, the State Department appealed to the Europeans for a "restrained" statement on Palestine. The request was less than effective.

In its maximalism, the Venice Declaration was a path-breaker for the Community. It stated:

> The Palestinian people . . . must be placed in a position . . . to exercise fully its right to self-determination. . . . The Nine stress the need for Israel to put an end to [its] territorial occupation. . . . [T]he Israeli settlements . . . as well as modifications in population and property in the occupied Arab territories, are illegal under international law. . . . [The Palestine Liberation Organization] . . . will have to be associated with [Arab-Israeli] negotiations.

The appeal was for "self-determination," not merely a homeland; for Israeli territorial withdrawal without reference to UN Security Council Resolution 242 and its stipulation of "safe and secure" boundaries; for inclusion of the PLO in future negotiations, without imposing upon Arafat and his colleagues the obligation to renounce their stated objective of destroying the State of Israel.

The Europeans had overreached themselves. Prime Minister Menachem Begin's outrage could have been anticipated. But this time even Israeli nonrightists expressed shock at the declaration's palpable imbalance. In August 1980 Luxembourg's Foreign Minister Gaston Thorn, then president of the EC Council of Ministers, toured the Middle East in an effort to sell the Venice Declaration's guidelines. Received coldly in Israel, Thorn and his colleagues departed the Jewish state humiliated and empty-handed. They got no further in Cairo. If Begin wanted no part of a European initiative, neither did Sadat. The Egyptian president continued to pin his hopes on Washington. Thus, in November 1980, sensing the way the wind was blowing, Britain's Lord Carrington proposed that the incoming Reagan administration be given its own chance to resolve the Palestine issue. In any case, Israeli elections were scheduled for the following year, and Shimon Peres, the Labor candidate and an advocate of territorial moderation, had urged a hiatus on EC Middle East diplomacy. Unwilling to jeopardize Peres's electoral chances, the Europeans concurred. They had made their gesture, had extended themselves further than ever before in behalf of Arab demands. There was reason to hope that the

Arab governments had taken due notice—and that their oil would continue to flow.

A SOCIALIST BETRAYAL?

Although Israel had been losing ground in the international arena well before the Yom Kippur War, it was manifestly the 1973 conflict and the ensuing Arab oil embargo that compounded the Jewish state's diplomatic vulnerability. Moreover, for Golda Meir, presiding over a Labor cabinet, it was particularly unfathomable that she should have been "betrayed" at the hands of her Socialist comrades in Europe. Indeed, three weeks after the 1973 war, in a telephone call to Chancellor Willy Brandt in Bonn, Mrs. Meir ventilated her dismay that the Continent's Socialist governments had refused to lend their facilities to the American airlift operation:

> Willy . . . I have no demands to make of anyone, but I want to talk to my friends . . . I need to know what possible meaning socialism can have when not a single Socialist country in all of Europe was prepared to come to the aid of the only democratic nation in the Middle East. Is it possible that democracy and fraternity do not apply in our case?

At the Israeli prime minister's request, a special leadership meeting of the Socialist International then was convened in London in January 1974. Everyone came. Mrs. Meir herself was the opening speaker, and, typically, she did not mince words:

> We are all old comrades, long-standing friends. . . . On what grounds did you make your decisions not to let those [American] planes refuel? . . . [I recognize] that we are only one tiny Jewish state and that there are over twenty Arab states with vast territories, endless oil and billions of dollars, but what I want to know . . . is whether these things are decisive factors in Socialist thinking, too?

Not a single person answered her.

Nor, for many years, would satisfaction be forthcoming from any ideological soul mate. With few exceptions the political orientation of European cabinets would remain irrelevant to their perceived national interests. Even in Denmark, whose long tradition of Social Democratic incumbency was matched by genuine public goodwill for Israel, government and media alike had become critical of Israel's ongoing occupation of Arab territory. After joining the European Community in 1973, Denmark felt obliged to accept the EC line, including the 1980 Venice Declaration. Oil possibly was less a factor in the Danes' stance than fear of Palestinian irredentist terrorism, and a politic inclination to adapt to EC collegiality. Yet even in the case of Norway and Sweden, both outside the Community, the Socialist coloration of their governments was irrelevant in determining their Middle East policies. Like Denmark, both nations periodically had contributed troops to United Nations peacekeeping units along Israel's frontiers. In 1971 Prime Minister Meir had embarked on a ten-day "working vacation" through Scandinavia, and in Copenhagen, Oslo, Stockholm, and Helsinki alike she was warmly received by political leaders. Nevertheless, the future of Israel's occupied territories placed a question mark over that North European friendship.

It was Sweden whose attitude was the most problematic. Whatever their country's rather smug diplomatic neutralism, the Swedes' pragmatic role in international affairs by and large was active and responsible. Between 1945 and 1980 they provided 57 billion kronor to Third World nations, and some forty thousand troops for United Nations peacekeeping service in Africa and Asia, including the volatile demilitarized zones along Israel's borders. It had been specifically Swedish participation in the initial, 1948 United Nations mediation effort in Palestine that claimed the first of Sweden's postwar casualties. This was Count Folke Bernadotte, chief of the UN mediation unit, who was assassinated by Jewish terrorists in Jerusalem. Neither then nor later did Israel succeed in tracking down and prosecuting the murderers, and it was uncertain that the Ben-Gurion government, overwhelmed by the pressures of military and economic survival, ever significantly exerted itself to bring the killers to justice.

Stockholm did not accept this lapse with forbearance. In ensuing years it periodically raised with Israel the issue of Bernadotte's murder, and pressed for yet another official apology—which was always dutifully forthcoming. By the 1980s, however, the ritual was functioning as a thinly disguised judgment on Israel's Palestine policy. No government in Europe was harsher in its criticism of the Jewish state than Prime Minister Olaf Palme's in Sweden. During Palme's tenure, between 1982 and 1986, Swedish antipathy to Israeli "oppression" had become so vocal and apparently so indiscriminate that Moshe Yegar, Israel's ambassador to Stockholm, persuaded Jerusalem simply to abandon its political dialogue with the Palme government. Afterward Yegar confined his activities in the Swedish capital to the barest functional amenities.

From Austria, on the other hand, the Israelis had anticipated little diplomatic support from the outset. Early in the postwar period, both of Austria's political factions, the Social Democrats and the People's party (conservative), embraced the fiction that their nation had been a victim, not a collaborator, of Nazi Germany, and consequently bore no responsibility for the indemnification of Austrian Jews. Under this rationale survivors of one of Europe's largest Jewish communities were all but disenfranchised from *Wiedergutmachung*. The Austrians similarly evinced little interest in prosecuting their own Nazi criminals. It was an unsavory record. Nevertheless, when the Allies restored Austrian independence in 1955, Israel's government was among the first to appoint an ambassador to Vienna. The reason was entirely pragmatic. Austria served as a vital transit route for Jews departing Eastern Europe; and once in Vienna, the emigrants could be transshipped to Israel. Indeed, in 1967, when the Communist bloc severed diplomatic relations with the Jewish state, Austria's role as entrepôt between East and West, between the Soviet Union and Israel, became even more indispensable.

Yet it was Austria's unique intermediary status that also exposed the ultimate irrelevance of Socialist "fraternalism," even of putative ethnic *Judenschmerz*, of sensitivity to the plight of fellow Jews. Bruno Kreisky incarnated that paradox. A Viennese Jew, Kreisky had served brief stints in prison in 1934 under the reactionary Dollfuss chancellorship and in 1938 following the Anschluss. Early in 1939 he found refuge in Stockholm, and in 1945 he became Austria's first postwar diplomatic representative in Sweden. Politics, however, not diplomacy, was Kreisky's métier. A veteran Social Democrat, he began his parliamentary career in Austria in 1951. Later, as state secretary between 1953 and 1959, and then as foreign minister until 1966, it was Kreisky who charted Austria's neutralist role in world affairs. With Willy Brandt and Olaf Palme, he was also a powerfully influential figure in the Socialist International. Throughout those years, nevertheless, Kreisky was certain that as a Jew he was precluded from ever becoming head of his party or government. But in the party congress of 1969, and in the national elections of 1970, he suddenly became both. The achievement evidently posed no ideological difficulties for the new chancellor. As an atheist he no longer identified himself with the Jewish community. Neither did Kreisky's version of socialism permit him an accommodation with Zionism. Once in office, he maintained a rigorously "objective" attitude toward the Jewish state.

Yet Kreisky was also a humanitarian. He kept Austria's frontiers open to arriving East European Jews and even provided transit facilities for them. At his orders an unused former baronial residence, Schönau Castle, was turned over to the Jewish Agency as a housing-and-classification center for Soviet Jewish transients. In the early 1970s, as a precautionary move against threatened Arab terrorism, Kreisky authorized increased security measures at Schönau, with some one hundred police assigned there on round-the-clock duty. Indeed, Schönau soon became a kind of extraterritorial Israeli enclave, doubly protected by armed Israeli guards. Austrian police were not allowed inside. Few sovereign governments would have tolerated this arrangement. And none, possibly, would have accepted the use of its territory as a surrogate battleground.

On September 28, 1973, three Palestinian terrorists boarded a Soviet train as it arrived at a railroad station outside Vienna. Kidnapping five Soviet Jewish emigrants and an Austrian customs official, the hijackers then demanded to be flown to Libya or Syria, where the hostages could be exchanged for Palestinian prisoners in Israel. They also demanded that the government halt all further transit of Soviet Jews through Austria. Kreisky immediately called an emergency session of his cabinet. After a four-hour meeting, the chancellor and his colleagues produced a "compromise." The Jewish Agency hostel at Schönau was closed. Soon afterward the terrorists released the hostages, and were themselves then flown out of Vienna to Libya. In response to Israeli protests, Kreisky explained that Austria could not be allowed to become a secondary theater of operations in a Middle Eastern conflict. He also reminded Israel that Austria had allowed thousands of Soviet Jewish émigrés (by then, slightly more than one hundred thousand) to enter the country, and would continue to do so. It was the argument Kreisky used with Israel's Prime Minister Golda Meir, who flew to Vienna in a vain attempt to change his mind (p. 243).

In the ensuing years the chancellor kept his promise of humanitarian aid. Notwithstanding Arab warnings and ultimatums, Austria's frontiers remained continually open to Soviet Jewish emigrants. Periodically, too, when Israel needed intercession with Moscow on behalf of Soviet Jewish "prisoners of Zion," Kreisky could be counted on to undertake that task. In the aftermath of Israel's 1982 invasion of Lebanon, the chancellor's personal emissary, Herbert Amry, embarked on numerous missions to the Middle East in efforts to negotiate the release of Israeli prisoners of war. Within the Socialist International, Shimon Peres maintained equable relations with Kreisky. But so did Yasser Arafat. The chancellor had always evinced a warm sympathy for the Palestinian cause. In Peres's recollection, Kreisky often "waxed poetic" in his admiration of Arafat, and pleaded with the Israelis to recognize and negotiate with the PLO. In 1978, with the Egyptian-Israeli peace process apparently stalled, it was Kreisky, together with ex-chancellor Willy Brandt, who invited Sadat and Peres (then leader of Israel's Labor opposition) to Vienna to explore the possibilities of a Middle East diplomatic breakthrough.

Although Kreisky left office in 1983, his party remained in control of the Austrian government coalition. The new chancellor, Fred Sinowatz, rather less fixated on the Palestine issue, was able to maintain correct relations even with Israel's right-wing Likud government. Yet the "thaw" endured barely three years. In 1986 elections were scheduled for the presidency of Austria. One of the candidates was Kurt Waldheim, the former United Nations secretary-general. By then Waldheim's wartime presence as a Wehrmacht lieutenant in the killing fields of the Balkans had been revealed and extensively publicized by the World Jewish Congress. In voting Waldheim into office, the Austrian people appeared deliberately to be flouting international and specifically Jewish outrage. Israel's Ambassador Michael Elizur was immediately summoned home for "consultations." He did not return. Through the ensuing six years of Waldheim's presidency, Israel was represented in Vienna only by a chargé d'affaires, and even the latter declined to attend any ceremonial affair at which Waldheim was present.

THE SOCIALISM OF GREAT-POWER DIPLOMACY

In Britain's parliamentary elections of February 1974, Edward Heath's Conservative government was defeated and replaced by the Laborites under Harold Wilson. For Israel the return of a trusted friend as British prime minister was a source of cautious hope. During his four and a half years in opposition, Wilson had been a relentless critic of Foreign Secretary Douglas-Home's pro-Arab diplomacy, and had blisteringly excoriated the cabinet for its arms embargo during the Yom Kippur War. Wilson's son, working as a volunteer at Kibbutz Yagur during the conflict, had written home describing the magnitude of Israel's losses. The father was moved. Now, back in power, he would be in a position to repair Labor's former solidarity with the Jewish state.

Indeed, it was soon after his election that Golda Meir paid her "private" visit to London, to address the leaders of the Socialist International. Wilson greeted the Israeli prime minister with an affectionate embrace. The next day, hosting an intimate luncheon for her at 10

Downing Street, Wilson explained that Britain would be independent of Arab oil supplies within five years, once the North Sea fields were in full operation; but for the time being his government would have to move carefully. At best he would seek to block France from leading the European Community into an irretrievably punitive stance on Israel. It was at this luncheon, too, that Mrs. Meir asked Wilson to give special consideration to Israel's trade imbalance with the United Kingdom. Britain was Israel's third largest trading partner, she reminded him, exporting to Israel three times more than it was importing. Additionally, as a new member in the European Community, Britain would be obliged to raise its tariffs on Israeli citrus fruit to the EC level. Would the Labor government not join with such friends as Germany and the Netherlands in negotiating a better trade deal for Israel within the Community? Here Wilson gave full assurances of cooperation. He kept his promise (p. 217).

It was above all on the issue of Palestine that the Wilson government offered Israel its most decisive support. The prime minister would resist French pressure for unilateral Israeli withdrawal. Although in England as elsewhere, the Palestine Liberation Organization evoked much public and media sympathy, both Wilson and Foreign Secretary James Callahan rejected any notion of granting the PLO official status until it abandoned its endorsement of terrorism. In October 1974 Britain was one of the few European nations to oppose Yasser Arafat's appearance before the UN General Assembly. It similarly resisted all EC demands in favor of Palestinian "self-determination." In March 1976, exhausted by the country's mounting economic problems, Wilson stepped down as prime minister, to be replaced by James Callahan. There was no alteration in the government's Middle East policy. Under Callahan in June of the same year, the government hosted the state visit of Israel's President Ephraim Katzir, and did so with much pomp and ceremony. Nevertheless, with Wilson's departure the Israelis lost their best friend in Europe.

They had believed, earlier, that they could depend on another "loyal Socialist." This was Willy Brandt of the Bundesrepublik, whose friendship for Israel had been one of the certitudes of the Jewish state's international position. All the greater the shock, therefore, during the Yom Kippur War, when the chancellor denied the United States use of German airport facilities for its emergency supply effort. In that moment of crisis, Israel's Ambassador Eliashiv Ben-Horin threw diplomacy to the winds and angrily condemned the embargo. The Israeli newspaper *Ma'ariv* described the Bundesrepublik's reaction as a "neutrality which indirectly contributes to genocide." National outrage was compounded when the EC's Brussels Declaration of November 6, alluding to the "legitimate rights of the Palestinians," bore West Germany's imprimatur.

In fact Willy Brandt made no secret of his discomfiture with this adversarial stance. On November 11, 1973, he explained in a radio interview that the Brussels Declaration had not blocked the way to minor territorial adjustments in Israel's favor. Only the day before he had dispatched his party deputy, Heinz Kühn, to Jerusalem to express his, Brandt's, personal "solidarity and sympathy." And for their part, Shimon Peres and even Golda Meir had never doubted the chancellor's basic friendship for Israel and the Jewish people. Yet it did not escape the Israeli leaders that, since 1969, Brandt appeared to be carving out a more "even-handed" Middle East policy as a feature of his *Ostpolitik* (p. 208). Under his leadership, Foreign Minister Walter Scheel was dispatching missions to Arab governments in almost mathematical balance with visitations to the Jewish state. Given Europe's palpable dependence on Arab oil, Bonn's "even-handedness" was likely to continue.

Israeli premonitions soon were borne out. In May 1974, only a month after Golda Meir's resignation as prime minister of Israel, Brandt resigned as chancellor of the Bundesrepublik. A domestic spy scandal had unseated him. He was replaced by his finance minister, Helmut Schmidt. A member of the Social Democratic party's conservative wing, Schmidt regarded it as vital that "objective" economic factors determine Bonn's Middle East policy. The most critical of those factors of course were rising oil prices and the Bundesrepublik's balance-of-payments deficit to the Gulf states. These had to be made good by increased German exports to the Arab nations. Even more than his predecessor, therefore, the new chancellor encouraged ministerial and business visits to the Arab world.

The initiative soon began to pay dividends. German exports to the Arab states rose from DM3.6 billion in 1973 to nearly DM30 billion in 1981. At the same time, Arab governments invested substantial quantities of their oil profits in German industry. The Kuwaiti royal family purchased a 30 percent share of Kohr Stahl AG, one of the Bundesrepublik's biggest steel firms; 10 percent of Metallgesellschaftsverein, a huge metals-and-engineering conglomerate; and 14 percent of Daimler-Benz, Germany's largest vehicle manufacturer. Kuwait and Qatar purchased a 14 percent share of the two giant chemical corporations Höchst and BASF. During a 1980 state visit to the Bundesrepublik, King Khaled of Saudi Arabia announced his intention to award German firms a $920 million contract for a water pipe system in his country, and to give "favorable consideration" to other German bids on desalinization and petrochemical projects.

In cultivating the Arab world, Schmidt manifestly was not seeking a crisis in bilateral relations with Israel. Unlike Giscard d'Estaing in France, he refused to condemn the Egyptian-Israeli peace treaty. He consistently opposed the award of observer status to the PLO in the United Nations "as long as [the PLO] does not agree to Israel's right to exist within secure and recognized boundaries, and does not renounce acts of force and terror." Within the European Community, German spokesmen defined their special role as the formulation of an "independent European position" between those of the Americans and of the Israelis. If the Bundesrepublik shared in the EC's gravitation toward a pro-Arab stance, its position never was as extreme as France's.

A confrontation with Israel was inevitable, however. Pro-Israel sentiment in the Bundesrepublik had ceased to be an inhibiting factor. As late as October 1973, during the Yom Kippur War, German opinion surveys had indicated 57 percent support for Israel over the Arabs. By 1978, a year into Menachem Begin's prime ministry, the percentage favoring Israel had dropped to 24 percent. Under Schmidt, then, Bonn's policy statements on the Middle East became increasingly matter-of-fact. References to the Holocaust became rarer. In June of 1979, interviewed by an Israeli journalist, the chancellor expressed hope that German-Israeli relations could be based on something more solid than a "bad German conscience about Hitler." The following August, with Schmidt's approval—and possibly also with that of President Jimmy Carter in Washington—a German representative met with Yasser Arafat in Beirut. The German was Jürgen Möllmann, foreign affairs spokesman for the Free Democrats, partners in Bonn's government coalition. The two men discussed an "informal document" that envisaged direct negotiations between Israel and the PLO, a return by Israel to its pre-1967 borders, and a Palestinian home in a "state organization." When the conversation leaked, an explosion of Israeli outrage prompted Bonn to disavow the conversation.

Yet German Foreign Minister Genscher launched into his own tour of the Arab Middle East during the summer of 1979, and in a series of Arab capitals he unambiguously stressed the Palestinians' right to full self-determination. Discreet queries from Jerusalem evoked no retractions. Two months later Israel's Foreign Minister Moshe Dayan met with Genscher in Bonn, seeking to resuscitate Germany's earlier role as friend and patron. Genscher assured Dayan that the Bundesrepublik would not recognize the PLO or allow it to open an office in the German capital. But neither would the Bundesrepublik abandon its support for Palestinian self-determination. How could it, asked Genscher, when Bonn was advocating similar rights for East Germany?

The German foreign minister might have added that Bonn also was in search of even more pragmatic advantages in the Middle East. While on a visit to Saudi Arabia in 1980, Chancellor Schmidt promised to review his government's ban on the sale of German weapons to "areas of tension." The statement betokened a policy shift of far-reaching implications. Since 1965, as justification for terminating its secret military shipments to Israel, Bonn had imposed seemingly ironclad restrictions on German weapons sales abroad (pp. 146–7). But in ensuing years the Arab arms market, aflush with petrodollars, burgeoned as the West's single most dramatic export opportunity. French weapons manufacturers already were rushing to stake out a proprietary claim to this bonanza. By the latter 1970s, as a result, the Schmidt government tended increasingly to finesse the earlier legal constraints.

At first, Bonn continued to disallow the export of such high-visibility hardware as tanks or aircraft. Yet it turned a blind eye as German arms manufacturers began to ship laser range finders to Syria, rocket- and bomb-manufacturing equipment to Algeria, and entire naval weapons systems, including submarines, to Iran, Turkey, Bahrain, and Tunisia. Eventually, through the device of joint production with Italy and France, the Bundesrepublik managed to evade its export restrictions altogether and deliver antitank missiles and jet training planes to Egypt, Morocco, and Qatar. And at last, in 1980, during the first of his two visits to Riyadh, Chancellor Schmidt suggested that Bonn might now respond favorably to a Saudi request for tanks, inasmuch as Saudi Arabia was not a "confrontation state" in the Arab-Israel conflict. Immediately, then, the Saudis placed an order for three thousand late-model Leopard tanks, as well as one thousand self-propelled antiaircraft guns.

It was an unfortunate historical concatenation that the Schmidt chancellorship overlapped the Begin prime ministry. In his own way, Schmidt was as brusque and peremptory as Begin. Witnessing the Israeli leader's aggressive settlements policy and his evident indifference to treaty commitments on Palestinian autonomy, the German chancellor confided to his cabinet that Begin was "a danger to peace." In Schmidt's view, "Israel is on a very dangerous path.... If Israel goes on with its present political course, it will be difficult to remain a friend." These evaluations leaked to the press. Beyond their resonance in Israel, they also had the effect of focusing world attention on the impending tank sale to the Saudis. Editorial comment in the United States was not favorable. In Germany, too, important elements within the Social Democratic party expressed reservations. Eventually, in April 1981, Schmidt felt obliged to inform Riyadh that the sale was not feasible "for the present" but would be "reconsidered later."

At the same time, in his chagrin, the chancellor could not refrain from asserting publicly that "one must recognize also the moral claim of the Palestinian people to self-determination . . . and to me this includes their right to organize themselves as a state." The observation was too much for Begin. The Israeli prime minister then loosed an equally public but even more violent expostulation: "[Schmidt] doesn't care if Israel goes under. He saw this almost happen to our people in Europe not so long ago. He served in the armies that encircled the cities, until the work was finished by the [SS] *Einsatzgruppen*." The statement outraged virtually every echelon of the German people. This time, opting for restraint, Schmidt did not comment. Nevertheless, German-Israeli diplomatic relations by then plainly had fallen to their lowest ebb since the 1963 crisis of German rocket scientists in Egypt.

ISRAEL'S GREAT SOCIALIST HOPE

Possibly the deterioration of Israeli hopes for the Bundesrepublik was at least partially balanced by a revival of expectations from France. It was also in 1981, in France's presidential elections of that year, that Valéry Giscard d'Estaing was defeated in the second round of voting by a newly united Socialist party. Then it was that François Mitterrand, for twenty years a perennial as candidate of the French left, at long last achieved his nation's highest office. Son of a railway stationmaster, Mitterrand as a young man had served briefly in the French army during World War II. Taken prisoner by the Germans, he apparently managed to escape. Information on his subsequent wartime career remains skeletal, but recent biographical research suggests that he may have been an official of the Vichy regime. If so, evidence of his youthful collaboration mysteriously disappeared in the postwar years. Indeed, Mitterrand resurfaced as minister of veterans' affairs in the short-lived Ramadier cabinet of 1947. As parliamentary leader afterward of a left-of-center non-Socialist faction, he was in and out of other coalition governments, and did not identify himself with mainstream socialism until the accession of de Gaulle in 1958. In ensuing years, however, rising to leadership of the Socialist party, Mitterrand attracted enough middle-class support to make an impressive run for the presidency in 1974, and finally to triumph in May 1981.

In his domestic agenda Mitterrand as president subsequently produced a mixed record of audacious ideological initiative and cautious tactical retrenchment. It was rather in the arena of international affairs that he kept virtually all his campaign promises. For twenty-three years the government had been committed to a revival of French *grandeur* on the world scene. Mitterrand's objective was very different: It was to a European partnership of shared liberal values, to a more flexible, cooperative relationship with the United States, and not least to the security of a tiny Middle Eastern nation whose raison d'être was asylum for refugees. During his years of political apprenticeship, Mitterrand had developed warm friendships with Jews, including the Socialist leaders Pierre Mendès-France and Jacques Attali. Indeed, Mitterrand's knowledge of Jewish history often exceeded theirs. Endlessly sensitive to Jewish concerns, he spoke out on behalf of Soviet Jewry and interceded in Damascus on behalf of Syrian Jews and in Cairo on behalf of Egyptian-Israeli peace. Within the Socialist International, Mitterrand had come to know and respect Golda Meir, Yigal Allon, and Shimon Peres. He became an especially devoted friend of Peres, with whom he shared political and personal confidences until the end of Mitterrand's life. In 1978, on Israel's thirtieth birthday, he and Peres marched side by side through the streets of Paris as thousands of French Jews cheered.

A majority of those Jews by then were of North African origin. In a French Jewish population of 600,000, fully 350,000 had arrived as postwar immigrants from Algeria, Morocco, Tunisia, and the Middle East. Intensely ethnocentric, they reinvigorated the somewhat pallid cultism of the older European Jewish establishment. As a profoundly Zionist community, too, they reacted in scalded bitterness to the pro-Arab foreign policies of de Gaulle, Pompidou, and Giscard d'Estaing. Mitterrand vigorously exploited their outrage, appearing at one pro-Israel rally after another. He visited Israel twice during the 1970s, and his son worked briefly as a volunteer in an Israeli kibbutz. By 1981 Mitterrand had the bulk of French Jewry in his camp; for them he was "Comrade François." In that year's national election their voting bloc was decisive in the victory of some forty Socialist deputies. The Israelis were thrilled. Prime Minister Begin rushed off a congratulatory message, praising Mitterrand for evoking "the heroism of Jewish combatants in the Resistance," and inviting him to visit Israel, where "you will be received with all the honor and warm enthusiasm due . . .

to a friend who has never turned his back on Israel and who is continually preoccupied with its security and welfare." Mitterrand responded in the same spirit, promising that his first overseas visit would indeed be Israel.

On assuming office the president moved swiftly to distance himself from his predecessors' approach to the Jewish state. Within the domestic sphere, he canceled the "Barre decree," the 1977 ruling of former Prime Minister Raymond Barre that had peremptorily weakened France's antiboycott law. Nevertheless, Mitterrand was too shrewd to jettison the seven years of good relations Giscard had developed with the Arab world. He did not disguise his concern for the rights of the Palestinian people. "I am a friend of Israel and will do nothing that will threaten its existence," he affirmed, "but I do not believe it realistic to ignore the Palestinian problem." During his election campaign Mitterrand had forthrightly declared his support of a Palestinian homeland, and subsequently he remained firm on this point. His foreign minister, Claude Cheysson, even spoke in terms of "state-type structures" for the Palestinians. Yet, far less equivocally than their predecessors, Mitterrand and Cheysson linked their concern for Palestinian rights with unqualified support of the Egyptian-Israeli treaty, and of Israel's right to security within safe and recognized borders. Mitterrand made clear, too, his disapproval of the 1980 Venice Declaration, and of the European Community's diplomatic initiatives in the Middle East altogether. Favoring a policy of "incremental steps," he supported direct Israeli-Arab negotiations, and voiced no objection to Washington's ongoing intermediary role in the peace process.

Only days after taking office, ironically, the French president encountered a crisis that challenged the promising new ambience in French-Israeli relations. At stake was the preservation of Israel's nuclear supremacy within the Middle East. For twenty years, since construction of the Dimona reactor, the little nation had regarded its atomic edge as the ultimate deterrent against its enemies. In 1975, however, Iraq's Saddam Hussein regime began laying its own plans for the Osiraq Project, construction of a nuclear reactor outside Baghdad. Like Israel in the 1950s, Iraq was able to rely on cooperation with France. The Giscard d'Estaing government did not regard the provision of two nuclear reactors as too high a price for access to Iraqi oil supplies, and to the vast Iraqi market for industrial and military equipment. News of the Franco-Iraqi nuclear deal reached Washington early in 1976. Concerned, the Ford administration sought to intercede with Giscard. The reply from Paris was glacial:

"We cannot let our American and European allies continue their offensive against our nuclear industry," it stated. Israel's appeals were spurned even more decisively.

It was the Begin cabinet that decided to adopt more vigorous measures on its own. In April 1979 Mossad agents broke into a French warehouse near Toulon and blew up the casings that had been stored there for imminent shipment of uranium fuel to Iraq. Although costly for Saddam Hussein, the setback was not irretrievable. The French produced new casings in the autumn and delivered the first installments of enriched uranium in June 1980. With the Osiraq reactor scheduled to become operational early in 1981, the Iraqis could be expected to move directly into the production of plutonium. Accordingly, in the late summer of 1980, Israel's Foreign Minister Yitzchak Shamir presented his case directly in Paris, where Giscard d'Estaing received him at the Élysée Palace. Courteously the president heard Shamir out. "Please believe me," he assured his guest, "if ever we have reason to suspect Iraq of trying to produce nuclear weapons, we will see to it that this does not happen." When Shamir returned for a second visit in December, Giscard repeated the assurance, adding that "nothing untoward has been seen." By then diplomatic intercession with France had become an exercise in futility. As Menachem Begin saw it, more drastic steps were now required. If the Toulon operation had produced only limited effect, there remained only the alternative of destroying the reactor itself.

In December 1980 the prime minister explored this alternative with his cabinet members. Their reaction was hesitant. A bombardment of the reactor might provoke international repercussions, they feared, possibly even diplomatic quarantine. When Begin then discussed the issue with Shimon Peres, the Labor party leader also expressed reservations. But several weeks later, at a Paris gathering of the Socialist International, Peres raised the question of the nuclear reactor with his friend Mitterrand, who was then preparing for the French presidential election. Peres explained that the Giscard government already had provided the first of two scheduled deliveries of enriched uranium for the Iraqi reactor. Mitterrand interrupted. "If I become president," he said firmly, "France will not make the second delivery." Peres subsequently reported the conversation to Begin. The Israeli prime minister reserved his judgment; but several months afterward, Peres learned that the bombing would proceed, and that it would take place in late May 1981. Mitterrand by then had been elected president of France, and the bombing was scheduled for the very day he was to be sworn into office. With much emotion, Peres implored Begin at least to postpone the bombing for a fortnight. The prime minister agreed. It would be his single concession.

Upon assuming office, Mitterrand instructed the foreign ministry to produce a fail-safe plan for limiting the Osiraq reactor exclusively to peaceful purposes. Foreign Minister Cheysson turned the project over to a ministerial task force. After ten days of intensive effort, the committee produced a formula. It envisaged a "spacing out" of uranium deliveries to ensure that each shipment of bomb-grade material would be promptly irradiated—in effect consumed—by the reactor; and a limitation of all subsequent French deliveries to "caramel-2," a less "transformable" uranium. Yet before Mitterrand or even Cheysson had an opportunity to review the plan, the Israelis resolved the issue on their own. Their famous air strike of June 7, 1981, proved devastatingly effective. Indeed, its accuracy was ensured by a French technician working at Osiraq, Damien Chassepied, who had been recruited by Israel's Mossad. It was the signal issued from his transmitter, hidden in a briefcase, that guided the Israeli fighter-bombers to their target. Ironically, Chassepied had not distanced himself sufficiently from the reactor, and he became the only human casualty of the bombing raid.

The attack's diplomatic repercussions were far-reaching, as Peres and others had warned. In Washington, President Reagan foreclosed Israeli access to United States satellite photographs of the Middle East. A scheduled shipment of American F-16 jets to Israel was halted. Begin's effort to block the sale of AWACS—early warning aircraft—to Saudi Arabia was firmly rebuffed by Reagan, with the support of the United States Senate. In France, however, the repercussions were less diplomatic than personal. An aggrieved Mitterrand sent back word to Jerusalem that the Israelis might have placed greater confidence in his promise to them. Yet it was testimony to the French president's goodwill that he refrained from repeating Cheysson's public censure, which had characterized the bombing as a "violation of law," and an "unacceptable act." Whatever his distaste for Begin's aggressive territorialism, Mitterrand was intent on keeping the relationship between the two governments viable. The French leader simply decided to make his first overseas trip as president not to Israel but to Saudi Arabia, and subsequently to Algeria. In his meetings with Moslem leaders, too, Mitterrand urged forbearance, expressing hope that the Egyptian-Israeli negotiations on Palestinian autonomy might yet bear fruit. He then rescheduled his visit to Israel for January 1982.

On December 14, 1981, Prime Minister Begin surprised and outmaneuvered his political opposition by steamrolling a bill through the

Knesset that in effect annexed the Golan Heights to Israel. Europe and the United States were angered. At this point, Mitterrand felt obliged to join other leaders of the European Community in public condemnation. "Israel must understand," he warned, "that its friends . . . will not indifferently tolerate being presented with forceful faits accomplis." Even then, however, the president declined to share in the Community's appeal for an emergency meeting of the UN Security Council. Once more, he simply postponed his trip to Israel, and at the same time emphasized his government's equivalent commitment to Palestinian self-government. In discussions with Israel's Ambassador Meir Rosenne, Foreign Minister Cheysson repeatedly emphasized the need to enlarge the "dialogue" between Israel and the Palestinians.

It was the argument Mitterrand stressed as well on March 3, 1982, when finally he arrived in Israel for his twice-postponed official visit. The first French president ever to come to the Jewish state, he was greeted with an enthusiasm bordering on rapture. Over the next three days, conferring with Begin and other political leaders and then addressing the Knesset, Mitterrand tactfully but forthrightly interwove his professions of friendship with his expressed hope that "the Palestinians [may] decide their fate themselves . . . in a dialogue that accepts the right of each party to live in a state." Begin and his colleagues tolerated their guest's admonitions with equanimity. After all, he had not invoked the imprimatur of the European Community, and assuredly not the spirit of the Venice Declaration. Instead, he had rehabilitated the concept of bilateral Arab-Israel discussions based on Camp David and the Egyptian-Israeli treaty. "Venice est dépassé," Foreign Minister Cheysson affirmed. If the French-Israeli relationship did not yet quite approach the *entente* of the 1950s, it apparently revived something of that earlier period's mutual understanding and goodwill.

THE BACK OF A EUROPEAN HAND

On June 6, Menachem Begin launched "Operation Peace for the Galilee," a full-scale military invasion of southern Lebanon. The assault had been in preparation for months, and its intent was nothing less than the destruction of the PLO's extensive infrastructure of guerrilla bases along Israel's northern borders, and ultimately eradication of the PLO as a political force throughout the Palestine West Bank. In ensuing weeks, however, with PLO guerrillas retreating to "safe" positions in the Moslem sector of West Beirut, the Israeli invasion evolved into a congested siege, replete with thunderous air bombardments that devastated civilian and military enclaves alike, inflicting many hundreds of casualties. Not until August 12 did a cease-fire come into effect. Brokered by the United States, it permitted Yasser Arafat to move his guerrillas and his headquarters out of Beirut, and transfer them to other Arab lands.

Civil war between Moslems and Christians was an old story in Lebanon. During the 1970s, fighting between the two communities had devoured not hundreds but thousands of lives. Nevertheless, for Europeans, the intramural carnage had evoked little more than a fatigued sense of déjà vu. But this time the European reaction was quite different. It was the Jews, perennial victims of European persecution and claimants on the European conscience, who were inflicting havoc on others. Western newspaper and television reportage gave sharply biased accounts of the war, often accepting PLO figures on civilian dead and wounded. Even in countries as traditionally pro-Israel as Norway and the Netherlands, journalists drew portentous analogies between the "genocide" of Beirut and the genocide of Warsaw in World War II. On June 9 the European Community denounced the invasion as a "flagrant violation of international law and of the most basic humanitarian principles."

In the Bundesrepublik, the upsurge of anti-Israel and even anti-semitic sentiment became quite palpable. In February 1983, a leading German poll hinted at a sharp decline in German-Israeli relations, as 52 percent of the respondents agreed that "[w]e should not place our good relations with Israel above all else. The Arab countries are important for our oil needs. Therefore, we should not become enemies of these countries on Israel's account." Only 18 percent favored the alternative choice: "It is still important today for the Bundesrepublik to attend to its especially friendly relations with Israel." Bonn's official reaction was somewhat more restrained. Beyond its support of the EC declaration, the Helmut Schmidt government declined to endorse proposals for UN Security Council condemnations. At a Council of Ministers gathering in Brussels on June 17, when Greece's Prime Minister Papandreou characterized Israel's invasion as "Nazi" and "Fascist," it was Schmidt who protested that such terms should be banned from Community discussions.

In some degree, the show of "even-handedness" was paralleled in Britain, where Middle East policy no longer was determined either by Harold Wilson or by his successor, James Callahan. In 1979 new elections had returned the Conservatives to office, this time under a formidable, business-oriented leader, Margaret Thatcher. Daughter of a grocer, Mrs. Thatcher had known many Jews in her middle-class Finchley (north London) neighborhood, and had developed a warm respect for their family values and work ethic. Her personal assistant was a nephew of the Jewish multimillionaire Sir Isaac Wolfson, and her intellectual guru, the veteran Conservative cabinet member Sir Keith Joseph, was also a Jew. In 1974, as minister of education in the Heath cabinet, Mrs. Thatcher had visited Israel. Years later, as prime minister, she would pay two additional goodwill visits to Israel, in 1985 and again 1986, although essentially as gestures of support for the moderate leadership of Shimon Peres.

But despite Mrs. Thatcher's bedrock sympathy for the Jewish state, neither she nor her foreign secretary, Lord Carrington, could acquiesce silently in Israel's aggressive settlements program in the West Bank. Nor was trust between the two governments enhanced by recollections of Menachem Begin's earlier career as an anti-British terrorist. The late 1970s and early 1980s also were years when wealthy Arabs were becoming major players in the British economy. The largest institutional investor in London real estate was the Kuwait Investment Office, even as Arab money was becoming the single largest source of British urban funding altogether. If not a decisive influence on British foreign policy, the torrent of Arab capital pouring into the nation's financial and banking systems was impossible to ignore.

In 1980, therefore, Foreign Secretary Carrington played an active role in formulating the EC's Venice Declaration, and later in expressing sharp criticism of the unification-of-Jerusalem law and the ensuing Golan annexation. During the 1982 Lebanon invasion Sir John Thomson, Britain's ambassador to the UN Security Council, harshly criticized Israel for "taking the law into its own hands in someone else's territory." It was then too that London reimposed its 1973 arms embargo against Israel. In ensuing years Mrs. Thatcher, Carrington, and later Carrington's successor, Geoffrey Howe, pressed Israel's Likud government to accept the legitimacy of Palestinian self-determination. Although London thus far had conducted only lower-level meetings with PLO representatives, the portents for Israel were ominous.

But so, even more, was the palpable shift in François Mitterrand's threshold of toleration. Menachem Begin had launched his invasion of Lebanon only three months after the French president's state visit. As the Israeli siege of Beirut intensified, Mitterrand became visibly confused and depressed. He still rejected Greece's appeals for sanctions against the Jewish state, and spoke only in terms of France's "deep reprobation." But on June 15, 1982, he firmly rebuffed Israel's Foreign Minister Shamir, who had flown to Paris in quest of the president's understanding. Nine days later, entreating the European Community to request an immediate withdrawal of Israeli troops from Lebanon, Mitterrand went so far as to compare Israel's "smashup" offensive through Lebanon with the Nazi wartime destruction of the French village of Ouradour (an analogy that offended Israelis of all political affiliations).

Henceforth, in demanding a Palestinian solution to the ongoing Middle Eastern crisis, Mitterrand dropped virtually all his earlier qualifications. On July 28, 1982, France's representative at the UN Security Council coupled a draft appeal for Israeli withdrawal with a proposal for accelerated Palestinian autonomy. The formula still was less than extreme. It advocated a Camp David–style process intended first to "normalize" relations between Israel and the Palestinians, and only later to nurture the Palestinians to possible sovereignty. In fact it was the approach favored by Shimon Peres and Israel's Labor leadership, and by a number of moderate Arabs. Mitterrand's willingness now to press the issue constituted statesmanship of the highest order and in some measure even restored France's leadership in the European Community.

It was not so regarded by the Begin government, of course, or by Jewish irredentists elsewhere. But the Israelis at least were grateful that, in September 1982, Mitterrand had contributed three hundred French troops to the multilateral buffer force assigned to monitor the PLO guerrilla evacuation from southern Lebanon. A year later, in September 1983, Ovadia Sofer, Israel's newly appointed ambassador to Paris, almost immediately established a cordial relationship with Foreign Minister Cheysson. And all the while Peres and Mitterrand remained the warmest of comrades. Indeed, the president was overjoyed at Peres's accession as Israel's prime minister in 1984, and during Peres's two-year incumbency he muted his own views on Palestine to allow his old friend the widest diplomatic latitude. Thus, in 1985 France abstained in the UN Security Council vote against Israel's ongoing occupation of the southern Lebanon "security zone." In 1986, at Mitterrand's request, King Hassan II of Morocco invited Peres to Rabat to explore Arab-Israeli peace opportunities. In 1988, when President Chaim Herzog paid a state visit to France, Mitterrand tendered his guest a reception of such magnificence that it touched the hearts of Israelis and French Jews alike. In no sense had Mitterrand revived the intense, pro-Israel solicitude of his own first months as president. But the connection had recovered at least a certain measure of its earlier reciprocal candor and forbearance.

REALPOLITIK IN THE VATICAN

From June 27, 1967 on, the issue of Jerusalem, initially resolved by de facto Israeli-Hashemite partition in 1948, was foreclosed even more decisively by the Knesset's annexation of the captured Arab sector of the city. The move infuriated the Moslem world, but so did Israel's conquest of Palestine altogether. No Israeli was quivering in terror of Arab retribution, or given pause over the next four years by successive United Nations resolutions of condemnation. Still less, then, was the Israeli government impressed by Pope Paul VI's renewed spate of appeals for the internationalization of Jerusalem. It held firm.

Rather sooner than in the pre-1967 era, therefore, the Vatican this time felt obliged to accept the military and political realities of Israel's strength and evident permanence. In July 1967 Prime Minister Eshkol held a series of cordial meetings in Jerusalem with Monsignor Angelo Felici, Vatican undersecretary of state for "extraordinary affairs." The discussions in turn laid the groundwork for a special visit to the pope by Ya'akov Herzog, director-general of Israel's Prime Minister's Office. Herzog brought with him Eshkol's personal guarantee of security for the Christian holy places, of free and unqualified access to Christian shrines. The ensuing months bore out the prime minister's commitment. Remaining under the exclusive supervision of their own clerics, the holy places continued to be accorded the fullest protection and security. At last, in December 1968, Paul VI moderated his position and spoke of his wish for an "internationally guaranteed agreement on the question of Jerusalem and the Holy Places." In contrast to the language of earlier years, the reference now was only to "agreement," no longer to a "special international regime."

Yet, whatever its gradual accommodation to Jewish rule in Jerusalem, the Vatican watched in mounting concern as Israel set about confiscating public land and constructing large Jewish housing projects in and around the eastern, Arab sector of the city. By the early 1970s *L'Osservatore Romano* was appealing editorially for "an international body that would truly guarantee the particular character of Jerusalem and the rights of its minority communities." In March 1974 Paul VI issued an apostolic censure, *Nobis in Animo*, of extrajudicial confiscations that, "far from constituting a fair and acceptable solution that takes account of everyone's rights, can only make such an achievement more difficult." The Vatican persisted on this issue. Clearly its preoccupation was no longer with shrines but with people.

The people Rome had in mind were the Arabs of the Holy Land. In its 1967 victory Israel had become de facto ruler of over 540,000 former Palestinian refugees. Thereafter nearly half the Palestinians in the Middle East would live under Israeli control, and the Vatican, too, now had to take acute cognizance of this political transformation. As early as December 1968, addressing the question of the Palestinians, Paul VI in his Christmas Eve sermon expressed solicitude for their "dignity, their rights, and their legitimate aspirations," and in ensuing Christmas Eve messages the pontiff harked back repeatedly to that concern. Invariably Rome was careful to deplore guerrilla atrocities, to condemn such episodes as the Lod Airport and Munich Olympics massacres. Yet, in the post-1967 years, the Vatican adverted again and again to the fundamental source of the violence—the desperate circumstances of the Palestinian refugees. Several factors influenced this new preoccupation. One was humanitarian, a genuine compassion for the fate of tens of thousands of uprooted Palestinian families. A second factor was political, awareness of the destabilizing threat to the Middle East of a large, embittered Palestinian refugee populaton that had become even more vastly augmented by Israel's recent conquest of the West Bank and Gaza.

Of still greater importance, however, was the Vatican's concern specifically for Palestine's Christian population. It was this element that now was threatened by the essentially Moslem constituencies of Fatah and of other PLO guerrilla factions. While directed principally at Israel, PLO irredentism also spilled over to the better-educated and more affluent Arab Christians in Palestine. The largest number of these people lived in Jerusalem and nearby Bethlehem, and it was their communities, fearful of both Israeli rule and Moslem radical extremism—which in turn was fostered by the clumsiness of Israeli rule—that produced most of the Palestinian émigrés. By 1973 fully 100,000 Christians had departed the Holy Land, a third of Palestine's Christian population. It was not merely Jews, therefore, who were the "beneficiaries" of their departure, but Moslems; and, in consequence, the Church's fragile demographic base in the Holy Land was steadily eroding. So it was, in its Middle East diplomacy, that Rome would devote its principal efforts no longer to a theologically based opposition to Israeli statehood, or to a feckless quest for a *corpus separatum* in Jerusalem, but to the human plight and "legitimate aspirations" of the Palestinian people.

At the same time, given the Six-Day War's dramatic evidence of Israel's staying power, the earlier modus vivendi between the papacy and the Jewish state continued to develop. In Jerusalem the apostolic delegate remained in frequent contact with Israel's ministry of religions. In Rome, Israel's ambassadors to Italy often were received by the Vatican. During the 1970s those ambassadors were Amiel Nejjar and then Moshe Sasson, both experienced Sephardi experts on Mediterranean affairs. Swiftly mastering the labyrinth of Vatican bureaucracy, they dealt for the most part with the Congregation for Non-Christian Communities. Through this office, in turn, arrangements periodically were made for receiving other Israeli dignitaries, including Foreign Ministers Eban, Dayan, and Shamir, on "private" visits.

In January 1973, too, Prime Minister Golda Meir, in Europe for a meeting of the Socialist International, was invited to a papal audience. The experience this time was sobering. Paul VI began the interview by inquiring how it was that the Jews, who of all peoples should have displayed mercy toward others, now behaved so harshly to the non-Jews under their rule. Mrs. Meir was not the person to cloak her response in diplomatic banalities. She recalled the conversation later:

> Your Holiness . . . [l]et me assure you that my people know all about real "harshness" and also that we learned all about real mercy when we were being led to the gas chambers of the Nazis. . . . Then I went on to tell him, very respectfully but very firmly . . . that now that we had a state of our own, we were through with being "at the mercy" of others.

The conversation subsequently became more relaxed. In favor of a "continuing dialogue" between Israel and the Vatican, Paul expressed appreciation for the care Israel had taken of the Christian holy places. Mrs. Meir acknowledged his thanks, but emphasized that Jerusalem would remain the capital of Israel. The audience ended with mutual expressions of regard.

Yet its immediate aftermath disclosed the gulf still remaining between Israel and the Church. Within the hour the papal spokesman, Professor Federico Alessandrini, issued a press statement that was obviously intended to appease the Arab world. The papal audience had not been granted "as a gesture of preference or exclusive treatment," Alessandrini noted. "The pope accepted the request of Mrs. Meir because he considers it his duty not to let slip any opportunity to act . . . in defense of all religious interests, particularly of the weakest and most defenseless, and most of all the Palestinian refugees." Apprised of this statement, the prime minister angrily instructed Ambassador Najjar to protest to the Vatican in her name. "I didn't mince words, either," Mrs. Meir wrote later. "I hadn't broken into the Vatican, and I told that to the [Italian] journalists at [an afternoon] press conference." Embarrassed by Alessandrini's heavyhandedness, the pope then dispatched a gift to Mrs. Meir, a sculptured silver dove and a catalogue of Hebrew publications in the Vatican Library.

"Misunderstandings" continued throughout the decade. On February 5, 1976, at the close of a four-day "Seminar on Islamic-Catholic Dialogue," held in Tripoli, Libya, the assembled Christian and Moslem clerics issued a joint communiqué that threatened to reopen old wounds. It endorsed the recent, November 1975, UN General Assembly resolution equating Zionism with racism, affirmed "the national rights of the Palestinian people and their right to return to their lands," and emphasized "the Arab character of the city of Jerusalem." There could be no doubt of Vatican approbation, for the communiqué was prominently reported that same February 5 in *L'Osservatore Romano*.

Israeli reaction was instantaneous. At 2:00 a.m. on February 6, Ambassador Moshe Sasson was awakened in Rome by a phone call from Jerusalem. It was from Yigal Allon, foreign minister in the Rabin government. With cold fury Allon instructed Sasson to demand an immediate meeting with Monsignor Augustino Casaroli, the Vatican assistant secretary of state for Middle Eastern affairs. Casaroli was to be informed that, if the Libyan communiqué was not repudiated "within forty-eight hours," the government of Israel would declare publicly that it regarded the statement as the Church's "declaration of war on the Jewish people." Allowing five hours to go by, the ambassador then put in an early-morning call to Casaroli at the latter's Vatican apartment and requested an interview forthwith, before "normal" office hours. Shortly afterward the ambassador arrived to deliver Allon's ultimatum. At first Casaroli sought to equivocate, to "reinterpret" the Libyan declaration. "Within forty-eight hours, Your Eminence," repeated Sasson firmly, "and in the same prominent place in *L'Osservatore Romano*." The shaken Casaroli then concurred. The next morning a Vatican statement of repudiation was duly featured on the newspaper's front page.

The papacy's tactical retreat signified no fundamental change in its campaign in behalf of the Palestinian refugees. During his fifteen-year incumbency, Paul VI advocated their cause with increasing deliberation and urgency, appealing repeatedly for their "legitimate rights." More than any of his predecessors, in fact, Paul VI came to be known as the "pope of the Palestinians." Yet, at the same time, the Vatican was edging away from its historic rejection of Zionist statehood. Its refusal to establish diplomatic relations with Israel became increasingly a conditional refusal. With all the Church's interests in the Holy Land under Israeli rule, it was evident that recognition of the Jewish state would become increasingly "negotiable." It was equally apparent that much would depend upon the occupant of the papal throne. And then, in August 1978, Paul VI died.

Following an incumbency of only a few weeks, Paul's successor, John Paul I, died unexpectedly. It was the latter's successor, in turn, Karol Wojtyla, who assumed office as John Paul II. Wojtyla, a Pole, became the first non-Italian pontiff in centuries, and the first among recent popes who had not served his apprenticeship in the Vatican diplomatic service. The fact would be relevant in Wojtyla's attitude toward the Palestinians, which was that of a novice. But if the new pope was unfamiliar with Arabs, he possessed extensive knowledge of Jews, and specifically of East European Jews. During the war Wojtyla had served in the Polish underground, where he had sought to save Jewish lives. For many years afterward he had been associated with Zanak, a Cracow-based group of Roman Catholic intellectuals. In reaction to Poland's notorious antisemitism, Zanak had always been unreservedly pro-Jewish. It had also been pro-Zionist, understanding well that Zionism would become a useful antidote to communism among East European Jewry.

As John Paul II, therefore, Wojtyla evinced an uncharacteristic papal restraint on the Arab-Israeli conflict. In March 1979, declaring his support of the impending Egyptian-Israeli peace treaty, the pope alluded only to his goodwill for all "populations" in the region. Shortly afterward he elevated Augustino Casaroli to the post of secretary of state. Casaroli in turn entrusted Middle Eastern affairs to Monsignor Achille Silvestrini, a career diplomat who lately had developed serious reservations about Third World liberation movements. It was plain by then that the Vatican was formulating a new approach to the Middle East. Thus, in April 1979, John Paul granted a long private audience to David Kimche, director-general of Israel's foreign ministry, and agreed "to promote dialogue and more extensive contacts between the Holy See and Israel." With growing frequency, Israel's ambassadors to Italy were received in papal audience.

So were representatives of the World Jewish Congress and of other international Jewish organizations. Intermittently the Vatican continued to issue dutiful allusions to the plight of the Palestinians, but thus far not to their option of self-determination, or even to their "legitimate rights."

Over the turn of the decade, however, alarmed by the depletion of the Holy Land's Christian communities, John Paul at last began appealing in his speeches for a "just settlement of the Palestine question." And in July 1980 the good-natured pontiff felt impelled to abandon his stance of even-handedness. It was in that month that Menachem Begin rushed through the Knesset his bill proclaiming "united" Jerusalem as the capital of Israel. Although the Vatican did not resuscitate its earlier demands for internationalization of the Holy City, or even of the holy places, it severely condemned the Israeli action. In January 1982 Israel's Foreign Minister Shamir traveled to the Vatican, hoping to "interpret" his government's actions. But the audience with John Paul went badly; the pope expressed stern opposition to Israel's actions. By then the Palestine issue had emerged as no less central to John Paul's diplomacy than to that of Paul VI. Papal statements on behalf of "the legitimate rights of the Palestinian people" became more frequent.

The revived tensions between Rome and Jerusalem approached their climax with Israel's invasion of Lebanon in the summer of 1982. On June 26, fully sharing Europe's shock and horror at the siege of Beirut, John Paul dispatched a personal message to Israel's President Yitzchak Navon (a known moderate), beseeching "honorable treatment" for the Palestinians and recognition of their "just aspirations." And then, in September 1982, following the evacuation of PLO guerrillas from Beirut, John Paul took a step even his predecessor had not ventured. He invited Yasser Arafat to an audience. Widely publicized, the event provoked an unprecedented Israeli governmental denunciation of Vatican policy. Issued by Foreign Minister Shamir, it declared:

> The same Church that did not say a word about the massacre of Jews for six years in Europe, and did not say much about the killing of Christians in Lebanon for seven years, is willing to meet the man who . . . is bent on the destruction of Israel which would complete the work done by the Nazis of Germany. If the Pope is going to meet Arafat, it shows something about the moral standards of the Church.

It was not an outburst that the Vatican could accept in silence. In an official communiqué, the Holy See branded the accusation of Vatican silence in World War II as "an outrage to the truth, couched in language completely lacking in respect for the person of the Pope." The September 1982 exchange was the most acrimonious in thirty-four years of Israeli-Vatican dialogue.

Months of grim silence followed on both sides. But in April 1984 John Paul issued a document on the Middle East that was given the forceful cachet of an apostolic letter, *Redemptionis Anno.* On the one hand, the statement besought peace and tranquillity for the "Jewish people who live in the State of Israel." On the other, it affirmed that the Palestinians too had "the natural right in justice to find once more a homeland and to be able to live in peace and tranquillity with the other peoples of the area." Ten months later, in February 1985, Shimon Peres, who lately had returned as Israel's prime minister in a rotation government, visited Rome to assure the pope of his intention to resolve the Palestinian issue in a "fair and just" manner. John Paul was friendly but noncommittal. In that same month he received a Jordanian-Palestinian delegation and again expressed support for "Palestinian dignity and rights." And in April, when Peres launched the bombing raid that destroyed PLO headquarters outside Tunis, *L'Osservatore Romano* editorialized: "One cannot affirm a desire to support . . . negotiations and then . . . lash out in merciless ways like the bombing raid into Tunisia."

The months passed; Yitzchak Shamir resumed the prime ministry of Israel's rotation government in October 1986, Jewish settlement activity in the territories continued, and the search for a Middle East solution remained frozen. In December 1987, when the Palestinian *intifada* erupted in the West Bank, Israel's policy of repression struck Europe as unduly harsh. The Vatican affirmed that it, too, maintained "serious concern about Israel's handling of Palestinian unrest." Addressing a group of pilgrims in Saint Peter's Square, John Paul observed sadly that the Holy Land "cannot continue being a theater of violence, of opposition, and of injustice." In late December 1988 the pope received Yasser Arafat a second time, on this occasion extending the PLO chairman the deference normally accorded a head of state.

As pope, Karol Wojtyla remained available to his Jewish friends, visiting their synagogues, repeatedly affirming the depth of his respect for Judaism and the Jewish people, sternly denouncing antisemitism in its every coloration and disguise. By the end of his first decade on the pontifical throne, nevertheless, the Polish pope had moved with an equivalent forthrightness to criticize Israel's territorialism, and eventually to condemn the Jewish state's perceived transgressions against the Palestinian people. In his diplomatic odyssey through the Middle Eastern quagmire, John Paul II had become a paradigm of Europe itself.

XIII   A EUROPEAN
     EMBRACE

A THAWING PARALYSIS

European goodwill toward Israel sank to its nadir in the wake of Menachem Begin's invasion of Lebanon in 1982. In official dispatches and media coverage alike, Britain, Germany, France, the Benelux and other Western nations, as well as the Vatican, expressed their condemnation more vigorously and unambiguously than at any earlier period in the Jewish state's history. Yet, within the institutional structure of the European Community, the attitude toward Israel during the mid-1980s was rather more equivocal. In common with its participant governments, the EC's Council of Ministers had denounced the Lebanon invasion. Afterward, however, as the world oil crisis eased with the growing availability of North Sea reserves, the Community was prepared to heed the advice of François Mitterrand in France and Helmut Kohl in Germany to defer its own collective Middle East initiatives.

On occasion the Community issued routine platitudes in support of "legitimate Palestinian aspirations," even of the need for PLO involvement in Middle East peace negotiations, but nothing more. In the spring of 1984, Shimon Peres, chairman of Israel's Labor party, became prime minister of his country's rotating National Unity government. Trusted for his moderation, Peres was able to secure a moratorium on EC diplomatic pressure. Even afterward, in January 1987, speaking this time as foreign minister in a Shamir coalition, Peres addressed the EC's Council of Cooperation in Brussels and won its forbearance on Middle Eastern issues. For the time being, the Community chose to refocus on its traditional economic responsibilities.

Those functions, as it happened, included the accommodation of a complex structural enlargement. In 1981 Greece qualified for participation, and in 1986 Spain and Portugal similarly were admitted as the Community's eleventh and twelfth members. The timing of their

accession was significant. The Third World by then was fracturing
into rival blocs. Dissension had become the rule among the Moslem
OPEC nations, with Iraq pitted against its Gulf "sisters" Kuwait,
Saudi Arabia, and Iran. Vietnamese forces were occupying Cambodia;
Libyan troops were occupying Chad; while the Soviet Union, its own
army occupying Afghanistan, failed to sustain its earlier image as a
champion of "anti-imperialism." By the mid- and latter 1980s, with
the West no longer as reflexively sensitive to Afro-Asian concerns, the
Israeli government in turn began to discern a certain room for
maneuver among the Europeans.

Greece was a case in point. As in earlier years, Prime Minister
Andreas Papandreou's leftist PASOK government continued its doctrinaire vilification of Israel and the United States. Yet, by mid-decade,
Islamic fundamentalism was emerging as a threat to other Mediterranean nations, including a still extensive Greek diaspora scattered
throughout the Middle East. Meanwhile, Greece's persistent courtship of Arab diplomatic support on the Cyprus issue lately had re-
sulted in a certain equivocation. Appraising these shifting political
circumstances, Moshe Gilboa, who arrived in Athens in 1986 as
Israel's "diplomatic representative," sensed an opportunity to win
greater understanding for his nation's position. The initial portents
for change in Athens admittedly were not promising. Government
agents continued to organize public meetings in behalf of the PLO.
PASOK newspapers denounced Gilboa as an "American agent," and
crowds periodically gathered outside his office shouting insults.
Undaunted, the Israeli emissary now concentrated on Greece's political opposition party, the rather less doctrinaire Neo-Democrats.

Thus, in the summer of 1986, Gilboa set about organizing a David
Ben-Gurion centennial celebration. Through cajolery and sheer bull-
dog tenacity, he managed to persuade ex-president Constantine Tsa-
tsos, a friend of the Jews, to accept the chairmanship. Miltiadis Evert,
mayor of Athens and son of a famous wartime police chief who had
saved numerous Jews from Nazi capture, was another prominent
Neo-Democrat who agreed to serve on the centennial committee.
The event then took place before a large crowd in the Athens City
Hall. Among the guests was Constantine Mitsoutakis, leader of the
Neo-Democratic party, as well as the metropolitan of the Greek
Orthodox Church. As Gilboa suspected, the celebration prefigured a
tentative reassessment, at least within Greece's political opposition.
An implacably anti-Israel stance evidently had become obsolescent.

In September 1987 Gilboa moved on to the government itself. He
urged the PASOK foreign minister, Karolos Papoulias, to pay an

unofficial "exploratory" visit to Israel. Papoulias needed little persuasion. He too had become disillusioned with Arab ambivalence on the Cyprus issue, and no longer was inclined to ignore Israel's manifest economic and military strength in the eastern Mediterranean. The visit took place in November 1987, Papoulias spending four days conferring with Israel's political leaders and inspecting several of the country's largest industrial enterprises. He returned home impressed and sobered. With Papoulias's discreet approval, then, Gilboa managed to develop ties with other, private-sector groups: with an elite collection of business executives, who agreed to sponsor a Greek-Israel Chamber of Commerce; with the president of Plato University and a collection of senior professors, who arrived in Israel as honored guests of the Jewish state's leading academic figures.

Nevertheless, Gilboa continued to focus his principal efforts on the Greek political opposition. In May 1988 he succeeded in organizing a visit to Israel by Constantine Mitsoutakis and a bloc of Neo-Democratic parliamentarians. Beyond the official banquets and private hospitality, Mitsoutakis shrewdly appraised the Jewish state's palpable muscularity. He then promised Gilboa that, if elected, he would seek to establish diplomatic relations with Israel. He kept his word. In the spring of 1990 the Neo-Democrats won a narrow second-round electoral victory, and Mitsoutakis became prime minister. Afterward, in the first session of parliament, he requested approval for *de jure* recognition of Israel, and successfully pressed the issue through on May 21 as a vote of confidence. Gilboa himself then submitted his credentials as Israel's first ambassador to Greece. For the Greek government and people, still deeply committed to the Palestinian cause, the new departure was less than a gesture of friendship to Israel. At best it signified an exercise in diplomatic realism.

Even earlier, at the western end of the Mediterranean, *Realpolitik* similarly had produced a critical shift in Spain's diplomatic stance. Throughout the latter 1970s and early 1980s, Adolfo Suárez's centrist government had maintained its pro-Arab orientation. Even the election of a Socialist government in 1982 produced no fundamental change in Spain's Middle Eastern policy. The incoming prime minister, Felipe González, was an old friend of Shimon Peres and other Israeli Labor figures. Yet he too felt obliged to proclaim support for Palestinian statehood and to condemn Israel's invasion of Lebanon. In the spring of 1983, Peres himself visited Madrid for urgent discussions with González. The Spanish premier was cordial. Personally he favored relations between the two nations, he explained. He was merely awaiting evidence of a more moderate Israeli foreign policy.

That reassurance was forthcoming in Israel's elections of the following year, when Peres again became prime minister. Afterward Peres appointed as his emissary to Madrid Micha Harish, a Labor Knesset member who had developed numerous Spanish contacts within the Socialist International. In ensuing months Harish and Peres were able to count on an unlikely ally. It was the EC Commission, which for nearly eight years had been negotiating the terms of Spain's entry into the European Community. The arrangements were complex. Spanish membership would oblige the Community to absorb into its institutions an economy far larger and more diversified than Greece's or Portugal's. There were bound to be economic repercussions among the other Mediterranean participants. Led by the Germans, the EC Commission emphasized to the Spaniards that it anticipated a certain political reciprocity. If the Community was to play a credible role in encouraging moderation and forbearance in the Middle East, it would be useful for its members at least to normalize their relationship with Arabs and Israelis alike.

González was listening. In January 1986 he led his country into the European Community, and that same month announced his intention to establish diplomatic relations with Israel. Three months after that, the Buenos Aires–born Shmuel Hadas presented his ambassadorial credentials to King Juan Carlos. In 1992, on the quincentennial of Spain's expulsion of its Jews, Israel's President Chaim Herzog arrived in Madrid on a state visit. Amid the pageantry of governmental and royal receptions, the most poignant moment was the joint presence of Herzog and King Juan Carlos in the capital's synagogue. Wearing a skullcap, the king addressed the Israeli president, the congregation, and the Jewish world at large, and asked their "forgiveness" for the "cruel and unjust" events of 1492. Clearly, Israel had secured its flanks at both ends of the Mediterranean.

A FINAL SPASM OF EUROPEAN OBLOQUY?

By the mid-1980s, its Lebanon adventure liquidated, the Israeli government sought to refocus its dialogue on the economic issues that had drawn it closer to Europe in earlier decades. In 1975, it will be recalled, the Community had awarded Israel a form of de facto associate status. At first, the little nation appeared to have profited handsomely from that connection. Its trade deficit with Europe was reduced. Its industry grew and diversified. Yet the progress, if impressive, also was uneven. Israeli agriculture was encountering formidable competition from the subtropical produce of Italy, Greece, and the associated

Maghreb nations. A more serious challenge yet was the impending membership in the Community of Spain and Portugal, whose flourishing citriculture, avocado, and cut-flower plantations threatened Israel's once impressive share of the European market. Indeed, upon becoming members of the EC, Spain and Portugal would be eligible for Community subsidies that were certain to erode Israel's competitiveness even further.

To cope with this challenge, Israel's agricultural representative in Brussels, Eva Gover, entered into painstaking negotiations with the European Commission. A technocrat of uncommon persuasiveness and charm, Gover succeeded between 1986 and 1987 in winning a major additional "protocol" to the treaty. In essence, the amendment permitted Israeli agricultural exports a grace period before the EC's subsidies of Spanish and Portuguese imports came into effect. At the same time, the Community lowered its tariffs and enlarged both the quotas and categories of Israeli agricultural imports.

The protocol was duly signed by the European Commission in December 1987 and normally would have gone into effect without delay. Yet a final "constitutional" procedure remained. The year before, the Community's twelve members had passed the Single European Act, one of whose features incrementally strengthened the role of the European Parliament. In earlier times that body's function in Strasbourg had been essentially consultative. Now the assembly was authorized to give or withhold ratification of revised protocols. And in March 1988 the parliament announced that it was withholding ratification of the Israeli protocol. The veto was not gratuitous. It was intended as a political statement of support for the Palestinians; for by then the issue of Israel's "administered" territories had flared up again.

The crisis erupted on December 8, 1987. An Israeli civilian trucker, driving through the Gaza Strip, lost control of his vehicle and smashed into an oncoming automobile filled with local Arabs. Four of the Arab passengers were killed. Instantly riots broke out. Detachments of Israeli troops had to be rushed in. By the next day clamorous demonstrations were spreading rapidly to other Arab population centers in the West Bank. Additional thousands of Israeli troops were dispatched to suppress the unrest. The effort was unavailing. Violence soon assumed the character of a spontaneous *intifada*, an "upwhirling" of bitterness and rage against all the constraints and indignities of Israel's twenty-year rule in Palestine. In its most militant physical expression the *intifada* would continue on and off for the next three and a half years. Arab youths hurled stones at Jewish settlers on the West Bank.

Israeli soldiers, confused and frightened, often overreacted, clubbing indiscriminately, firing into threatening crowds with tear gas, plastic bullets, and occasionally live ammunition. Widely photographed by foreign television services, the image of Israeli repression was disseminated throughout the world. Among Europeans it evoked only revulsion.

Months even before the outbreak of the *intifada*, the European Community had begun to revive its criticism of Israel's stance on the territories. Only three weeks after a rather mild declaration in February 1987, recommending an international peace conference for the Arab-Israel impasse, the EC foreign ministers issued a new statement. This one condemned as "illegal" Israel's Jewish settlements in the territories. In July 1987 yet another EC declaration cited a committee report describing Israel's violation of human rights in Gaza and the Palestine West Bank. And then, in December 1987, the *intifada* erupted. Subsequently, in March 1988, the European Parliament made its gesture, withholding its ratification of the new trade protocol. As the *Financial Times* noted afterward: "The Parliament's failure to endorse [the protocol] is the first decisive mark of international censure of Israel since the Palestinian unrest began three months ago."

In Israel, Foreign Minister Peres, although a vigorous opponent of Shamir's settlements policy, expressed concern that the parliament had not separated "an essentially technical and economic issue from [its] opinions regarding the situation in the territories." He then directed his ambassadors in Europe to lobby the parliament for a reversal. As always the campaign achieved its greatest success among the foreign minister's extensive network of friends in Germany's Social Democratic party, who then dutifully interceded with their colleagues in other European countries. Thus, in October 1988 the European Parliament ended its "sanction" by assenting to the protocol. Yet the Community had not made its final statement. In February 1990, complying with still another parliamentary recommendation, the EC Commission imposed a new series of restrictive measures. These blocked Israel's access to some fifteen projects submitted by the EC-Israel Joint Scientific Committee, and postponed a cooperative agreement in the field of energy. None of the restrictions inflicted serious harm on Israel, and within a year most of them were reversed. But they, too, represented a plainspoken warning to the Jewish state, on the very threshold of its widening partnership with the Continent, that European forbearance once again was hanging in the balance.

OPERATION DESERT STORM
AND A REVISION OF PERSPECTIVE

It would be restored by events at the farthest perimeter of the Arab Middle East. Saddam Hussein, the president of Iraq, had long been intent on winning for his near-landlocked nation a more extensive maritime outlet to the world's oil markets. Such was the origin of his eight-year war against Iran, from 1980 to 1988. Inconclusive in results, the murderous struggle devoured hundreds of thousands of Iraqi and Iranian lives. Beyond its human toll, moreover, the war cost Iraq over $500 billion and saddled its economy with a foreign debt of $80 billion. Saddam Hussein wasted little time in seeking relief from his Arab creditors. The largest of these, the Sultanate of Kuwait, was not forthcoming. Worse yet, it rejected Saddam's long-standing claim to a pair of Kuwaiti-ruled islands facing the Shatt al-Arab estuary that functioned as Iraq's single maritime outlet to the Persian Gulf. For a man of Saddam's temperament, there could be only one course of action. On August 1, 1990, he dispatched his army across the Kuwaiti border, easily investing the little nation.

The aggression, and with it the palpable danger of an even-farther-ranging Iraqi thrust southward into the oil-rich Gulf, was unacceptable to Western Europe, even to the largest numbers of Arab nations. It was altogether unacceptable to the United States, principal guarantor of the Gulf. Immediately, then, President George Bush set about mobilizing some four hundred thousand American troops, and within six months deployed this force at Saudi bases for the imminent liberation of Kuwait. Bush's diplomatic achievement transcended even his military feat. Within the same half-year period he orchestrated a coalition of European and Middle Eastern nations, including such unlikely participants as the Soviet Union, Egypt, and Syria. At the president's behest each of these states contributed military units to the joint liberation effort. Finally, on January 17, 1991, the Allies launched their bombardment of Iraq.

Saddam Hussein was not without important resources of his own, however. In the last weeks before the onset of war, the Iraqi dictator formulated a shrewd stratagem to divide the Arab front arraying against him. He threatened to loose his planes and missiles on Israel, the common Zionist enemy. The Israelis took the threat seriously. They always had. In 1981 they had preemptively attacked and destroyed the Osiraq nuclear reactor before it became operative. Since then, Saddam Hussein had used poison gas to murder irredentist elements within his own country, Kurds and Arabs alike. It seemed unlikely that he would stay his hand against Israel. Indeed, on January 18, 1991, he made good his warning. His instrument of choice was the Scud missile. Of Soviet manufacture, the surface-to-surface rocket was unreliable as a military weapon, but as a weapon of terror it could inflict serious harm. Thus, in the dawn hours, eight Scuds were launched from western Iraq. Most of them struck in and around Tel Aviv, destroying several apartment buildings and wounding a dozen civilians. The next day four more Scuds struck Tel Aviv, again inflicting property damage and wounding a small number of civilians.

In response, the government of Prime Minister Yitzchak Shamir prepared to launch its own not inconsiderable air power against Iraq. At the last moment, however, George Bush dissuaded the Israeli cabinet from intervention. The American president could not allow his Arab partners to be distracted from the common venture against Saddam Hussein. Rather, in ensuing days, Bush ordered units of the United States Air Force to hunt and destroy the Scuds. The counter-campaign was only marginally effective. Tel Aviv would endure eighteen more attacks until the ordeal ended, on February 25, with the Allied ground assault on Iraqi forces and the liberation of Kuwait. Although the human cost of this assault was negligible to Israel, at least four thousand of the nation's buildings had been destroyed or damaged. Even more painful than the physical trauma and the tense discipline of nonretaliation was the psychological pressure of civilian vulnerability. Sooner or later, it was suspected, the incoming weapons would carry biological or chemical warheads, the kind Saddam Hussein had used earlier on civilians in his own country. But hardly less shattering to Israel was awareness of the source of much of Iraq's extensive military and technological capability. It was a nation whose role in the annals of genocide would remain forever seared in the memory of the Jewish people.

Other recent European developments lately had revived the image of Germany as the dominant power on the Continent. The Soviet Union's Communist empire was imploding. In November 1989, with the fall of the Berlin Wall, it became clear that all efforts to sustain even a decommunized Deutsche Demokratische Republik were futile. Eventually, in July of the following year, the Bundesrepublik's chancellor, Helmut Kohl, responded to overwhelming popular demand in both East and West Germany by accepting the daunting challenge of unification. Would the Allied Powers—and specifically the Soviet Union—agree to a single, undivided Germany? In fact, the Soviet Union itself was in the throes of liberalization by then, and

President Mikhail Gorbachev was urgently in need of Western good-will and investment for his own country. Accordingly, in negotiations with Bonn, and in return for massive Bundesrepublik payoffs in grants and credits, Gorbachev agreed not to block the process of union. In turn, spared the threat of a Soviet veto, Kohl's government promptly launched into separate discussions with the governments of the United States, Britain, and France. These too now agreed to relinquish their postwar claims on East Germany.

To dispel misgivings among Western, liberal circles, Bonn as always placed much reliance on the Jews and Israel. It was not an easy sell this time. Among American and international Jewish organizations, the unfolding spectacle of German unification evoked only confusion and consternation. The official response from Israel was necessarily more cautious, for Germany was a major source of economic support for the Jewish state. Thus, in April 1991, Prime Minister Shamir issued a distinctly restrained statement of acknowledgment. "The Jewish people have memories, doubts, and questions," he proclaimed. "It is therefore difficult to say that we are pleased by German unity. Nevertheless, we understand that the time for German unity has arrived." In October 1991, Israel's President Chaim Herzog was rather more forthcoming. "Ben-Gurion laid down Israel's policy toward Germany," he declared, "and that is the applicable policy to this very day, even with Germany reunited." Well into 1992, however, fears of an arrogant, xenophobic new Germany were exacerbated by a series of "skinhead" attacks against Turks and other foreigners. A December 1992 poll in Israel revealed that 75 percent of the respondents anticipated a flagrant revival of neo-Nazism in newly unified Germany.

These Israeli and Jewish misgivings were a source of genuine concern to Helmut Kohl. The German chancellor had not negotiated his formidable political achievements by insensitivity to public opinion, either in Germany or abroad. A dynamic Catholic politician from the Rhineland-Palatinate, where he rose to become prime minister and twice win reelection, Kohl in 1973 was elected chairman of the Christian Democratic Union and first ran for the chancellorship in 1976. Unsuccessful then, he subsequently lured the Free Democrats from their alliance with the Social Democrats, and in the 1982 national elections won barely enough votes to put together his own Christian Democrat–Free Democrat coalition. Thereafter, under Kohl's aegis, the Bundesrepublik entered into its second *Wirtschaftswunder,* a period of sustained economic growth and favorable trade balances. Reelected twice in the ensuing decade, to become the

longest-serving German chancellor since Bismarck, it was Kohl who
then fearlessly moved into the vacuum of disintegrating East Germany to engineer the nation's structural reunification.

When he first assumed office in October 1982, the new chancellor
was intent on dissipating the mistrust generated in Israel during the
predecessor Schmidt incumbency. To that end he visited the Jewish
state a year later, and was correctly received by Prime Minister Shamir
and other Israeli officials. Moreover, during his stay Kohl was careful to proclaim his nation's unique historical obligation to Israel and
the Jewish people. In contrast to the Schmidt and even Brandt eras,
the chancellor's speeches contained no visions of "normalized"
relations between the two countries. Israel accepted the event with
equanimity. More successful yet, in 1985, was the state visit of
Bundesrepublik President Richard von Weizsäcker. A man of great
moral rectitude, Weizsäcker touched the hearts of the Israeli nation
with his transparent commitment to German atonement. Reciprocating in 1986, Israel's President Chaim Herzog paid a return visit to the
Bundesrepublik, where he was tendered a reception of near-royal dignity. In the struggle against guerrilla terrorism, too, Kohl authorized
the Bundesrepublik's intelligence agencies to cooperate intimately
with Israel's Mossad. Other cooperative ventures were equally far-
reaching. During the mid-1980s, when Saddam Hussein was engaged
in his debilitating Gulf war with Iran, Israel estimated that its national
interests would be served by providing selective quantities of advanced
weaponry to the Iranians. To help camouflage the Israel-Iran connection, the Bundesrepublik and individual German Länder discreetly
made their harbors and airports available to the Israeli supply effort.

But an unanticipated reassessment developed with the 1990 Iraqi
invasion of Kuwait, and the ensuing Allied countercampaign against
Saddam Hussein. The Bundesrepublik was precluded by its constitution from using its armed forces beyond NATO's European ambit.
Instead, as a measure of compensation, Bonn eventually would reimburse the Allied coalition and Israel (p. 328) to the tune of $11.4 bil-
lion in military hardware, supply services, and cash payments. The
assistance was hardly trivial. Even so, during the six months of Allied
military preparations, Western and German journalists alike carefully
reappraised the Bundesrepublik's earlier contributions to Saddam Hussein's war-making ability. It soon became evident that, between 1982
and 1989, West German manufacturers had provided Iraq with weapons and related technology worth $700 million. The legal constraints
on German military exports to the Middle East had proved a sham
from beginning to end. Indeed, the German government itself had

winked at a weapons-export program that had transformed the Bundesrepublik into Europe's third largest merchant of arms to the Middle East, after the Soviet Union and France. One company alone, Thyssen Rheinstahl Technik, had constructed Iraq's extensive chemical weapons program, upgraded Iraq's Scud missiles, and constructed an elaborate bunker system to protect Iraq's military control centers and political leadership.

Thus it was, as Iraqi Scuds began descending on Tel Aviv and Haifa on January 18, 1991, that both Israel and Germany were convulsed by paroxysms of acute anxiety. The year before, an Israeli public-opinion survey revealed that 72 percent of all respondents believed in a new, "good" Germany. In March 1991 the same question evoked a mere 56 percent response (and in December 1992, 41 percent). In the Bundesrepublik itself the emotional roller coaster was even more palpable. Until the revelations of German involvement in Iraqi military technology, polls had revealed a widespread exhaustion of sympathy for the Jewish state and its moral claims on the German people (p. 306). But now, in January 1991, with the threat of mass destruction confronting a Jewish population, German reaction shifted almost 180 degrees. By substantial majorities German media and German political parties agreed that Israel was entitled to the fullest measure of compensation.

In Bonn, during the height of the January 1991 Scud crisis, Israel's Ambassador Binyamin Navon met with Foreign Minister Hans-Dietrich Genscher to present extensive documentation of the missile havoc. Genscher was shaken. The next day, following an emergency cabinet meeting, the foreign minister departed for Israel to survey the damage personally. Navon joined him (in the airplane, en route, they engaged in a gas-mask drill). After touring Tel Aviv's more heavily damaged neighborhoods, Genscher and Israel's Foreign Minister David Levy went into immediate consultations. Within hours, following urgent back-and-forth telephone calls to Bonn, Genscher informed Levy that his government would provide Israel with DM250 million for reconstruction—a commitment that later would be raised to DM1 billion. Ambassador Navon, meanwhile, was holding his own urgent consultations with the Israeli cabinet. Soon afterward, accompanied by Defense Minister Moshe Arens, he returned to the Bundesrepublik with a shopping list that far transcended the cost of short-term repairs. Navon had shrewdly gauged the Kohl government's psychological defensiveness.

Indeed, upon landing at Frankfurt, Navon and Arens found a Luftwaffe helicopter awaiting them to carry them directly to the chancellor's office in Bonn. In attendance with Kohl were Germany's military commanders and a half-dozen cabinet ministers. It was a defining moment, and Navon exploited it to the hilt. *"Herr Bundeskanzler,"* he declared, *"drei Begriffe können niemals nebeneinander stehen: Juden, Deutsche, und Giftgas"*—"Mr. Chancellor, three concepts can never be linked with one another: Jews, Germans, and poison gas." Navon had chosen the phrase carefully. There were several moments of dead silence in the room. *"Herr Bundeskanzler,"* the ambassador then continued, "our first, second, and even tenth priorities are submarines." The shopping list in fact had been prepared even before the current crisis. Several years earlier, as Bonn indiscriminately loosened the ban on arms shipments to the Middle East, Israel had ordered two submarines from German shipyards at a cost of DM900 million, but later was obliged to cancel the contract for lack of funds. Now it was seeking the submarines again, as gifts. Kohl was listening. Before the day was over, he informed Navon and Arens that the government would indeed provide the two submarines gratis, and eventually would agree to fund half the cost of a third. It was a stupendous coup for Israel.

Meanwhile, with the return of Yitzchak Rabin as Israel's prime minister in June 1992 at the head of a Labor government, the relationship between Bonn and Jerusalem became progressively warmer. In March 1993 the two governments established a German-Israeli Cooperation Council to foster shared research in environmental technologies. The venture of course was but one of many cooperative undertakings that had been in place since the 1960s (pp. 209–11). As recently as 1986, a jointly funded German-Israeli Foundation for Scientific Research and Development, the brainchild of Peres and Kohl, had been launched with a start-up capital of DM150 million. By 1992 the operating capital was doubled, and was generating sixty grants a year for approved ventures. As always, the Minerva Foundation sustained and even enlarged the network of research-and-exchange projects between the two countries. Germany's three principal political parties, its trade union federation, and some eighty German municipalities funded exchange programs that brought selected groups of Israelis to the Bundesrepublik.

More than any single factor, however, it was the PLO-Israeli "Oslo" agreement of the following year (pp. 338–9) that vastly accelerated German investment and tourism in Israel. Well before then Germany had become Israel's second most important commercial partner, after the United States. Yet, by the same token, Israel's trade deficit with the Bundesrepublik also was climbing, at an annual rate of $600 million. It was the dramatic new prospect for peace, after 1993, and the ensuing relaxation of the Arab secondary boycott, that provided new opportunities for German investment in the Jewish state, and for narrowing the balance-of-payments gap between the two countries. Thus, by mid-decade the Daimler-Benz Investment Corporation had opened an office in Israel to explore likely prospects for its capital. Establishing an Israeli branch for the same investment purpose, Siemens launched its venture by purchasing a local computer firm, Or Net, for $30 million. Volkswagen in 1992 formed an investment relationship with Israel's Dead Sea Works for the extraction of magnesium, and poured $350 million into the venture over the ensuing four years. In 1996, the Henkel Detergents and Cosmetics Corporation purchased a 50 percent share in So'ad, a subsidiary of Israel's Koor conglomerate. Operating jointly with Clal, Israel's largest public investment company, Schneider Optical Works was committing $80 million to Robomatics and ELOP Optronics. Frankfurt's FG Bank AG and Israel's Bank HaPoalim were opening joint departments in Haifa and Jerusalem, specializing in Israel's foreign trade with the Bundesrepublik.

At all times, Bonn gave its official encouragement to these projects. Like Israel, it authorized special tax advantages for private German investors in the Jewish state. When Chancellor Kohl paid his second visit, in June 1996, he brought with him some twenty German business executives. Germany's Minister of Economics Gunther Rexrodt and the economics ministers of individual German Länder also were frequent visitors. Their arrival by no means reflected Europe's traditional interest in the Middle East as a source of cheap labor. Rather, Israel's principal attraction was its high-tech industry and its educated work force. By 1996, too, some 200,000 private German tourists were coming to Israel annually, more than to any other nation outside Europe, except for the United States. With 125,000 Israelis also visiting Germany yearly, *Geschichtspolitik*—the politics of historical memory—evidently was being paralleled by the exigencies of mild and pragmatic self-interest.

A BELATED RECONCILIATION WITH MOSCOW

Even before the 1992 advent of the Rabin government, it was the Gulf War that began to restore Israel's humanistic image after the earlier debacles of Lebanon invasion and *intifada*. Few European nations were unappreciative of the Jewish nation's stoicism and forbearance during the Scud attacks on its cities. Afterward, in April

1991, Prime Minister Yitzchak Shamir squeezed in a quick trip to London, ostensibly to attend the inauguration of the European Bank for Reconstruction and Development, but in fact to test Europe's "atmospherics" toward his country. He wrote later:

> The praise, the compliments, the warmth that flowed in my direction were extraordinary. Everyone wanted to talk to me, including heads of state I had never met before. . . . Everyone who could, shook hands . . . everyone stressed the "wisdom and courage" of our policy during the Gulf War. . . . [A]s if from being a frog, I had suddenly turned into a prince.

In some measure it was Shamir's positive reading of European opinion that dissipated his reluctance to participate in a Geneva-style peace conference with the Arab nations. Under the formula devised by the Bush administration in Washington, the conclave would enjoy joint American-Soviet sponsorship, and the simultaneous participation of the major Arab "confrontation" states. Israel of all nations traditionally had distrusted this format, and indeed had achieved peace with Egypt specifically by avoiding it. In the late winter of 1991, however, Secretary of State James Baker was intent on sustaining the diplomatic momentum that had produced the recent Gulf military victory. His priority henceforth was to exploit Arab and Israeli gratitude by maneuvering both sides into negotiations that would resolve their own historic impasse.

To that end, beginning in March 1991, Baker embarked on a series of whirlwind visits to the Middle East. Remarkably, under his vigorous persistence, the Syrian, Lebanese, and Jordanian governments all agreed to participate. Shamir decided then not to risk an open confrontation with Washington, and a possibly indefinite postponement of additional American financial aid packages to Israel. In any case, Baker had assured the prime minister that American-Soviet cosponsorship would serve essentially as an umbrella for direct negotiations between "regional committees," to consist of Israel and each separate Arab nation.

The selected venue was Madrid. Eager to display its bona fides as a once-historic fount of Islamic and Jewish culture, Spain had offered the participants every assurance of security and comfort. Thus it was, on November 1, 1991, that delegations from Jordan-Palestine, Lebanon, Syria, and Israel arrived in the Spanish capital. President George Bush and President Mikhail Gorbachev had flown in to launch the conclave, and in their opening remarks each expressed the usual pious hopes for Middle Eastern peace. In fact, not even Shamir was willing to denigrate Gorbachev's remarks as typical Soviet hypocrisy. Moscow after all had lent its diplomatic support to the recent Allied campaign against Saddam Hussein. It was a cooperation in turn that bespoke a profound metamorphosis of Soviet policy in the Middle East—and in triangular Soviet-Israeli-American relations. Without that transformation, not even Secretary of State Baker's adroit diplomacy could have brought Shamir to the peace table.

By the mid-1970s, it is recalled, much of the Arab world had begun to gravitate out of the Soviet sphere of influence. In ensuing years, and surely by the time of the 1991 Gulf War, the United States had emerged as the uncontested power broker in the Middle East. Long outside the diplomatic loop, the Soviets had become almost entirely irrelevant to American and Israeli policy in the region. In Moscow's view, then, a new approach was required, one that conceivably might elicit a forthcoming Israeli response. The reappraisal evinced not only diplomatic opportunism but economic desperation. Since the 1970s, the Soviets had come to regard Israel as an indispensable conduit to the United States, and specifically to American technological and investment resources. Access to that Western cornucopia was urgent. In recent decades the Soviet Union had become hardly less than a basket case of industrial and agricultural stagnation. Indeed, it was specifically to address this malaise that the Communist Central Committee elevated Mikhail Gorbachev, an energetic, university-trained technocrat, to the general secretaryship in 1985 (and to the nation's presidency three years later). On assuming office Gorbachev wasted little time in adopting a program of *perestroika*, economic decentralization. A year later *perestroika* was coupled with *glasnost*, a new openness of political and cultural expression in public and private life.

Yet, however valid in theory, *perestroika* in operation had come too late to rescue the nation's foundering economy; while *glasnost* triggered a rash of separatist movements among the USSR's heterogeneity of republics and ethnic factions. Moreover, the late 1980s witnessed a simultaneous deterioration of Communist control over the Warsaw Pact regimes in Poland, Hungary, Romania, Yugoslavia, East Germany, Bulgaria, Czechoslovakia. In each of these nations, party rule was supplanted by popularly elected governments. By the same token, free emigration to Israel at long last became a viable option for the residual Jewish populations of these former satellites. Not all of them rushed to avail themselves of it, however. Hungary's eighty thousand Jews had long since accommodated to the liberal "goulash communism" of the earlier, Janos Kadar government, and evinced little interest in mass departure afterward. A quiet, systematic emigration over the decades had left Romanian Jewry a geriatric relic of less than ten thousand souls. In Poland, Czechoslovakia, Yugoslavia, and Bulgaria, whose acculturated, extensively intermarried Jewish populations did not collectively exceed twenty thousand, emigration to Israel in the late 1980s and early 1990s was fitful and minimal.

Rather, it was the structural transformation of the Soviet Union itself that proved decisive for Israel. At first, Soviet Jews shared in the heady new atmosphere of free expression. Once again, they were admitted to better universities, reemployed in their traditional elite professional vocations, allowed to reopen shuttered synagogues, to publish books and newspapers on Jewish themes, to participate in a significant renaissance of Hebrew teaching and Zionist education. But among other, unanticipated consequences of the new liberalization was the virtual collapse of the Soviet economy, a free fall precipitous enough to unsettle a traditionally middle-class minority like the Jews. Worse yet, the Soviet behemoth soon was mired in ethnic upheavals and nationalist unrest, and the Jews as always became favored targets for chauvinist extremism. For them, as a result, emigration appeared the safer alternative.

Gorbachev was prepared to allow it. Desperate to gain access to American trade and technology on a most-favored-nation basis, the Soviet president had learned well from his predecessors the value of Jewish goodwill and the price of forfeiting it. Here it was, at last, that the 1972–75 struggle over the Jackson-Vanik Amendment belatedly began to pay off. In March 1987 Gorbachev tentatively lifted the ban on Jewish departure. A year later he acquiesced in another key Israeli request. To ensure that Jewish émigrés no longer would bypass Israel for the United States, as thousands had in earlier years once they reached their initial transit station of Vienna, the Soviets agreed this time to issue exit permits exclusively for Romania, and afterward for Bulgaria. In these latter countries, also by arrangement with Jerusalem, the Romanian and Bulgarian authorities then would issue their own exit visas and limit their use strictly for Israel. In Washington, meanwhile, the Bush administration cooperated in the new arrangement by refusing any longer to designate Soviet Jews as collective victims of Soviet persecution, who thereby automatically were eligible for refuge in the United States.

The consequences of these multilateral alterations soon became dramatically evident. With most Soviet barriers down, and those in the United States going up, the numbers of Jewish emigrants to Israel began climbing exponentially. In 1989 alone 71,000 departed the USSR for Israel. In 1990 the figure reached 182,000; in 1991, 145,000. Although the emigration rate afterward leveled off to a yearly average of 65,000, some 460,000 Soviet newcomers reached Israel by 1998, supplementing the 250,000 who had arrived over the three previous decades. For the little Zionist republic the influx was nothing less than a demographic revolution, increasing the country's Jewish population by one-fifth. Moscow of course expected reciprocity from the United States—and got it. In December 1990, at the request of the National Conference on Soviet Jewry (p. 262), the Bush administration at long last granted the Soviets their most-favored-nation status and their cherished goal of wider purchasing access to American technological and agricultural products.

Nevertheless, within both the Israeli and Soviet governments, sharp disagreement remained in 1991 on the price Moscow should pay for yet another of its key objectives. This was Soviet reentry into the Middle East peace process. Shimon Peres, chairman of Israel's Labor opposition, was inclined to regard the emigration revolution as a decisive Soviet gesture of moderation on the Arab-Israel impasse. Prime Minister Shamir was unconvinced. In any case, he regarded the Soviets as unacceptable even as nominal cosponsors of a peace conference until they restored diplomatic relations with Israel. On this issue nothing would shake the prime minister. For his part, Gorbachev in Moscow similarly had been exploring ways of establishing contacts with Israel. Yet he too faced objections within his own government. As late as the mid-1980s, Arabists still dominated the Soviet foreign and defense ministries; even as right-wing nationalist elements, surfacing in the wake of *glasnost*, were strenuously opposed to dealings of any kind with the Jewish state. Nevertheless, in his determination to present a "reasonable" face to the West and Israel, Gorbachev eventually managed to win his colleagues over.

Soon cautious meetings began taking place between Soviet and Israeli diplomats. The first occurred as far back as July 1985. In Paris that month, Soviet Ambassador Yuli Vorontsev sat with his Israeli counterpart, Ovadia Sofer. Vorontsev hinted at a package deal: Moscow would drop all restrictions on Jewish emigration, he suggested, in return for "partial" Israeli withdrawal from the Golan Heights. The Soviet ambassador also mooted the possibility that diplomatic relations might be "partially" renewed if the Soviets were included in any future Middle East peace process. It was an intriguing formula, but Sofer was obliged to reject it. No Israeli government yet was prepared to countenance even an incremental evacuation of the Golan, or a Geneva-style peace conference. No more than Moscow was prepared yet to accept full diplomatic relations with the Jewish state. Yet both sides expressed interest at least in a gradual enlargement of informal contacts, possibly even a reestablishment of consular ties.

In the autumn of 1986 the Soviets took the next step. They assigned their own consular "representatives" to the Finnish embassy in Tel Aviv, the diplomatic mission that had protected Soviet interests in Israel since 1967. Israel then requested a quasi-consular presence of its own in Moscow. After months of hesitation the Soviets consented. In July 1988 a group of Israeli "consular officials" was returned to the Soviet capital, setting up shop in the Netherlands embassy, which similarly had protected Israeli interests after the Six-Day War. And, all the while, unofficial bilateral contacts were broadened. In 1988 Prime Minister Shamir met with Soviet Foreign Minister Eduard Shevardnadze in New York, as did Israel's Foreign Minister Moshe Arens the following year. On each occasion Shevardnadze intimated that full diplomatic relations might yet be feasible, but only after a peace conference had been well launched—with Soviet participation.

There were human factors, too, that helped dissipate suspicions between the two countries. In November 1988 a massive earthquake wreaked havoc in Soviet Armenia. The Israeli government immediately offered to provide the Soviets with a full military field hospital, together with several doctors and a rescue team. Moscow accepted the offer, and an Israeli Air Force transport accordingly flew the personnel and equipment to Yerevan, the Armenian capital. The following spring two El Al passenger jets were dispatched to Yerevan to bring hundreds of Armenian amputees to Israel, where they were fitted with prosthetic limbs. The humanitarian mission was widely publicized in the Soviet Union. So, too, was another even more dramatic example of Israeli assistance. In December 1988 a group of Georgian criminals hijacked an Aeroflot passenger jet en route from Tbilisi to Moscow and—unaccountably—ordered the crew to fly to Israel. On landing at Ben-Gurion Airport, the abductors demanded a Soviet ransom of money and freedom. They got neither. Well experienced in coping with hijacking crises, Israeli police promptly seized and jailed the Georgians, then consented almost immediately to hand them over to Soviet custody. Soon afterward a KGB unit flew into Israel to bring the criminals home.

The Soviet government was genuinely grateful. In the aftermath of the hijacking episode, Foreign Minister Shevardnadze granted an interview to Aryeh Levin, Israel's ranking consular "official" in Moscow. Expressing appreciation for Israel's "humane and noble gesture," the foreign minister added his "personal opinion in saying that . . . the actions of the government of Israel reflect the will of the Israeli people." He then promised Levin improved consular facilities. The promise was kept. In January 1989 Levin and his staff were allowed to move their offices from the Netherlands embassy to the former Israeli embassy building, which had been closed since June 1967. Nominally identified as the "Visas to Israel" department of the Netherlands embassy, the building in fact became the symbol of a revived and officially acknowledged Israeli presence in the USSR. Its reopening, after twenty-two years of nonuse, became an intensely emotional moment for Soviet Jewry. Before a crowd of over five thousand Jews, and some non-Jews, the chief rabbi of Moscow was present to intone his ceremonial blessings.

Ironically, the ensuing implosion of the Soviet empire by then produced a reversal of diplomatic order, with the former satellite nations taking the initiative in reviving the Israeli "connection." Romania's special relation with Israel was an old story, of course. Hungary, too, seeking an improved atmosphere in Washington, cautiously widened its mercantile contacts with Israel during the 1980s. Then, in 1991, with the collapse of the Soviet bloc, the governments of Hungary, Czechoslovakia, and Poland all formally resumed diplomatic ties with Israel. Only Moscow now lagged behind, unwilling to take the final step of reviving official relations with the Jewish state. The Caucasus was in flames and Central Asian irredentism was festering ominously. The time did not appear opportune to risk further alienating the Moslem world.

As early as December 1989, however, Mikhail Gorbachev had presided over a major policy discussion on the Middle East with his foreign-affairs advisers, and the decision was reached to move even more forthrightly toward normalization of contacts with Israel. Both the Soviet consular "representation" in Tel Aviv, and the Israeli consular "representation" in Moscow, would be upgraded to formal consular status. In May 1990 Yuli Vorontsev, the former Soviet ambassador to Paris, was appointed director of the foreign ministry's Middle East department. Aware of the importance of Western liberal goodwill, it was Vorontsev now who pressed the case for a straightforward, unqualified institutionalization of relations with the Jewish state.

In September 1990, a month after the Iraqi invasion of Kuwait, Israel's Foreign Minister David Levy attended a session of the UN General Assembly in New York. In an informal meeting with Soviet

Foreign Minister Shevardnadze, he engaged in a cordial and lengthy tour d'horizon of the Middle East, including the possibility of restored diplomatic ties. Shevardnadze reserved his answer. But four months afterward, in January 1991, the Kremlin authorized yet another upgrading of the Israeli consulate in Moscow, this time to consulate general. At the same time, government propaganda against Israel, which had been muted in recent months, now stopped entirely. Aryeh Levin, Israel's consul general, was interviewed with growing frequency on Russian television, and his comments were broadcast uncensored.

The following May, the newly appointed Soviet foreign minister, Aleksandr Bessmertnykh, embarked on a tour of Arab capitals. By then the Soviets had participated in the recently completed Gulf campaign against Saddam Hussein, and Bessmertnykh decided also to make a one-day stopover in Israel on the pretext of inspecting Christian Orthodox holy places in Jerusalem. Nothing of diplomatic consequence took place during his brief visit, but the impending shift in Soviet policy toward Israel was unmistakable. To that end, Prime Minister Shamir had remained adamant on his terms for Soviet cosponsorship of a Middle East peace conference. Now, clearly, Moscow was preparing to accept his condition. In ensuing months additional Soviet ministers visited the Jewish state. In August 1991 an agreement was negotiated between El Al and Aeroflot for direct flights between the two countries.

As the Soviet regime crumbled, Gorbachev was replaced as president of Russia (although not of the USSR) by Boris Yeltsin, and Bessmertnykh was replaced as Soviet foreign minister by Boris Pankin. It was Pankin in turn who persuaded Gorbachev that the moment had come to spare their nation the final ignominy of exclusion from the Madrid Conference. On October 16, 1991, the foreign minister flew to Israel. Following two days of discussions, Pankin and Yitzchak Shamir jointly announced that their respective consulates general would be raised to embassy status. On October 24, finally, to great ceremonial fanfare, the Israeli flag was raised over the old embassy building in Moscow. And thus it was, two weeks later, that Mikhail Gorbachev addressed the gathering of Arabs and Israelis in his official capacity as cohost of the Madrid Peace Conference. His role was palpably a nominal one, but no more so now than his role as president of the Soviet Union. Indeed, the following month, Yeltsin would replace Gorbachev in that office, only to preside over the USSR's subsequent liquidation.

In its collapse, the great wounded empire was suffering the torments not only of political dysfunctionalism but of economic chaos and interethnic hatreds approaching civil war. It was no terrain any longer for the smallest and most vulnerable of the Soviet peoples. In the last hours of December 1991, as Gorbachev made his dramatic resignation speech as president, his departure anticipated by three weeks the death of Lazar Kaganovich. Ninety-two years old, the only Jew to have served in the Communist Politburo and remain alive, Kaganovich had become a nonperson following the death of Stalin. Alone and brooding in his Moscow apartment, the grizzled old apparatchik over the years had rejected all requests for interviews with the Soviet or international press, or even with members of his own family. As he neared his end, however, Kaganovich permitted his grand-niece to visit him. She asked his advice on her future life choices. In his response, he did not hesitate. "Go to Israel," he told her.

A PRECARIOUS SECOND HONEYMOON

By then, under the nominal aegis of the Madrid Conference, the Israelis were engaged in protracted bilateral negotiations with the Syrians, Lebanese, Jordanians, and Palestinians. The discussions actually took place at the State Department in Washington, and they would continue, month after month, from December 1991 through all of 1992 and into 1993. Progress was negligible. As the summer of 1993 approached, the entire "Madrid process" appeared to have ground to a stalemate. Within Israel itself, however, a major political transfiguration had occurred. In the June 1992 Knesset elections, the right-wing Likud government had suffered a decisive defeat. Yitzchak Rabin had replaced Shimon Peres as chairman of the Labor party, and it was under Rabin as prime minister that a Labor-dominated coalition was positioned to embark on a more vigorous effort to resolve the Arab-Israeli impasse.

Together with Peres, who had again returned to his familiar post of foreign minister, Rabin sensed that the moment was ripe for a breakthrough. One factor was the recent collapse of the Soviet empire, and the unavailability of further Russian military support to Syria, Israel's most truculent neighbor. Another was the impact of the recent Gulf War on Yasser Arafat and the PLO. Diplomatically isolated after its fulsome support of Saddam Hussein, deprived of its traditional Gulf subsidies, the refugee confederation no longer was able to maintain its extensive welfare services among the Palestinians. And, meanwhile, with the avalanche of Soviet immigration, Israel plainly was gaining in demographic mass. Fearful then of a possibly irretrievable Jewish grip on the West Bank, Arafat informed his contacts of his interest in an accommodation. Those contacts in fact were not made on Israeli-occupied territory. Rather, both sides preferred other, neutral venues.

By 1992 Norway proved to be the likeliest of these. Its government for the most part had adopted a pro-Israel stance in Middle Eastern affairs, yet had proved sufficiently "objective" to merit Arab trust. Until 1992 the Norwegian secret service had cooperated with the Mossad in the struggle against terrorism, had even allowed Mossad operatives to interrogate Arab suspects on Norwegian soil. But when the Israelis coupled their interrogations with threats of deportation, the local media broke the story. With memories of the 1974 Lillehammer killing (p. 242), the public reacted angrily to this latest violation of national sovereignty. The Norwegian minister of justice then called for an investigation, and NOAS, the Council of Norwegian Organizations for Asylum Seekers, filed a lawsuit against Svein Urdel, chief of the Norwegian secret service, for his role in Israeli intimidation. Urdel resigned soon afterward, and it was the Mossad agents, not the Palestinians, who were ordered out of the country. Jerusalem was hardly in a position to protest: Norway's commitment to human rights was internationally renowned.

Indeed, the record of that dedication was evident in Norwegian public service programs extending over many decades and countries. One of these private undertakings was Norway's Institute for Applied Social Science. Functioning under the unofficial imprimatur of the country's foreign ministry, the institute was a respected "think tank" devoted to the resolution of international disputes. In the spring of 1992 its director, Terje Rod Larsen, who had developed numerous PLO contacts while conducting field studies in the Gaza Strip, sought out Dr. Yossi Beilin, a protégé of Shimon Peres. Larsen informed Beilin that senior PLO members had confided to him their fatigue with the *intifada*, and their willingness to explore political alternatives. Beilin was interested.

After Labor's June electoral triumph, Peres appointed Beilin his deputy in the foreign ministry. At almost the same time, Larsen's wife, Mona Juul, was appointed assistant to Norwegian Foreign Minister Johan Jørgen Holst, and consequently was in a position to offer Beilin the services of the Norwegian government. Thereupon, sensing that the bilateral Arab-Israeli Madrid discussions had reached a dead end, Beilin brought his proposal for Israeli-PLO meetings to Peres. The foreign minister did not veto it, yet he cautioned Beilin to avoid "official" Israeli involvement. Operating under this guideline, Beilin then selected two dovish academicians, Yair Hirschfeld and Ron Pundak, as his personal, "unofficial" representatives. Arafat then selected as his own negotiator Ahmed Suleiman Khoury, the PLO "minister of finance." In January 1993, under cover of Larsen's institute, Hirschfeld, Pundak, and Khoury were secretly accommodated in a luxurious mansion outside Oslo, the estate of the Borregard Paper Company.

Over the ensuing months, there would be fourteen meetings here. Although security was tight, the Norwegians ensured that the atmosphere was relaxed (Khoury even attended one meeting in his pajamas). Foreign Minister Holst, his wife, Marianne Heiberg, as well as Larsen and Mona Juul, recruited a team of assistants from the social science institute to handle all details of travel, security, recreation, food, transcription, and typing. Holst and Larsen also played a vital substantive role, coming up with alternative negotiating proposals, functioning as mediators between the two sides. On one occasion, Holst was obliged to fly to PLO headquarters in Tunis for consultation with Arafat, even as Larsen traveled to Jerusalem to confer with Peres and Beilin. The exertion was a prodigious one for Holst, who suffered from a heart ailment, and twice he required hospitalization. Yet he would not relent. By spring of 1993, Prime Minister Rabin had been brought into the picture, and authorized an upgrading of Israel's representatives in Oslo to "official" status. Together with Uri Savir, director-general of Israel's foreign ministry, Beilin himself now paid intermittent, secret visits to Oslo to share in the discussions.

By August 1993 the basic outline of a "Declaration of Principles" was emerging. Even then Arafat in Tunis was hesitant to take the final step. On August 17, however, Shimon Peres flew to Stockholm, ostensibly to attend an international Socialist congress. Again, through Norwegian Foreign Minister Holst, who was at his side, a series of back-and-forth telephone calls to Arafat clarified the few remaining points at issue. Once the PLO chairman's final agreement was secured, Peres then flew secretly to Oslo the next day, and was present at the Borregard estate for the signature of agreements. Later, on September 13, 1993, when the final Declaration of Principles was ceremonially signed in the White House Rose Garden, public attention focused on the seated dignitaries: on Arafat, Rabin, and Peres; on President Bill Clinton, Secretary of State Warren Christopher, and Russian Foreign Minister Andrei Kozyrev, all of whose appearances maintained the original, Madrid Conference façade of Soviet-American "cosponsorship." Virtually no attention was given to the presence—in the audience—of Johan Holst or Terje Larsen. Even after the September signing, as the Israeli-PLO agreement became ensnarled in technical difficulties, Holst was obliged to press on in his diplomacy, traveling again to Jerusalem and Tunis. In January 1995, in the midst of these exertions, he was stricken by a last, fatal heart attack, at the age of fifty-nine.

By then the United States had resumed its earlier initiative in orchestrating a wider, regional accommodation for the Middle East. Largely through the persistence of Secretary of State Christopher, Israel and the Hashemite Kingdom of Jordan institutionalized their long, pragmatic modus vivendi by signing a formal peace treaty on October 26, 1994. Afterward, with the state of war officially terminated between Israelis, Egyptians, and Jordanians (and unofficially with the Palestinians), it was possible for Christopher to seek reciprocal gestures from other Arab moderates—from Saudi Arabia, the Gulf emirates and sultanates, from Morocco and Tunisia. He secured his concessions. Early in 1995 all these governments agreed to terminate their secondary boycott against Israel. They themselves would not enter into commercial relations, let alone peace relations, with the Jewish state, but neither any longer would they impose punitive sanctions on foreign companies that did. In truth, since the 1979 Egyptian-Israeli peace treaty, a growing number of European companies already had devised ways to evade the secondary boycott and to engage in trade with Israel. Now all official barriers were down.

No European nation exploited the new trade opportunity more aggressively than did Britain. Until recently, under the Conservative governments of Margaret Thatcher and John Major, the British had remained implacable in their criticism of Yitzchak Shamir's hard line. In December 1987 and January 1988, Britain's delegate at the UN Security Council supported resolutions condemning Israel's repression in the West Bank. In the June 1989 meeting of the EC Council of Ministers, Foreign Secretary Geoffrey Howe had joined with his colleagues in reaffirming the sharply critical 1980 Venice Declaration (pp. 290, 292). But from the advent of the Rabin government in 1992, and the progress afterward toward Middle Eastern peace, London's approach to Israel softened. In March 1995 Prime Minister Major paid his first official visit to the Jewish state.

It was significant that Major brought with him some thirty leaders of British industry. Several of their corporations, like Unilever, already had invested heavily in Israeli firms. Others now joined in the quest for likely Israeli business prospects. Thus Madge, a British network giant, made an outright purchase of Lannet, a promising Israeli software firm. Rolls-Royce purchased 30 percent of the Iscar tool-and-cutting conglomerate. As other British companies sought out attractive purchases or joint ventures, they availed themselves of the recently established Israel-UK Business Council, as well as the commercial office of the British Embassy in Tel Aviv. Under the direction of Wavell Megar, an energetic Cornishman, the commercial office's eight staffers scouted Israel for promising business ventures, analyzed their operations, and alerted likely investors in Britain. The latter were arriving in growing numbers, well aware of Israel's impressive labor skills and rising purchasing power. Indeed, by 1997, of Britain's £1.6 billion in exports to the Middle East and North Africa, £1.1 billion were going to Israel.

In 1992 Italian Foreign Minister Emilio Columbo, who served that year as president of the European Union, paid a courtesy visit to Israel. His meetings with Rabin and Peres signified more than the usual exchanges of amenities. In earlier years, fear of guerrilla terrorism and distaste for Israel's creeping annexationism had mandated a cautious approach to the Jewish state. So had Italy's fuel requirements, which were met principally by Libya's vast oil and gas fields. Those reservations in some measure were dissipated now by the inauguration of the Rabin cabinet, and by the availability of North Sea oil, which lately had begun to reduce Italian dependence on the Libyan wells.

Still another cautionary influence in earlier years was the Christian Democratic party's traditional domination of Italian political life. Unofficially linked with the Vatican, the Christian Democrats had long been sensitive to the papacy's reservations on Zionism and Israel. But now the Vatican itself was beginning to reevaluate its stance. Under the broad-spirited John Paul II, theological animus no longer played a role in church policy. Neither, any longer, did the security of Christian holy places in Jerusalem. Political considerations were decisive, and specifically the fate of Christian communities dispersed throughout the Arab world. Formerly it had been a Vatican certitude that recognition of Israel would place those communities at risk. But once the Gulf War ended and the Madrid Conference began, the Arab world itself appeared to be inching toward a possible de facto accommodation with the Jewish state. Indeed, other nations, with their own long traditions of reserve toward Israel, similarly had begun appraising the usefulness of direct interaction with the Jerusalem government. One of these, of course, was the Soviet Union. Then, in January 1992, within a single two-week period, India and China—encompassing a third of the world's population—also announced the establishment of formal ambassadorial relations with Israel.

Soon, the rapid new sequence of Middle Eastern developments impelled the church to abandon its traditionally Byzantine convolution and procrastination. The Oslo Agreement of August 1993, the ceremonial White House signing of the Israeli-PLO Declaration of Principles, the ongoing Egyptian, PLO, Hashemite, and Israeli quadrilogue—all appeared likely to transform the very political topography of the Middle East. These were changes that almost certainly would affect the fate of hundreds of thousands, perhaps millions of Christians in the region. In its own dealings with Israel, therefore, the Vatican no longer could afford to forfeit a comparable symmetry of official status.

So it was, in December 1993, following months of accelerated negotiations, that Israel and the Vatican jointly announced their agreement to establish diplomatic relations. In February 1994 Shmuel Hadas, Israel's former envoy to Madrid, presented his ambassadorial credentials to John Paul II; and in Jerusalem, four months afterward, Archbishop Andrea Cordero Lanza di Montezemolo presented his letters of credence to Israel's President Chaim Herzog as the Vatican's appointed papal nuncio to the Jewish state. Three years later yet, Montezemolo and Israel's Foreign Minister David Levy signed a compact redefining the church's legal status in the Holy Land for the first time in half a millennium. Beyond the traditional diplomatic immunities enjoyed by foreign legations and embassies, Roman Catholic institutions in Israel henceforth would enjoy near-total internal autonomy, including exemption from Israeli taxes on church property serving religious purposes (although not for income derived from revenue-producing property). Among the first of the Mediterranean's historic presences, the Vatican and the Jewish people now were the last to recognize the equivalence of their respective diplomatic sovereignties.

A STRUCTURAL REEVALUATION

Following the Oslo Agreement, and its sequence of ensuing diplomatic achievements, the Rabin government felt sufficiently assured of international goodwill to reassess its attitude toward the European Union. Until recently the (predecessor) European Community had felt obliged to transcend its once exclusively economic role in the hope of projecting itself into the arena of statecraft, and—among other diplomatic objectives—of chivvying Israel into fulfillment of its political obligations to the Palestinians. But now, ironically, it was Rabin and Peres, invoking the format established at the original Madrid Conference, who took the initiative in pressing the EU to play a wider role in Middle Eastern affairs. Specifically the Israelis urged the Europeans to take an active part in the various multilateral committees that had been organized under the Madrid guidelines for developing Middle Eastern security and prosperity. In fact the Israelis went further, entreating the EU, the World Bank, Japan, and individual Western nations to commit substantial sums to the envisaged new Palestinian Authority. Without a sound economic infrastructure, they warned, political viability might yet escape the fragile new Palestinian experiment.

Beyond concern for its Palestinian partner, Israel manifestly had its own, national agenda to resolve with the European Union. In May 1992 the Twelve had signed an agreement with yet a new constellation of states—with Austria, Finland, and Sweden—to enlarge the great trading bloc to an unprecedented membership of fifteen by 1995. Additionally the Maastricht Treaty of 1992 ensured that in time the EU members would be linked together in common monetary, fiscal, and social policies, even in a single currency. Israel's own economic future accordingly would be linked with an undifferentiated unit, in effect, with the totality of Western Europe.

Could a small, non-European nation compete with a behemoth of these dimensions? Israel's economy was barely 1 percent that of the EU nations. For its part, the European Union responded forthrightly, even generously, to the concerns both of Israel and of others of its Mediterranean "poor cousins." In November 1995 it negotiated a new "Europe-Mediterranean Partnership" agreement (pp. 353–4), a document that for Israel represented a significant refinement of the landmark 1975 treaty. Under its terms the Jewish state, and other Mediterranean states, would share in a series of new relationships with the EU, well beyond simple commerce. These included the right to compete freely for public procurements (bids) and intellectual property, and to share equally in the European Union's opportunities for scientific, technological, cultural, and audiovisual cooperation.

Yet trade remained the defining emphasis of the new pact, and its provisions similarly required the Jewish state to open its own market without further qualification to all European exports, agricultural and industrial alike. There would be no further grace periods. If Israel's exports enjoyed virtually unlimited access to that vast European emporium, so, by the same token, did Europe's exports to Israel. The agreement accordingly represented a challenge to the Jewish state no less than an opportunity. While Israeli exports to the EU had grown from $526 million in 1976 to $6.7 billion in 1997, Israel's imports from the EU had climbed in the same period from $1.3 billion to a staggering $14.8 billion. The nation's agricultural exports already were being gravely buffeted in competition with the EU's Mediterranean members and associate members. What, now, would be the fate of the nation's industry in competition with the Union's sophisticated production facilities? In the long run, a free and open trade association with Europe unquestionably would rationalize Israel's industrial base. But the process would not be easy. Its painful social costs already were evident in the failure of many scores of larger and smaller companies throughout the 1990s, and a growth in the unemployment rate by 1997 to 9 percent. Moreover, the trauma was inflicted on a nation whose vaunted boast of rising affluence obscured a grievously widening income gap between rich and poor.

Would Israel enjoy leeway to survive the critical transition from a parochial and protected economy to one of openness and competitiveness? Much would depend on Western, and specifically on European, goodwill. For the nearer future Washington was almost certain to maintain its role as Israel's principal guarantor and benefactor. Yet the Jewish state in its longer-term viability would falter or flourish less in its relationship with the distant United States than with its closest geographical and ideological hinterland. If that hinterland was never other than Europe, by the end of the twentieth century it was a Europe whose diplomatic and economic solicitude no longer could be equated with philanthropy or even with institutionalized guilt-consciousness. Mutual forbearance and cooperation would have to produce tangible mutual benefits. Doubtless Yitzchak Rabin grasped the changing equation. By signing his accords with the Palestinians and the Jordanians, the Israeli prime minister appeared to be offering Europe the most tangible benefit of all. This was a promise of Middle Eastern quietude, of a hiatus in the murderous confrontation that in four Arab-Israeli wars had threatened the Continent with economic paralysis, and conceivably worse.

On the evening of November 4, 1995, Rabin addressed a peace rally of some one hundred thousand citizens who overflowed Tel Aviv's Municipality Square. Afterward, his spirits buoyed by the warmth of the audience's reception, the prime minister made ready to depart. Lurking undetected near his limousine was a twenty-five-year-old law student, a fanatical Orthodox opponent of Palestinian self-rule. As Rabin approached, the young man fired three pistol shots into his back. Emergency surgery failed to save the prime minister. He died within the hour.

Two days later he was buried in Jerusalem. He had been the leader of a small country, with a population of less than six million. Yet his funeral was attended by statesmen from North and South America, from Asia, Africa, Australia, and, without an exception, from every nation of Europe. Among the latter were President Sali Berisha of Albania; Chancellor Franz Vranitsky of Austria; Foreign Minister Vladimir Senko of Belarus; President Zhelyu Mitev Zhelev of Bulgaria; Acting President Alexis Galanos of Cyprus; Prime Minister Vaclav Klaus of the Czech Republic; Prime Minister Poul Rasmussen of Denmark; President Lennart Meri of Estonia; President Martti Ahtisaari and Prime Minister Paavo Lipponen of Finland; President Jacques Chirac of France; President Eduard Shevardnadze of Georgia; President Roman Herzog and Chancellor Helmut Kohl of Germany; Prince Charles and Prime Minister John Major of Great Britain; Prime Minister Gyula Horn of Hungary; Prime Minister John Burton of Ireland; Prime Minister Umberto Dini of Italy; Prime Minister Maris Gailis of Latvia; Prime Minister Adolfas Slezevicius of Lithuania; Prime Minister Jean-Claude Juncker of Luxembourg; President Mircea Snegur of Moldova; Queen Beatrix and Prime Minister Wim Kok of the Netherlands; Parliamentary President Kirsti Kolle Grondahl and Foreign Minister Tore Godal of Norway; President Mario Soares of Portugal; President Ion Iliescu of Romania; Prime Minister Viktor Chernomyrdin of Russia; Prime Minister Vladimir Meciar of Slovakia; President Milan Kucan of Slovenia; Prime Minister Felipe González of Spain; Prime Minister Ingvar Carlsson of Sweden; Prime Minister Tansu Ciller of Turkey; President Leonid Kuchma of Ukraine; Deputy Prime Minister Nikola Sainovic of Yugoslavia.

Rabin had been born in Israel. Yet his forebears, as well as a majority of his fellow citizens, and their forebears, had drawn their initial breaths in Europe. Standing now under a Middle Eastern sun, could these hushed and thoughtful eminences have shared a sense of common loss, and a premonitory vision of their own continent, deracinated of its Jews only half a century earlier, now entwined with a nation of Jewish survivors in a possible common future destiny: of sterility or creativity, privation or prosperity, volatility or stability— war or peace?

XIV AN AFTERWORD
AT HALF-CENTURY

PEACE IN THE BALANCE

For Yitzchak Rabin and Yasser Arafat, the 1993 Oslo Agreement had represented the barest initial stage in an ongoing process of peace. The accord would require translation into pragmatic arrangements for Gaza and the West Bank. To that end, over the ensuing two years, Arafat and Foreign Minister Peres painstakingly negotiated detailed schedules for Palestinian self-rule. At last, on September 24, 1995, the second-phase agreement was consummated, in Taba, Egypt. By its terms, Israel would withdraw from the major Palestinian population centers within the ensuing hundred days, release some five thousand Palestinian prisoners, and allow elections for the Palestinian Authority's Legislative Council. Like the original Oslo understanding, the Taba accord, to be known henceforth as "Oslo II," was given the cachet of a White House signing four days later, on September 28. The ceremony would be Rabin's final diplomatic legacy.

Shimon Peres, who acceded to the prime ministry upon Rabin's assassination, was intent on preserving their joint achievement. His commitment was shared by Arafat, and evidently by an overwhelming majority of the Palestinian people. Polls taken as late as December 1995 by Turje Larsen's Institute for Applied Social Science (p. 338) indicated 81 percent support among the Palestinians for continuation of the peace negotiations. Altogether, the prognosis for an even broader Arab-Israeli normalization appeared encouraging. Face-to-face discussions between Israeli and Syrian diplomats had been going on in Washington since late 1993, and these too evinced a certain incremental progress on the critical issue of the Golan Heights. In a calculated gamble, therefore, Peres decided to exploit the peace momentum by advancing the scheduled national-election date by half a year, to May 29, 1996. The groundswell of emotion released by the murder of Rabin and by his, Peres's, own diplomatic achievements presumably would return the Labor coalition to office with a more substantial Knesset majority.

As in earlier elections, the prime minister underestimated the near-atavistic insecurities of the Israeli people. By the opening days of 1996, Binyamin Netanyahu, chairman of the Likud opposition, already had forged ahead of Peres in several polls. Then, soon afterward, Palestinian guerrillas of the militant Hamas faction intensified their suicide-bombing campaign as a means of sabotaging the peace negotiations. In late February 1996, a bomb exploded on a bus in New—Jewish—Jerusalem, killing twenty-four Israelis, as well as the bomber. A week later, on March 3, a second bomb was detonated in Jewish Jerusalem, killing nineteen people, together with the bomber. The next day, still another bomb went off in a Tel Aviv shopping center, killing twelve people, again including the bomber. Other bombs exploded at bus stops or were discovered and disarmed only at the last moment. In response, the government sealed off the Palestinian territories, thereby blocking tens of thousands of commuting Arabs from employment in integral Israel. The Israeli public was not reassured. Even moderates among them wondered if Arab hatred had not become irreversible, if peace negotiations should not at least be slowed.

It was against the background of these suicide bombings that Likud and other right-wing factions denounced Peres for his declared willingness to countenance a future Palestinian mini-state in the West Bank and Gaza, and even a partial Israeli withdrawal from the Golan Heights. For the sake of final peace accords with Israel's Arab neighbors, the prime minister insisted, he was obliged to maintain a certain diplomatic flexibility on these issues. Yet his forthrightness ultimately cost him dearly. So, too, in April 1996, did a sudden onslaught of Hizballah—Iranian-sponsored—guerrilla rocket attacks. Launched from southern Lebanon against Israel's northern border communities, the salvoes once again raised the question of Peres's bona fides as guarantor of his nation's security. With the election barely six weeks off, the beleaguered prime minister then authorized a series of heavy artillery bombardments against suspected guerrilla bases in Lebanon. Dubbed "Operation Grapes of Wrath," the shelling continued intermittently for two weeks and sent over 200,000 hapless Lebanese villagers fleeing to the north. It was a clumsy and indiscriminate retaliation, and it outraged Israel's Arab minority no less than the neighboring Arab countries. In the subsequent Israeli election, not a few of these local Arabs for the first time would cast blank ballots rather than deliver them to the Labor coalition. While hardly the principal factor swinging public opinion against the government, those blank ballots proved just sufficient to deny Labor a renewed incumbency.

When the votes were counted on May 29–30, 1996, it developed that Binyamin Netanyahu had achieved his victory by a margin of less than 1 percent. Accordingly, with both Likud and Labor emerging far weaker than in previous elections, Netanyahu was obliged to patch a cabinet together by negotiating alliances with several ultrarightist minority factions and a constellation of distinctly illiberal religious parties. These were the elements in turn that steered the new government toward a much harder line on territorial issues, both on the Golan and in the West Bank. Thus, within weeks of taking office, Netanyahu allowed the discussions with Syria effectively to lapse, then interposed new delays in negotiating further stages of withdrawal in Palestine. For the first three months of his incumbency, the new prime minister disdained even to confer with Yasser Arafat. When at last, on September 4, 1996, he consented to a brief, perfunctory "audience" with the Palestinian leader, the meeting was essentially cosmetic, intended to placate the Clinton administration on the eve of Netanyahu's visit to Washington.

Otherwise, the months passed, and implementation of the next stage of "Oslo II," including Israeli withdrawal from Hebron and other Arab population centers, was repeatedly postponed. Intent upon finding ways of protecting Hebron's tiny Jewish enclave and of widening Israel's transportation infrastructure in the territories, the Netanyahu government played for time. By the end of the year, as a result, armed clashes between Jews and Arabs in the West Bank were approaching the threshold of the previous decade's *intifada*. Not until early January 1997, through intensive American mediation, was agreement reached on the future of Hebron, giving over control of some 95 percent of the town to the Palestinian Authority, but keeping its minuscule Jewish settlement under direct Israeli jurisdiction and protection.

It appeared to be Netanyahu's final concession. Henceforth, the prime minister committed his government to the "thickening" of the Jewish presence in the West Bank, most specifically in and around Greater Jerusalem. Arafat's anguished entreaties, and Washington's persistent appeals, went for nought. By late 1997, as the peace process seemingly had withered into inanition, Jordan's King Hussein and Egypt's President Mubarak hinted that diplomatic relations with the Jewish state might not remain viable. Several moderate Arab nations—Morocco, Tunisia, Oman, Muscat—already had allowed their consular relations with Israel essentially to lapse. Within the Arab League, the Saudis even proposed reviving the secondary boycott against the Zionist state.

JACQUES CHIRAC TAKES A WALK

It was not alone the recalcitrance and political fragility of the Netanyahu government that deepened the Israeli-Palestinian impasse. The irresolution of Washington's Middle East diplomacy also played a role. Throughout his term of office, under continual political harassment, President Bill Clinton appeared unwilling to jeopardize the support even of marginal, irredentist elements within the American Jewish community. Moving cautiously, he relegated the United States presence in the post–Oslo II negotiations to an assistant secretary of state, Dennis Ross. Ross, in turn, uncertain of his bargaining power, intermittently laid down and then withdrew deadlines for Israeli or (less frequently) Palestinian acceptance of American proposals. Here it was, in mounting consternation, that a number of European spokesmen began venturing occasional initiatives of their own. Among these, Terje Larsen and his wife, Mona Juul, the Norwegian researchers who had inspired the original 1993 Oslo negotiations, continued to function as a secret channel between the Palestinian leadership and the Israeli government. It was through the Larsens' intercession in the summer of 1996 that Netanyahu consented to his last-minute September 4 meeting with Arafat.

Other European initiatives were less clandestine. In June 1995, during the last year of the Rabin government, Ireland's Foreign Minister Dick Spring visited Israel. Over Rabin's objections, Spring insisted upon stopping off at Orient House, an East Jerusalem building used by Palestinian activists as their unofficial "capital" headquarters. The gesture of political support was unmistakable. In May 1998, Britain's Prime Minister Tony Blair persuaded Arafat and Netanyahu to visit London for tripartite discussions on Palestine. Blair's effort to play the honest broker proved as unavailing as Dennis Ross's. Yet his willingness to risk failure reflected Europe's mounting frustration with the flaccidity of Washington's mediation, and with the evident obdurateness of the Israeli government.

It was Jacques Chirac, however, drawing on precedents from the pre-Mitterrand era, who issued the most vigorous reminder that Europe would not indefinitely tolerate an Israeli-Palestinian deadlock. In May 1995, Chirac acceded to the presidency of France in his third campaign, defeating the Socialist Lionel Jospin in a runoff that ended fourteen years of Socialist incumbency. A veteran Gaullist, a perennial mayor of Paris and cabinet member in the de Gaulle and Pompidou governments, Chirac served as prime minister during the presidencies of both Giscard d'Estaing and Mitterrand. Now, as chief of state, he was too experienced a politician to project French *grandeur* frontally and flagrantly into the world arena. His technique was more oblique. In dealings with other West European leaders, he emphasized his commitment to the European Union. In visits to Washington, he stressed his loyalty to NATO. Touring Asia, he invoked a "Euro-Asian partnership." Chirac plainly intended to function through, rather than outside, Europe. In this fashion, with the weight of the Continent behind it, France, a middle-sized power, once again could play a global role.

Would Chirac's approach necessarily prove inimical to Israel? In fact, the new president's warm-spirited relationship with French Jewry would have suggested the opposite. In July 1995, only two months after assuming office, Chirac acknowledged France's responsibility for deporting Jews to Nazi death camps in World War II. "Yes, the criminal folly of the [German] occupier was assisted by French people, by the French state," he declared at a ceremony commemorating the 1942 roundup of Paris's Jews by the French police. "These dark hours tarnish forever our history. . . ." Even Mitterrand had not gone as far in admitting France's wartime role. Nor was the gesture intended to cloak a shift in French policy toward Israel. Chirac admired Yitzchak Rabin, came as a mourner to Rabin's funeral, and assiduously supported Shimon Peres in the latter's quest for a full and final accommodation with the Palestinians.

Goodwill for the Israelis, however, in no sense precluded a reaffirmation of France's extensive ties with the Arab world. During a state visit to Egypt in April 1996, Chirac recalled for his hosts France's long cultural relationship with the southern Mediterranean peoples. In Beirut, he reminded the national parliament of France's traditional solicitude for the Lebanese, then issued a pointed admonition that neither Lebanon nor Israel could enjoy full security amid millions of unfriendly neighbors without accepting a *"pact de stabilité,"* in which Europe (read France) should participate. Within a matter of days, ironically, Chirac would have occasion to demonstrate France's concern for *stabilité,* when the Peres government in that same month launched its "Grapes of Wrath" bombardment of southern Lebanon. Responding then to an anguished appeal from Lebanon's Prime Minister Rafiq Harari, Chirac on April 14 dispatched his foreign minister,

Hervé de Charette, to mediate between Israel, Lebanon, and Syria (by whose sufferance Hizballah guerrillas passed into southern Lebanon). De Charette continued his negotiations for some two weeks, much to the annoyance of the Israelis and Americans alike. On May 16, United States Secretary of State Warren Christopher finally arrived from Washington to nail down a formula for limiting, if not ending, hostilities. Yet the price for the agreement was Israel's willingness to accept a monitoring team that included delegates from Israel, Lebanon, Syria, the United States—and France. Chirac afterward would boast that French intercession was decisive in achieving the qualified cease-fire.

Then, two weeks later, on May 29, 1996, Israel's election sent shock waves far beyond the Middle East. At first the Europeans, even the French, adopted a stance of cautious reserve, waiting to assess the extent of Netanyahu's commitment to the Oslo accords. But little time passed before the new cabinet's aggressive settlements program evoked a rising tide of Palestinian violence. In September 1996, President Clinton invited Arafat and Netanyahu for a conference in Washington. It produced no tangible results. With congressional elections pending in the United States, Clinton remained unprepared to lay down a firm line, to withhold financial or diplomatic "entitlements" from either side. Hereupon, in considerable dismay, Arafat decided to stop off in Paris en route home. At the Élysée Palace, he implored Chirac to adopt a more active posture on the Palestine issue. The French president required no further inducement. In late October 1996 he departed on a renewed series of whirlwind visits to the Middle East. This time Israel figured prominently in his agenda.

Arriving at Ben-Gurion Airport at noon of the 21st, Chirac almost immediately deviated from the tradition established by earlier visiting heads of state. His schedule did not include the customary address to the Knesset. Instead, after a brief lunch in Jerusalem with Israeli President Ezer Weizman, Chirac flew off to Haifa for a low-key, honorary-degree ceremony at Israel's Institute of Technology (the Technion). He returned that evening to Jerusalem for a state dinner. The following day, October 22, comprised the single full day of Chirac's visit, and its schedule left no doubt toward whom he was orienting his diplomacy. In the morning, he set out on a walking tour through Arab East Jerusalem. His scheduled route extended from the Church of the Holy Sepulchre along the Via Dolorosa to Saint Anne's Church, where a meeting was planned with Palestinian notables. Chirac had emphasized in advance that he would not pass through the city's Arab neighborhoods under the protection of uniformed

Israeli police. On that understanding, and surrounded now only by Israeli plainclothesmen, he set off on his walk. At the last moment, however, the French president quite spontaneously changed his route, choosing to pass through the heart of the crowded Arab market area. If the shift was intended as an additional gesture of goodwill to the Palestinians, it evoked only consternation among the Israeli escort. They were obliged now to shepherd their guest through "unsecured" terrain. Thus, as Chirac moved through the "Street of the Butchers," and as excited Arab civilians crowded in upon him, the Israeli bodyguards vehemently pushed them away. Chirac was outraged. In full view of accompanying journalists and television cameramen, he shouted to the Israelis in English: "Stop this! Stop this! What do you want? Do you want me to go back to my plane and fly back to France? Is that what you want?" The guards stepped back, and the presidential entourage then continued on without further incident to Saint Anne's Church.

Saint Anne's was a French institution, and traditionally enjoyed the extraterritorial status of a consulate. It had been agreed that no Israeli police would be allowed inside for the reception. Yet the Israeli foreign ministry, apparently "overlooking" the prior understanding, stationed a police unit in the church courtyard. Apprised of the change, Chirac refused to set foot inside until the police were withdrawn. Only then did he enter to address the waiting Arabs, to express his sympathy with them, and to offer his support for their political rights in East Jerusalem and the West Bank altogether. The entire episode was publicized throughout the world. The French president's afternoon conferences with Netanyahu and Foreign Minister David Levy were held in private, but an official communiqué made clear that Chirac had forthrightly pressed the case for Palestinian empowerment. Later that afternoon, after brief ceremonial visits to the Holocaust Memorial Museum and to Rabin's grave, Chirac hosted an official reception of his own for Palestinian leaders at the French consulate-general in Jerusalem. In the early evening, at a French embassy reception in Tel Aviv, the guest list was restricted to French nationals. No Israeli was invited.

The next morning, October 23, Chirac was off by helicopter to the West Bank Arab town of Ramallah, where Yasser Arafat and the members of the Palestinian Council awaited him. In his remarks to them, the French president urged firmness of resolve. "The Palestinians are the victims of history," he declared, "a people without a territory. You, too, have known the trials of an exodus and have held up well. Stick to your principles." The Palestinians were thrilled. Ahmed

Qurai, president of the Council, recalled for journalists de Gaulle's famous 1967 characterization of the Jews as an "elite," "domineering" people (p. 184). "History repeats itself today," exulted Qurai. Chirac then flew back to Jerusalem, bade farewell to President Weizman, and embarked for Amman. In the Hashemite capital, addressing the Jordanian parliament, he repeated the sentiments he had expressed in Ramallah.

Had Chirac projected a revived Gaullist image to the Arab world? Possibly he had taken an important step along that road, first by his overt gestures toward the Palestinians, then by canceling most of Syria's $350-million debt to France. In a brief stopover in Egypt, too, on the final leg of his journey, he pledged a "dramatic" increase in Franco-Egyptian economic relations. Washington, meanwhile, followed Chirac's visit with muted reservations. Pressing for an Israeli-Palestinian accommodation in the West Bank, the Americans did not welcome the intrusion of another player into their Middle East diplomacy. Nor did Chirac's European colleagues rush to endorse his initiative. Germany's Chancellor Helmut Kohl, still Israel's most powerful friend in Europe, took pains to dissociate himself from the French president's coup de théâtre. Oslo I and II had been achieved without significant European participation, after all. In contrast to the 1970s, no oil crisis was looming. There did not yet appear to be need for another Venice-style declaration.

EUROPE PROBES A VACUUM

Nevertheless, the European Union would not indefinitely refrain from discreet exploratory efforts of its own. There was recent precedent for new initiatives. In 1992, President Jacques Delors of the EC Commission reminded his fellow commissioners that the (then) European Community was exerting five times the effort in behalf of East European, former Communist nations than for the southern Mediterranean countries. The asymmetry was hazardous, Delors argued, for the south's poverty and rapid population growth, its metastasizing unemployment, corruption, crime, and political terrorism, were propelling waves of North African and Middle Eastern immigrants into Europe. The influx was threatening large areas of the Continent with economic and social instability.

Delors's warning registered. The Community launched into intensive discussions with Mediterranean governments. The negotiations eventually culminated in November 1995 with the signing in Barcelona of the Europe-Mediterranean Partnership agreement. The new

venture encompassed the fifteen nations of the European Union and
twelve southern Mediterranean countries extending from Algeria and
Morocco to Egypt, Syria, Turkey—and Israel. Far more than a trade
agreement, the Barcelona pact transcended all earlier economic-
cooperation treaties between Europe and the Mediterranean "poor
cousins." Its projected goal was nothing less than development of a
Euro-Mediterranean "zone of peace and stability."

The expectation was not altogether fanciful. The Barcelona
partners soon became enmeshed in a cat's cradle of multinational
committees devoted to joint programs for agriculture, industry, communications, transportation, and immigration, and to campaigns
against drugs, white slavery, and terrorism. From the outset, there
were skeptics who envisaged the partnership as merely a huge smoke
screen for the control of illegal immigration from the south. They
questioned whether an undertaking so vast and complex would not
eventually bog down, even share the fate of the 1973 Euro-Arab Dialogue (p. 286). Yet, if the reservations were legitimate, so was
Barcelona's potential as an alternative to America's four-decade role as
guardian of Western interests in the Middle East. Through the new
enterprise, the Europeans were now engaged in a more profound
commitment to Mediterranean stability than at any time since the
pre-1956 years of Anglo-French domination.

The EU-Mediterranean paradigm was not designed specifically to
advance the Arab-Israeli peace process. But as Ephraim Halevy,
Israel's ambassador to the EU, insisted, it was the only framework in
which "Israel and Syria still meet and talk regularly," and for that reason alone constituted a "major breakthrough." "Breakthrough" or
not, the Barcelona structure tended to loom larger as Washington fal-
tered in its own Middle East diplomacy. Indeed, the United States
itself had obliquely involved the Europeans in the peace process by
recruiting their help in the 1990–91 Gulf War. Although they were
not themselves participants in the ensuing Madrid Conference, the
Europeans were invited to share afterward in the specialized multilateral economic committees established under the Madrid format.

Following Oslo I and Oslo II, moreover, both Rabin and Arafat
requested Europe's economic help for the emergent Palestinian
Authority. In truth, the EU required no encouragement whatever to
offer its largesse, so boundless was its gratification at the unfolding
vista of Arab-Israeli peace. As early as September 8, 1993, five days
even before the initial Israeli-Palestinian signing ceremony in Washington, the EU Commission proposed a $600-million aid package for
the Palestinians, to be applied over the ensuing five years; and before

the first year was out, the Commission approved a $104-million grant simply to help underwrite the new Palestinian police force. In January 1996, as Arafat and his staff prepared to organize the Palestinians' first "national" election, it was again the EU that provided most of the funds and some three hundred monitors to help administer the actual balloting. Meanwhile, in the Israel-Jordan equation of the peace process, the EU similarly was involved on the operational level, and in fact had been so well before the 1994 peace treaty between the two nations. As far back as the Gulf War, the predecessor European Community supplied tens of millions of dollars to help the Hashemite government cope with the influx of Palestinian refugees from Iraq. In 1993, too, the Jordanians were extended virtually the identical free-trade access to the EU that Israel had achieved earlier.

So it was, by mid-decade, that the Europeans had earned the right to begin registering their collective impatience with the pace of Palestinian empowerment. In August 1995, the EU Commission took note of the Rabin government's plans for organizing an elaborate "three-thousandth" anniversary celebration the following year to mark the founding of Jerusalem. Traditionally, the Union and its predecessors had helped fund international cultural programs. Not this time. It did not escape the EU Commissioners that the "Jerusalem 3000" extravaganza was intended for political rather more than for cultural purposes. Their reaction accordingly carried political overtones of its own. Unless the program, they warned, gave additional weight to the diverse strands of non-Jewish traditions enmeshed in Jerusalem's history, Israel risked losing EU subventions for Jerusalem's annual international music and film festivals, and its annual international medical conventions. The Commission's warning registered. The format was modified.

The following year, in the aftermath of Chirac's October 1996 visit to Israel, the EU Council accepted the French president's suggestion to appoint its own special emissary to Israel for "Middle Eastern Affairs"—a thinly disguised euphemism for the Israeli-Palestinian peace process. The envoy of choice was Miguel Angelo Moratinos, formerly Spain's ambassador to Israel. In November 1996, Moratinos opened an office in Tel Aviv, then periodically approached the Netanyahu government to seek an observer's role in the Palestine discussions. Politely, but firmly, the Israelis fended him off. Yet the European Union was not entirely without recourse in registering its concern on the lagging peace negotiations. In Paris the year before, Arafat and Peres had signed an agreement under EU sponsorship authorizing Palestinian exports to Europe on the same basis—that is, essentially without duties—as Israeli products. Then, three years later, in 1998, with the Netanyahu government adopting its hardest line toward the Palestinians, Miguel Moratinos informed Israel's foreign ministry of the Union's current position on the Paris pact. The window for Palestinian goods applied exclusively to commodities produced for Palestinian profit, he explained, not to Palestinian goods produced for Israeli companies and Israeli profit. These latter would not be admitted into the European market without duties, under either the Israeli or the Palestinian category. The financial import of the decision in fact was minimal. As in 1988, when the European Parliament chose not to ratify a new EC-Israeli agricultural protocol (p. 322), the Europeans barely troubled to disguise the essentially political implications of their new administrative measures.

There appeared little chance that the EU would engage in serious economic retaliation. Its trade agreements with the Jewish state were locked in place, and almost certainly would remain intact into the distant future. By the same token, the commercial benefits to Israel of its European relationship were similarly being projected for the distant future. As the little nation's balance-of-payments gap widened under the impact of European imports, Israel's leaders accordingly chose to emphasize the political significance of de facto membership in the European Union. For Netanyahu, as for Peres and Rabin before him, that association represented Israel's acceptance into the ambit of a wider European "family," into nothing less than the broadest spectrum of European civilization.

There was reason nevertheless to question the Israeli people's willingness to accept the challenges, no less than the blessings, of European cooperation. The auguries were mixed. As the Jewish state commemorated the fiftieth anniversary of its independence, its citizens doubtless could look back on near-miracles of collective fulfillment. Not the least of these was the achievement of plain and simple survival. Following World War I, after all, the newly established successor-states of Central and Eastern Europe had managed to sustain their independence for barely a single generation. Israel, in contrast, stripped by World War II of its potential demographic mass, of its very life's essence, had managed somehow to function as a vibrant republic, and to flourish mightily for not one but two generations. On the threshold of the twenty-first century, the nation's physical survival conceivably no longer was at issue. Yet its identity in history was. Would the Israeli people survive a third generation only by maintaining a state of siege, retreating behind a wall of parochialist suspicion and fundamentalist exclusivity? Or would they adopt alternative paths at a time when their maritime and air routes were entirely open at last to the flow of goods, visitors, immigrants, and ideas from the West?

It had not always been a humanistic—and assuredly not a hospitable—West, not for the Jews in their Diaspora incarnation. But dynamic peoples large or small learned to adopt and adapt the best resources of mind and heart that other civilizations could offer, whenever opportunity allowed. In October 1998, as Binyamin Netanyahu and Yasser Arafat tortuously negotiated and grudgingly signed yet another incremental redeployment accord for Palestine, opportunity still allowed. For the Jews, reestablished in their ancient homeland, the reservoir of European goodwill had not yet been depleted, and possibly once again even had been replenished. Its bounty then remained still to be exploited on both sides of the Mediterranean, still to be mobilized for productive application by Europeans and Israelis alike in a potential effulgence of shared and synergistic creativity.

BIBLIOGRAPHY

OVERVIEW

Allen, David, and Alfred Pijpers, eds. *European Foreign Policy-Making and the Arab-Israel Conflict.* The Hague, 1984.

Ben-Gurion, David. *Israel: A Personal History.* New York, 1971.

Eban, Abba. *Personal Witness.* New York, 1993.

Eytan, Walter. *The First Ten Years: A Diplomatic History of Israel.* New York, 1958.

Peres, Shimon. *David's Sling.* New York, 1971.

Rafael, Gideon. *Destination Peace: Three Decades of Israeli Foreign Policy.* New York, 1981.

Sharett, Moshe. *Yoman M'dini* [Diplomatic diary]. Tel Aviv, 1968.

EUROPEAN ECONOMIC COMMUNITY
(European Community, European Union)

Alençon, F. d'. "The EC Looks to a New Middle East," *Journal of Palestine Studies,* No. 2, 1994.

Bartur, Moshe. "Israel und die europäische Integration," *Europäische Wirtschaft,* No. 18, 1961.

Chorin, Yaacov. "Israeli Citrus and the Common Market," *New Outlook,* Mar.–Apr. 1966.

Cohen, Yaacov. *Israel and the EEC: Israel's Integration in the Economic Structure of the European Community.* Jerusalem. 1979.

———. "Israel and the EEC, 1958–1978: Economic and Political Relations," in Giersch, Herbert, ed. *The Economic Integration of Israel into the EEC.* Tübingen, 1980.

Dajani, H. al-. "The PLO and the Euro-Arab Dialogue," *Journal of Palestine Studies,* No. 3, 1980.

Einhorn, Talia. *The Role of the Free Trade Agreement between Israel and the EEC.* Baden-Baden, 1994.

European Community. *Protocols of the EEC-Israel Agreement.* Brussels, 1993.

Fishelson, Gideon. *The Economic Integration of Israel into the European Economic Community.* Tel Aviv, 1977.

Garfinkle, Adam M. *Western Europe's Middle East Diplomacy and the United States.* Philadelphia, 1993.

Giersch, Herbert, ed. *The Economic Integration of Israel into the EEC.* Tübingen, 1980.

Gorce, Paul-Marie de la. "Europe and the Arab-Israel Conflict," *Journal of Palestine Studies*, No. 3, 1997.

Greilsammer, Ilan, and Joseph Weiler. *Europe's Middle East Dilemma: The Quest for a Unified Stance*. Boulder, Colo., 1987.

———. "The Non-Ratification of the EC-Israel Protocols by the European Parliament, 1988," *Middle East Studies*, No. 2, 1991.

Hallaba, S. A. S. *The Euro-Arab Dialogue*. Brattleboro, Vt., 1984.

Hurewitz, J. C., ed. *Oil, the Arab-Israeli Dispute, and the Industrial World*. Boulder, Colo., 1976.

Mani, Saleh A., al-, ed. *The Euro-Arab Dialogue: A Study in Associative Diplomacy*. New York, 1983.

Minerbi, Sergio. "The Accession of Spain to the EEC and Its Implications for Mediterranean Third Countries: The Israeli Case," *Jerusalem Journal of International Affairs*, No. 3, 1982.

———. "Europe and the Middle East: An Israeli Perspective," *Jerusalem Journal of International Affairs*, No. 3, 1988.

Mushkat, M. "Israel and the Common Market," *Israel Year Book*, 1980.

Olson, R. K. "Partners in the Peace Process: The United States and Europe," *Journal of Palestine Studies*, No. 4, 1997.

Palmieri-Billig, L. EC-Israeli Relations and the Middle East Peace Process," *Jerusalem International Economic Revue*, No. 22, 1993.

Sarna, Aaron J. *Boycott and Blacklist: A History of Arab Economic Warfare against Israel*. Totowa, N.J., 1986.

Serre, F. de la. "L'Europe des Neuf et le conflit israélo-arabe," *Revue française de science politique*, No. 4, 1974.

Shlaim, Avi, and G. N. Yannopoulos. *The European Economic Community and the Mediterranean Countries*. Cambridge, England, 1976.

Sowayegh, Abdulaziz al-. *Arab Petro-Politics*. New York, 1984.

Taylor, Alan R. "The Euro-Arab Dialogue: Quest for an Interregional Partnership," *Middle East Journal*, Autumn 1978.

Tovias, Alfred. "From Twelve to Fifteen: The Impact of the Last European Union's Enlargement on Israel's Political Economy," *Israel Affairs*, Winter 1995.

Tovias, Alfred, and Ephraim Ahiram, eds. *Whither EU-Israel Relations?* New York, 1995.

Uri, Pierre. *Israel and the Common Market*. London, 1972.

———. "Israel and the European Economic Community: The Prospects for Integration," *Middle East Information Series*, Dec. 1972.

FRANCE

Aggiouri, René. *Le Conflit de Palestine dans le jeu des puissances, 1950–1967*. Beirut, 1968.

Amson, Daniel. *De Gaulle et Israël*. Paris, 1991.

Aron, Raymond. *De Gaulle, Israel, and the Jews*. New York, 1968.

Association France-Israël. *France-Israël: le livre de la fidélité*. Paris, 1972.

Azeroual, Yves. *Mitterrand, Israël, et les juifs*. Paris, 1990.

Balta, Paul. *Le politique arabe de la France: de Charles de Gaulle à Pompidou*. Paris, 1973.

Bar-Zohar, Michael. *Ben-Gurion: The Armed Prophet*. Englewood Cliffs, N.J., 1967.

———. *Embassies in Crisis: Diplomats and Demagogues Behind the Six-Day War*. Englewood Cliffs, N.J., 1970.

———. *Gesher al HaYam HaTichon* [Bridge over the Mediterranean]. Tel Aviv, 1964.

Beaufré, André. *L'expédition de Suez, 1956*. Paris, 1968.

Binder, Leonard, Stanley Hoffman, J. C. Hurewitz, and François Rouillon. "Les États-Unis, la France, et le conflit israélo-arabe," *Politique Étrangère*, Nos. 5–6, 1971.

Bourdeillette, Jean. *Pour Israël*. Paris, 1968.

Carrol, R. "FOB Cherbourg: Israel Gets Its Boats," *Newsweek*, Jan. 12, 1970.

Clement, Claude. *Israël et la Cinquième Republique*. Paris, 1978.

Cohen, Samy. *De Gaulle, les gaullistes et Israël*. Paris, 1974.

Crosbie, Sylvia K. *A Tacit Alliance: France and Israel from Suez to the Six-Day War*. Princeton, N.J., 1974.

Dan, Uri. *De Gaulle contre Israël*. Paris, 1969.

———. *L'embargo*. Paris, 1970.

Davenport, Elaine, Paul Eddy, and Peter Gillman. *The Plumbat Affair*. London, 1978.

Dayan, Moshe. *Diary of the Sinai Campaign*. New York, 1965.

———. *The Story of My Life*. New York, 1976.

Derogy, Jacques, and Hesi Carmel. *The Untold Story of Israel*. New York, 1979.

Duclos, Jean-Louis. "Un essai de rapprochement égypto-israélien," *Maghreb-Machrek*, Jan.–Mar. 1978.

Evron, Y. "French Arms Policy in the Middle East," *World Today*, Feb. 1970.

Feldman, S. "The Bombing of Osiraq Revisited," *International Security*, No. 2, 1982.

Galard, Henri de. "Pompidou et Israël," *Nouvel Observateur*, Nov. 10, 1969.

Gendzier, Irene. "Arabs and Israelis: French Views," *Middle East Journal*, Spring 1968.

Ginewski, Paul. *L'antisionisme*. Brussels, 1973.

Godin, M. "What Do the French Want? A Look at De Gaulle's Mideastern Policy," *New Middle East*, Mar. 1969.

Kagan, Benjamin. *Combat sécret pour Israël*. Paris, 1963.

Lankin, Eliahu. *The Story of the* Altalena. Tel Aviv, 1967.

Lapierre, Jean W. *L'Information sur l'État d'Israël dans les grands quotidiens français en 1958*. Paris, 1968.

Lazar, David. *L'opinion français et la naissance de l'État d'Israël, 1945–1949*. Paris, 1972.

Levey, Zach. *Israel and the Western Powers, 1952–1960*. Chapel Hill, N.C., 1997.

———. "Israel's Pursuit of French Arms, 1942–1958," *Studies in Zionism*, No. 2, 1993.

Lucas, W. "Redefining the Suez 'Collusion,' " *Middle East Studies*, No. 1, 1990.

Moutet, E. "Les français et le sionisme," *L'Arche*, May 1976.

Nicault, Catherine. *La France et le sionisme, 1897–1948*. Paris, 1992.

Nouschi, André. *La France et le monde arabe*. Paris, 1994.

Peres, Shimon. *David's Sling*. New York, 1971.

Rabinovich, Abraham. *The Boats of Cherbourg*. New York, 1980.

Rash-Cohen, Yehoshua. *Déminer un champs fertile: les catholiques français et l'État d'Israël*. Paris, 1982.

Rondot, P. "France and Palestine: from Charles de Gaulle to François Mitterrand," *Journal of Palestine Studies*, No. 3, 1987.

Rouleau, Eric. "French Policy in the Middle East," *World Today*, May 1968.

Saint-Prot, Charles. *La France et le renouveau arabe: de Charles de Gaulle à Valéry Giscard d'Estaing*. Paris, 1980.

Snyder, Jed C. "The Road to Osiraq: Baghdad's Quest for the Bomb," *Middle East Journal*, Autumn 1983.

Soustelle, Jacques. *La longue marche d'Israël*. Paris, 1968.

Sullivan, A. "The Dynamics of French Resistance to Zionism in the 19th and Early 20th Centuries," *Mid-East Forum*, No. 4, 1968.

Thomas, Abel. *Comment Israël fut sauvé*. Paris, 1978.

Tourneau, J. R. *Secrets d'État*. Paris, 1960.

Tsur, Ya'akov. *Prélude à Suez: Journal d'une ambassade, 1953–1956*. Paris, 1968.

Wajsman, Patrick. *Nos politiciens face au conflit israëlo-arabe*. Paris, 1969.

Wood, Pia Christina. "France and the Israeli-Palestinian Conflict: The Mitterrand Policies, 1981–1992," *Middle East Journal*, Winter 1993.

GERMANY

Abediseid, M. *Die deutsch-arabische Beziehungen*. Stuttgart, 1976.

Adenauer, Konrad. *Erinnerungen*. 2 vols. Frankfurt, 1967, 1969.

———. "Bilanz einer Reise: Deutschlands Verhältnis zu Israel," *Politische Meinung*, No. 115, 1966.

Albazaz, A. "Germany's Economic Relations with the Arab World," *Journal of Arab Affairs*, No. 2, 1993.

Balabkins, N. *West German Reparations to Israel*. New Brunswick, N.J., 1971.

Bar-Zohar, Michael. *The Avengers*. London, 1968.

———. *Ben-Gurion: A Biography*. New York, 1977.

———. *The Hunt for German Scientists*. London, 1967.

Bator, Angelika. "Bilanz des westdeutsch-israelischen Bundnisses 1969/70," *Dokumentation der Zeit*, No. 16, 1970.

Benda, Roswitha von. *Dieses Land pack ich nicht: junge Deutsche in Israel und Westbank*. Munich, 1991.

Ben-Gurion, David. *Ben-Gurion Looks Back*. London, 1965.

Ben-Natan, Asher. *Briefe an den Botschafter*. Frankfurt, 1971.

Ben-Vered, A. "Deutschland und Israel: Bedeutung der Aufnahme von diplomatischen Beziehungen für den jüdischen Staat," *Europa-Archiv*, No. 13, 1965.

———. "Über die Entwicklung der deutsch-israelischen Beziehungen," *Europa-Archiv*, No. 7, 1967.

Birrenbach, Kurt. "Die Aufnähme der diplomatischen Beziehungen zwischen der Bundesrepublik Deutschland und Israel," in *Ludwig Erhard: Beiträge zu seiner politischen Biographie*. Frankfurt, 1972.

Böhm, F. "Die deutsch-israelischen Beziehungen," *Frankfurter Hefte*, Sept. 1965.

Büttner, F. "German Perceptions of the Middle East Conflict: Images and Identifications during the 1967 War," *Journal of Palestine Studies*, No. 2, 1977.

Brecher, Michael. "Images, Process, and Feedback in Foreign Policy: Israel's Decisions on German Reparations," *American Political Science Review*, June 1973.

Chubin, Shahran, ed. *Germany and the Middle East*. New York, 1972.

Cygielman, V. "Trusting Bonn Again," *New Outlook*, No. 2, 1965.

Deligdisch, Yekutiel. *Die Einstellung der Bundesrepublik Deutschland zum Staate Israel*. Bonn–Bad Godesberg, 1974.

Deutschkron, Inge. *Bonn and Jerusalem: The Strange Coalition*. Philadelphia, 1970.

Dittmar, P. "Die DDR und Israel: Ambivalenz einer Nich beziehung" (two articles), *Deutschland Archiv*, Nos. 2, 3, 1977.

Eban, Abba. "Bestandteile der Beziehungen zwischen der Bundesrepublik Deutschland und dem Staat Israel," *Diplomatischer Kurier*, No. 6, 1970.

Famchon, Yves, and Maurice Lerautay. *L'Allemagne et le Moyen Orient*. Paris, 1957.

Feldman, Lily Gardner. *The Special Relationship between West Germany and Israel*. Boston, 1984.

Frei, N. "Die deutsche Wiedergutmachungspolitik gegenüber Israel im Urteil der öffentlichen Meinung der USA," in Herbst, L., and C. Goschler, eds. *Wiedergutmachung in der Bundesrepublik Deutschland*. Munich, 1989.

Gegenwartskunde. "Die BRD zwischen Israel und den Arabischen Staates," No. 1, 1975.

Gerlach, F. *The Tragic Triangle: Israel, Divided Germany, and the Arabs, 1956–1965*. Ph.D. dissertation, Columbia University, 1968.

Gilleson, Gunther. *Konrad Adenauer and Israel*. London, 1986.

Ginor, Fanny. "The Impact of German Reparations and Restitution Payments on the Israeli Economy," *Wiener Library Bulletin*, Nos. 3–4, 1972–73.

Goldmann, Nahum. *Sixty Years of Jewish Life*. New York, 1969.

Gollwitzer, H. "Zur Frage der deutsch-israelischen Beziehungen: ein überblick," *Blätter für deutsche und internationale Politik*, No. 12, 1964.

Grossman, Kurt. *Germany and Israel: Six Years Luxemburg Agreement*. New York, 1958.

———. *Germany's Moral Debt: The German-Israeli Agreement*. Washington, D.C., 1954.

Hadi, Hakam Abdel. *Bundesrepublik, Israel, und die Palästinenser: eine Fallstudie*. Cologne, 1973.

Harel, Isser. *The House on Garibaldi Street*. Boston, 1975.

Hausner, Gideon. *Justice in Jerusalem*. New York, 1966.

Herbst, Rudolf, and Constantin Goschler. *Wiedergutmachung in der Bundesrepublik Deutschland*. Munich, 1989.

Hottinger, Arnold. "Die arabische Welt zwischen der Israel-Front und der 'Erdölwaffe,'" *Europa-Archiv*, No. 7, 1973.

———. "Die Hintergründe der Einladung Ulbrichts nach Kairo," *Europa-Archiv*, No. 7, 1973.

Jelinik, Yeshayahu, ed. *Zwischen Moral und Realpolitik, deutsch-israelische Beziehungen, 1945–1965*. Gerlengen, 1997.

Jena, K. von, "Versöhnung mit Israel? Die deutsch-israelischen Verhandlungen bis zum Wiedergutmachungsabkommen von 1952," *Vierteljahrsheft für Zeitgeschichte*, No. 4, 1982.

Jochum, Herbert, and Udo Steinbach, eds. *Juden, Judentum, und Staat Israel im christlichen Religionsunterricht in der Bundesrepublik Deutschland*. Paderborn, 1980.

Josephthal, Giora. *The Responsible Attitude: Life and Opinion of Giora Josephthal*. New York, 1966.

Kloke, Martin W. *Israel und die deutsche Linke*. Frankfurt, 1990.

Kreysler, J., and K. Jungfer. *Deutsche Israel-Politik: Entwicklung oder politische Masche?* Diessen, 1965.

Lang, Jochen von. *Das Eichmann-Protokol: Tonbandaufzeichnungen der israelischen Verhöre*. Berlin, 1982.

Lavy, George. *Germany and Israel: Moral Debt and National Interest*. London, 1996.

Lewan, Kenneth M. "How West Germany Helped to Build Israel," *Journal of Palestine Studies*, No. 4, 1975.

Lüth, Erich. *Die Friedensbitte an Israel 1951: Eine Hamburger Initiative*. Hamburg, 1976.

Malone, Joseph J. "Germany and the Suez Crisis," *Middle East Journal*, Winter 1966.

Man, Peter. *Eichman b'Yadai* [Eichmann is in my hands]. Tel Aviv, 1983.

Medzini, Meron. "Israel's Changing Image in the German Mass Media," *Wiener Library Bulletin*, Nos. 3–4, 1972–73.

Meroz, Yohanan. *In Schwieriger Mission: als Botschafter Israels in BDR*. Berlin, 1986.

Neustadt, Amnon. *Die deutsch-israelischen Beziehungen im Schatten den EG-Nahostpolitik*. Frankfurt, 1983.

Ollenhauser, Erich. "German Social Democracy and Reparations," in Infield, Henry, ed. *Essays in Jewish Sociology, Labour and Cooperation*. London, 1962.

Piekalkiewicz, Janusz. *Israels langer Arm: Geschichte der Israelischen Geheimdienste und Kommandounternehmen*. Frankfurt, 1975.

Poschinger, Georg. *Der Palästina-Konflikt: unsere Medien und wir.* Frankfurt, 1992.

Robinson, Nehemiah. "The Luxemburg Agreements and their Implementation," in Infield, Henry, ed. *Essays in Jewish Sociology, Labour and Cooperation*. London, 1962.

Rolef, Susan Hattis. *The Middle East Policy of the Federal Republic of Germany*. Jerusalem, 1985.

Sachar, Howard M. *Diaspora: An Inquiry into the Contemporary Jewish World*. New York, 1985.

Sachar, Howard M., ed. *The Unlikely Partnership: Germany and Israel*. Washington, D.C., 1997.

Sagi, Nana. *German Reparations: A History of the Negotiations*. Jerusalem, 1980.

Schürholz, Franz. *Ergebnisse der deutschen Wiedergutmachungsleistungen in Israel*. Bonn, 1968.

Seelbach, J. *Die Aufnähme der diplomatischen Beziehungen zu Israel als Problem der deutschen Politik seit 1955*. Meisenheim, 1970.

Shafir, Shlomo. *HaSozialdemokratim HaGermanim v'Yachasam la'Yehudim u'l'Yisrael baShanim 1945–1967* [German Social Democrats and their relations to Jews and Israel, 1945–1967]. Tel Aviv, 1986.

Shinnar, Felix. *Bericht eines Beauftragten: Die deutsch-israelischen Beziehungen, 1951–66*. Tübingen, 1967.

Strauss, Franz-Josef. *Erinnerungen*. Berlin, 1989.

Theis, Rolf. *Wiedergutmachung zwischen Moral und Interesse: eine Bestandsaufnahme der deutsch-israelischen Regierung*. Frankfurt, 1989.

Vogel, Rolf. *The German Path to Israel*. London, 1969.

Wagner, Heinz. *Der arabisch-israelische Konflikt in Völkerrecht*. Berlin, 1971.

Wagner, W., "Rückschläge der Bonner Politik in den arabischen Staaten," *Europa-Archiv*, No. 10, 1965.

Wetzel, Dietrich. *Die Verlängerung von Geschichte: Deutsche, Juden, und der Palästinakonflikt*. Frankfurt, 1983.

Wewer, H. "Israel und das politische Selbtsverständnis der Deutschen," *Diskussion*, No. 18, 1966.

Wolffsohn, Manfred. *Deutsch-Israelisch Beziehungen*. Munich, 1986.

———. *Eternal Guilt? Forty Years of German-Jewish-Israeli Relations*. New York, 1993.

"Wiedergutmachungsabkommen von 1952 im internationalen Zusammenhang," *Viertel jahrsheft für Zeitgeschichte*, No. 4, 1988.

———. "Globalentschädigung für Israel und die Juden? Adenauer und die Opposition in der Bundesregierung," in Rudolf Herbst & Constantin Goschler, eds. *Wiedergutmachung in der Bundesrepublik Deutschland*. Munich, 1989.

Zimmermann, Moshe, ed. *25 Years of Israeli-German Relations*. Jerusalem, 1990.

GREAT BRITAIN

Abadi, Jacob. *Britain's Withdrawal from the Middle East, 1947–1971*. Princeton, N.J., 1982.

Abdullah, King of Jordan. *My Memoirs Completed*. Washington, D.C., 1954.

Adams, Michael. *Publish It Not: The Middle East Coverup*. London, 1975.

Aldrich, Richard J., and John Zametica. "The Rise and Decline of a Strategic Concept: The Middle East," in Aldrich, Richard J., ed. *British Intelligence, Strategy and the Cold War, 1945–51*. London, 1992.

Bar-On, Mordechai. *The Gates of Gaza: Israel's Road to Suez and Back, 1955–1957*. New York, 1994.

Bar-Yosef, Uri. *Intelligence Intervention in the Politics of Democracies: United States, Israel, and Britain*. University Park, Pa., 1995.

Bialer, Uri. *Between East and West: Israel's Foreign Policy Orientation, 1948–56*. Cambridge, England, 1990.

Brown, N. "Israel and the British Left," *Venture*, Dec. 1967.

Buzzard, A. "Israel, the Arabs, and British Responsibilities," *World Today*, July 1971.

Cana'an, Haviv. *B'tzet HaBritim* [The departure of the British]. Tel Aviv, 1958.

Childers, Erskine B. *The Road to Suez*. London, 1962.

Cohen, Michael J. *Churchill and the Jews*. London, 1985.

———. *Fighting World War Three from the Middle East: Allied Contingency Plans, 1945–1954*. London, 1997.

———. *Palestine and the Great Powers, 1945–1948*. Princeton, N.J., 1982.

———. *Palestine to Israel: From Mandate to Independence*. London, 1988.

———. *Palestine: Retreat from the Mandate: The Making of British Policy, 1936–1945*. New York, 1978.

———. "Why Britain Left: The End of the Mandate," *Wiener Library Bulletin*, No. 45, 1978.

Darby, Philip. *British Defense Policy East of Suez, 1947–1968*. London, 1973.

Devereux, David R. *The Formulation of British Defence Policy Towards the Middle East, 1948–56*. London, 1990.

Eban, Abba. *An Autobiography*. New York, 1977.

Fulleck, Roy, and Geoffrey Powell. *Suez: The Double War*. London, 1979.

Glubb, Lieutenant General Sir John B. *A Soldier with the Arabs*. London, 1957.

Great Britain. Central Office of Information. *Britain and the Arab-Israeli Conflict*. London, 1993.

Hahn, Peter L. *The United States, Great Britain, and Egypt, 1945–1956*. Chapel Hill, N.C., 1991.

Haron, Miriam J. *Palestine and the Anglo-American Connection*. New York, 1986.

Kimche, Jon, and David Kimche. *Both Sides of the Hill: Britain and the Palestine War*. London, 1960.

Kyle, Keith. *Suez*. New York, 1991.

Laskier, Michael. *The Jews of Egypt, 1920–1970*. New York, 1992.

Louis, William R. "Britain at the Crossroads in Palestine, 1942–1954," *Jerusalem Journal of International Relations*, No. 3, 1990.

———. *The British Empire in the Middle East, 1945–1951*. Oxford, 1986.

Love, Kenneth. *Suez: The Twice-Fought War*. New York, 1969.

Lucas, W. Scott. "Redefining the Suez 'Collusion,'" *Middle Eastern Studies*, Jan. 1990.

Pappé, Ilan. *Britain and the Arab-Israeli Conflict, 1948–1951*. New York, 1988.

Pattison, W. Keith. "The Delayed British Recognition of Israel," *Middle East Journal*, Summer 1983.

Prittie, Terence. "The British Media and the Arab-Israeli Dispute," *Middle East Review*, No. 1, 1980.

———. *The Fourth Arab-Israeli War: The Propaganda Battle.* London, 1974.

Rahman, Habibur. "British Post–Second World War Military Planning for the Middle East." *Journal of Strategic Studies*, No. 4/5, 1982.

Robertson, Terence. *Crisis: The Inside Story of the Suez Conspiracy.* New York, 1965.

Sachar, Howard M. *Europe Leaves the Middle East, 1936–1954.* New York, 1972.

Sheffer, Gabriel. "British-Israeli Relations since Suez." *Wiener Library Bulletin*, No. 1, 1970.

Shlaim, Avi. *Collusion Across the Jordan: King Abdullah, the Zionist Movement, and the Partition of Palestine.* Oxford, England, 1988.

Shuckburgh, Evelyn. *Descent to Suez: Diaries, 1951–56.* New York, 1987.

Teveth, Shabtai. *Ben-Gurion of Israel: The Burning Ground.* Boston, 1987.

———. *Moshe Dayan.* London, 1972.

Wilson, Harold. *The Chariot of Israel: Britain, America, and the Soviet Union.* London, 1981.

ITALY, SPAIN, SMALLER NATIONS, TERRORISM

Abbas, Mahmoud (Abu Mazen). *Through Secret Channels.* New York, 1995.

Alexander, Yonah, ed. *Middle East Terrorism: Current Threats and Future Prospects.* New York, 1994.

Alexander, Yonah, and Kenneth A. Myers, eds. *Terrorism in Europe.* New York, 1982.

Alexander, Yonah, with Michael Noone. *Three Nations' Response to Terrorism.* The Hague, 1996.

Alexander, Yonah, and Joshua Sinai. *Terrorism: The PLO Connection.* New York, 1989.

Alexander, Yonah, and Eugene Sochor, eds. *Aerial Piracy and Aviation Security.* Dordrecht, the Netherlands, 1990.

Asociación de Periodistas Españolas. *España-Israel: horizonte de un reencuentro.* Toledo, 1988.

Bar-Ilan, David. *Eye on the Media.* Jerusalem, 1993.

Bar-Zohar, Michael. *The Quest for the Red Prince.* New York, 1983.

Ben-Asher, A. *Yachsei HaChutz shel Israel* [Israel's foreign relations]. Tel Aviv, 1955.

Berg, Arthur. *Med Israel i kemp for fred.* Oslo, 1979.

Black, Ian, and Benny Morris. *Israel's Secret Wars.* New York, 1991.

Boer, Connie de. *Western European Public Opinion and the Palestine Question.* Kingston, Ont., 1987.

Boyd, James. *United Nations Peace-Keeping Operations: A Military and Political Appraisal.* New York, 1971.

Brecher, Michael. *The Foreign Policy System of Israel.* London, 1972.

Corbin, Jane. *Gaza First: The Secret Norway Channel to Peace between Israel and the PLO.* London, 1994.

Eisenberg, Dennis, Eli Landau, and Menahem Portugali. *Operation Uranium Ship.* Tel Aviv, 1978.

Elizur, Michael. "Israelis and Austrians: Toward the Future," Paper Delivered at a Hebrew University Symposium, Jerusalem, 1989.

Goldstaub, Adriana, and Laura Wofsi Rocca. *La Guerra nel Libano e l'opinione pubblica italiana*. Milan, 1983.

Grazzone, L. "Security in the Mediterranean: Italy's Perceptions and Policies," *Journal of Arab Affairs*, No. 2, 1991.

Greilsammer, Ilan. "Economic Sanctions against Israel: Are They Credible?" *Jerusalem Quarterly*, No. 3, 1990.

———. *European Sanctions Revisited*. Jerusalem, 1989.

Greilsammer, Ilan, and Joseph H. M. Weiler, eds. *Europe and Israel: Troubled Neighbors*. Torence, N.Y., 1988.

Grimaldi, F. "Denmark and the Middle East," *Middle East*, November 1978.

Hadar, C. "The United States, Europe, and the Middle East," *World Policy Journal*, No. 3, 1991.

Halevi, N. "Israele e la Communità Mediteranea," *Lo Spettatore Nazionale*, June–Aug. 1970.

Heradstveit, D. "Norwegian Policy in the Middle East," *International Politik*, No. 1, 1969.

Horowitz, David. *In the Heart of Events: Israel and the World Community*. Jerusalem, 1980.

Houten, Annelies van den. *Wij staan schter Israel, wis stonden schter Israel, wif hebben schter Israel gesteen: de evenwichtige politiek van Nederland*. Amsterdam, 1981.

Ibañez de Ibero, Carlos (Mulhacén, Marques de). *Politica Mediterranea de España*. Madrid, 1952.

Inbar, Ephraim. "The Emergence of Pariah States in World Politics: The Isolation of Israel," *Korean Journal of International Studies*, No. 1, 1983.

Ishai, Moshe. *Eretz B'ruchat Shemesh* [The sun-drenched land (Italy)]. Tel Aviv, 1975.

"Italy and the Middle East: Special Survey," *Middle East*, July 1983.

Jalbert, P. "'News Speak' about the Lebanon War," *Journal of Palestine Studies*, No. 1, 1984.

Jonas, George. *Vengeance: The True Story of an Israeli Counter-Intelligence Team*. New York, 1984.

Karetzky, Stephen. *The Media's Coverage of the Arab-Israel Conflict*. New York, 1989.

Khadduri, Majdia, ed. *The Arab-Israeli Impasse: Expressions of Moderate Viewpoints on the Arab-Israeli Conflict by Well-Known Western Writers*. Washington, D.C., 1969.

Khader, Bichara. "L'Europe et le conflit israëlo-arabe," *Études Internationales*, No. 14, 1973.

Kirisci, Kemal. *The PLO and World Politics: A Study of the Mobilization of Support for the Palestinian Cause*. New York, 1986.

Klieman, Aaron. *Israel and the World After 40 Years*. Washington, D.C., 1990.

———. *Statecraft in the Dark: Israel's Practice of Quiet Diplomacy*. Boulder, Colo., 1988.

Kline, Ray. *State-Sponsored Terrorism*. New York, 1986.

Leydesdorff, Selma. *Israel: een blanco cheque?* Amsterdam, 1983.

Melman, Yossi, and Dan Raviv. *The Imperfect Spies: The History of Israeli Intelligence*. London, 1989.

Mesa, R. "L'Espagne et les Espagnols en face au problème palestinien," *Revue d'Études Palestiniennes*, No. 5, 1987.

Meülen, J. W. van der. "Israel: Exception and Example in Dutch Politics," in Heradstveit, Daniel, and Gunnar Stave, eds. *European Policies in the Arab-Israeli Conflict*. Oslo, 1972.

Minerbi, Sergio. *L'Italie et la Palestine, 1914–1920.* Paris, 1970.

Moisi, E. "L'Europe et le conflit israélo-arabe, 1948–1979," *Politique Étrangère,* Dec. 1980.

Nachmani, Amikam. *Israel, Turkey, and Greece: Uneasy Relations in the East Mediterranean.* London, 1987.

Norton, Augustus R., and Martin H. Greenberg, eds. *The International Relations of the Palestine Liberation Organization.* Carbondale, Ill., 1989.

Ostrovsky, Victor J. *By Way of Deception.* New York, 1990.

———. *The Other Side of Deception.* New York, 1994.

Peres, Shimon. *Battling for Peace.* New York, 1995.

———. *For the Future of Israel.* Baltimore, 1998.

———. *The New Middle East.* New York, 1993.

Perry, Mark. *A Fire in Zion: The Israeli-Palestinian Search for Peace.* New York, 1994.

Piason, Frank J. "Italian Foreign Policy: The *Achille Lauro* Affair," in Leonardi, Robert, and Raffaella Y. Nanetti, eds. *Italian Politics: A Review.* Vol. 1. London, 1986.

Posner, Steve. *Israel Undercover: Secret Warfare and Hidden Diplomacy in the Middle East.* Syracuse, N.Y., 1987.

Questar, G. A. "Israel and the Nuclear Non-Proliferation Treaty," *Bulletin of Atomic Sciences,* June, Oct. 1969.

Rabie, M. "The US-PLO Dialogue: The Swedish Connection," *Journal of Palestine Studies,* No. 4, 1992.

Raeymaeker, O. "La Belgique et les conflits israélo-arabes, 1948–1978," *Studia Diplomatica,* No. 5, 1980.

Segal, Aaron. "Spain and the Middle East: A 15–Year Assessment," *Middle East Journal,* Summer 1991.

Servicio de Publicaciones. *España-Israel: Horizonte de un Re-encuentro.* Toledo, 1988.

Sicherman, Harvey. "The Politics of Dependence: Western Europe and the Arab-Israeli Conflict," *Orbis,* Winter 1980.

Silvestro, Stephano. "Italy's Mediterranean Role," in Heradstveit, Daniel, and Gunnar Stave, eds. *European Policies in the Arab-Israeli Conflict.* Oslo, 1972.

Simon, R. "The Print Media's Coverage of the War in Lebanon," *Middle East Review,* No. 1, 1983.

Smith, P. A. "European Leaders Unhappy with Sadat-Begin Treaty," *MERIP Reports,* September 1979.

———. "European Reactions to Israel's Invasion," *Journal of Palestine Studies,* No. 1, 1982.

Sorge, B. "Sionismo e razzismo," *Rivista Studie Politische Internazionale,* Jan.–Mar. 1976.

Stanger, Cary D. "A Haunting Legacy: The Assassination of Count Bernadotte," *Middle East Journal,* Spring 1988.

Voorhoeve, J. C. *Peace, Profits, and Principles: A Study of Dutch Foreign Policy.* The Hague, 1979.

Weiler, Joseph H. H. *Israel and the Creation of a Palestinian State: A European Perspective.* London, 1985.

Weiler, Joseph H. H., and Ilan Greilsammer. *Europe and Israel: Troubled Neighbors.* New York, 1988.

Yegar, Moshe. *Neutral Policy—Theory Versus Practice: Swedish-Israeli Relations.* Jerusalem, 1993.

SOVIET UNION AND EASTERN EUROPE

Altshuler, Mordechai. *Ma'amadah shel M'dinat Yisrael b'Kerev Yehudei B'rit HaMo'atzot* [The position of Israel among Soviet Jewry]. Jerusalem, 1983.

Andreski, S. "Communism and Jewish Eastern Europe," *International Journal of Comparative Sociology*, March, June 1979.

Axelbank, Albert. *Soviet Dissent, Intellectuals, Jews, and Détente*. New York, 1975.

Bar-Zohar, Michael. *Spies in the Promised Land: Isser Harel and the Israeli Secret Services*. London, 1972.

Ben-Ami (Arieh Eliav). *Between Hammer and Sickle*. Philadelphia, 1967.

Ben-Horin. *Ma Koreh Sham? Sipuram shel Yehudei B'rit HaMo'atzot* [What is happening there? The story of Soviet Jewry]. Tel Aviv, 1970.

Bialer, Uri. *Between East and West: Israel's Foreign Policy Orientation, 1948–56*. Cambridge, England, 1990.

Dagan, Avigdor. *Moscow and Jerusalem: Twenty Years of Relations Between Israel and the Soviet Union*. London, 1970.

Davis, Michael. "Armenia: IDF to the Rescue," *Israel Defense Forces Journal*, Winter 1989.

Dawisha, Karen. *Soviet Foreign Policy Towards Egypt*. New York, 1979.

Freedman, Robert O. *Soviet Policy toward Israel under Gorbachev*. Westport, Conn., 1991.

———. *Soviet Policy toward the Middle East since 1970*. New York, 1978.

Freedman, Robert O., ed. *Soviet Jewry in the 1980s: The Politics of Anti-Semitism and Emigration and the Dynamics of Resettlement*. Durham, N.C., 1989.

Friedgut, Theodore H. "The Middle East in Soviet Global Strategy," *Jerusalem Journal of International Relations*, No. 1, 1980.

Gaysteygar, Kurt. "Moscow and the Mediterranean," *Foreign Affairs*, July 1968.

Gilboa, Yehoshua A. *The Black Years of Soviet Jewry*. Boston, 1971.

Gitelman, Zvi. "Moscow and the Soviet Jews: A Parting of the Ways," *Problems of Communism*, Jan. 1980.

Glassman, Jon D. *Arms for the Arabs? The Soviet Union and War in the Middle East*. Baltimore, 1975.

Golan, Galia. "Gorbachev's Middle East Strategy," *Foreign Affairs*, Jan. 1988.

———. *The Soviet Union and the Arab-Israeli War of October 1973*. Jerusalem, 1974.

———. *The Soviet Union and the PLO: An Uneasy Alliance*. New York, 1980.

———. "Syria and the Soviet Union since the Yom Kippur War," *Orbis*, Winter 1978.

Goldberg, Itche, and Yuri Suhl. *The End of a Thousand Years: The Recent Exodus of the Jews from Poland*. New York, 1971.

Goodman, Jerry. *The Jews in the Soviet Union*. New York, 1981.

Heikal, Mohamed Hassanein. *The Road to Ramadan*. New York, 1975.

Hoffman, Charles. *Gray Dawn: The Jews of Eastern Europe in the Post-Communist Era*. New York, 1992.

Horelick, Arnold L. "Soviet Involvement in the Middle East and the Western Response," *Middle East Information Series*, June 1972.

Husseini, Mohrez Mahmoud al-. *Soviet-Egyptian Relations 1945–1985*. New York, 1987.

Institute of Jewish Affairs. *The Use of Antisemitism against Czechoslovakia*. London, 1968.

Jones, Clive. *Soviet Jewish Aliyah 1989–1992: Impact and Implications for Israel and the Middle East*. London, 1996.

Karsh, Efraim. *The Soviet Union and Syria: The Asad Years*. London, 1988.

Klieman, Aaron S. *Soviet Russia and the Middle East.* Baltimore, 1970.

Klinghoffer, Arthur J., and Judith Apter. *Israel and the Soviet Union.* Boulder, Colo., 1985.

Kochan, Lionel, ed. *The Jews in Soviet Russia since 1917.* London, 1978.

Kohler, Foy D., Leon Goure, and Mose L. Harvey. *The Soviet Union and the October 1973 Middle East War.* Coral Gables, Fla., 1974.

Korey, William. *The Soviet Cage.* New York, 1973.

Korn, David A. *Stalemate: The War of Attrition and Great Power Diplomacy in the Middle East, 1967–1970.* Boulder, Colo., 1992.

Krammer, Arnold. *The Forgotten Friendship: Israel and the Soviet Bloc, 1947–53.* Urbana, Ill., 1974.

Laqueur, Walter. *The Struggle for the Middle East: The Soviet Union in the Mediterranean, 1959–1968.* New York, 1969.

Lendvai, Paul. *Antisemitism Without Jews.* Garden City, N.Y., 1971.

———. "Jews Under Communism," *Commentary,* Dec. 1971.

Levin, Aryeh. *Envoy to Moscow: Memoirs of an Israeli Ambassador 1988–92.* London, 1996.

McLanvin, Ronald D. *The Middle East in Soviet Policy.* Lexington, Mass., 1975.

Meerson-Aksenov, Michael. "The Jewish Exodus and Soviet Society," *Midstream,* April 1979.

Meir, Golda. *My Life.* New York, 1975.

Meyer, Peter, B. D. Weinryb, E. Duschinsky, and N. Sylvain. *The Jews in the Soviet Satellites.* 2nd ed. Westport, Conn., 1971.

Namir, Mordechai. *Shlichut b'Moskva* [Mission to Moscow]. Tel Aviv, 1971.

National Council for Soviet Jewry. *Hostages for Trade: Soviet Jews.* Miami, 1979.

Pennar, Jaan. *The USSR and the Arabs: The Ideological Dimension.* New York, 1973.

Primakov, Yevgeni. "Soviet Policy Toward the Arab-Israel Conflict," in Quandt, William, ed. *The Middle East Ten Years After Camp David.* Washington, D.C., 1988.

Quandt, William. "Soviet Policy in the October Middle East War: I," *International Affairs,* July 1977.

Ra'anan, Uri. "Soviet Policy in the Middle East, 1960–1973," *Midstream,* Dec. 1973.

Rafael, Gideon. "Divergence and Convergence of American-Soviet Interests in the Middle East: An Israeli Viewpoint," *Political Science Quarterly,* Winter 1985.

Ro'i, Yaacov. *From Encroachment to Involvement? A Documentary Study of Soviet Policy in the Middle East.* Jerusalem, 1974.

———. *Soviet Decision-Making in Practice: The USSR and Israel 1947–1964.* New Brunswick, N.J., 1980.

Rothschild, Joseph. *Return to Diversity: A Political History of East Central Europe since World War II.* 2nd ed. New York, 1993.

Rubenstein, Alvin. *Red Star on the Nile.* Princeton, N.J., 1977.

———. "The Soviet Union and the Peace Process since Camp David," *Washington Quarterly,* Winter 1983.

Sachar, Howard M. *Diaspora: An Inquiry into the Contemporary Jewish World.* New York, 1985.

———. *A History of the Jews in America.* New York, 1992.

Sayigh, Yezid, and Avi Shlaim, eds. *The Cold War and the Middle East.* New York, 1997.

Schroeter, Leonard. *The Last Exodus.* Seattle, 1981.

Smolansky, Oleg M. "Soviet Policy in the Arab East, 1945–47," *Journal of International Affairs,* Summer 1959.

———. *The Soviet Union and the Arab East under Khrushchev*. Lewisburg, Pa., 1974.

Teller, Judd L. *The Jews, The Kremlin, and the Middle East*. Syracuse, N.Y., 1957.

Weinland, R. "Superpower Naval Diplomacy in the October 1973 Arab-Israeli War," *Washington Papers*, No. 61, 1979.

Whetton, Lawrence L. "June 1967 to June 1971: Four Years of Canal War Reconsidered," *New Middle East*, June 1971.

Yodfat, Aryeh. *Arab Politics in the Soviet Mirror*. Jerusalem, 1973.

Zak, Moshe. *Yisrael u'Brit HaMo'atzot: Arbayim Shanah shel Dusiach* [Israel and the Soviet Union: A forty-year dialogue]. Tel Aviv, 1988.

VATICAN

Bovis, H. Eugene. *The Jerusalem Question, 1917–1968*. Stanford, Calif., 1971.

Chouraqui, André. *La reconnaissance: le Saint-Siège, les juifs, et Israël*. Paris, 1992.

Ellis, Kail C. *The Vatican, Islam, and the Middle East*. Syracuse, N.Y., 1987.

Feldblum, E. "Israel in the Holy Land: Catholic Responses, 1948–1950," *Journal of Ecumenical Studies*, No. 2, 1975.

Ferrari, Silvio. "The Vatican, Israel, and the Jerusalem Question (1943–1984)," *Middle East Journal*, Winter 1985.

Irani, George E. *The Papacy and the Middle East: The Role of the Holy See in the Arab-Israeli Conflict*. Notre Dame, Ind., 1986.

Kenny, Anthony J. *Catholics, Jews, and the State of Israel*. New York, 1993.

Kreutz, Andrej. *Vatican Policy on the Palestinian-Israeli Conflict: The Struggle for the Holy Land*. Westport, Conn., 1990.

Mendes, Meir. *HaVatikan v'Yisrael* [The Vatican and Israel]. Jerusalem, 1983.

———. "The Vatican and Israel," in Kent, Peter, and John P. Pollard, eds. *Papal Diplomacy in the Modern Age*. Westport, Conn., 1994.

Metzger, A. "Israël et le Vatican," *L'Arche*, Feb.-Mar. 1973.

Montoisy, J. "Israël-Vatican: Le nouveau dialogue," *Studia Diplomatica*, No. 6, 1981.

Pollard, John F., and Peter Kent, eds. *Papal Diplomacy in the Modern Age*. Westport, Conn., 1994.

Rokach, Livia. *The Catholic Church and the Question of Palestine*. London, 1987.

Stevens, P. "The Vatican, the Catholic Church and Jerusalem," *Journal of Palestine Studies*, No. 1, 1982.

Tincq, Henri. *L'étoile et la croix: Jean-Paul II–Israël*. Paris, 1993.

Tomeh, George J. *Jerusalem at the United Nations*. Beirut, 1974.

INDEX

A Note About the Author

Born in St. Louis, Missouri, and reared in Champaign, Illinois, Howard Morley Sachar received his undergraduate education at Swarthmore and took his graduate degrees at Harvard. He has taught extensively in the fields of Modern European, Jewish, and Middle Eastern history, and lived in the Middle East for six years, two of them on fellowship, the rest as founder-director of Brandeis University's Hiatt Institute in Jerusalem. Dr. Sachar has contributed to many scholarly journals and is the author of thirteen previous books: *The Course of Modern Jewish History* (1958), *Aliyah* (1961), *From the Ends of the Earth* (1964), *The Emergence of the Middle East, 1914–1924* (1969), *Europe Leaves the Middle East, 1936–1954* (1972), *A History of Israel: From the Rise of Zionism to Our Time* (1976), *The Man on the Camel* (1980), *Egypt and Israel* (1981), *Diaspora* (1985), *A History of Israel from the Aftermath of the Yom Kippur War* (1987), *A History of the Jews in America* (1992), *Farewell España* (1994), *A History of Israel from the Rise of Zionism to Our Time, Revised and Updated* (1996). He is also the editor of the thirty-nine-volume *The Rise of Israel: A Documentary History*. Based in Washington, D.C., where he serves as Professor of Modern History and International Affairs at George Washington University, Dr. Sachar lectures widely throughout the United States and abroad. He lives in Kensington, Maryland.

A Note on the Type

This book was set in Janson, a typeface long thought to have been made by the Dutchman Anton Janson, who was a practicing type-founder in Leipzig during the years 1668–1687. However, it has been conclusively demonstrated that these types are actually the work of Nicholas Kis (1650–1702), a Hungarian, who most probably learned his trade from the master Dutch typefounder Dirk Voskens. The type is an excellent example of the influential and sturdy Dutch types that prevailed in England up to the time William Caslon (1692–1766) developed his own incomparable designs from them.

Composed by NK Graphics, Keene, New Hampshire
Printed and bound by Haddon Craftsmen, an R. R. Donnelley
& Sons Company, Bloomsburg, Pennsylvania
Designed by Anthea Lingeman